SHARE
the
Music
McGRAW-HILL

AUTHORS
Michael Jothen, Vincent Lawrence,
Barbara Staton, Merrill Staton

CONTRIBUTING AUTHOR
Jeanne Ruviella (Knorr)

McGraw-Hill School Division
A Division of The McGraw-Hill Companies

McGraw-Hill School Division
Two Penn Plaza
New York, NY 10121

Printed in the United States of America

ISBN 0-02-295383-3

4 5 6 7 8 9 058 03 02

McGraw-Hill
School Division
New York   Farmington

Contents

MEET THE MUSICIAN

Recorded interviews with composers, arrangers, performers, producers, and engineers—a career motivator.

TECHNOLOGY

- **Music with MIDI** allows students to play, improvise, create, and analyze music with the MIDI sequencer. Builds upon musical concepts and skills presented in the *Share the Music* program.

- **Videos** make music come alive through movement, signing, and authentic performances.

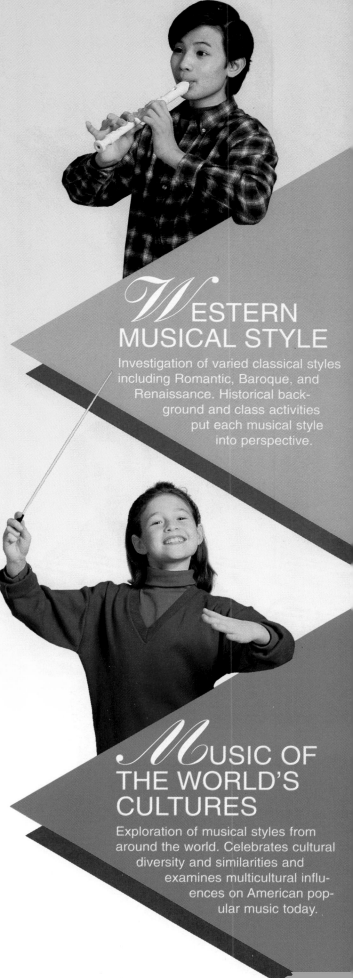

WESTERN MUSICAL STYLE

Investigation of varied classical styles including Romantic, Baroque, and Renaissance. Historical background and class activities put each musical style into perspective.

MUSIC OF THE WORLD'S CULTURES

Exploration of musical styles from around the world. Celebrates cultural diversity and similarities and examines multicultural influences on American popular music today.

MUSIC IN YOUR LIFE

Students explore the manifold impact of music on life in today's world. The impact of technology on the musical scene is emphasized through hands-on activities.

MUSIC LIBRARY

Appealing songs that accommodate the singing capabilities of young adolescent and changing voices. Preparation activities develop vocal and music-reading skills.

OUR AUTHORS

SHARING A UNITY OF PURPOSE AND A DIVERSITY OF TALENTS

DR. MICHAEL JOTHEN

Michael is an Associate Professor of Music and Coordinator of the Graduate Program in Music Education at Towson State University in Maryland. He is a nationally-known music educator, choral clinician, and conductor. Michael has received many commissions for choral compositions and has been recognized by ASCAP for his contributions as a composer of choral music. He has served as President of the National Board of Directors of Choristers Guild. Michael is an author of *Music and You* and of *Share the Music* (Grades K-6).

BARBARA STATON

During her eight years as a music television teacher for the State of Georgia, Barbara pioneered the teaching of music through movement on television. Her diverse teaching experience spans pre-kindergarten through graduate courses. Barbara is the author of the *Move Into Music* series and is a recognized ASCAP composer. A popular clinician, she has conducted music and movement workshops for teachers throughout the U.S. and Canada. Barbara is a senior author of *Music and You.*

DR. VINCENT LAWRENCE

Vincent is widely recognized as an expert in secondary general music education. For 21 years he was Professor of Music at Towson State University in Maryland, where he was the chairperson of Music Education and directed the University Chorale. During that time he was actively involved in teaching general music in the middle school. Vincent is an author of *Music and You,* a coordinating author of *Share the Music* (Grades K-6), and an author of the leading high school text *Music! Its Role and Importance in Our Lives.*

DR. MERRILL STATON

Merrill is nationally known as a music educator, choral conductor, singer, ASCAP composer and producer of recordings. He has been music director of and has conducted the Merrill Staton Voices on many network TV series and recordings. A leader in the field of music education recordings for over thirty years, Merrill pioneered the separation of instrumental and vocal tracks and the use of children's voices on recordings. He is a senior author of *Music and You.*

JEANNE RUVIELLA (KNORR)

Jeanne teaches music education and theory at Towson State University in Maryland. She has taught vocal and instrumental music at all levels and is a noted teacher trainer in the Orff, Kodály, and Dalcroze approaches. Jeanne holds a Dalcroze-Orff-Kodály Certificate from the Manhattan School of Music and a Dalcroze Certificate from the Longy School of Music. She is a contributing author of *Music and You.*

A PHILOSOPHY

SHARING YOUR COMMITMENT FOR SUCCESSFUL LEARNING

SHARE THE MUSIC is an activity-centered program that involves students of all learning styles. Sequenced and thematic activities develop the cognitive, affective, and psychomotor domains of learners.

SHARE THE MUSIC helps you address the issues of today and tomorrow. Here's how!

OUTSTANDING SONGS, LISTENINGS, AND NEW SONG RECORDINGS	• Present the highest-quality materials in a variety of musical styles. • Highlight the natural sound of young adolescent voices recorded with artistic and captivating accompaniments.
CULTURALLY AUTHENTIC MUSIC	• Celebrates cultural diversity and similarity through motivating multicultural materials and recordings. • Broadens the students' experiences with diverse vocal techniques used around the world while building vocal skills.
SEQUENCED LEARNING PROCESS	• Helps students to understand the different elements of music and analyze the reasons they enjoy their favorite musical styles. • Integrates Kodály, Orff, Dalcroze, and traditional music approaches. • Builds music literacy and understanding through singing, listening, moving, creating, music reading, critical thinking, and meaningful assessment.
ACTIVE STUDENT INVOLVEMENT	• Engages students' interest through composition, creative movement, critical listening, and instrumental playalongs. • Encourages students to become musically independent.
FLEXIBLE ORGANIZATION FOR DIVERSE NEEDS	• Presents multiple options to fit 6-week, 9-week, full-semester, or full-year course offerings. • Provides a wide range of activities and materials to meet the varied interests, needs, and skill abilities of the young adolescent student.

AN  RGANIZATION

DEDICATED TO MEETING DIVERSE TEACHING NEEDS

- **FLEXIBLE FORMAT TO ACCOMMODATE 6-WEEK, 9-WEEK, FULL-SEMESTER, OR FULL-YEAR COURSE**

- **8 UNITS OF GENERAL MUSIC INSTRUCTION AND SUPPLEMENTARY SECTIONS**

GENERAL MUSIC

- **Unit 1, the "core" unit, forms the basic structure for all other units. Designed to be taught first.**

- **Listening lessons, songs, motivational music topics, concepts, music reading, and playalong accompaniments are integrated throughout.**

- **Unit reviews assess student content and skill mastery.**

SPECIAL STUDY SECTIONS

Grade 7
- American Popular Music
- Making a Recording

Grade 8
- Western Musical Styles
- Music of the World's Cultures
- Music in Your Life

INSTRUMENTAL SECTIONS

Grade 7
- Keyboard and Guitar
- Accompaniments and Lyrics to Songs in *American Popular Music*

Grade 8
- Keyboards of Today
- Playing the Guitar

MUSIC LIBRARY

Grades 7 and 8
- Song Anthology
- Choral Anthology

THE *LESSON PLAN* DESIGNED FOR CREATIVE

SHARE THE MUSIC builds on our tradition of sequential instruction.

Each lesson outlines specific objectives, step-by-step teaching procedures, and appraisals that save you time in reaching and teaching your students.

Teaching suggestions are easily organized by color coding and placement on the teacher's page.

- **Lesson preparation information**
- **Basic teaching plan**
- **Extended activities for in-depth study**

LESSON PLANNER
A quick outline of the lesson.

1 SETTING THE STAGE
A creative "lesson starter."

2 TEACHING THE LESSON
Sequenced lesson steps.

EXTENSION
Optional resources for meeting individual needs. Includes more music teaching ideas, biographies, curriculum connections, cooperative learning, suggestions for special learners, critical thinking strategies, and additional background information.

Reproduced lesson pages

LESSON 4

2. Introduce polyrhythms in different musical styles. Have the students:
- Listen to "Polyrhythm Montage" and match the photo with the music they are hearing. (steel band, *Cats, The Rite of Spring*, African music)
- Discuss each photo.

CD2:27 **Listening to Polyrhythm**

Polyrhythms are found in many
Match the picture with the music
listen to "Polyrhythm Montage."

"Polyrhythm Montage"

Above, a scene from *Cats*. The "garbage" on the stage is the same size it would appear to a real cat.

LESSON 4

Focus: Polyrhythms

Objectives
To identify, perform, and define polyrhythms
To create and notate a composition using polyrhythms

Materials
Recordings: "Hay Que Trabajar"
"Polyrhythm Montage"
"Weather"
Percussion instruments
Pitched or unpitched classroom instruments

Vocabulary
Polyrhythm, salsa, coro

1 SETTING THE STAGE
Tell the students they will be learning about a style of dance music called *salsa*.

2 TEACHING THE LESSON
1. Introduce polyrhythms. Have the students:
- Discuss the information on "Hay Que Trabajar" and *salsa*.
- Listen to "Hay Que Trabajar" to hear polyrhythms and the sound of *salsa*.

CD2:26 **PERFORMING POLYRHYTHMS**

Polyrhythm is the simultaneous combination of two or more contrasting rhythmic patterns.

"*Hay Que Trabajar*" (ī kä trä-bä-här') contains *polyrhythms*. The style of "*Hay Que Trabajar*" is known as *salsa*. This style was born in New York City when Cuban and Puerto Rican music met big band jazz. *Salsa* is dance music that combines the rhythms and harmonies of Latin America and Africa with those of blues, jazz, and rock.

- Listen to "*Hay Que Trabajar*" to hear polyrhythms and the sound of salsa. In addition to the very active rhythm section, the large band you will hear includes saxophones, trombones, and trumpets, which give it a bright sound. *Salsa* vocals typically feature a soloist and the *coro*, or chorus, which is usually the band members themselves.

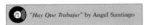 "*Hay Que Trabajar*" by Angel Santiago

You can accompany the A sections of "*Hay Que Trabajar*" with many different rhythm patterns.

- Practice each of the rhythms on page 71.
- Follow the listening map and perform with the recording.

Tito Puente, whose band is heard in this recording, is a very popular Latin music performer, with more than a hundred albums.

70

E X T E N S I O N

THE PERFORMER
Tito Puente—composer, arranger, performer, and Latin jazz band leader, was born of Puerto Rican descent in the Spanish Harlem neighborhood of New York City. He is best known for his work as a percussionist, and particularly as a *timbalero* (timbale player). Tito Puente has recorded with many bands since the 1940s, averaging two albums per year. He is currently performing with his *Latin Jazz Ensemble*. He has been recognized by the National Academy of Recording Arts and Sciences with several Grammy awards for excellence in Latin music categories.

CURRICULUM CONNECTION: SOCIAL STUDIES
Salsa—the Spanish word meaning "sauce"—is a term that was coined in the 1970s. *Salsa* originally referred to a style of music that had evolved in the USA when the multi-cultural influences and musical innovations of the more modern era mixed with the big band Cuban sounds of the 1940s–50s. The style quickly gained popularity in Latin America and the Caribbean. Since that time, many distinct varieties of *salsa* have developed as various cultures have added their own flavors. The word is now used loosely and often refers to a broad variety of fast Latin dance music, including older styles such as *mambo*.

LISTENING
You may wish to use the Listening Map overhead transparency to help guide the students through the listening selection.

LISTEN
You ma
overhe
studen

70 UNIT 3

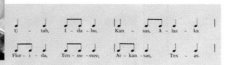

Creating Polyrhythms

CD2:28

You can combine words to create different rhythm patterns.

- Read and perform each of the five rhythms in "Weather."
- Perform "Weather" to create polyrhythms.

Weather

1. Fair — Fair — V.L.
2. Sun–shine, oh it's hot! Sun–shine, oh it's hot!
3. Part – ly cloud – y, part – ly cloud – y
4. Rain! Rain! Snow! Snow!
5. Now it's clear! Now it's clear!

- Use other words to create compositions with polyrhythms. Here are two examples.

U – tah, I – da – ho, Kan – sas, A – las – ka

Flor– i – da, Ten – ne – ssee, Ar – kan –sas, Tex – as.

- Choose names of states, classmates, or automobiles to create your own rhythm patterns. Perform the compositions you created for your classmates. Learn and perform the polyrhythms created by your classmates. Mix and match rhythms from different

73

LESSON 4

3. Introduce creating a polyrhythmic speech composition. Have the students:
- Read and perform each of the five speaking rhythms.
- Form two to five groups and perform "Weather" beginning at different times to experience polyrhythms. ("Weather" can be performed as a round.)

REINFORCING THE LESSON

Have the students create their own compositions with polyrhythms as indicated.

3 APPRAISAL

The students should be able to:
1. Identify and verbally define polyrhythm.
2. Perform a polyrhythmic accompaniment to "Hay Que Trabajar" with accuracy.
3. Create and notate an original polyrhythmic composition using word rhythms.

REINFORCING THE LESSON
Lesson strategies for application, reinforcement, and synthesis of concepts.

3 APPRAISAL
A check for student understanding and accomplishment of each objective.

CURRICULUM CONNECTION: SCIENCE

Weather—Meteorologists constantly observe weather conditions around the world. Observation stations measure temperature, humidity, wind direction and speed, and other conditions every hour. Weather balloons with special instruments measure conditions in the atmosphere and transmit data to ground stations. Cameras on satellites take and transmit photographs of cloud patterns and areas of ice and snow on earth. Meteorologists prepare various maps and charts from this information and analyze them to make weather predictions. Forecast maps are also prepared using computers that solve complex formulas to project ahead from current data.

UNIT 3 **73**

LESSON 4

- Practice clapping the individual rhythm patterns in ⅜ meter found in the playalong sections of the Listening Map for "Hay Que Trabajar." (Each student should learn every rhythmic pattern.)
- Follow the listening map, and with the recording, perform only the new rhythm pattern given for each playalong section.
- Divide into seven groups, each group taking a different part. (Some students may volunteer to perform rhythm patterns as solos.)
- Combine parts. (Have the students in the first group perform their steady beat throughout this process. Add one part at a time, repeating each new combination as necessary.)
- Follow the listening map and perform the rhythm patterns as they listen to "Hay Que Trabajar."

SPECIAL LEARNERS

Prepare an overhead transparency of pupil page 71 if there are exceptional students in the class who are visually impaired or have difficulty coordinating visual and audio skills. Point to each new section as the students listen to the selection to help these students visually and aurally perceive the components of the selection.

UNIT 3 **71**

Piano Accompaniments
Conveniently bound in a separate booklet for each grade.

COMPREHENSIVE EVALUATIONS
- *Review* and *Just Checking* at the end of each unit of the Pupil Book.
- Unit written/recorded evaluations in the Teacher's Resource Masters.

TEACHER'S RESOURCE MASTERS
- Blackline masters to extend and evaluate learning.

ACTIVE PARTICIPATION

Special study sections focus on high-interest topics that help students link music learning with their everyday lives.

Grade 7
- American Popular Music
- Keyboard and Guitar
- Making a Recording

Grade 8
- Western Musical Styles
- Music of the World's Cultures
- Keyboards of Today
- Playing the Guitar
- Music in Your Life

PLAYALONG ACCOMPANIMENTS

Throughout the text, students have an opportunity to perform simple rhythmic, melodic, and harmonic scores. Students play keyboard, guitar, percussion, and recorder with their favorite groups.

MUSIC IN YOUR LIFE

Students explore the manifold influences of music on life in today's world. The impact of technology on the musical scene is emphasized through hands-on activities.

MEET THE MUSICIAN

Recorded interviews with composers, arrangers, performers, producers, and engineers serve as a career motivator for students.

MUSIC LIBRARY

Appealing songs that accommodate the singing capabilities of young adolescent and changing voices. Preparation activities develop vocal and music-reading skills.

SONG ANTHOLOGY

The **Song Anthology** contains lively arrangements of folk and recreational songs.

CHORAL ANTHOLOGY

The **Choral Anthology** contains vocal arrangements suitable for performance.

NEW RECORDINGS

OUTSTANDING SOUNDS AND INNOVATIVE CHOICES

SONG RECORDINGS

- Teen and young adult voices that provide exemplary and motivating vocal models.

- Rich, contemporary instrumental arrangements that inspire participation.

- The warm sound of analog recordings mixed and mastered with state-of-the-art digital technology.

- **Divided Tracks** allow students to hear the vocal and instrumental tracks separately by adjusting the balance control on the CD player.

- **Divided Vocal Parts** in part songs allow students to hear selected vocal parts over a stereo accompaniment by adjusting the balance control.

PERFORMANCE MIXES

- Stereo accompaniments without vocals for selected songs and choral arrangements.

RECORDED INTERVIEWS

- Recorded interviews, entitled MEET, bring the voices and music of famous musicians into the classroom to help motivate and inform young people about musical careers.

MUSIC ACROSS CULTURES

Open a new world of understanding and a rich heritage for your students with song recordings representing many American cultures.

- Pronunciation guides by native speakers.

- Variety of ethnic instruments.

- Native singers, speakers, and instrumentalists provide authentic regional music and cultural background.

PERFORMING GROUPS selected from around the country.

INTEGRATED ARTS

VISUAL ARTS • DANCE • THEATER • MUSIC

Motivating materials invite students to explore connections among the visual arts, dance, theater, and music.

REPETITION WITH VARIATION

• What is the original idea in each picture?
• What has been changed in each picture to provide visual interest and contrast?

Variation results when an idea is changed or altered.

I Saw the Figure 5 in Gold, by Charles Demuth

Teke, by Victor Vasarely

153

Mixing Musical Cultures

In this first section you will listen to music that mixes the characteristics of music of the United States with characteristics of the music of another culture. Some ways musicians do this are to combine instruments, rhythm, melodies, or harmonies of both cultures.

Kogoklaras (kō-gō-klä′räs) is one example of this mix. It combines characteristics of Indonesian music and music of the United States.

Right and below, dancers from the island of Bali, Indonesia. The dancers must practice for years to master these difficult techniques.

• Listen and identify musical characteristics of Indonesia and the United States.

Kogoklaras, by Vincent McDermott

211

A consistent Teaching Plan focuses on concepts and skills that are first experienced, then identified and labeled, creatively reinforced, and finally evaluated.

Boldface type indicates a *basic concept or skill* is measured.

Concepts and skills are measured informally in the Pupil books at the end of each unit.

Written Unit Evaluations are provided in *Teacher's Copying Masters*.

ELEMENTS OF MUSIC	UNIT 1 EXPLORING MUSICAL STYLES Objectives	UNIT 2 RHYTHM PLAYS A ROLE Objectives	UNIT 3 RHYTHM SETS THE BEAT Objectives
Dynamics	Identify contrasting dynamics in different style periods **Define and identify $<$ and $>$** Identify *forte, piano*	Identify dynamic changes in a composition	
Tone Color	Identify and show understanding of tone color Identify instruments and their sounds	Identify tone color changes Perform melodic accompaniments on bells, recorder, or keyboard	Identify tone colors
Tempo	Identify contrasting tempos (slow, moderate, fast)		Conduct patterns to fit the tempo
Duration/ Rhythm	**Perform rhythms to a steady beat** Identify meter contrasts **Experience and label syncopation**	**Identify duple, triple, and quadruple meter** **Identify meter changes** Perform, listen to, and identify irregular meter in $\frac{5}{4}$ and $\frac{7}{8}$	**Identify, define, perform, and conduct in compound meter** Identify meter changes **Identify polyrhythms**
Pitch	Identify major and minor in a composition **Read and perform a melody**	Hear, sing songs within a range of B-e'	Hear, sing songs within a range of C-e'
Texture	Experience musical textures	Perform a melodic accompaniment	Perform a polyrhythmic accompaniment
Form	**Identify contrast between A and B sections** Identify verse and refrain	Conduct a musical composition having a strophic form	Follow a listening map of a composition having the form: A, A, B, A, B, A, B, Bridge, Bridge, C, A, Bridge, C, A, Coda
Style	**Identify compositions from different cultures and style periods** Create and perform music	Listen to and discuss the jazz style Discuss nationalism in the romantic style period **Classify musical examples according to style period**	Listen to songs from musicals and music that combines jazz and classical style Discuss salsa
Reading	Read percussion, melodic and harmonic scores using [musical notation symbols]	Practice known notations Use [musical notation symbols]	Read [musical notation symbols] in $\frac{6}{8}$ Read [musical notation symbols] in $\frac{4}{4}$

UNIT 4	UNIT 5	UNIT 6	UNIT 7	UNIT 8
MELODY	**HARMONY**	**FORM AND STYLE**	**ELEMENTS OF FORM**	**TONE COLOR IN DIFFERENT STYLES**
Objectives	Objectives	Objectives	Objectives	Objectives
	Identify dynamic changes Determine how dynamics create a mood in the music	**Discuss ways in which dynamics affect mood in music** Listen to, identify, and perform contrasting dynamics	Follow dynamics from a listening map Listen to and identify contrasting dynamics	Listen to, identify, and perform contrasting dynamics
Perform retrograde on percussion instruments Perform a song on bells or keyboard and classroom instruments	Identify bright and dark tone colors Determine appropriate tone colors for a composition	Creatively explore tone colors **Perform melodic accompaniment on bells, guitar, keyboard, or recorder**	Listen to and identify the orchestra	**Discuss traditional and nontraditional tone colors** **Perform vocal tone colors** **Listen to prepared piano and steel band** **Identify new sounds from found objects** **Identify synthesizer**
	Determine appropriate tempo for the composition	**Discuss ways in which tempo affects mood in music** **Identify tempo of a composition**	Perform a free form composition keeping a steady tempo	Read and perform sounds at different tempos
Clap the rhythm of the melody as a canon Perform rhythms containing meter changes		**Perform a rhythmic motive** Perform steady beat Perform music with changing meters	**Identify rhythmic motives** **Define *legato* and *staccato* articulation**	**Read and perform a rhythm score**
Learn pitch organization **Define twelve-tone music** **Perform a tone row and its retrograde**	Listen to and identify key changes **Define register and modulation** **Identify bitonality**	**Discuss how mode can express the mood of music**	Follow a melodic listening map Create a melodic motive Identify pitch levels and major/minor tonality Read and perform spoken music	**Read and perform pitch sounds from a score**
Define harmony and consonance **Identify and define polyphonic, monophonic, and homophonic texture** **Perform melodic accompaniment**	Perform accompaniments in minor tonality **Identify, play tonic, subdominant, dominant chords in C**	Perform melodic accompaniments		
Analyze phrase length	**Perform the twelve-bar blues progression** Listen to, discuss, and create variations	**Listen to and identify phrases of different lengths** Identify, create, and perform rhythmic and melodic motives **Identify motive**	**Discuss and identify motives** **Discuss sonata allegro form** **Listen to and identify free form** Discuss, create, and perform a composition in free form	
Discuss a composer from the baroque period Discuss the music of Schoenberg **Identify atonal music**	Sing a song in Spanish Discuss the blues and music by an African American composer **Identify and discuss bitonal music** **Discuss and identify the art song**	Discuss musical characteristics of the romantic period and the 20th century	**Identify musical characteristics of the classical and neoclassical style period** **Identify program music**	**Discuss the pipe organ and synthesizer** Discuss composers **Discuss ways to produce new sounds from voices and traditional instruments** Discuss the electronic revolution **Identify composer Vangelis**
Follow listening map using ♪♪, ♩♩, ♩, ♪	Read and play ♩. on g, a, b♭, b♮, c	Read and play melodic accompaniments using pitches g♩ b♩ c♩ d♩ e♩ f♯♩ g, a, b, c, d, e Read and play Em, D, G, and C chords Use ♩, ♩, ♩, ♩♩	Read *staccato* and *legato* patterns:	Read and play rhythm scores for contemporary music using

XV

UNIT 1 • OVERVIEW

ELEMENTS OF MUSIC	UNIT 1 OBJECTIVES	Lesson 1 CORE Focus: Style, Reggae	Lesson 2 Focus: Western and Non-Western Styles	Lesson 3 Focus: Recognition of I and V Chords, Syncopation	Lesson 4 Focus: Instrumental Tone Color, Dynamics
Dynamics	Identify contrasting dynamics in different style periods **Define and identify** $<$ **and** $>$ Identify *piano/forte*				Identify contrasting dynamics Demonstrate understanding of dynamics Define and identify *piano (p)*, *forte (f)*, $>$ and $<$
Tone Color	Identify and show understanding of tone color Identify instruments and their sounds	Identify vocal and instrumental tone colors Perform accompaniments on recorder or keyboard	Perform a rhythm accompaniment on percussion instruments	Play harmonic patterns with song on bells, keyboard, or guitar Select percussion instruments for performing rhythms	Identify sounds of Japanese instruments Demonstrate understanding of tone color
Tempo	Identify contrasting tempos (slow, moderate, fast)		Identify contrasting tempos (fast, slow)		Identify contrasting tempos (slow, moderate, fast)
Duration/ Rhythm	**Perform rhythms to a steady beat** Identify meter contrasts **Experience and label syncopation**	Tap a steady beat	Tap steady beat and clap beat subdivision Perform a rhythm accompaniment Create rhythm patterns	Perform syncopated rhythm patterns	
Pitch	Identify major and minor in a composition **Read and perform a melody**	Perform a melody Read and perform a chord sequence Create a melodic accompaniment		Create melodic patterns Sing a song with a range of e-d' 	Describe methods of tone production in a Japanese instrument
Texture	Experience musical textures			Define, identify, perform tonic and dominant chords, roots	
Form	**Identify contrast between A and B sections** Identify verse and refrain			Identify verse and refrain of a song	
Style	**Identify compositions from different cultures and style periods** Create and perform music	Identify, discuss, and listen to the reggae style	Discuss, identify, and compare musical styles	Identify, discuss, and listen to calypso music	Discuss and listen to Japanese song Create and perform a sound composition
Reading	Read percussion, melodic, and harmonic scores using ♩, 𝄆 𝄇, ⌢, ♪, 𝄾, ♫, ♩, 𝄿, ♩., ♩, —, 𝅝, ‿	Read melodic and harmonic notation using ♩	Read rhythm scores with ♪, 𝄿, ♩, 𝄾	Read melodic notation using ♩	Identify $<$ (cres.), $>$ (decres.), *p*, *f*

PURPOSE Unit 1: EXPLORING MUSICAL STYLES

In this unit the students will review and/or experience rhythm, pitch, tone color, meter, texture, and form. They will gain an understanding of musical styles through listening and performing.

SUGGESTED TIME FRAME

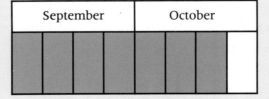

September	October

FOCUS

- Style, Reggae
- Western and Non-Western Styles
- I and V Chords, Syncopation
- Instrumental Tone Color, Dynamics
- Historical Style Periods
- Baroque Style
- Major and Minor, Romantic Style
- Synth-Pop Style, Steady Beat

Lesson 5 Focus: Historical Style Periods	Lesson 6 Focus: Baroque Style	Lesson 7 Focus: Major and Minor, Romantic Style	Lesson 8 Focus: Steady Beat
Listen for different functions of dynamics in various style periods	Follow dynamic changes indicated on a musical map while listening to a composition (p, f, $<$)	Discuss the contrast of dynamics in a composition	
Perform a melody on recorder, bells, or keyboard Listen to and identify tone colors associated with various style periods	Identify contrasts in tone color Identify tone colors on a musical map while listening to a composition		Perform rhythm and melodic accompaniments
	Discuss tempo contrasts in a composition Identify a *ritardando*		
Listen to and identify the use of rhythm in various style periods	Identify meter contrasts Identify duple and triple meter Define meter, measure, and bar line **Play steady beat**		Read and perform a rhythmic accompaniment pattern using drumsticks Identify accent
Perform a melody with accuracy Listen for characteristics of melody in the various style periods		Identify major and minor chords Perform D major and D minor chords Determine how to change a chord from major to minor Analyze the tonality of a composition Sing a song with a range of B♭–e♭'	Perform a melodic accompaniment
Experience textures of various styles			
	Follow a musical map showing the form of a composition Define and identify ternary (ABA) form	Identify major and minor sections Analyze the form of a composition Identify the themes in a composition	Identify contrast between A and B sections
Listen to, discuss, and classify representative compositions from each historical time period Identify musical characteristics of the major historical time periods	Identify and discuss characteristics of baroque style Analyze a composition in baroque style Discuss the French composer Jean Baptiste Lully	Identify the musical characteristics of the romantic period Study a composition by the French composer Georges Bizet	Discuss the influence of vocal style and rhythm on musical expression
♩. ♪	Follow listening map Use duple meter, triple meter, measure, bar line, ritardando, $\frac{2}{2}$ $\frac{3}{4}$, 𝄽 ♩ 𝅝 ▬ 𝄐		Read melodic and percussion scores using 𝄴, 𝄆 𝄇, 𝄐, ♪, 𝄾, ♫, ♩, 𝄽, ♩, ♩, ▬, 𝅝, ▬

TECHNOLOGY

MUSIC WITH *MIDI*

MIDI technology allows students to manipulate musical elements and make musical decisions.

- Lesson 1, page 1: Perform/Improvise in the **Reggae Style**
- Lesson 2, page 6: Create Using Elements of **West African Music**
- Lesson 3, page 10: Tutorial: *"The Entertainer"* by Scott Joplin
- Lesson 3, page 10: *"The Wabash Cannonball"*
- Lesson 7, page 24: Analyze **Major and Minor:** *"Farandole"* by G. Bizet
- Lesson 8, page 30: Perform/Improvise in **Funk Style**

VIDEO RESOURCES

Use video resources to reinforce, extend, and enrich learning in this unit.

WORLD WIDE WEB

Visit Macmillan/McGraw-Hill's Web site at **http://mhschool.com**

UNIT 1

EXPLORING MUSICAL STYLES

LESSON 1

Focus: Style, Reggae

Objectives
To identify and define style
To perform melodic and harmonic accompaniments
To identify and define reggae style

Materials
Recordings: "Style Montage"
          "Serious Reggae Business"
Keyboard or recorder

Vocabulary
Quarter note, quarter rest, repeat signs, half note, chord, reggae, ska, dancehall

1 SETTING THE STAGE

Tell the students that they will be discussing contrasting musical styles and studying the Caribbean style called reggae.

1

THE ARTIST

Jan Van Eyck (yän van īk) (ca 1380–1441)—was one of the first artists to use oil painting. He is known for using natural lighting, vivid colors, and precise details of clothes and jewelry. Jan Van Eyck probably worked with his brother Hubert on *The Ghent Altarpiece*, a huge painting that is filled with many figures and consists of 26 panels in a frame. A detail of the altarpiece is shown here.

LESSON 1

2 TEACHING THE LESSON

1. Introduce style. Have the students discuss the information on style.

2. Introduce different musical styles. Have the students:

• Discuss the pictures representing music styles.

• Listen to "Style Montage" and follow the pictures that represent each musical selection.

• Listen to and describe "Serious Reggae Business," using the musical terms suggested on page 2. (Students should note the alternation of solo vocalists and solo with back-up group, the prominent use of percussion and brass instruments, and syncopated rhythms.)

CD1:1 Musical styles differ throughout the world. The many styles of music reflect the cultures and people who created them. Becoming familiar with a variety of music can help you identify the source of a specific type of music.

• As you listen, look at the pictures on the previous pages. Follow the pictures that represent the musical selections in "Style Montage."

 "Style Montage"

A Caribbean Style

CD1:2 Musical styles are often made up of elements from several cultures. Styles of music today also reflect the influences of the latest technology. These influences may be heard in the instrumental and vocal tone colors, the types of rhythms used, the interplay between voices and instruments, and the overall form of a musical composition.

• Listen to a piece based on Jamaican musical traditions. What instruments do you hear? What vocal sounds do you hear? What musical elements can you identify that you have heard before?

Lucky Dube

 "Serious Reggae Business" by Lucky Dube

2

Tap the steady **quarter note** (♩) beat with your foot, and clap the rhythm pattern as you listen again. Make a silent palms-up motion on each **quarter rest** (𝄽). The **repeat signs** (𝄆 𝄇) mean play the pattern again.

clap 𝄆 𝄽 ♩ 𝄽 ♩ 𝄇

tap 𝄆 ♩ ♩ ♩ ♩ 𝄇

Making music at Montego Bay, Jamaica

3

3. Introduce steady beat in "Serious Reggae Business." Have the students:
• Clap the rhythm patterns as they listen to "Serious Reggae Business," and identify the tempo. (tempo is moderate)

SPECIAL LEARNERS

Exceptional students who are visually impaired or who need a visual cue for coordinating motor and reading tasks will benefit from enlarged notation for the rhythm pattern accompaniment. Some mainstreamed students may also need a teacher cue to clap on the correct beats.

LESSON 1

4. Perform accompaniments "Serious Reggae Business." Have the students:
• Practice the melodic and harmonic accompaniments. (You may wish to use the keyboard section that begins on pupil page 232 for instruction on the playing of chords.)
• Perform the melodic and harmonic accompaniments with the recording as indicated.

• Play this melody on a recorder or keyboard instrument. Each **half note** (♩) sounds as long as two quarter notes.

• Play these chords on a keyboard instrument. A **chord** consists of three or more pitches sounded together. To play **B♭** (**B-flat**) on the keyboard, find the black key to the right of **A**.

• Listen to "Serious Reggae Business" again. Play the melody above during the Verse and the chords during the Refrain.

Bob Marley

Ziggy Marley

4

SPECIAL LEARNERS
Use an overhead transparency of pupil page 4 to assist students in following the notation for the melodic and harmonic accompaniments to "Serious Reggae Business." Point to the beginning of each phrase.

Reggae

"Serious Reggae Business" is an example of the musical style **reggae** (rĕ′gā). This style developed during the 1960s on the island of Jamaica in the Caribbean. Reggae has since become very popular in the United States and other parts of the world.

Reggae grew out of the Jamaican **ska** music. Ska was a fast, lively style that featured the trumpet, trombone, and saxophone. Over time the ska ensemble grew to feature a prominent rhythm section of electric guitar, bass guitar, and drums. Eventually some ska songs became slower, and rhythms and melodies became catchier. Reggae is one of the few styles to feature the bass guitar. The guitar sounds, combined with reggae drum patterns, give the music its distinct rhythmic style. The electric guitar generally plays a simple off-beat strum, while organ and brass instruments are often used to punctuate and fill out the sound.

The first song to name this musical style was "Do the Reggay," recorded by Toots and the Maytals in 1968. Reggae music in the United States can trace its popularity to a 1973 film "The Harder They Come." The film starred Jamaican singer Jimmy Cliff, who was one of the creators of the reggae music used in the film's popular soundtrack. Bob Marley made reggae popular in the 1970s with his unique vocal melodies, full harmonies, and lyrics containing political and social statements. The reggae style influenced rock groups in America and Britain—most notably The Police in the 1980s.

In addition to creating reggae music, Jamaican culture contributed to the creation of rap. As early as the 1960s, long before rap was developed in the United States, Jamaican disc jockeys would improvise rhymes over recordings of instrumental music. This practice was called "toasting" and was linked to a musical style called **dancehall**. Dancehall survives in Jamaica as a more melodic style of rap. Dancehall and reggae have continued to be influential in American music. Prominent reggae performers today include Michael Rose (formerly the lead singer of Black Uhuru), Shabba Ranks, Buju Banton, Ziggy Marley, and Beenie Man.

Michael Rose

Buju Banton

5. Introduce reggae style. Have the students:
• Discuss the background information on reggae.
• Discuss reggae as an example of a musical style that was created at a specific time, in a specific place—the Caribbean island of Jamaica. Reggae incorporates sounds and rhythm patterns characteristic of that particular culture and geographical area. Select several cultural groups or countries and discuss the characteristics of their musical styles. (Fiddles and guitars are often associated with bluegrass music; music from many parts of Africa is marked by complex rhythms.)

Reinforcing the Lesson

Discuss with the students why they chose certain pictures on pages x–1 to represent a particular style as they heard "Style Montage."

3 APPRAISAL

The students should be able to:
1. Listen to two stylistically contrasting compositions and discuss similarities or differences in the composers' use of such elements as tempo, form, tone color, and accompaniment.
2. Read and perform the melodic and harmonic accompaniments to "Serious Reggae Business" with accuracy.
3. Verbally identify reggae style to include at least three characteristic sounds specific to this style.

MORE MUSIC TEACHING IDEAS

Have the students:
1. Create their own melodic accompaniments to "Serious Reggae Business."
2. List other popular performers whose music reflects the reggae style. (Answers will vary.)

LESSON 2

Focus: Comparing Western and Non-Western Styles

Objectives
To identify and define contrasting styles
To perform a rhythmic accompaniment containing eighth notes and eighth rests

Materials
Recordings: *Bwala*
            Kyrie
            African Sanctus
Percussion instruments

Vocabulary
Style, eighth note, tempo, eighth rest

1 SETTING THE STAGE

Review the qualities of musical style and recall the elements of reggae style heard in "Serious Reggae Business" (page 2). Tell students that they will learn about a style of music that combines musical characteristics from different cultures.

2 TEACHING THE LESSON

1. Introduce contrasting styles. Have the students:
• Listen to and contrast *Bwala* and Kyrie. Try to identify their origins.
• Examine the photos and determine which musical selection they would associate with each of the sculptures. (Kyrie—English sculpture; *Bwala*—African sculpture)

• Listen to *Bwala*, a dance from Uganda, and the Kyrie (kir′ ē-ā) from the Mass in G Minor by Ralph Vaughan Williams. What characteristics of each composition might help you identify its origin? Answers may vary.

Bwala (dance from Uganda)
Kyrie from Mass in G Minor, by Ralph Vaughan Williams

In different cultures many things vary. The people may speak different languages. The foods they eat and the clothes they wear also may be different. The art and architecture produced by different cultures also have their own unique characteristics.

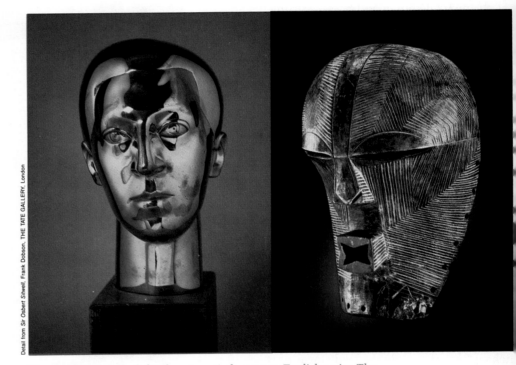

Detail from *Sir Osbert Sitwell*, Frank Dobson. THE TATE GALLERY, London

The sculpture on the left is by a twentieth-century English artist. The sculpture on the right is by an artist of the Songe tribe in Zaire. Although they both have the same subject, their styles are quite different.

6

EXTENSION

THE COMPOSER

Ralph Vaughan Williams (1872–1958) was born in Gloucestershire, England. His interest in music was sparked by his grandmother, who encouraged him to study piano and violin. He later went on to study composition and organ at Trinity College, Cambridge.

Vaughan Williams had great pride in his homeland. He loved his country's folk music—"the lilt of the chorus in a music hall . . . the children dancing to a barrel organ . . . the cries of street peddlers." His own music was greatly influenced by the many songs he collected and wrote down.

Besides composing, Vaughan Williams taught, wrote about music, conducted at choral festivals, and always encouraged young musicians.

Music from different times and cultures sounds different. The **style** of a culture is a unique mixture of its characteristics. The style of a musical composition is the unique mixture of its musical and cultural characteristics.

In *African Sanctus*, a new musical style results from combining the musical characteristics of different cultures. *Bwala* with its percussion, strong steady beat, and accents is combined with the choral singing tradition of Western cultures.

• Listen to *African Sanctus*. As each number is called, decide whether the music sounds more African or more Western. In which sections is it hard to make a choice? Western: 1, 3, 4, 6, 10, 11; African: 2, 5, 9; both: 7, 8

 African Sanctus, by David Fanshawe

The style of *African Sanctus* is unique. The musical characteristics of two cultures have been combined to create music in a new style.
• Tap the steady quarter-note beat played on the drum as you listen to the opening choral part of *African Sanctus*. Then tap the following patterns as you listen again. Make a palms-up, silent motion for each quarter rest.

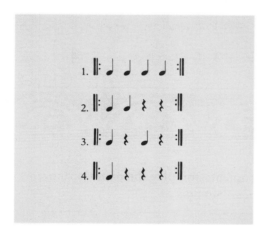

7

LESSON 2

2. Introduce *African Sanctus*. Have the students:
• Discuss the information on style.
• Discuss the combination of musical styles in *African Sanctus*.
• Listen to *African Sanctus* (with call numbers).
• Determine which selections are in an African or a Western style, or both.

3. Prepare students to perform the percussion part to *African Sanctus*. Have the students:
• Listen to the recording of *African Sanctus* (call number 1) and tap the steady beat played by the drum. (Assign the note value of quarter note to the steady beat.)
• Tap the rhythm patterns as they listen again.

THE COMPOSER

David Fanshawe—English composer, was born in Paignton, Devonshire, in 1942. He was educated at St. George's Choir School and Stowe. He later won the Foundation Scholarship to the Royal College of Music, where he studied composition. His professional debut as a piano soloist–composer was at Queen Elizabeth Hall in 1970. Fanshawe has written scores for radio, film, and television programs. Journeys through Europe, the Far East, and Africa have resulted in compositions that merge local folk melodies and rhythms with Western musical traditions.

LESSON 2

• Listen to the recording of *African Sanctus* again (call number 1) and clap two sounds for each beat, counting aloud from 1 to 8. (Assign the note value of eighth notes to each subdivision.)

• Listen to the second and third sections of *African Sanctus* and clap and count the eighth-note subdivisions in the new tempo.

• Form six groups, with each group performing a line of the percussion score.

• Practice lines 1 and 2, 3 and 4, and 5 and 6 separately and then together.

• Perform with the recording of *African Sanctus* beginning with call number 3.

• Select percussion instruments and perform the patterns as an accompaniment to *African Sanctus*.

• Respond to the Challenge! by creating their own rhythm patterns to *African Sanctus*.

Reinforcing the Lesson

Discuss what distinguishes an African style from a Western one. (more complicated rhythms, different instruments)

3 APPRAISAL

The students should be able to:

1. Listen to a composition representative of Western style and one representative of non-Western style, and identify salient musical characteristics of each. Discuss at least two similarities and two differences in the cultures' music.

2. Read and perform with accuracy a percussion accompaniment to *African Sanctus* containing eighth notes and eighth rests.

Each quarter note can be divided into two **eighth notes** (♪♪).

• Listen again to the opening choral section of *African Sanctus*, and clap two eighth-note sounds for each beat. As you clap, count aloud from 1 to 8, giving each clap one count.

• Listen to the second and third sections of *African Sanctus*. Clap and count the eighth notes in these sections. Is the new **tempo**, or speed of the beat, faster or slower than that of the first section? faster

• Listen to the complete *African Sanctus*. Perform these patterns with the choral sections by clapping and counting each line. Make the silent, palms-up motion for the **eighth rest** (❼).

• Select percussion instruments and play the patterns above as an accompaniment to *African Sanctus*.

 CHALLENGE Create your own patterns to accompany *African Sanctus*.

8

E X T E N S I O N

EXTRA HELP

The success of the *African Sanctus* activity will be enhanced if the groups are paired—1 and 2, 3 and 4, and 5 and 6—to perform the rhythms.

SPECIAL LEARNERS

Divide the class into two groups, each having a mixture of mainstreamed and regular students. Use an overhead transparency of pupil page 8 with different color cues for each pair of lines. Have each group play the even- or odd-numbered lines as you point to each pair of lines on the color-coded overhead transparency.

MORE MUSIC TEACHING IDEAS

Have the students:

1. Create their own rhythmic accompaniments to *African Sanctus*.

2. Create their own musical style by combining two or more contrasting styles, for example, melodies from the classics set with a rock-style rhythmic accompaniment.

Left, drummers at a festival in Vuaben, Ghana. Above, celebration at a baby-naming ceremony in Accra, Ghana. Below, South African women perform a mine dance.

9

LESSON 3

Focus: Recognition of I and V Chords, Syncopation

Objectives
To identify calypso style
To become familiar with syncopation
To identify and perform the I and V chords (and their roots)

Materials
Recordings: "Run Joe"
　　　　　 "Run Joe" (performance mix)
　　　　　 "Serious Reggae Business"
Keyboard, bells, recorder, guitar

Vocabulary
Calypso, syncopation, tonic, key tone, dominant, root

1 SETTING THE STAGE

Tell the students that they will be learning about another Caribbean style.

2 TEACHING THE LESSON

1. Introduce calypso. Have the students:
• Discuss the information on calypso and syncopation.
• Listen to the recording and sing the refrain (changing voices can sing an octave lower).

2. Introduce "Run Joe." have the students:
• Perform the rhythm patterns on the verse and refrain with the recording. (The pattern to be performed during the verse can be introduced by rote.)
• Sing the verses and refrain with the recording.

CALYPSO STYLE

Key: G major　　Starting Pitch: G　　Scale Tones: *la, ti, do re mi fa so*

"Run Joe" is a **calypso** song about two brothers who get into trouble. Calypso texts are usually witty, making fun of political and economic issues. The music is rhythmic, danceable, and cheerful. It achieves its unique lilt by stressing melodic notes just ahead of or just behind the steady beat. This type of off-the-beat rhythm is called **syncopation.** Calypso music evolved in Trinidad, in the West Indies, toward the end of the nineteenth century. It also exhibits a strong African influence.

Run Joe

Words and music by Dr. Walt Merrick,
Joe Willoughby, and Louis Jordan

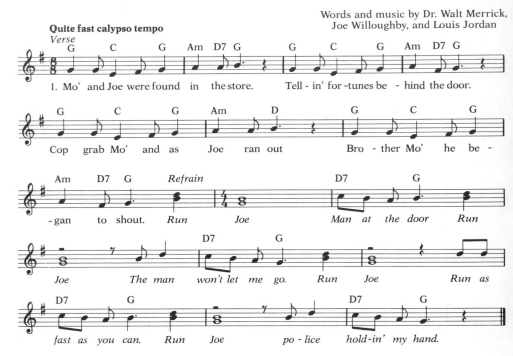

2. When you get home, you get to bed
   Call a doctor and tie your head.
   Can't tell Ma to invent a lie.
   Got to have a good alibi.

3. When the Judge ask me how I plea
   Not guilty, sir, most decidedly.
   You can see, judge, at a glance
   I'm the victim of circumstance.

4. If the judge believe what I say
   I'll be home by the break of day.
   If he don't, I'll be looking cute
   Behind the bars in my striped suit.

5. Mother told me not long ago
   Keep away from that worthless Joe.
   If I heard what my mama say
   Wouldn't be in this mess today.

Words and Music by Dr. Walt Merrick, Joe Willoughby and Louis Jordan
Copyright © 1947 (Renewed) CHERIO CORP.
International Copyright Secured. All Rights Reserved.

10

E X T E N S I O N

CURRICULUM CONNECTION: SOCIAL STUDIES

Calypso—a type of folk music that comes from Trinidad. It originated in the work songs of the African slaves. The word *calypso* is thought to have come from the African word *kai-so,* which means bravo.

In calypso the words are more important than the music. They usually reflect local events, gossip, or personal philosophy. Cleverness in making up words and rhymes on the spot is the sign of a virtuoso calypso singer. Almost any instrument can be used to accompany the calypso singer. Commonly used instruments are bamboo pieces, rattles, drums, flutes, and guitars.

MORE MUSIC TEACHING IDEAS

Have the students select rhythm instruments to perform the rhythm patterns while singing "Run Joe."

- Perform this pattern during the verses of the song.

- Perform this pattern during the refrain. Pat your lap with your right and left hands.

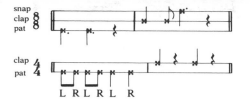

You can accompany the refrain of "Run Joe" on guitar or keyboard using two chords built on G, the first (I), and D, the fifth (V), pitches of the **G major scale**.

The G or I chord is called the **tonic** chord and is built on the most important pitch or tone of this scale, the **key tone** or home tone. The D or V chord is built on the fifth pitch of this scale and is called the **dominant** chord.

- Listen to the refrain of "Run Joe." Place your palms down on your desk when you hear the I chord. Turn your palms upward when you hear the V chord.

The lowest pitch of each of these chords is called the **root**.

- Give the letter names of the roots of the I and V chords. G and D
- Play the root of each chord on keyboard as you sing the refrain.
- Play the chords (I and V) as you sing the refrain.
- Play this pattern on bells or keyboard as you sing the refrain.

 CHALLENGE Create your own melodic pattern on keyboard, bells, or recorder to play on the word *Joe* as you sing the refrain. Use these five pitches. Play your accompaniment as you sing the song.

G A B D E

11

3. **Introduce the chord accompaniments to the refrain of "Run Joe."** Have the students:
- Discuss the information on the G-major scale and chords.
- Label the I and V chords.
- Listen to the refrain of "Run Joe" and identify tonic and dominant chords as indicated.
- Identify and label the root of each chord to the refrain of "Run Joe."
- Form two groups and choose bells, guitar, or keyboard. Each group will play one of the chords as it is heard on the recording.

4. **Introduce the melodic accompaniment to "Run Joe."** Have the students:
- Play the melodic accompaniment to "Run Joe" on bells or keyboard as they sing the refrain.
- Respond to the Challenge! by creating their own four-beat melodic patterns. Use the five pitches of the G pentatonic scale.

Reinforcing the Lesson
Have the students review "Serious Reggae Business" on page 2 to distinguish between syncopated and non-syncopated styles.

3 APPRAISAL
The students should be able to:
1. Listen to a composition in calypso style and list at least three musical characteristics that can be identified with calypso style.
2. Perform the I and V chords and roots in "Run Joe" on keyboard, guitar, or bells.
3. Listen to several musical examples of syncopated and non-syncopated melodies and identify each example using pencil and paper procedures.

MORE MUSIC TEACHING IDEAS
Have the students perform other selections that use the I and V chords, for example, "Tom Dooley."

VOCAL DEVELOPMENT
Sing the refrain on a sustained *oo* vowel to contrast with the marcato articulation of the verse.

SPECIAL LEARNERS
Speech cues that reinforce the rhythms will help exceptional students perform the accompaniments. Have the class make up their own speech patterns from "Run Joe" such as, "Run, Joe, po-lice here" for the rhythm during the verse, or "Mo and Joe are run-ning fast-er" for the rhythm in the refrain. (Or you may wish to invent the speech patterns.)

LESSON 4

Focus: Instrumental Tone Color, Dynamics

Objectives
To identify instrumental tone color
To identify and label dynamic changes
To create an original composition

Materials
Recordings: *Hiryu Sandan Gaeshi*
               Bwala
               Kyrie
High and low drums
Pitched and unpitched classroom instruments

Vocabulary
Tone color, dynamics, piano, forte, crescendo, decrescendo

1 SETTING THE STAGE

Tell the students they will be identifying the sounds of instruments in Japanese music and creating their own sound compositions.

2 TEACHING THE LESSON

1. Introduce *Hiryu Sandan Gaeshi*. Have the students:
• Listen to *Hiryu Sandan Gaeshi* and describe the moods of the piece.
• Summarize how the changes in tempo and instrumentation take place (abruptly? quickly? gradually?)

Hiryu Sandan Gaeshi (hē´ rē-yōō sän´ dän gī´ shē) features *taiko* (tī´ kō) ensemble and bamboo flute. Taiko is a large Japanese barrel drum of ancient origin. In this piece, the drummers express hope for good fortune, peace, and long life.

• Listen to *Hiryu Sandan Gaeshi*. You will hear several instruments. The flute begins the piece alone. In what ways does the mood of the piece change after the drums enter?

 Hiryu Sandan Gaeshi

12

E X T E N S I O N

CURRICULUM CONNECTION: SOCIAL STUDIES

Taiko—the Japanese barrel drum whose origin is mentioned in legend from as early as the 7th century. Taiko has been used for such diverse purposes as animating battling warriors, scaring away insects, and religious ceremonies. Taiko ensembles regained their popularity in Japan in the 1950s, and interest in the music has subsequently grown in the USA and throughout the world. Soh Daiko, the group heard in the recording and pictured on the pupil page, is from New York City.

A procession crossing a river at a Japanese festival

• Listen to *Hiryu Sandan Gaeshi* for the variety of tone colors. (flute, drums, and voice)
• Identify the techniques used by the drummers to achieve the varied tone colors. (sticks on drum head, sticks on barrel, and stick on stick)
• Discuss the information on dynamics.
• Listen again to *Hiryu Sandan Gaeshi* for dynamic changes.
• Describe the use of dynamics in this piece.

In *Hiryu Sandan Gaeshi*, contrast is achieved through the use of different *tone colors*, *tempos*, and *dynamic* changes.

    Tone color refers to the sounds of the different instruments.

• Listen again. Name three ways that the drummers create different tone colors.

    Dynamics are the levels of loudness and softness in music. They are often shown by the abbreviations of the Italian words *piano* (*p*) for soft and *forte* (*f*) for loud. To show gradual changes from one dynamic to another, symbols and words are used.

            crescendo (*cresc.*) gradually grow louder

            decrescendo (*decresc.*) gradually grow softer

• Listen to *Hiryu Sandan Gaeshi* once again for dynamic changes. Do the drums first enter on a crescendo or on a decrescendo? Describe the overall dynamic level of this piece.

13

MORE MUSIC TEACHING IDEAS

Have the students create an improvised percussion part on high and low drums in the style of *Satto* to demonstrate contrasts of tone color and dynamics.

LESSON 4

2. Prepare to create a sound composition. Have the students:
• Discuss the information about creating a sound composition.
• Read the poems aloud.
• Choose one poem and create a composition that will make a sound picture of the poem. (Help the students decide which tone colors, dynamics, and tempo they will use.)
• Practice and perform the composition. (Provide a limited time framework in which to complete the composition. You may wish to tape record each composition for appraisal. You may wish to use one of the poems to develop a composition as a model for the class.)

Create a Sound Composition

Composers often get ideas from other art forms such as theater or poetry. You, too, will have the opportunity to be a composer and create a sound composition based on one of these poems.

• Read the poems aloud. Select one of them and create an original composition that will make a sound picture of the poem. Decide what tone colors, dynamics, and tempo you will use.
• Practice and perform your composition. Have other students guess which poem inspired your composition.

Rainbow Writing

Nasturtiums with
their orange cries
flare like trumpets;
their music dies.

Golden harps
of butterflies;
the strings are mute
in autumn skies.

Vermilion chords,
then silent gray;
the last notes of
the song of day.

Rainbow colors
fade from sight,
come back to me
when I write.

—*Eve Merriam*

14

E X T E N S I O N

CURRICULUM CONNECTION: READING

Eve Merriam—born in 1916, is a writer of poetry, fiction, nonfiction, and plays for both adults and children. She has won several awards for her writing. Her poetry often contains humorous plays on words and expresses a joyful exploration of the world.

Langston Hughes (1902–1967)— was born in Joplin, Missouri, and grew up in other cities of the Midwest. Known mainly for his poetry, he also wrote fiction, nonfiction, and drama. His poetry portrays the urban African American experience in everyday language. It conveys the rhythms of colloquial speech and of popular music.

TEACHER INFORMATION

Share the Music uses the term *African American* when referring to Americans of African descent.

COOPERATIVE LEARNING

Have the students work in cooperative groups of four to create a sound composition based on the poems on pages 14 and 15. Have the group decide on a poem for the project. For creating the sound picture of the poem, all four members of the group should decide on the tone colors, dynamics, and tempo that will be used. Possible roles to be assigned are recorder, to notate a graph score that includes one idea from each group member, and conductor, to research and lead the performance once the basic decisions have been made. Each cooperative group will perform its sound piece for the rest of the class. For another day, duplicate the graph score of each co-

Dreams

Hold fast to dreams
For if dreams die
Life is a broken-winged bird
That cannot fly.

Hold fast to dreams
For when dreams go
Life is a barren field
Frozen with snow.

—*Langston Hughes*

Bravado

Have I not walked without an upward look
Of caution under stars that very well
Might not have missed me when they shot and fell?
It was a risk I had to take—and took.

—*Robert Frost*

15

operative group and have other members of the class perform the sound pieces by reading the graph scores. Discuss the results.

Reinforcing the Lesson

Review *Bwala* and Kyrie on page 6. Discuss the contrasts in dynamics.

3 APPRAISAL

The students should be able to:

1. Identify the tone color of Japanese woodwind and percussion instruments and the method of tonal production for each.

2. Listen to several musical examples demonstrating clear examples of piano, forte, crescendo or decrescendo, and identify the correct dynamic symbol for each.

3. Create a composition to represent a sound picture of a poem and, within the composition, include contrasts in tone color, dynamics, and tempo.

CURRICULUM CONNECTION: READING

Robert Frost (1874–1963)— was one of the greatest of twentieth-century poets. His poetry is characterized by plain language, a graceful style, and powerful images. Born in the West, Frost moved to New England at age eleven and was influenced by the region's countryside, colloquial speech, and attitudes. He briefly attended Dartmouth College and Harvard University. Frost also worked for a short time as a schoolteacher, newspaper editor, mill worker, and farmer. His first books, published in England, brought him international recognition. He later won four Pulitzer Prizes for his poetry.

LESSON 5

Focus: Historical Style Periods

Objectives
To identify the major historical style periods and their musical characteristics
To perform a melody on keyboard, bells, or recorder

Materials
Recordings:　"Historical Style Montage"
　　　　　　"Style Montage"
Keyboard, bells, or recorder

Vocabulary
Renaissance, baroque, classical, romantic, twentieth century

1 SETTING THE STAGE
Tell the students European musical styles can be organized into major historical style periods.

2 TEACHING THE LESSON

1. Introduce European-Western styles.
Have the students:
- Discuss the information on "Ode to Joy" and Beethoven's Symphony No. 9.
- Listen to the "Historical Style Montage."
- Prepare to perform "Ode to Joy" melody on keyboards, bells, or recorders.
- Identify phrases that are similar. (1, 2, and 4) (If students are having difficulty with the third phrase, have them play phrases 1, 2, and 4.)
- Perform "Ode to Joy" as they listen to the "Historical Style Montage." (The students should begin after the Beethoven excerpt.)
- Identify the number of times they played "Ode to Joy" as they listened to "Historical Style Montage." (five times)
- Describe the musical characteristics of each of the five settings. (Encourage the students to use general descriptions of tempo, rhythm, dynamics, and tone color.)

E X T E N S I O N

SPECIAL LEARNERS
Prepare an overhead transparency of pupil page 16 if the class contains mainstreamed students who have visual impairments or difficulty reading notation. Write the names of the notes under phrases 1 and 3. It may also be necessary to point to the beginning of each phrase as the students are performing the theme. This will enable the mainstreamed students to coordinate the auditory with the visual activity.

Symphony No. 9 by the German composer Ludwig van Beethoven (lōōd′ vig vän bā′ tō-ven) contains one of the most famous melodies ever written, the "Ode to Joy."

- Listen to the "Historical Style Montage." It first presents the "Ode to Joy" as Beethoven used it in his Symphony No. 9 and then as it might have sounded if used by composers who lived as much as four hundred years before Beethoven, or as much as one hundred fifty years after.

How is each performance different? Think about tone color, instruments, dynamics, and tempo to help you decide. Answers will vary.

 "Historical Style Montage"

- Perform the "Ode to Joy" on keyboard, bells, or recorder as you listen to the "Historical Style Montage." Begin after the Beethoven example.

"Ode to Joy" from Symphony No. 9, Fourth Movement

Ludwig van Beethoven

16

Each time you performed the "Ode to Joy," it was in a different musical style. In European-Western music the terms *Renaissance, baroque, classical, romantic,* and *twentieth century* are used to describe each of the musical styles.

Renaissance Both religious and secular music, predominantly vocal, instruments used in secular music

Baroque Steady rhythm, organ used to accompany religious music, secular music written for small groups

Classical Short, tuneful melodies, gradual dynamic changes, restrained expression of emotions

Romantic Longer, often complex melodies, more open expression of emotions

Twentieth Century Unusual rhythms, emphasis on unusual tone colors, great emphasis on experimentation

• Listen to the "Historical Style Montage" again. Identify the order in which the style periods are presented. Use the musical descriptions above to explain your choices.

17

2. Introduce the European-Western style: the differences. Have the students:
• Identify the major historical style periods and their major characteristics.
• Listen to the "Historical Style Montage." Identify the order in which the style periods are presented. (The five styles are: baroque, Renaissance, classical, twentieth century, romantic.)

Reinforcing the Lesson

Review "Style Montage" on page 2. Have the students follow the pictures that represent each musical section.

3 APPRAISAL

The students should be able to:
1. Match the names of the major historical style periods—Renaissance, baroque, classical, romantic, and twentieth century—to brief written descriptions of salient musical characteristics of those styles.
2. Perform "Ode to Joy" on keyboard, bells, or recorder with melodic and rhythmic accuracy.

MORE MUSIC TEACHING IDEAS

Have the students listen to, identify, and classify selected recordings representative of the major style periods if available.

LESSON 6

Focus: Baroque Style

Objectives
To identify duple and triple meter
To review and identify orchestral tone colors
To identify ternary (ABA) form of a composition
To identify the musical characteristics of a baroque composition

Materials
Recordings: ''Marche'' (excerpt)
   ''Marche''
   ''Historical Style Montage''
   ''Spring'' from *The Four Seasons* (optional)
Keyboard, recorder, percussion instruments

Vocabulary
Meter, duple meter, triple meter, measure, bar line, ritardando, coda, ternary

1 SETTING THE STAGE
Play Lully's ''Marche'' as the students enter the room. Tell them this music is typical of baroque style.

2 TEACHING THE LESSON
1. Introduce duple meter and triple meter conducting patterns. Have the students:
• Discuss the information on duple meter and triple meter.
• Perform the duple meter and triple meter rhythms.
• Listen to the excerpt from Lully's ''Marche.''
• Identify which conducting pattern shows the meter for each section.
• Describe the contrast in tempo between the two sections.
• Listen to the entire ''Marche'' and conduct showing duple and triple meter.

Conducting a Baroque Composition

''Marche'' by Jean Baptiste Lully (zhän′ bäp-tēst′ lyoo-lē′) has sections in different **meters,** or groupings of beats. Beats grouped in twos are **duple meter.** Beats grouped in threes are in **triple meter.** Groups of beats are shown in **measures** that are separated by **bar lines.**

These are the conducting patterns for duple and triple meter. The photographs show the patterns when the conductor faces you.

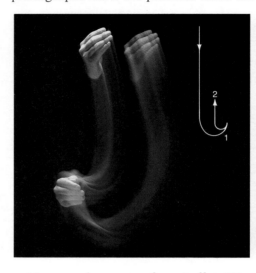
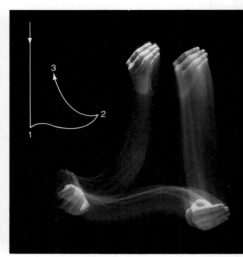

• Listen to the excerpt from Lully's ''Marche.'' It has A and B sections. Tell which conducting pattern to use for each section. Describe the contrast in tempo between the two sections. duple, triple; B is faster than A

🎵 ''Marche'' (excerpt) by Jean Baptiste Lully

• Listen to the entire ''Marche'' and conduct showing duple and triple meter.

🎵 ''Marche'' by Jean Baptiste Lully

18

Jean Baptiste Lully

JEAN BAPTISTE LULLY

Jean Baptiste Lully (1632–1697) became King Louis XIV's most important and influential composer, producing operas and ballets to entertain the French court. For fifteen years Lully controlled much of the music performed in Paris. He was so popular that he was able to persuade King Louis XIV to force other composers to move away from Paris. Thus Lully managed to eliminate most of his competition. He earned enormous sums of money, but no amount ever seemed enough.

An unusual accident caused Lully's death. Instead of using a baton, conductors in those days often kept the steady beat by tapping a large stick on the floor. While conducting this way, Lully struck his own foot. An infection developed, which resulted in his death a month later.

During his career Lully wrote a great deal of dance music. His interest in orchestral tone color can be seen in the wide range of instruments he used in his works.

LESSON 6

2. Introduce the composer. Have the students discuss the information on Lully. You may wish to use some of the following items as a basis for further discussion.

1. Discuss the use of the words *important* and *influential*. Name people in the twentieth century who have been "important and influential" in political and social affairs. (Martin Luther King, Jr.—social justice, Eleanor Roosevelt—social reform; Mahatma Gandhi—social and political reform; Winston Churchill—political leadership)

2. Lully died a rich and famous man. Discuss the concept of fame. Name some famous contemporary musicians. (Philip Glass, Bruce Springsteen, Andrew Lloyd Webber, Leonard Bernstein, and so on)

19

LESSON 6

3. Introduce the listening map of "Marche." Have the students:

• Become familiar with the format of the map. As each number is called:

Section A

1. Follow each measure of the notation in rhythm.
2. Touch the picture of the instrument family that is heard. (strings, then woodwinds)
3. Follow each measure of notation in rhythm.
4. Follow the bridge section followed by the ritardando.

Analyzing a Baroque Composition

• Listen to Lully's "Marche" again and follow the map by pointing to each measure when the music is provided. When no music is shown, point to the pictures that represent the meter, tone color, dynamics, and form. At call number 4, **ritardando** (ri-tär-dän' dō) means a gradual slowing down of the tempo. At call number 9, the **coda** is the concluding section.

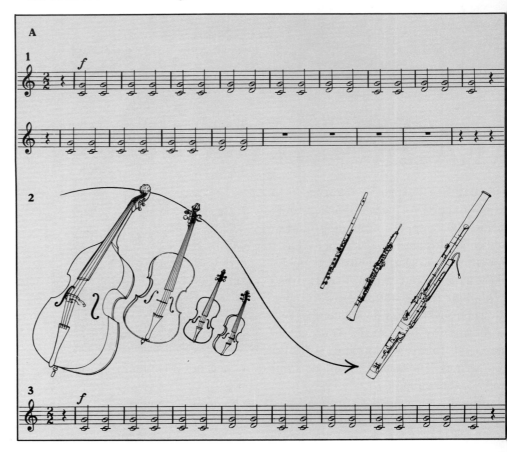

20

SPECIAL LEARNERS

Prepare an overhead transparency of pupil pages 20 and 21 if your class contains exceptional students who will have difficulty following notation. Point to each measure of the notation. It may help these students first to listen to the A section and tap the beat before following the listening map.

LISTENING

You may wish to use the Listening Map overhead transparency to help guide the students through the listening selection.

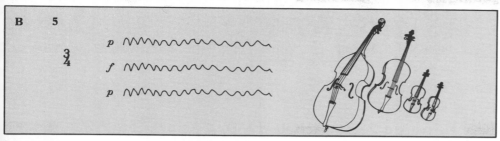

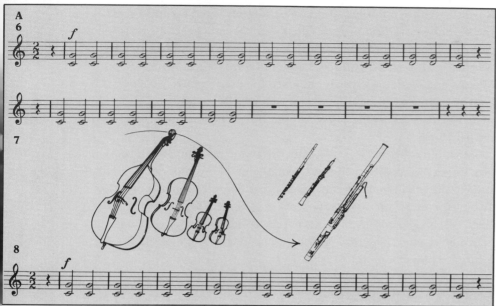

Repetition after a contrasting section creates an ABA, or ternary, form. **Ternary** means having three parts.

- Describe the contrasts between the A and B sections of Lully's "Marche." Identify contrasts in meter, tempo, and tone color.

- Play the A section and the coda of the "Marche" on recorder or keyboard.

A section is duple meter, moderate tempo, uses strings, woodwinds, and brass. The B is triple meter, faster tempo, and uses strings only.

LESSON 6

Section B
5. Follow the dynamic markings as the volume of the music changes.
Section A
6. Follow each measure of the notation in rhythm.
7. Follow the picture of the family of tone color that is heard. (strings then woodwinds)
8. Follow each measure of notation in rhythm.
Coda
9. Follow each measure of notation in rhythm.
- Define ternary form.
- Describe the contrast of meter, tempo, and tone color between the A and B sections.
- Play the A section and coda of the "Marche" on keyboard or recorder.

21

LESSON 6

4. Introduce the baroque period. Have the students:
• Discuss the information focusing on the musical characteristics of the period.

The Baroque Period (1600–1750)

Royalty, wealthy families, and large churches hired composers of the baroque period to provide music for special occasions or for entertainment. Operas, ballets, and instrumental compositions were written for the world at large. Large religious choral works— Masses and cantatas—were composed for use in churches. For contrasts in tone color composers used a wide variety of instruments such as the organ, violin, flute, oboe, trumpet, and harpsichord.

Most baroque music has steady, rhythmic patterns. Each section of a larger composition conveys a single mood or emotion. Improvements in instruments made more complex music possible. Two of the most famous composers of all time, Johann Sebastian Bach (yō' hän se-bäs' tē-än bäкн') and George Frederick Handel (hän' del) lived during this period and produced some of the finest examples of baroque music.

Staircase at the Residenz (with frescos by Tiepolo), Würzburg

• Identify the characteristics of baroque style in "Marche." (steady rhythms, a single mood in each movement, and contrasting tone colors)

Reinforcing the Lesson

Review "Historical Style Montage" on page 16 to identify contrasting tone colors.

3 APPRAISAL

The students should be able to:

1. Listen to a composition in duple and triple meter and identify the meters.

2. Demonstrate duple and triple meters using appropriate conducting patterns or movements.

3. Listen to musical examples demonstrating the tone color of brass, woodwind or string families and name, in writing, the tone color.

4. Verbally identify ternary form as a contrasting section followed by a return of the first section.

5. Verbally describe at least three salient musical characteristics of baroque style.

During the baroque period, elaborate styles of architecture, art, and clothing were popular. The exterior scene is of a palace in Vienna, Austria. The interior scene is in Würzburg, West Germany. The musicians in the painting are gathered for a formal portrait.

The Concert. Antonio Domenico Gabbiani

Characteristics of Baroque Music

Steady rhythms

Single mood in each section of a musical composition

Wide variety of instruments used for contrasts in tone color and dynamics

elvedere. Vienna

23

MORE MUSIC TEACHING IDEAS

Have the students:

1. Play the steady beat on percussion instruments to accompany the B section of "Marche" as a contrast to the melodic performance activity in Section A.

2. Listen to "Spring" from *The Four Seasons* by Vivaldi, another baroque composer (see page 192).

LESSON 7

Focus: Major and Minor, Romantic Style

Objectives
To identify major and minor chords
To identify the contrasting sections in ·a twentieth-century song
To identify the musical characteristics of a romantic composition

Materials
Recordings: "Farandole"
Chopin, Etude in E Minor (optional)
"Our World"
"Our World" (performance mix)
"Marche"
Keyboard, bells, or guitar
Tennis balls
Copying Master 1-1: Listening Map (optional)

Vocabulary
Suite, natural

1 SETTING THE STAGE

Tell the students they will study music in three different styles but with the same basic harmonies.

2 TEACHING THE LESSON

1. Introduce "Farandole." Have the students:

• Listen to "Farandole." As each number is called, write on a sheet of paper which of the themes they hear. (You may wish to use Copying Master 1-1: Listening Map at this time.)

CD1:11

A Romantic Composition

"Farandole" (fä-rän-dôl') is the final selection in the second *L'Arlésienne* (lär-lā-zē-en') Suite by the French romantic composer Georges Bizet (zhorzh' bē-zā'). A **suite** consists of several individual forms linked together. Bizet wrote the suite as background music for a play called *L'Arlésienne,* or "The Woman of Arles." You may recognize the first of the two themes as the Christmas carol "The March of the Three Kings."

• Listen to "Farandole." Each time you hear a number decide whether you are hearing Theme A or Theme B. 1: A; 2: B; 3: A; 4: B; 5: A; 6: B; 7: A and B

 "Farandole" from *L'Arlésienne* Suite No. 2, by Georges Bizet

Georges Bizet (1838–1875), great opera composer, was born in Paris into a family of professional musicians. His father and uncle were singing teachers, and his mother was an excellent pianist. Bizet showed great promise as a musician at an early age. He entered the Paris Conservatory at nine. At nineteen he had won several prizes for piano, organ, and composition.

Although Bizet was a brilliant pianist, his main interest was composing, especially opera. *Carmen* is his best-known work. His music is very melodic with simple orchestral accompaniments. His music for the play *L'Arlésienne* was ignored by the public when it was first presented in 1872. It was not appreciated until the play was revived after his death.

24

EXTENSION

Theme A of "Farandole" begins with the D minor chord. Theme B begins with the D major chord.

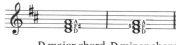

D major chord   D minor chord

To play F# (F sharp) on the keyboard, find the black key to the right of F. The symbol ♮ is called a **natural.** It tells you to play F rather than F#. Changing this middle pitch from F# to F changes the D major chord to a D minor chord.

Play the D minor and D major chords one after the other on keyboard, bells, or guitar to hear the difference between minor and major.

Bizet uses changes between major and minor, and changes in dynamics, to create the romantic style in "Farandole."

Listen to "Farandole" again. In each section identify the use of major or minor, and changes in dynamics. A: minor, loud; B: major, soft or <

Arles, a city in southern France, was founded almost twenty-five hundred years ago. Many of its ancient buildings have been preserved.

25

• Discuss the information on Bizet and *L'Arlésienne* Suite No. 2.
You may wish to use the following as a basis for further discussion.
Bizet wrote *L'Arlésienne* as background music for a play. Music in theater has many functions. It can set a mood, announce an event, or add a dimension to the plot. Name specific examples of each of the above in movies or television. Discuss some techniques for using music to create a mood or scene.

2. Introduce major and minor chords.
Have the students:
• Discuss the information on the D major and D minor chords.
• Practice playing the chords on keyboard, bells, or guitar to hear the difference.
3. Prepare analysis of "Farandole."
Have the students listen to the recording of "Farandole" again. As each number is called, determine if the themes are presented in major or minor and the appropriate dynamic marking (piano or forte). (You may wish to use Copying Master 1-1: Listening Map at this time.)

SPECIAL LEARNERS

Exceptional students who need visual cues to coordinate visual and reading tasks will benefit from an overhead transparency and individual copies of Copying Master 1-1: Listening Map. As the listening selection is played, pause at the end of each section to allow the students to fill in the chart with the correct responses. Then mark the correct response on the transparency. This will enable the mainstreamed students to coordinate the auditory activity with the visual task.

LESSON 7

4. Introduce the historical and musical characteristics of the romantic period. Have the students:

• Discuss the information focusing on the musical characteristics of the period.

• Summarize the romantic characteristics of "Farandole." (telling a story without words; long complex melodies; prominence of certain instruments; contrasting tone colors; and use of a large orchestra)

The Romantic Period (1830–1900)

Much of the music in movies and on television can be traced back to the kind of music written in the nineteenth-century romantic period. Romantic artists and musicians tried to express their feelings, their outlook, and their hopes and dreams openly. Composers wrote instrumental works that told a story without words. Music became more descriptive, with changes in moods occurring within sections. Long, complex melodies were used to express these moods or emotions. As orchestras became larger and improved instruments were added, tone color became more important than it had been in earlier periods.

Left, the
Opéra, Paris,
built 1861–7?

Music of the romantic period is very popular today. Many famous romantic works have been used as background music for extremely successful motion pictures. Some of the best known composers of this period were Ludwig van Beethoven (bā' tō-ven), Franz Schubert (shoo' bert), Robert Schumann (shoo' män), Hector Berlioz (ber' lē-ōz), Frédéric Chopin (shō' pan), Richard Wagner (väg' ner), Giuseppe Verdi (ver' dē), Johannes Brahms (bräms'), Peter Ilyich Tchaikovsky (chī-käv' skē), and Nicolai Rimsky-Korsakov (rim' skē kor' sä-kôv).

26

EXTENSION

COOPERATIVE LEARNING

Have the students form cooperative groups of four. Two readers (one for page 22 and one for page 26), a recorder and a reporter should be assigned in each group. The readers should read page 22 and 26 out loud for the group. Then each group member should write down at least two statements that focus on the similarities and differences between the baroque and romantic musical styles. The group should decide at least four of the most common statements that best describe the differences between baroque and romantic music. The recorder should record the six common statements. The reporter reads the descriptive statements to the class. Class members should require each cooperative group to provide a rationale as to why they think their statements best describe the differences between baroque and romantic music.

You may wish to vary this activity by having the students read the material and write their statements before you divide the class into groups. The students could then compare lists, choosing several of the most common statements describing the differences between baroque and romantic music.

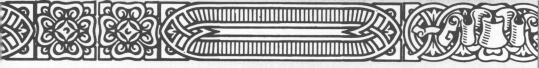

Florentine Story-teller, Vincenzo Cabianca, MUSEO DELL'ARTE MODERNA, Florence

The Ball, James Tissot, MUSÉE D'ORSAY, Paris

Characteristics of Romantic Music

■ Changes of mood within sections of a composition
■ Direct expression of emotions
■ Long, often complex melodies
■ Use of large orchestra

Artists of the romantic period often depicted scenes of earlier times. Top, an imaginary scene of medieval Italy. Right, women's fashions in the nineteenth century often were quite elaborate.

27

MORE MUSIC TEACHING IDEAS

Have the students:
1. Choose eight to ten selections from current popular music. Listen and identify selections in major and minor.
2. Listen to "Farandole." Pass a tennis ball to the right on the strong beat when the music begins in minor; pass the tennis ball to the left when the music begins in major. (The order is: 1: m; 2: M; 3: m; 4: m, 5: m; 6: m; 7: M)
3. Listen to the Etude in E minor Op. 25, by Chopin, to hear the musical characteristics of the period (see page 199).

LESSON 7

5. Introduce a song in major and minor. Have the students:
• Listen to the repeated and contrasting sections in "Our World" and identify which are major and which are minor.
• Sing "Our World," emphasizing the contrasting sections.

Reinforcing the Lesson

Review "Marche" by Lully, page 18, and compare the major and minor sections.

3 APPRAISAL

The students should be able to:
1. Listen to aural examples of major and minor chords and identify the chords using pencil and paper procedures.
2. While watching the music for "Our World" (with numbered measures) write the measure numbers for the A section repeat and the B contrasting section.
3. Verbally describe at least three salient musical characteristics of romantic style.

CD1:12, **A Song in Major and Minor**

Key: E♭ major   Starting Pitch: B♭

CD8:31   "Our World" is a twentieth-century song that has sections in both major and minor.

• Listen to the repeated and contrasting sections. You will hear the A section repeat before you hear the B section. Which section is in major and which is in minor? A is in major; B is in minor.
• Sing the song. Be sure to emphasize the contrasting sections.

Scale Tones: E♭ major: *so, la, ta, ti, do re ma mi fa so la ta ti do'*
              G minor: *mi si la ti do'*

Our World

Piano Accompaniment on page PA 2

Words by Jane Foster Knox
Music by Lana Walter

28

E X T E N S I O N

SPECIAL LEARNERS

Students who are slow readers or who have visual impairments may have difficulty following the notation when the song changes from single to double staff format. Prepare an overhead transparency of pages 28–29 of the pupil edition and point to the staff that has the melody. This procedure will enable different learners to follow the order of the song. Mainstreamed students also may need a visual starting cue since "Our World" does not begin on the downbeat.

VOCAL DEVELOPMENT

Have the students sing the pitches of "Our World" on short *doo* sounds to aid rhythmic and melodic accuracy.

SIGNING FOR "OUR WORLD"

In sign language the meaning of the phrase is signed. For example, to "make it so" means to make it happen or succeed; therefore the sign is "succeed."

Think

The index finger points to the brain.

Human Race (People)

Using "P" palms down hands circle alternately in front of the body.

Find

With palm down, index finger and thumb close, as in picking up something.

16   17 *poco rit.*   18   *a tempo*   19 unison *mp*   20 *soft and intense*

flash-ing in the sun. Jour-ney just be-gun!   What   fu -ture will there

flash-ing in the sun. Jour-ney just be-gun!   What   fu -ture will there

21 no breath 22   23   24   25

be   for land and_ air and   sea?   Liv-ing things like_ you and   me?_____

26   27   28 Ⓐ   *mp*   29

I'd   like to think a   fu -ture hu -man

I'd

30   31

race   would find the world a   fair and love -ly

like to think a   fu -ture hu -man   race   would

32   33 *mf*   34

place.   Lov – ing and car – ing,   we can make it   so,

find the world a   fair and love-ly   place. By   car – ing   we can make it   so,

35   36   *rit.*   37 *p*   38   39

shar-ing what we know: lov -ing, we can make   it   so._____

shar-ing what we know: lov -ing, we can make   it   so._____

29

World   Circle the right "W" forward, down, up and around the left "W" as in the world revolving.

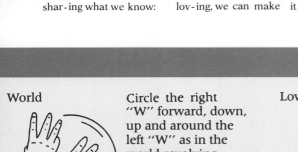

Fair/Lovely   The "O" hand starts at the chin, opens while circling the face, coming back to rest again at the chin.

Loving   With closed fists, cross hands over the heart.

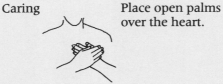

Caring   Place open palms over the heart.

Make It So (Succeed)   Index fingers move up, making two loops, as in moving up the ladder toward success.

Sharing   Move the upright, open-palm of the right hand back and forth across the open, palm-up left hand.

Know   Fingers touch forehead.

LESSON 8

Focus: Steady Beat

Objectives
To explore aspects of the history of rock and roll
To perform quarter notes and eighth notes in a rhythm score
To perform rhythmic and melodic accompaniments

Materials
Recordings: "Believe"
          African Sanctus
Drumsticks (or substitutes)
Keyboard, bells, or recorder
Copying Master 1-2 (optional)

Vocabulary
rock and roll

---

1 SETTING THE STAGE

Ask students to share the titles of their favorite songs or name their favorite types of music, then tell them that they will be learning about the history of the most influential style of popular music in the last 50 years—"rock" music or "rock and roll."

2 TEACHING THE LESSON

1. Introduce the history of rock and roll. Have the students:
• Read pages 30–31 and discuss any of the rock artists mentioned with whom they might already be familiar.
• Predict which current music figures will be remembered in the future and share opinions about why they might be remembered.

ROCK AND ROLL

The term **rock and roll** was invented to describe a new kind of music that captured the energetic spirit of the 1950s. Rock and roll borrowed elements from various styles of music. For example, it took blues scales and blues progressions from rhythm and blues. It took vocal styles from rockabilly, a style of country western music. Its rhythms came from rhythm and blues, rockabilly, and many other styles. The combination of these elements created a unique beat that shook the nation and eventually the world.

Chuck Berry was an early rock and roll innovator. His guitar playing came from the rhythm and blues style. He brought the lead guitar to the forefront of the band, and is remembered as the first great showman of rock and roll. His energetic performances often included his trademark "duck walk" step. Other early rock and rollers were Elvis Presley and Buddy Holly. They became famous stars with their captivating singing, which was influenced by rhythm and blues as well as rockabilly.

Soon after rock and roll became popular in America, its influence spread abroad. In the early 1960s, rock and roll became very popular in Britain. It influenced British groups such as The Rolling Stones and Cream, which featured the guitar playing of Eric Clapton. Another British group influenced by rock and roll was The Beatles, whose impact on popular music has lasted for decades. In the mid-1960s these groups began the "British Rock Invasion," which captured the American rock and roll stage. During the 1970s other English super-groups such as Led Zepplin and The Who added new sounds to rock music.

Left to right:
The Beatles,
Elvis Presley,
Melissa Etheridge,
Sting.

30

MORE MUSIC TEACHING IDEAS
Have students work individually or in pairs to select an innovator from the history of rock and roll. Have them research biographical details and find examples of their chosen person's music. Share the results of their research (including recorded examples) with the rest of the class, giving special attention to what specific innovations the performer or composer brought to the rock-and-roll style.

America in the late 1960s was an important place and time for rock and roll. Jimi Hendrix amazed audiences with his electrifying guitar playing. Janis Joplin captivated audiences with her powerful and expressive voice. The group The Doors combined the musical elements of jazz with spoken poetry to create their own unique style. The Grateful Dead began experimenting with long, intricate improvisations at live concerts. These concerts started their reputation as a great live band. All of these artists created innovative music that captured the spirit of their era.

In the early 1990s a new kind of rock music developed called "alternative rock." This music contained elements such as rough and distorted guitars, heavy drum sounds, and emotional singing. It is exemplified by groups such as Pearl Jam and Nirvana. Like the rock groups that preceded them, they added new expressive elements to the music and created their own personal styles.

Rock music is also a reflection of the times. As our culture has changed over the last few decades, rock has also changed and evolved. These changes are easy to hear by contrasting a classic 1950s Chuck Berry song like "Johnny B. Goode" against a 1990s alternative rock song like Pearl Jam's "Even Flow." These and many other artists were honored in the summer of 1995 with the opening of the Rock and Roll Hall of Fame in Cleveland, Ohio. Through its vast collection of memorabilia, the Rock and Roll Hall of Fame pays tribute to the great innovators who have made this music an important part of American culture.

31

LESSON 8

2. Meet Elton John. Have the students:
• Read page 32.
• Listen to the recording of "Believe," following the printed text on page 35. Identify words or phrases emphasized by the singer and discuss how vocal inflection can contribute to the expressive impact of a performance.

3. Introduce rhythmic accompaniment to "Believe." Have the students:
• Prepare to perform the four rhythmic patterns on page 32 by patting the quarter notes and clapping the eighth notes. (Remind them to make no sound for the rests and observe the accents in Pattern 2.)
• Learn the matched-grip drumsticks position. (Hold both drumsticks in the same position, palms down.)
• Practice the four patterns, using the matched grip.
• Locate the patterns in the rhythmic accompaniment score to "Believe."
• Listen to "Believe" again, noticing the contrast between the sections marked "A" and those marked "B" in the rhythmic accompaniment.

Elton John

The pop star Elton John has combined rock and roll with other styles of music to create his own personal style. His well-crafted melodies and unique vocal style have made his ballads and up-tempo rock and roll songs long-lasting favorites.

Elton was born near London, England, in 1947 as Reginald Kenneth Dwight. As a young boy he received recognition for his classical piano playing. Instead of pursuing classical music he joined a rock band in his late teens. He developed a talent for writing catchy pop tunes and eventually changed his name to Elton John.

By the time of his American debut in 1970, he had gone from the shy Reginald to the outrageous Elton John. He is known for popular ballads such as "Daniel" and "Candle in the Wind" (about Marilyn Monroe) as well as rock classics like "Crocodile Rock," "Honky Cat," and "Benny and the Jets." In the 1990s he wrote much of the music for the award-winning Disney film "The Lion King." "Candle in the Wind, 1997," written for the funeral of Diana, Princess of Wales, became the best-selling single of all time.

• Listen to "Believe," composed by Elton John in 1995. How do the singer's vocal style and rhythmic emphasis help to express the lyrics?

 "Believe" by Elton John and Bernie Taupin

• Practice playing these rhythmic patterns. Stress, or emphasize, the accented notes ()

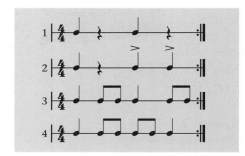

• Play the rhythm accompaniment to "Believe" on page 33 with the recording.

32

E X T E N S I O N

he symbol () in the score means you should listen and count
measures before beginning to play.

Believe
Rhythm Accompaniment

Introduction

Interlude

Coda

rest to end

**4. Perform a rhythmic accompaniment
with the recording of "Believe."** Have
the students:
• Form two groups. (One group will perform the "**A**" sections; the other will
perform the "**B**" sections. Both groups will
perform the Introduction and Coda.)
• Practice the parts on pupil page 33.
• Perform the rhythmic accompaniment
with the recording, continuing to alternate
parts from section to section.

MORE MUSIC TEACHING IDEAS

Have students with prior keyboard experience learn and perform a keyboard accompaniment to "Believe" (Copying Master 1-
2).

EXTRA HELP

You may wish to use an overhead transparency of pupil page 33. Point to each section of the accompaniment as it begins.

LESSON 8

5. Perform a melodic accompaniment to "Believe." Have the students:
• Practice the pattern at the top of page 34, and find the notes in the melodic accompaniment.
• Practice the melodic accompaniment.
• Perform the melodic accompaniment with the recording of "Believe."
• Perform both rhythmic and melodic accompaniments with the recording as the rest of the class sings along, using the text on page 35.

Reinforcing the Lesson

Review the rhythmic accompaniment to *African Sanctus* on page 8.

3 APPRAISAL

The student should be able to
1. Name key performers who played a part in the history of rock and roll.
2. Read and perform a rhythmic accompaniment to "Believe."
3. Read and perform a melodic accompaniment to "Believe."

• Play this pattern on bells or a keyboard instrument. Find these notes in the melodic accompaniment.

• Play this melodic accompaniment with "Believe."

34

E X T E N S I O N

Believe

Words and music by Elton John
and Bernie Taupin

I believe in love,
it's all we've got.
Love has no boundaries,
costs nothing to touch.
War makes money,
cancer sleeps,
curled up in my father
and that means something to me.
Churches and dictators,
politics and papers,
everything crumbles
sooner or later,
but love.
I believe in love.

I believe in love,
it's all we've got.
Love has no boundaries,
no borders to cross.
Love is simple.
Hate breeds
those who think difference
is the child of disease.
Fathers and sons
make love and guns.
Families together
kill someone
without love.
I believe in love.

Without love
I wouldn't believe
in anything
that lives and breathes.
Without love
I'd have no anger.
I wouldn't believe
in the right to stand here.
Without love
I wouldn't believe.
I couldn't believe in you
and I wouldn't believe in me
without love.
I believe in love.
I believe in love.
I believe in love.

REVIEW AND EVALUATION

JUST CHECKING

Objective
To review and test the skills and concepts taught in Unit 1

Materials
Recordings: Just Checking Unit 1
(Questions 1, 2, 5, 6, 7, 8, 10)
"Historical Style Montage"
"Run Joe"
"Serious Reggae Business"
African Sanctus
Hiryu Sandan Gaeshi
Unit 1 Evaluation (question 3)
For Extra Credit recordings
(optional)
Keyboard, recorder, or bells
Copying Master 1-3 (optional)
Evaluation Unit 1 Copying Master

TEACHING THE LESSON

Review the skills and concepts taught in Unit 1. Have the students:
• Perform the activities and answer the questions on pages 36–37. (For this review, examples for questions 1, 2, 5, 6, 7, 8, and 10 are included in the "Just Checking Unit 1" recording. Have the students answer these questions first. Then have them answer the other questions in the review, using the recordings in the unit where necessary.)
• Review their answers.
(You may wish to use Copying Master 1-3 at this time.)

REVIEW

JUST CHECKING

See how much you remember.

1. Listen to the recording of the steady beat and perform these patterns, patting the quarter notes and clapping the eighth notes.

2. Listen to a section of Lully's "Marche" and decide if the meter is duple or triple. Show your answer by conducting. Is the tempo slow, moderate, or fast? duple; moderate

3. Play the "Ode to Joy" on page 16 on keyboard, recorder, or bells as you listen to the "Historical Style Montage." Decide whether the style period of each version of the "Ode to Joy" is Renaissance, baroque, classical, romantic, or twentieth century. baroque, romantic, twentieth century, Renaissance

4. Perform this pattern as you listen to the verse of "Run Joe" to experience the syncopated calypso style.

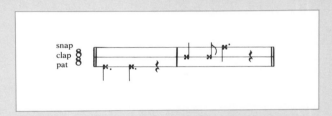

5. Use two movements to show the I and V chords as you listen to the refrain of "Run Joe." Show the chord changes by putting your palms on your desk when you hear the I chord. Put your thumbs up when you hear the V chord.

36

6. Listen to determine whether the style period of each of these compositions is Renaissance, baroque, classical, romantic, or twentieth century. baroque, romantic, classical, twentieth century

7. Listen to a section of Bizet's "Farandole" to determine whether its theme begins in major or minor. minor

8. Listen to determine whether the style of each example is African, rock and roll, Japanese, calypso, or reggae. reggae, Japanese, synth-pop, calypso

9. Listen and identify the instrument family you hear in these excerpts from Lully's "Marche." Show your answer by pointing to the appropriate picture as each number is called.
1. strings only; 2. woodwinds and strings

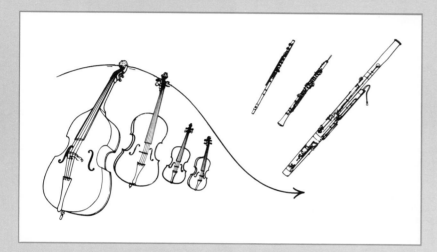

0. Listen to a section of *African Sanctus* and decide if the music sounds more African or more Western. African

1. Listen to a section of *Hiryu Sandan Gaeshi* and determine whether you are hearing a crescendo or decrescendo.

REVIEW AND EVALUATION

GIVING THE EVALUATION
Evaluation Unit 1 Copying Master can be found in the *Teacher's Copying Masters* book along with full directions for giving the evaluation and checking the answers.

FOR EXTRA CREDIT
You may want to have the students do one of the following activities.
1. Describe how tone color, meter, tempo, and dynamics are used to create contrast in the baroque style of "Marche." (The work is in ABA form. The A sections are in duple meter, slow tempo and use all of the families of instruments. The B section is faster than A, is in triple meter, and uses only the string section of the orchestra.)
2. Binary and ternary form are common in many aspects of our lives. Identify and describe one other object which either contains or is an example of binary form and one which is an example of ternary form. (architecture, buildings, and so on.)

UNIT 2 • OVERVIEW

ELEMENTS OF MUSIC	UNIT 2 OBJECTIVES	Lesson 1 Focus: Duple, Triple, and Quadruple Meter	Lesson 2 Focus: Changing Meter
Dynamics	Identify dynamic changes in a composition		
Tone Color	Identify tone color changes Perform melodic accompaniments on bells, recorder, or keyboard		Perform a melodic accompaniment on bells, recorder, or keyboard
Tempo			
Duration/ Rhythm	**Identify duple, triple, and quadruple meter Identify meter changes Perform, listen to, and identify irregular meter in $\frac{5}{4}$ and $\frac{7}{8}$**	Identify duple, triple, and quadruple meter by responding to the meter through body percussion, tennis ball activities, and conducting metric patterns Perform meter games by accurately saying and performing the meter patterns Identify duple, triple, and quadruple meter from listening examples Identify changes in meter	Identify changes of duple, triple, and quadruple meter through conducting and movement Listen to, conduct, and perform changing meters in a song Read and perform a melodic accompaniment with rhythmic accuracy Learn to conduct the pattern for $\frac{6}{4}$ Create changing meter patterns
Pitch	Hear, sing songs within a range of B-e′	Sing a song with changing meters	Sing a song with a range of B-e′
Texture	Perform a melodic accompaniment		Read and perform a melodic accompaniment on bells, recorder, or keyboard (d-b)
Form	Conduct a musical composition having a strophic form		Conduct a composition in strophic form
Style	Listen to and discuss the jazz style Discuss nationalism in the romantic style period **Classify musical examples according to style period**	Listen to rhythm use in different musical styles Classify listening examples according to style period	Discuss a contemporary Broadway musical
Reading	Practice known notations Use $\overset{3}{\underset{}{\sqcup\!\sqcup\!\sqcup}}$, $\sqcup$. $\sqcup$.	Read ♩, >, ‖: :‖ in $\frac{2}{4}$, $\frac{3}{4}$, $\frac{4}{4}$ Follow body motion score	Sing and play songs using $\frac{3}{4}$, $\frac{4}{4}$, $\frac{6}{4}$, ‖: :‖, 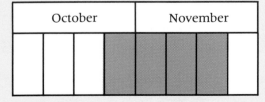

PURPOSE Unit 2: RHYTHM PLAYS A ROLE

In this unit the students will review and/or experience various aspects of rhythm. They will review duple, triple, and quadruple meter and be introduced to some unusual rhythm patterns.

SUGGESTED TIME FRAME

October				November			

FOCUS
- Duple, Triple, and Quadruple Meter
- Changing Meter
- Irregular Meter
- Irregular Meter in Sevens, Jazz

Lesson 3 Focus: Irregular Meter	**Lesson 4** Focus: Irregular Meter in Sevens, Jazz
Follow dynamic changes in a composition	
Follow tone color changes in a composition	Hear instruments in a jazz quartet
Identify, listen to, define, and perform irregular meter Identify meter changes in a composition through body percussion Read and perform a speech chant in $\frac{5}{4}$ meter Perform meter games in $\frac{5}{4}$	Identify, listen to, and perform irregular meter in seven Determine the grouping of twos and threes in a composition with seven beats per measure Tap steady beat while listening to irregular meter Perform a rhythmic ostinato on bells, recorder, or keyboard Play accented beats in $\frac{7}{4}$ meter
Listen to a melody in $\frac{5}{4}$ meter	Read and perform a melodic accompaniment in $\frac{7}{4}$ meter Sing a song with a range of d-e'
Listen to a jazz composition using irregular meter Discuss nationalism shown through musical style of Modest Mussorgsky Listen to a composition which reflects the romantic style period and uses changing and irregular meters	Discuss jazz style of Dave Brubeck Discuss musicians from the 1950s and 1960s who made unique contributions to popular music
Read body motion score, irregular meters Follow notation in $\frac{2}{4}$, $\frac{3}{4}$, $\frac{5}{4}$, $\frac{6}{4}$	Play ostinato in $\frac{7}{4}$ Sing song in $\frac{7}{8}$

TECHNOLOGY

MUSIC WITH *MIDI*

MIDI technology allows students to manipulate musical elements and make musical decisions.
- Lesson 3, page 48: Perform/Improvise in **Five-Four Meter**
- Lesson 3, page 48: Analyze **Tone Color:** *"Promenade" from Pictures at an Exhibition by M. Mussorgsky*

VIDEO RESOURCES

Use video resources to reinforce, extend, and enrich learning in this unit.

LESSON 1

UNIT **2**
RHYTHM
PLAYS A ROLE

38

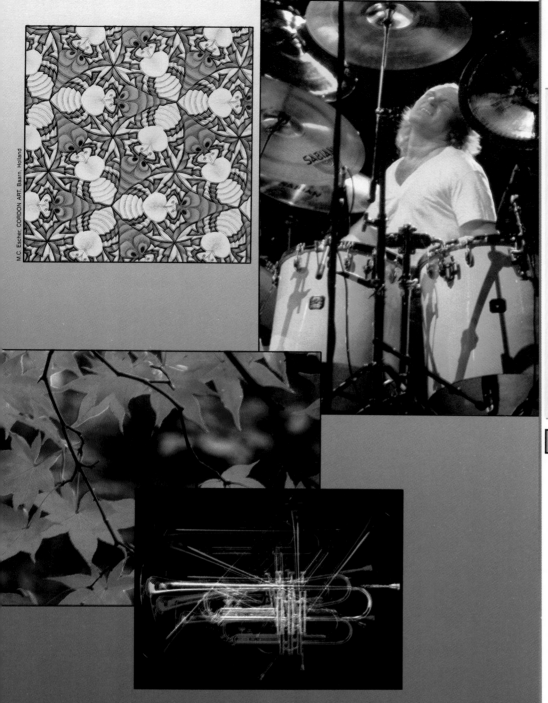

M.C. Escher, CORDON ART, Baarn, Holland

LESSON 1

Focus: Duple, Triple, and Quadruple Meter

Objectives
To identify and distinguish between duple, triple, and quadruple meter in recorded compositions.

Materials
Recordings: "Marche"
           "Music in Twos"
           "Music in Threes"
           "Music in Fours"
           "Meter Identification Montage"
           "That's What Friends Are For"
           "That's What Friends Are For" (performance mix)
Classroom pitched and unpitched instruments
Tennis balls (one for each student)

Vocabulary
Quadruple meter

1 SETTING THE STAGE
Review conducting "Marche" by Lully on page 18.

39

LESSON 1

2 TEACHING THE LESSON

1. Introduce duple, triple and quadruple meter. Have the students:

• Perform the body percussion in duple meter as shown while listening to "Music in Twos."

• Listen again to "Music in Twos" and perform the body percussion while saying their names as indicated.

• Perform the body percussion in triple meter as shown while listening to "Music in Threes."

• Listen again to "Music in Threes" and perform the body percussion while speaking their names as indicated.

• Perform the body percussion in quadruple meter as shown while listening to "Music in Fours."

• Listen again to "Music in Fours" and perform the body percussion while saying their names as indicated.

Beats can be grouped in sets. The first beat of each group is emphasized.

• Perform this rhythm in duple meter as you listen to the recording.

"Music in Twos"

• Listen again, perform the rhythm pattern in duple meter, and play this name game. Each of you, in turn, will say your first name on the accented beat of each measure until everyone has had a turn.

• Perform this rhythm pattern in triple meter as you listen to the recording.

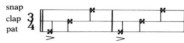

"Music in Threes"

• Listen again, perform the rhythm pattern, and play the name game in triple meter.

• Perform this rhythm pattern in **quadruple meter** as you listen to the recording.

"Music in Fours"

• Listen again, performing the rhythm pattern. Play a variation of the name game in which each of you says your first name on the accented first beat and your last name on the third beat.

40

E X T E N S I O N

- Show duple, triple, and quadruple meter by bouncing a tennis ball
on the first beat of each measure. "Change" means to change hands.

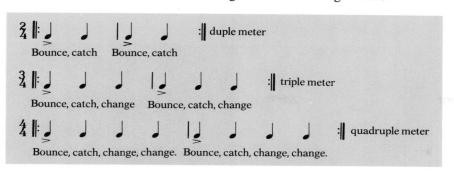

CD1:37

Bounce, catch   Bounce, catch   duple meter

Bounce, catch, change   Bounce, catch, change   triple meter

Bounce, catch, change, change.   Bounce, catch, change, change.   quadruple meter

- Show duple, triple, and quadruple by bouncing the ball and then
by conducting as you listen to "Meter Identification Montage." duple, quadruple, triple

 "Meter Identification Montage"

This diagram shows the conducting pattern for quadruple meter. The photograph shows how the pattern looks when the conductor faces you.

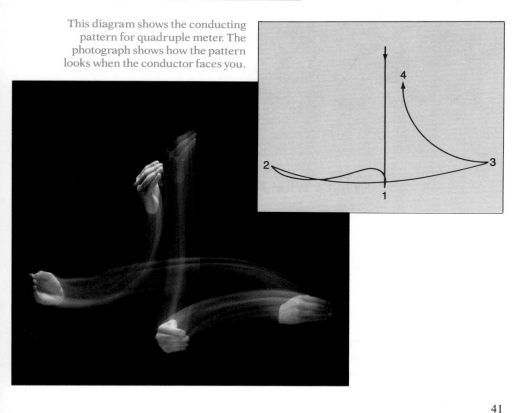

41

LESSON 1

2. Introduce tennis ball activity for reinforcing duple, triple and quadruple meter. Have the students practice duple, triple, and quadruple meter by bouncing a tennis ball on the first beat of each measure as indicated. Duple meter is performed as "bounce, catch." Triple meter is performed as "bounce, catch, change" (change hands). Quadruple meter is performed as "bounce, catch, change, change."

3. Introduce conducting patterns to reinforce duple, triple, and quadruple meter. Have the students:
- Review the conducting patterns for duple and triple meters on page 18.
- Examine the conducting pattern for quadruple meter.
- Practice each conducting pattern encouraging the use of two hands.
- Listen to "Meter Identification Montage" and bounce a tennis ball, then conduct, in the appropriate meter with the music.

COOPERATIVE LEARNING

Have the students show duple, triple, and quadruple meters by conducting as they listen to the music. Then working in cooperative groups of four, have the students create their own "Meter Identification Montage" using percussion and pitched instruments. (Encourage the students to use the pentatonic scale or Dorian mode if they know them.) Assign the role of recorder (to write down the order of the meters in the montage) and a conductor. One group may wish to quiz another group by having it determine the order of the meter in the "Meter Identification Montage."

SPECIAL LEARNERS

If a class includes exceptional students who have difficulty with coordination, or have physical handicaps, preplan an alternative activity for the body percussion and tennis ball activities, which emphasize metrical organization. Have these students pat a rhythm instrument on each downbeat. These students also may need a teacher cue for each downbeat.

EXTRA HELP

For beginning experiences with tennis balls, you may want to select two or three students to demonstrate the procedure for the class. Gradually add additional students to the group. You may want to have half the class use tennis balls while others observe. Alternate.

LESSON 1

4. Introduce changing meter. Have the students:

• Follow the score as they listen to "That's What Friends Are For" and notice when the meter changes.
• Sing the song.

Reinforcing the Lesson

Have the students classify the three listening examples from "Meter Identification Montage" according to style periods. Example 1—"Galop" by Igor Stravinsky. Twentieth century because of the emphasis on unusual rhythms and off-beat patterns. Example 2—Sinfonia from Cantata 140 by J. S. Bach. Baroque period because of the steady rhythm and sudden changes in dynamics. Example 3—"Procession of the Nobles" by Nicolai Rimsky-Korsakov. Romantic period because of the large orchestra.

3 APPRAISAL

The students should be able to listen to several musical examples in duple, triple, and quadruple meter and accurately identify the meter.

• Listen to "That's What Friends Are For." Decide when the meter changes. measures 9, 10, 22, 23
• Sing the song.

Key: F major   Starting Pitch: D   Scale Tones: *mi, fa, so, la, ti, do re mi fa so la*

That's What Friends Are For

Piano Accompaniment on page PA 6

Words and music by Carole Bayer Sager and Burt Bacharach

And I nev-er thought I'd feel__ this way—

1. and as far as I'm__ con-cerned__ I'm glad I got__ the chance__ to say__
2. well you came and o - pened me_____ and now there's so__ much more__ I see—

42

E X T E N S I O N

THE COMPOSER

Burt Bacharach—was born in 1928 in Kansas City, where he was raised in a cultured atmosphere. Bacharach studied music at McGill University and studied composition with Darius Milhaud and Henry Cowell. He played jazz piano in nightclubs at the same time. From 1958 to 1961 he was Marlene Dietrich's accompanist. Bacharach is best known for his popular songs, many of which were recorded by singer Dionne Warwick. During the 1960s he teamed up with Hal David to create such timeless songs as "Walk On By," "Raindrops Keep Fallin' On My Head," "What's New, Pussycat?" and "Alfie." "That's What Friends Are For" was written, arranged, and produced by Bacharach and his wife, Carole Bayer Sager.

VOCAL DEVELOPMENT

Have the students emphasize diction (consonant articulation) as a means of experiencing the rhythmic quality of this composition. Also, have them perform selected patterns of short vowels followed by long vowels to assist in achieving rhythmic accuracy, such as

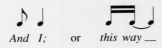

And I; or *this way* __

Have them find other examples of long and short vowels in the composition.

LESSON 2

Focus: Changing Meter

Objectives
To distinguish changes of duple, triple and quadruple meter
To conduct a six-beat pattern
To perform a composition in changing meters

Materials
Recordings: "Love Song"
"Love Song" (performance mix)
"Mix 'Em Up"
"Meter Identification Montage"
Keyboard, recorder, or bells
Tennis balls (one for each student)

1 SETTING THE STAGE

Tell the students they will be distinguishing changes of duple, triple and quadruple meter, and performing a composition in changing meters.

2 TEACHING THE LESSON

1. Introduce changing meters. Have the students:
• Listen to "Love Song" and read information on the musical *Pippin*.
• Listen to "Mix 'Em Up" and raise their hands when they hear a change in meter.

A STAGE STYLE

The musical *Pippin* is set in medieval times. However, because it is largely about young people growing up and learning to face the world around them, it has considerable contemporary appeal. Pippin's father, a character based on Charlemagne, wants his son to become a great warrior. Pippin, on the other hand, dreams of magic shows and miracles. Although Pippin never becomes the great warrior his father desired, he does learn to cope with the realities of being heir to the throne.

• Listen to "Love Song," which contains many changes of meter.

 "Love Song" from the musical *Pippin*, by Stephen Schwartz

A scene from the musical *Pippin*.

• Listen to "Mix 'Em Up" and raise your hand when you hear a change from one meter to another.

 "Mix 'Em Up"

44

EXTENSION

THE COMPOSER

Stephen Schwartz—composer and lyricist, was born in New York City in 1948. He studied at the Julliard School and Carnegie Mellon University. Schwartz is best known for his musicals. He wrote the music and lyrics to *Godspell,* for which he won the Drama Desk Award, two Grammy Awards, and a gold record. He also wrote the English text for Leonard Bernstein's *Mass.* Schwartz wrote *Pippin* in 1972. During its run on Broadway it won four Tony Awards, among other honors. In recent years, Schwartz has contributed music to the animated features *Pocahontas, The Hunchback of Notre Dame* and *Prince of Egypt.*

• Listen again and show when the composition is in duple, triple, or quadruple meter by conducting the appropriate pattern. duple; quadruple; triple

 CHALLENGE   As you listen to "Mix 'Em Up":

Walk forward and conduct in two when you hear duple meter. Stop and conduct in three when you hear triple meter. Stop and clap four beats in a square formation when you hear quadruple meter.

In "Love Song" Stephen Schwartz used meters of three, four, and six beats. Practice conducting the pattern for six beats in a measure.

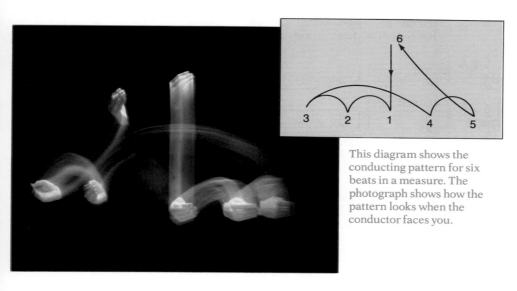

This diagram shows the conducting pattern for six beats in a measure. The photograph shows how the pattern looks when the conductor faces you.

• Look at the first four measures of "Love Song" on page 46 and decide which conducting pattern should be used in each measure. six beats; four beats; three beats; four beats

• Practice conducting the first four measures as you listen to "Love Song."

• Sing "Love Song" (pages 46–47). Play the descant (part tinted in yellow) on recorder, bells, or keyboard.

45

LESSON 2

• Listen again to "Mix 'Em Up" and identify the meter of the selection by conducting the appropriate pattern.
• Listen to "Mix 'Em Up" and respond to the Challenge! by performing the appropriate movement pattern to represent the meter they are hearing.

2. Introduce conducting changing meters. Have the students:
• Practice conducting the beat pattern for six beats in a measure.
• Examine the first four measures of "Love Song" and determine which conducting patterns should be used. (six, four, three, four)
• Practice conducting the first four measures as they listen to the song. (Note that the song is in strophic form so they will have the opportunity to conduct the pattern at least three times.)
• Analyze the conducting patterns for the entire song.

LESSON 2

• Sing the song with the recording and play the descant on keyboard, recorder, or bells.

Reinforcing the Lesson

Review "Meter Identification Montage" on page 41 to identify changes of meter.

3 APPRAISAL

The students should be able to:

1. Listen to "Mix 'Em Up" and with eyes closed, signal when they hear a change in meter.
2. Accurately conduct the changing meters in "Love Song" ($\frac{3}{4}$, $\frac{4}{4}$, and $\frac{6}{4}$).
3. Perform the melodic accompaniment to "Love Song" with rhythmic and melodic accuracy.

Key: E major   **Starting Pitch: F♯**   Scale Tones: *so, la, ta, ti, do re mi fa so la ta ti do'*

Love Song

Piano Accompaniment on page PA 10

Words and music
by Stephen Schwartz

Sit-ting on the floor and talk-ing 'til dawn. Can-dles and con-fi-
Pri-vate lit-tle jokes and sil-ly pet names. Lav-en-der soap and
how can you de-fine a look or a touch? How can you weigh a

-den-ces. Trad-ing old be-liefs and hum-ming old songs and
lo-tions. All of the cli-chés and all of the games and
feel-ing? Ta-ken by them-selves, now they don't mean much. To-

low-er-ing old de-fen-ces. Sing-ing a
all of the strange e-mo-tions. Sing-ing a   Love song,   la la la la__ la la
-geth-er they send you reel-ing in to a

3rd time cut to Coda ⊕

la la   la__ la la   Love song,   la la__ la la   la.____

46

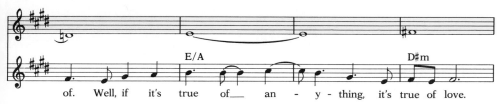

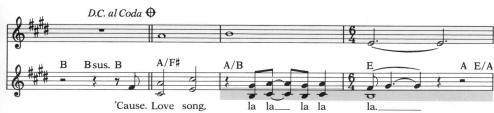

47

MORE MUSIC TEACHING IDEAS

Have the students:

1. Use the tennis ball–bouncing activity to show changing meter while they listen to "Mix 'Em Up."

2. Identify words with two syllables (U-tah) or (base-ball) and three syllables (Ar-kan-sas or bas-ket-ball) and create alternating measures of changing meters.

CURRICULUM CONNECTION: SOCIAL STUDIES

Charlemagne—also known as Charles the Great, was king of the Franks (the ancestors of the modern French people) from 768 to 814. He conquered most of western Europe and ruled as emperor. The arts and literature flourished during his reign. In 806, Charlemagne divided his empire among his three sons, Pepin, Charles, and Louis. Pepin and Charles died soon after, and Louis succeeded his father as emperor. Louis was a weak ruler; his sons warred against him for control of the empire. Finally, a treaty divided the empire into three parts. Without Charlemagne's strong rule, the empire fell into a period of confusion and decline.

LESSON 3

Focus: Irregular Meter

Objectives
To identify, perform, and define irregular meter
To listen to recorded compositions that use irregular meter
To follow changes of meter in a one-line score

Materials
Recordings: *Take Five* pattern
"Goin' Trav'lin'"
Take Five
"Promenade" from *Pictures at an Exhibition*
"Love Song"

Vocabulary
Irregular meter, program music

1 SETTING THE STAGE
Tell the students they will be identifying and performing irregular meters.

2 TEACHING THE LESSON

1. Introduce irregular meter. Have the students:
• Discuss and define irregular meter.
• Listen to the *Take Five* pattern and practice the rhythm pattern that is a combination of triple and duple meter.
• Practice the ⁵₄ pattern by patting the accented beats and clapping nonaccented beats while listening again to the *Take Five* pattern.
• Say their first names on the first beat of the measure and their last names on the fourth beat of the measure until every student has said his or her name.

IRREGULAR METER

Much of the music you have sung and played moves in either duple, triple, or quadruple meter throughout an entire composition. Sometimes composers use changing meter in a repeating pattern to produce **irregular meter.**

This painting by the American artist Romare Bearden illustrates the spirit of jazz.

A Little Jazz

• As you listen to the *Take Five* pattern, perform this rhythm pattern, which is a combination of triple and duple meter.

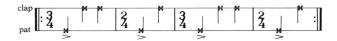

 Take Five pattern

This same pattern can be written with five beats in each measure with accents on the first and fourth beats.

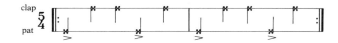

• Listen again. Show this irregular meter by patting your knees on beats 1 and 4 and clapping your hands on beats 2, 3, and 5.
• Continue patting and clapping as you play this variation on the name game. Say your first name on the first beat of your measure and your last name on the fourth beat of your measure.

48

EXTENSION

SPECIAL LEARNERS
Prepare an overhead transparency of pupil page 48 if you have mainstreamed students who have difficulty with motor coordination. Some of these students may not be able to coordinate the meter changes. Preplan the lesson so that these students pat or play a rhythm instrument on each downbeat. Exceptional students also may need a teacher cue for each downbeat.

THE ARTIST
Romare (Howard) Bearden (1914–1988)—was an American artist who lived across from the Apollo Theatre in Harlem and was inspired by the great jazz musicians who played there. He made collages with torn paper and paint, and showed his subjects' faces with several angles or colors to suggest African masks.

Traveling in Style

- Perform the pattern in $\frac{5}{4}$ as you recite "Goin' Trav'lin'." Pat the accented beats and make a palms-up motion on each quarter rest.

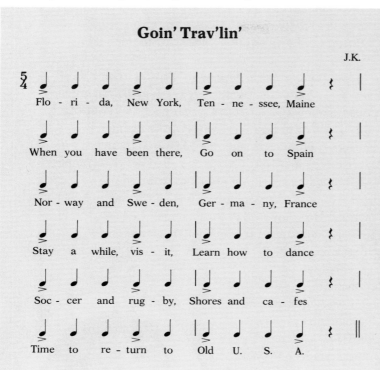

Goin' Trav'lin'

J.K.

Flo - ri - da, New York, Ten - ne - ssee, Maine

When you have been there, Go on to Spain

Nor - way and Swe - den, Ger - ma - ny, France

Stay a while, vis - it, Learn how to dance

Soc - cer and rug - by, Shores and ca - fes

Time to re - turn to Old U. S. A.

- Perform this pattern as you listen to *Take Five*. The composer, saxophonist Paul Desmond, was a member of the Dave Brubeck Quartet.

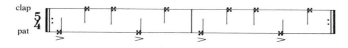

Take Five, by Paul Desmond, performed by the Dave Brubeck Quartet

49

---

2. Prepare "Goin' Trav'lin'." Have the students:
- Add to the $\frac{5}{4}$ pattern by patting the accented beat and substitute quarter rests for the claps.
- Perform the $\frac{5}{4}$ pattern as they recite "Goin' Trav'lin'."
- Perform the pat-clap pattern as they listen to *Take Five* by Dave Brubeck.

SPECIAL LEARNERS

Reading "Goin' Trav'lin'" and performing the body percussion or changing the pattern to sound and silence may be a difficult task for some exceptional students. This activity can be simplified by emphasizing only the accented beats by patting, using instruments, or through participation in only one part of the activity (speech or motion). Prepare an overhead transparency of pupil page 49 to help these students keep track of the words and the accents. For some students to participate in the sound and silence pattern with *Take Five*, a teacher visual cue on each accent will be necessary.

3. Introduce "Promenade" from *Pictures at an Exhibition*. Have the students:
• Read and discuss the information on Mussorgsky.
• Listen to "Promenade" and show the meter changes by pointing to the meter signature in each measure.

Changing Meter and a Change in Style

Changing meter and irregular meter are not unique to jazz. About one hundred years before Paul Desmond wrote *Take Five*, a Russian composer was using these same techniques.

The music of Modest Mussorgsky (mo-dest' mōō-sorg' skē) (1839–1881) reflects his great love for his Russian homeland. He often borrowed folk melodies to use as themes for his works. Sometimes he composed original melodies that sounded like Russian folk tunes.

One of his most famous compositions is *Pictures at an Exhibition*, which he composed in memory of an artist friend, Victor Hartmann. Following Hartmann's death, a number of his paintings were exhibited in a gallery. Mussorgsky decided to compose a collection of musical "pictures" inspired by the paintings. Descriptive music of this type is called **program music**.

Mussorgsky named each section after the painting it represented, for example, "The Gnome," "The Old Castle," and "The Great Gate of Kiev." He composed a "Promenade" theme to introduce the work and to lead the listener from "picture" to "picture" as if strolling through an art gallery. This famous "Promenade" theme makes use of changing and irregular meters.

Although Mussorgsky composed *Pictures at an Exhibition* for piano alone, the French composer Maurice Ravel later arranged the work for full orchestra. It is this orchestral version with its beautiful tone colors that most people hear today.

• Listen to "Promenade" and follow the score on page 51 by pointing to the meter signature changes in each measure.

50

EXTENSION

CURRICULUM CONNECTION: HISTORY

Nationalism—the sense of collective identity among the citizens of a country and the promotion of its interests. Examples of nationalism can be found in the arts, as in the case of the "Mighty Handful," a famous group of five Russian nationalistic composers. In the nineteenth century, nationalism developed in tandem with the struggle for democracy. As many European countries were attempting to overthrow monarchs and establish elected governments, the feelings that united the people also inspired loyalty and dedication to the movement. The spirit of reform spread to Russia, and nationalism grew proportionally.

COOPERATIVE LEARNING

Have one of the students write the following term and definition on the board:

Nationalism—the sense of collective identity among the citizens of a country and the promotion of its interests.

Divide the students into cooperative groups of four. Assign the role of reader and recorder in each group. The reader should read page 50 out loud for the group. After the materials have been read, each group member should write down one statement that he or she thinks supports the idea that Mussorgsky was a nationalistic composer. Each member of the group will present his or her statement. The validated examples for the entire group should be listed on a sheet of paper, which is then signed by all of the group members.

"Promenade" from *Pictures at an Exhibition,*
by Modest Mussorgsky

- Listen again and try to determine which instruments are used to create the tone color and dynamics of each section. See notations on score.

51

LESSON 3

- Listen again and try to determine which instruments are used to create the tone color and dynamics of each section.
- Respond to the following:
1. Many composers use folk melodies or create folklike melodies as themes for larger compositions. Why do they use folk tunes instead of melodies they wrote themselves? (To demonstrate a sense of Nationalism and enable the audience to identify with the music.)
2. Name composers besides Mussorgsky who used folk melodies in their music. (Copland: *Appalachian Spring*; Tchaikovsky: Symphony No. 4; Brahms: "Hungarian Dances"; Dvořák: *Slavonic Dances*).
3. How does *Pictures at an Exhibition* reflect the romantic period ideal? (There are many changes of mood within the composition and it reflects expressions of feelings and emotions.)

Reinforcing the Lesson
Review "Love Song," which also has changing meters (pages 46–47).

3 APPRAISAL
The students should be able to:
1. Accurately read and perform a speech canon in $\frac{5}{4}$ meter.
2. Follow changes of meter in a line score to "Promenade."

MORE MUSIC TEACHING IDEAS
Have the students perform the first four measures of "Promenade" on keyboard or bells with the recording.

LISTENING
You may wish to use the Listening Map overhead transparency to help guide the students through the listening selection.

SPECIAL LEARNERS
Prepare an overhead transparency of pupil page 51 if you have exceptional students in the class who have difficulty coordinating auditory and visual skills. Point to the name of each instrument group as the students follow the Listening Map to "Promenade" from *Pictures at an Exhibition.*

LESSON 4

Focus: Irregular Meter in Sevens, Jazz

Objectives
To identify, perform, and define irregular meter in sevens
To read and perform a melodic accompaniment in irregular meter

Materials
Recordings: *Unsquare Dance*
　　　　　　"Samiotissa"
　　　　　　"Promenade" from
　　　　　　Pictures at an Exhibition
Bells, recorder, or keyboard

Vocabulary
Ostinato

1 SETTING THE STAGE

Tell the students they will be studying jazz, which is a twentieth-century popular style.

2 TEACHING THE LESSON

1. Introduce 1950s jazz and Dave Brubeck. Have the students:
• Discuss the information on 1950s jazz and Dave Brubeck.
You may wish to use the following as a basis for extended discussion.
The Dave Brubeck Quartet made a unique contribution to the development of jazz through the use of meters that had been considered unusual in jazz. Name other musicians from the 1950s and 1960s who made unique contributions to popular music. (Chuck Berry, Bill Haley, Jerry Lee Lewis, and many others developed a style known as rock and roll. Bob Dylan used the tone color of folk guitar in developing the style of popular music known as folk rock.)

A JAZZ STYLE

Unusual meters, rhythms, harmonies, forms, and tone colors have been used in jazz since 1950. You listened to *Take Five*, a composition in $\frac{5}{4}$ meter.

Unsquare Dance, composed by Brubeck, is in $\frac{7}{4}$ meter. The composer writes that this unusual meter makes *Unsquare Dance* "a challenge to the foot-tappers, finger-snappers, and hand-clappers. Deceitfully simple, it refuses to be squared."

These photographs show famous jazz musicians. Right, the Dave Brubeck Quartet; below, Marcus Roberts; below right, Lionel Hampton (left) and Stan Getz (right).

52

EXTENSION

THE COMPOSER

Dave Brubeck—American jazz pianist and composer, was born in California in 1920 into a family of talented musicians. Brubeck studied with Darius Milhaud and Arnold Schoenberg in Los Angeles. During World War II he played in a military band in Europe. After the war he organized his own jazz band, which became extremely successful. Brubeck brings together elements of jazz and baroque textures in his compositions, which contain a great deal of improvisation.

THE COMPOSER

Marcus Roberts—was born in 1963 in Jacksonville, Florida. Blind since birth, he showed an early aptitude for music, and began formal training at the age of 12. Roberts studied at Florida State University in Tallahassee, where he was greatly influenced by Russian piano repertoire and technique. In 1982, Roberts won a competition sponsored by the Association of Jazz Educators and gained the attention of the Marsalis family. By 1985, he was the pianist for Wynton Marsalis' quartet and began extensive recording and touring with Marsalis. Roberts has also released numerous solo albums, featuring his own compositions as well as interpretations of others', and served as music director of the Lincoln Center Jazz Orchestra.

Above, Dizzy Gillespie;
left, Thelonius Monk

53

LESSON 4

2. Introduce meter in sevens. Have the students:
• Practice the rhythm pattern in seven, which is a combination of triple and duple meter.
• Transfer the rhythm pattern to sound and silence by stepping the quarter note and substituting quarter note rests for the claps as they listen to *Unsquare Dance*.
• Identify the meter signature as ⁷⁄₄.
• Perform ostinato on keyboard, recorder, or bells with the recording.

Meter in Sevens

• Perform this rhythm pattern, which is a combination of duple and triple meter. Step the accented beat.

This same pattern can be written with seven beats in each measure, with the first, third, and fifth beat accented.

• Step the accented beats and make a palms-up motion on each quarter rest as you listen to *Unsquare Dance*.

• Listen to *Unsquare Dance* again and perform this **ostinato** (äs-tin-ä′ tō), or repeated pattern, on bells, recorder, or keyboard as an accompaniment.

Unsquare Dance, by Dave Brubeck

"Samiotissa" means "girl from Samos." Samos is a Greek island in the Aegean (e-jē′ ən) Sea.

54

E X T E N S I O N

nother Meter in Sevens

he Greek song "Samiotissa" (Girl from Samos) is in $\frac{7}{8}$ meter. This
eter is similar to the meter of *Unsquare Dance*. It has seven beats
a measure. However, in "Samiotissa" different beats are accented.
his shift of accent creates a completely different rhythm.

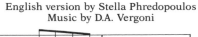

Listen to "Samiotissa" and tap the steady beat.
Sing "Samiotissa."

Samiotissa

English version by Stella Phredopoulos
Music by D.A. Vergoni

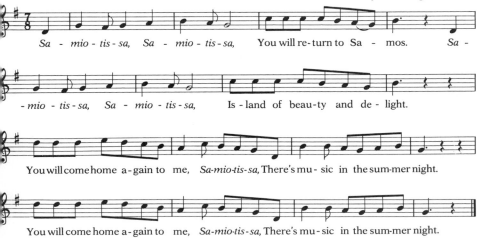

Sa - mio - tis - sa, Sa - mio - tis - sa,   You will re-turn to Sa - mos.   Sa -

- mio - tis - sa,   Sa - mio - tis - sa,   Is -land of beau-ty and de - light.

You will come home a - gain to   me,   *Sa-mio-tis-sa,* There's mu - sic in the sum-mer night.

You will come home a - gain to   me,   *Sa-mio-tis-sa,* There's mu - sic in the sum-mer night.

55

3. Introduce another meter in sevens.
Have the students:
• Compare the accented beats in *Unsquare Dance* and "Samiotissa."
• Listen to "Samiotissa" and tap the steady beat.
• Sing "Samiotissa."

Reinforcing the Lesson

Review "Promenade" on page 51 for changing and irregular meters.

3 APPRAISAL

The students should be able to:
1. Identify and define rhythm patterns in irregular meters of seven and perform them using body percussion.
2. Accurately read and perform the ostinato melodic accompaniment to *Unsquare Dance*.

MORE MUSIC TEACHING IDEAS

Have the students play the accented beats of *Unsquare Dance* (1, 3, and 5) on percussion instruments.

VOCAL DEVELOPMENT

Have the students perform the following rhythmic and melodic patterns at various pitch levels to expand their vocal range and rhythmic accuracy:

tee   tee tee   tee

tee tee tee tee tee tee tee

REVIEW AND EVALUATION

JUST CHECKING

Objective
To review and test the skills and concepts taught in Unit 2

Materials
Recordings: Just Checking Unit 2
                    Unit 2 Evaluation (question 2)
Recorder, bells, or keyboard
Copying Master 2-1 (optional)
Evaluation Unit 2 Copying Master

TEACHING THE LESSON

Review the skills and concepts taught in Unit 1. Have the students:
• Follow the recorded review with pages 56–57, perform the activities, and answer the questions.
• Review their answers.
(You may wish to use Copying Master 2-1 at this time.)

JUST CHECKING

See how much you remember.

1. Listen to the recording and decide if the meter is duple, triple, or quadruple. Show your answers by conducting. duple; quadruple; triple

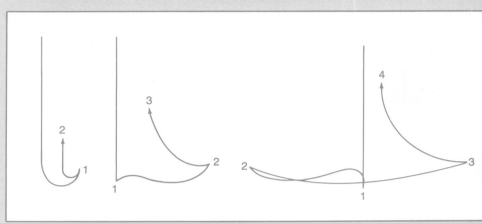

2. Listen to this musical selection, which is an example of changing meters. Identify when the meter changes by conducting the appropriate pattern. The selection begins in duple meter. duple; quadruple; triple

3. Perform this pattern in $\frac{5}{4}$ as you listen to "Goin' Trav'lin'" to review irregular meter.

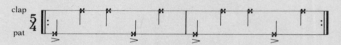

4. Perform this irregular meter pattern as you listen to *Unsquare Dance*.

56

5. Listen to *Take Five*. Perform a rhythm pattern that shows the meter. $\frac{5}{4}$

6. Play part of the descant accompaniment to "Love Song" below to review changing meter. The recording has an eight-beat introduction.

7. Listen to "Love Song" and show the changes of meter by conducting the first four measures as you listen. The recording has an eight-beat introduction.

8. Clap this pattern as you listen to "Samiotissa" to review irregular meter.

9. Listen to the "Promenade" from *Pictures at an Exhibition* and show the changes of meter by clapping or patting on the first beat of each measure.

GIVING THE EVALUATION

Evaluation Unit 2 Copying Master can be found in the *Teacher's Copying Masters* book along with full directions for giving the evaluation and checking the answers.

ELEMENTS OF MUSIC	UNIT 3 OBJECTIVES	Lesson 1 Focus: Compound Meter	Lesson 2 Focus: Compound Meter
Dynamics			
Tone Color	Identify tone colors	Read and perform on sticks or claves	
Tempo	Determine tempo relationships in the music Conduct patterns to fit the tempo		Listen for basic beat in a song with compound meter Read and discuss ♫♫ , ♪, ♫ , ♪♪♪ ♪, ♩♪, ♪ ♫♫ , ♪♪ , ♪♪ ; ♫♫ ♫♫ , ♪♪♪
Duration/ Rhythm	**Identify, define, perform, and conduct in compound meter** Identify meter changes **Identify polyrhythms**	Identify and define compound meter through body percussion ostinati Read and perform a speech chant in compound meter Determine the order of word rhythms in compound meter music Clap the steady beat (♩.)	Identify, define, and perform compound meter Read and discuss ♩. as the basic beat Listen for rhythmic patterns in compound meter
Pitch	Hear, sing songs within a range of C-e♭'		Listen to and perform a song in a compound meter with a range of C-e♭'
Texture	Perform a rhythm accompaniment		
Form	Follow a listening map of a composition having the form: A, A, B, A, B, A, B, Bridge, A, Bridge, C, A, Bridge, C, A, Coda		
Style	Listen to songs from musicals and music that combines jazz and classical style Discuss salsa		Listen to and perform a song in compound meter from a musical Listen to a song in changing meter from a musical
Reading	Read ♫♫ , ♪♩ , ♩. , ♩ ♩ in $\frac{6}{8}$ Read ♫♫♫ , ♪ , ♩ , ♪♪♪ , ♪, ♩♩, ♪ ♫♫ , ♪♪ , ♪♪ ♫♫ ♫♫ , ♪♪♪ , in $\frac{4}{4}$	Read and perform a speech composition using ♫♫ , ♪♩ , ♩. , ♩ ♩ in $\frac{6}{8}$	Read compound meter: $\frac{12}{8}$, $\frac{6}{8}$

PURPOSE Unit 3: RHYTHM SETS THE BEAT

In this unit the students will continue to investigate different aspects of rhythm. They will review compound meter and extend their experiences with polyrhythms.

GUIDE: Unit 2 Overview pages 58A and 58B

SUGGESTED TIME FRAME

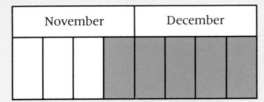

November			December			

FOCUS

- Compound Meter
- Compound Meters in Combination
- Compound Meter in Two Contrasting Tempos
- Polyrhythms

Lesson 3 Focus: Compound Meter in Two Contrasting Tempos	Lesson 4 Focus: Polyrhythms
	Follow a listening map while listening to a salsa song that uses vocals and a big band
Determine which conducting pattern fits the tempo of the music Listen for basic beat and tempo relationship in a song with changing meters	
Listen to and conduct compound meter in two tempi Listen to, read, and identify meter changes Listen to a composition combining compound and quadruple meter Identify tempo and metric organization of compound meter through body percussion and listening	Identify and perform polyrhythms Perform a polyrhythmic accompaniment Create and perform an original polyrhythmic composition based upon words
Sing a song with a range of B♭ - e♭¹	
	Perform a rhythmic accompaniment Identify contrasting sections by changing textures
	Follow a listening map having the form: A, A, B, A, B, A, B, Bridge, A, Bridge, C, A, Bridge, C, A, Coda
Listen to a composition that combines jazz and classical styles Compare two twentieth-century styles	Discuss the salsa style
$\frac{2}{4}, \frac{4}{4}, \frac{7}{4}, \frac{6}{8}, \frac{9}{8}$	Follow and play from listening map that uses ♩ ♩ ♫ ♪ ♫ ♪ ♩ ♫ ♩. ♪♩ ♫ ♫♫

TECHNOLOGY

MUSIC WITH *MIDI*

MIDI technology allows students to manipulate musical elements and make musical decisions.

• Lesson 4, page 70: Create Using Elements of **West African Music**

VIDEO RESOURCES

Use video resources to reinforce, extend, and enrich learning in this unit.

LESSON 1

Guigass #4, Victor Vasarely.
VASARELY CENTER, NY

UNIT 3

RHYTHM SETS THE BEAT

58

THE ARTIST

Victor Vasarely (vä-sä-rel′ē) (1908-1997)
—was born in Hungary and worked in
France. He was interested in optical patterns that seem to move, and experimented with geometrical shapes and bright
color combinations that give the illusion
of three dimensionality or movement. He
believed this kind of art is an expression
of the geometry found in nature and is
thus appealing to all viewers.

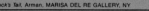
"Peacock's Tail, Arman, MARISA DEL RE GALLERY, NY

59

LESSON 1

Focus: Compound Meter

Objectives
To identify, perform and define compound meter
To perform a speech chant in compound meter

Materials
Recordings: "Cheers"
         "Marche"
Sticks and claves

Vocabulary
Dotted quarter note, dotted quarter rest, compound meter

1 **SETTING THE STAGE**

Tell the students that such familiar songs as "Row, Row" and "Three Blind Mice" are in compound meter.

LESSON 1

COMPOUND METER

2 TEACHING THE LESSON

1. Introduce compound meter. Have the students:

• Clap the steady beat as they recite "Cheers."

• Transfer the rhythm of the words to sticks or claves while listening to "Cheers."

• Read and discuss information on the system of notation which establishes the dotted quarter note as the basic beat.

• Clap the steady beat as you say this chant.

CHEERS

Cheers for soccer, basketball, volleyball,
Track and rugby, too.
We're for swimming, tennis, and racket ball!
Try them all—one's just right for you.

—*Jane Knox*

• As you listen to "Cheers," play the rhythm of the words on sticks or claves.

 "Cheers," by Jane Knox

In this chant the **dotted quarter note** (♩.) represents the steady beat. The basic dotted quarter-note beat can be divided into threes. The **dotted quarter rest** (𝄾·) represents one beat of silence and can also be divided into threes.

A meter that uses this steady beat might be represented as $\frac{2}{♩.}$ but is usually represented as $\frac{6}{8}$.

60

E X T E N S I O N

Use these words to read these rhythms.

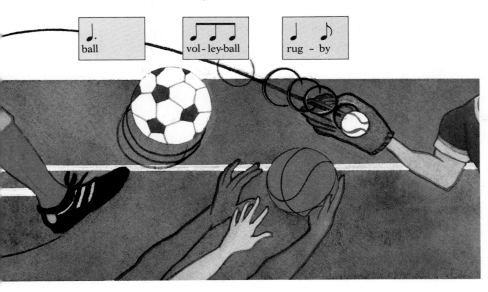

Pat the steady dotted quarter–note beat as you say the poem.

Meter whose basic beat is subdivided into threes and/or sixes is called **compound meter.** Some compound meters are written as $\frac{6}{8}$, $\frac{9}{8}$, or $\frac{12}{8}$.

61

2. Introduce word rhythms in combination. Have the students:
• Use the words from "Cheers" to read the compound time rhythms.
• Pat the steady dotted quarter note beat as they say the poem.
• Discuss the information on compound meter.

Reinforcing the Lesson
Review the B section of Lully's "Marche" (page 18), which can be conducted in compound meter.

3 APPRAISAL
The students should be able to:
1. Verbally define compound meter and give the time signatures of at least two compound meters.
2. Accurately read and perform a speech chant in compound meter.

COOPERATIVE LEARNING
Place the following rhythm patterns on the board:

Have the students pat the steady dotted quarter note beat as they say the poem on page 61. Assist the students in identifying the four separate rhythm patterns (mm. 1, 2, 4, and 8) found in the poem. Repeat each pattern and extend it. Point out that pattern 1 has two uneven sounds per beat; pattern 2 has three even sounds per beat; pattern 3 has one sound on the first beat; and pattern 4 is a combination of three sounds and one sound per beat.

Have the students work in cooperative groups of four to decide on new word rhythms for the four rhythm patterns on the board. The new words should all be from the same category: names of states, counties, automobiles, sports teams, and so on. Assign the role of recorder to notate the word rhythms for each pattern. Appoint a conductor to point to the different rhythm patterns the group is performing. Each cooperative group will perform its newly created word rhythms for the rest of the class.

CURRICULUM CONNECTION: READING
Poetry—Just as music has strong and weak beats, poetry has strong and weak syllables. Like music, poetry often can be organized into divisions of time. One of these divisions, similar to a measure in music, is called a *foot*. A foot contains two or three syllables, which can be stressed (´) or unstressed (˘). Four common types of feet are:
trochaic ´ ˘
iambic ˘ ´
dactylic ´ ˘ ˘
anapestic ˘ ˘ ´
The first line of "Cheers," for example, is composed of two trochaic and two dactylic feet:
Cheérs fŏr sóccĕr, básketbăll, vólleybăll.

LESSON 2

Focus: Compound Meter

Objectives
To identify and perform compound meters

Materials
Recordings: "Cheers"
"Consider Yourself"
"Consider Yourself" (performance mix)
"Memory"

1 SETTING THE STAGE
Review "Cheers" on page 60.

2 TEACHING THE LESSON

1. Introduce a song in compound meter. Have the students:
• Read about the musical *Oliver!*
• Clap the dotted-quarter-note pattern shown on page 62. Divide each dotted quarter note into three eighth notes; alternate clapping between divided and non-divided beats.
• Listen to "Consider Yourself" and pat the basic dotted-quarter-note beat in 6/8 .
• Sing the song.

EXTENSION

VOCAL DEVELOPMENT

Encourage students to use good posture to enhance their breathing for the performance of "Consider Yourself." Have the students experiment with different vocal emphases and dynamics to determine which expressive devices best communicate the energetic nature of the song.

A SONG IN COMPOUND METER

Oliver! one of the longest running British musicals, is based on Charles Dickens' novel about the adventures of the orphan Oliver Twist. In the song "Consider Yourself," a group of young pickpockets enthusiastically welcomes Oliver.

The dotted quarter note is the basic beat of "Consider Yourself." When dotted quarter notes (♩.) are grouped two to a measure, the meter is represented as 6/8.

• Listen to "Consider Yourself" as you pat the basic beat. Into how many parts is the basic beat divided? three

Is this song in compound meter? Why?
Yes; basic beat is divided into three parts.

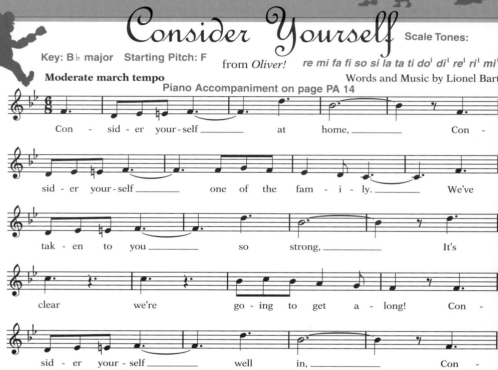

Consider Yourself

Scale Tones:
re mi fa fi so si la ta ti do¹ di¹ re¹ ri¹ mi¹

Key: B♭ major   Starting Pitch: F   from *Oliver!*

Moderate march tempo

Piano Accompaniment on page PA 14

Words and Music by Lionel Bart

Con - sid - er your-self _____ at home, _____ Con -

sid - er your-self _____ one of the fam - i - ly. _____ We've

tak - en to you _____ so strong, _____ It's

clear we're go - ing to get a - long! Con -

sid - er your-self _____ well in, _____ Con -

From the Columbia Pictures–Romulus Film OLIVER!
Words and Music by Lionel Bart
© Copyright 1960 (Renewed) Lakeview Music Co., Ltd., London, England
TRO–Hollis Music, Inc., New York, controls all publication rights
for the U.S.A. and Canada. Used by Permission.

62

sid - er your-self _____ part of the fur - ni - ture. _____ There

is - n't a lot _____ to spare; _____ Who

cares? What - ev - er we've got we share! If it should
No - bod - y

chance to be, we should see some hard - er days, _____ Emp - ty
tries to be lah - di - dah and up - pit - y, _____ There's a

lard - er days, _____ why grouse? _____ Al - ways a
cup o' tea _____ for all. _____ On - ly it's

chance we'll meet some - bod - y to foot the bill, _____ Then the
wise, to be han - dy with a roll - ing pin _____ When the

drinks are on the house! _____ Con -
land - lord comes to call! _____

sid - er your-self _____ our mate, _____ We

don't want to have _____ no fuss, _____ for

af - ter some con - sid - er - a - tion, we can state: Con -

ad lib. ending

sid - er your-self _____ one of us.

63

2. Practice hearing patterns in compound meter. Have the students:
• Discuss the photos and information on the musical *Cats*.
• Listen to "Memory," patting the basic dotted-quarter-note beat and feeling the division.
• Clap the rhythms on page 65, noting how the beat is divided under the notation.
• Listen to the song again to locate the patterns indicated and answer the questions.

Reinforcing the Lesson

Have the students tap the basic dotted-quarter-note beat with their foot while clapping the divided beat with their hands as they listen to the first four measures (following the introduction) of "Memory."

APPRAISAL

The students should be able to listen to the recording of "Memory" and pat the basic dotted-quarter-note beat, or divisions of the beat (threes), when cued by the teacher.

CD2:21, CD8:34

A Song from *Cats*

Imagine a musical set in a garbage dump. Imagine a musical that has songs based on the poetry of a Nobel Prize winner. Imagine a musical that has no human characters, only cats. Imagine a musical in which Grizabella, an old and tattered alley cat, finds release from her sorrows and rises to heaven on a discarded automobile tire. Imagine a musical in which story, song, and dance are uniquely combined. You have imagined *Cats*, one of the most successful musicals of the past two decades.

In the song "Memory," Grizabella wishes her youth and beauty could return. It is probably the most familiar song from *Cats*.

• As you listen to "Memory," pat the basic beat. Is the song in compound meter? Why? Yes; basic beat is divided into threes.

 "Memory," from the musical *Cats*, by Andrew Lloyd Webber, Trevor Nunn, and T.S. Eliot

Left, Grizabella, who sings "Memory" in the musical *Cats*. Below, the entire cast of *Cats*. Grizabella is at the far right. This musical has been performed around the world in many languages.

64

E X T E N S I O N

THE COMPOSER

Andrew Lloyd Webber—British theatrical composer, was born in 1948 into a musical family. His father was the director of the London College of Music, and his mother was a piano teacher. Lloyd Webber learned how to play piano, violin, and French horn at an early age. He later attended Magdalen College, Oxford, and the Royal College of Music. Lloyd Webber's first notable musical was *Joseph and the Amazing Technicolor Dreamcoat*, which he wrote when he was 19. His first commercial success came when he was 23 with *Jesus Christ Superstar*, which won several Tony awards. His list of successes includes *Evita, Song and Dance, Cats, Starlight Express, The Phantom of the Opera*, and *Sunset Boulevard*.

Sometimes dotted quarter notes are grouped four to a measure. This meter is represented as **12/8**.

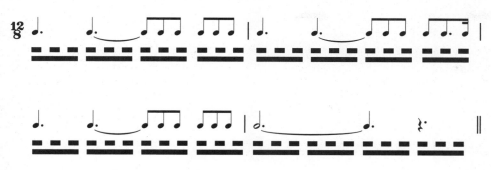

Listen to "Memory" again. Listen for this rhythm in the voice.

Now listen to "Memory" once more. Listen for a phrase that begins like this.

Below, a scene from *Cats*

CONDUCTING IN COMPOUND METER

LESSON 3

Focus: Compound Meter in Two Contrasting Tempos

Objectives
To identify, perform and define compound meter in two contrasting tempos
To identify the beat and tempo relationship in a song with changing meters

Materials
Recordings: "Cheers"
"Joyfully Sing," Version 1
"Joyfully Sing," Version 2
"Compound Meter Montage"
"Caprice"
Unsquare Dance (optional)

Tennis balls

1 SETTING THE STAGE
Review "Cheers" on page 60 as an example of compound meter.

2 TEACHING THE LESSON
1. Introduce conducting in compound meter. Have the students:
• Practice conducting the six-beat pattern.
• Listen to "Joyfully Sing," Version 1 as they conduct a slow six-beat pattern.
• Listen to "Joyfully Sing," Version 2 and decide which conducting pattern best fits with the music.
• Discuss the information on conducting compound meter in a slow and fast tempo.

"Joyfully Sing" is a folk song about the joy of singing in harmony.

• Listen to Version 1 of "Joyfully Sing." Conduct in a slow six-beat pattern.

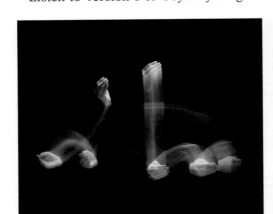

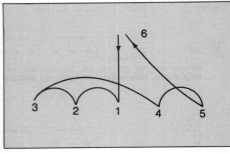

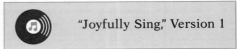
"Joyfully Sing," Version 1

• Listen to Version 2 of "Joyfully Sing," which is performed at a different tempo. Decide which conducting pattern best fits the music. duple meter pattern

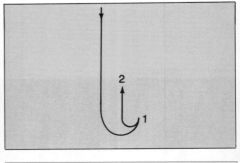

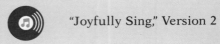
"Joyfully Sing," Version 2

When compound meter is performed at a slow tempo, it is usually conducted in the six-beat pattern. When compound meter is performed at a fast tempo, it is usually conducted in the two-beat pattern.

66

Joyfully Sing

Traditional German round
Arr. M.J.

67

VOCAL DEVELOPMENT

Build tonal focus and extend the development of breathing and rhythmic accuracy by having students perform "Joyfully Sing" without words, using only pure vowels and articulated consonants such as *vee, tee, tah, too.*

LESSON 3

2. Introduce conducting and body percussion patterns for "Joyfully Sing."
Have the students:
- Listen to "Joyfully Sing," Version 2 again and identify the changes in meter signatures by deciding which conducting pattern best fits with the music, and show the answer by conducting.
- Perform the body percussion pattern to the steady beat as they listen to "Joyfully Sing."
- Sing the song, looking for the meter changes in the score.

3. Introduce "Compound Meter Montage." Have the students listen to the three examples to decide which conducting pattern best fits with the music, and show the answer by conducting.

Fields surround the village of Kaub, West Germany.

- Listen to "Joyfully Sing" (Version 2) again and identify the changes in meter.

- Perform these rhythm patterns as you listen to "Joyfully Sing" one more time.

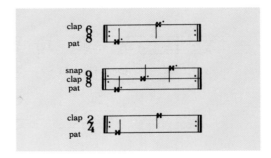

- Sing "Joyfully Sing." Look for the meter changes as you sing.

- Listen to "Compound Meter Montage" and decide which conducting pattern best fits each composition. two-beat pattern; six-beat pattern; two-beat pattern

 "Compound Meter Montage"

68

EXTENSION

SPECIAL LEARNERS

Preplan an alternative way to experience compound meters if exceptional students are unable to conduct patterns. Have the students illustrate the meter changes in "Compound Meter Montage" by patting the accented first beat or by playing a rhythm instrument.

Students with physical handicaps or who have difficulty with motor coordination may not be able to coordinate the meter changes in "Joyfully Sing." Prepare an overhead transparency of pupil page 68. Have the students pat or play a rhythm instrument on each downbeat. Mainstreamed students also may need a teacher cue for each downbeat.

Claude Bolling was born in Cannes, France, in 1930. He was a child piano prodigy and was studying harmony by the age of twelve. Bolling's interest in jazz also began at an early age. By age fifteen, he was making professional appearances throughout France as a jazz pianist. By the time he was in his mid-twenties, he had become one of the most popular jazz musicians in Europe. He has won several recording industry awards.

Bolling has also received international acclaim as an accompanist-composer. He has worked with such performers as Liza Minnelli, Jerry Lewis, Duke Ellington, and Jean-Pierre Rampal. Bolling has also written scores for dozens of French and American films.

Bolling's Suite for Violin and Jazz Piano is a unique combination of jazz and classical styles. "Caprice," a section of this suite, contains both compound and quadruple meter.

• Listen to this section of "Caprice" and raise your hand when you hear changes in meter.

"Caprice," from Suite for Violin and Jazz Piano, by Claude Bolling

---

LESSON 3

4. Introduce "Caprice," from the Suite for Violin and Jazz Piano by Claude Bolling. Have the students:
• Discuss the information on Claude Bolling and his Suite for Violin and Jazz Piano.
• Listen to the selection from "Caprice" and raise their hands when they hear a change of meter.

Reinforcing the Lesson
Have the students:
• Show the compound and quadruple meter in "Caprice" by bouncing and rolling a tennis ball as indicated by the metrical changes:
Compound $\frac{6}{8}$ (fast tempo); quadruple (moderate tempo); compound $\frac{6}{8}$ (fast tempo).
• Perform the tennis ball activity with the recording.

3 APPRAISAL
The students should be able to:
1. Listen to several examples from "Compound Meter Montage" and match the correct conducting pattern for each example.
2. Read and conduct the meter changes in "Joyfully Sing" in two contrasting tempos. Use appropriate conducting patterns to identify the beat and meter.

MORE MUSIC TEACHING IDEAS
Have the students compare "Caprice" from the Suite for Violin and Jazz Piano with Dave Brubeck's *Unsquare Dance*. (*Unsquare Dance:* small ensemble, irregular meter, no change of tempo; "Caprice": small ensemble, compound and quadruple meter, tempo changes between meters.)

LESSON 4

Focus: Polyrhythms

Objectives
To identify, perform, and define polyrhythms
To create and notate a composition using polyrhythms

Materials
Recordings: "Hay Que Trabajar"
"Polyrhythm Montage"
"Weather"
Percussion instruments
Pitched or unpitched classroom instruments

Vocabulary
Polyrhythm, salsa, coro

1 SETTING THE STAGE

Tell the students they will be learning about a style of dance music called *salsa*.

2 TEACHING THE LESSON

1. Introduce polyrhythms. Have the students:
• Discuss the information on "Hay Que Trabajar" and *salsa*.
• Listen to "Hay Que Trabajar" to hear polyrhythms and the sound of *salsa*.

PERFORMING POLYRHYTHMS

Polyrhythm is the simultaneous combination of two or more contrasting rhythmic patterns.

"*Hay Que Trabajar*" (ī kā trä-bä-här´) contains *polyrhythms*. The style of "*Hay Que Trabajar*" is known as *salsa*. This style was born in New York City when Cuban and Puerto Rican music met big band jazz. Salsa is dance music that combines the rhythms and harmonies of Latin America and Africa with those of blues, jazz, and rock.

• Listen to "*Hay Que Trabajar*" to hear polyrhythms and the sound of salsa. In addition to the very active rhythm section, the large band you will hear includes saxophones, trombones, and trumpets, which give it a bright sound. Salsa vocals typically feature a soloist and the *coro*, or chorus, which is usually the band members themselves.

 "*Hay Que Trabajar*" by Angel Santiago

You can accompany the A sections of "*Hay Que Trabajar*" with many different rhythm patterns.

• Practice each of the rhythms on page 71.

• Follow the listening map and perform with the recording.

Tito Puente, whose band is heard in this recording, is a very popular Latin music performer, with more than a hundred albums.

70

EXTENSION

THE PERFORMER

Tito Puente—composer, arranger, performer, and Latin jazz band leader, was born of Puerto Rican descent in the Spanish Harlem neighborhood of New York City. He is best known for his work as a percussionist, and particularly as a timbalero (timbale player). Tito Puente has recorded with many bands since the 1940s, averaging two albums per year. He is currently performing with his *Latin Jazz Ensemble*. He has been recognized by the National Academy of Recording Arts and Sciences with several Grammy awards for excellence in Latin music categories.

CURRICULUM CONNECTION: SOCIAL STUDIES

Salsa—the Spanish word meaning "sauce"—is a term that was coined in the 1970s. *Salsa* originally referred to a style of music that had evolved in the USA when the multicultural influences and musical innovations of the more modern era mixed with the big band Cuban sounds of the 1940s–50s. The style quickly gained popularity in Latin America and the Caribbean. Since that time, many distinct varieties of *salsa* have developed as various cultures have added their own flavors. The word is now used loosely and often refers to a broad variety of fast Latin dance music, including older styles such as *mambo*.

LISTENING

You may wish to use the Listening Map overhead transparency to help guide the students through the listening selection.

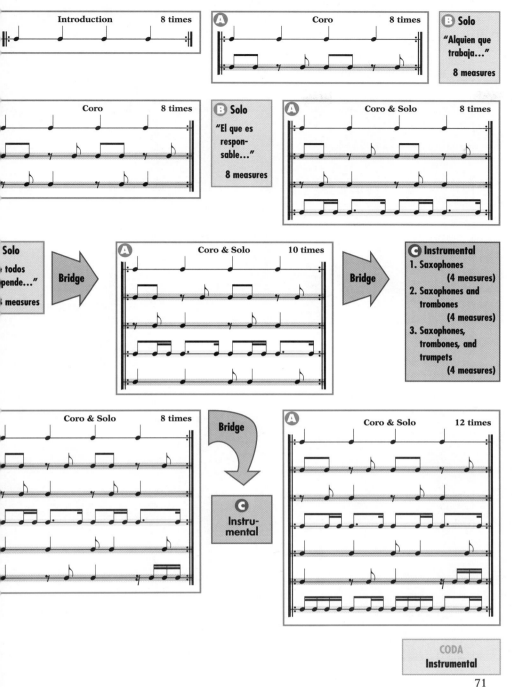

Hay Que Trabajar
Listening Map

Introduction — 8 times

A — Coro — 8 times

B — Solo
"Alquien que trabaja…"
8 measures

Coro — 8 times

B — Solo
"El que es respon-sable…"
8 measures

A — Coro & Solo — 8 times

Solo
todos pende…"
measures

Bridge

A — Coro & Solo — 10 times

Bridge

C — Instrumental
1. Saxophones
(4 measures)
2. Saxophones and trombones
(4 measures)
3. Saxophones, trombones, and trumpets
(4 measures)

Coro & Solo — 8 times

Bridge

C — Instru-mental

A — Coro & Solo — 12 times

CODA
Instrumental

71

- Practice clapping the individual rhythm patterns in $\frac{4}{4}$ meter found in the playalong sections of the Listening Map for "Hay Que Trabajar." (Each student should learn every rhythmic pattern.)
- Follow the listening map, and with the recording, perform only the new rhythm pattern given for each playalong section.
- Divide into seven groups, each group taking a different part. (Some students may volunteer to perform rhythm patterns as solos.)
- Combine parts. (Have the students in the first group perform their steady beat throughout this process. Add one part at a time, repeating each new combination as necessary.)
- Follow the listening map and perform the rhythm patterns as they listen to "Hay Que Trabajar."

LISTENING

You may wish to use the Listening Map overhead transparency to help guide the students through the listening selection.

SPECIAL LEARNERS

Prepare an overhead transparency of pupil page 71 if there are exceptional students in the class who are visually impaired or have difficulty coordinating visual and audio skills. Point to each new section as the students listen to the selection to help these students visually and aurally perceive the components of the selection.

LESSON 4

2. Introduce polyrhythms in different musical styles. Have the students:
• Listen to "Polyrhythm Montage" and match the photo with the music they are hearing. (steel band, *Cats*, *The Rite of Spring*, African music)
• Discuss each photo.

Listening to Polyrhythms

Polyrhythms are found in many different styles of music. Match the picture with the music you are hearing as you listen to "Polyrhythm Montage." steel band, *Cats*, *Rite*, African

"Polyrhythm Montage"

Above, a scene from *The Rite of Spring* in the Joffrey Ballet's re-creation of the original 1913 version

Above, a scene from *Cats*. The "garbage" on the stage is the same size it would appear to a real cat.

Above, a steel band from Trinidad. Left, the Ladzekpo Brothers, an African music and dance ensemble

72

EXTENSION

COOPERATIVE LEARNING

Have the students work in cooperative groups of four to explore the concept of polyrhythms. Each member of the group will create and perform a one-measure ostinato for unpitched or pitched instruments. (Encourage the students to use the pentatonic scale or Dorian mode if they know them.) Each cooperative group will perform its newly created rhythms for the rest of class. Perform the ostinati by starting with one and adding the others in succession. As each ostinato is added, the rhythmic density should become more complex. Assign a student the role of conductor to organize the entrances of the ostinatos.

MORE MUSIC TEACHING IDEAS

Have the students perform the following patterns on percussion instruments to experience polyrhythms.

Creating Polyrhythms

You can combine words to create different rhythm patterns.

- Read and perform each of the five rhythms in "Weather."
- Perform "Weather" to create polyrhythms.

Weather

V.L.

1. Fair　　　　　Fair
2. Sun-shine, oh it's hot!　Sun-shine, oh it's hot!
3. Part – ly cloud – y,　part – ly cloud – y
4. Rain!　Rain!　Snow!　Snow!
5. Now it's clear!　Now it's clear!

- Use other words to create compositions with polyrhythms. Here are two examples.

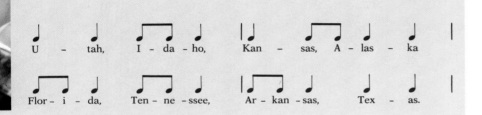

U – tah,　I – da – ho,　Kan – sas,　A – las – ka

Flor – i – da,　Ten – ne –ssee,　Ar – kan –sas,　Tex – as.

- Choose names of states, classmates, or automobiles to create your own rhythm patterns. Perform the compositions you created for your classmates. Learn and perform the polyrhythms created by your classmates. Mix and match rhythms from different compositions to create additional polyrhythms.

73

LESSON 4

3. Introduce creating a polyrhythmic speech composition. Have the students:
- Read and perform each of the five speaking rhythms.
- Form two to five groups and perform "Weather" beginning at different times to experience polyrhythms. ("Weather" can be performed as a round.)

REINFORCING THE LESSON

Have the students create their own compositions with polyrhythms as indicated.

3　APPRAISAL

The students should be able to:
1. Identify and verbally define polyrhythm.
2. Perform a polyrhythmic accompaniment to "Hay Que Trabajar" with accuracy.
3. Create and notate an original polyrhythmic composition using word rhythms.

CURRICULUM CONNECTION: SCIENCE

Weather—Meteorologists constantly observe weather conditions around the world. Observation stations measure temperature, humidity, wind direction and speed, and other conditions every hour. Weather balloons with special instruments measure conditions in the atmosphere and transmit data to ground stations. Cameras on satellites take and transmit photographs of cloud patterns and areas of ice and snow on earth. Meteorologists prepare various maps and charts from this information and analyze them to make weather predictions. Forecast maps are also prepared using computers that solve complex formulas to project ahead from current data.

REVIEW AND EVALUATION

JUST CHECKING

Objective
To review and test the skills and concepts taught in Unit 3

Materials
Recordings: Just Checking Unit 3
    Unit 3 Evaluation (question 2)
Copying Master 3-1 (optional)
Evaluation Unit 3 Copying Master

TEACHING THE LESSON

Review the skills and concepts taught in Unit 3. Have the students:
• Follow the recorded review with pages 74–75, perform the activities, and answer the questions.
• Review their answers.
(You may wish to use Copying Master 3-1 at this time.)

JUST CHECKING

See how much you remember. Listen to the recording.

1. Listen to the steady beat and perform these rhythm patterns individually and then together.

Coro & Solo

2. Listen to the steady beat and perform these rhythm patterns in $\frac{6}{8}$ meter by clapping as you say the words.

a. base - ball

b. track and rug - by

c. bask-et – ball, vol - ley- ball

d. just right for you.

74

. Listen to these recordings and decide if the style of each example
  is salsa, jazz, or Broadway musical. jazz, Broadway musical, salsa

. Listen to this excerpt from "Caprice" from Claude Bolling's Suite
  for Violin and Jazz Piano. Determine if this section is in
  compound or quadruple meter. Demonstrate your answer by
  conducting the appropriate pattern. compound meter

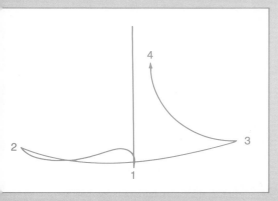 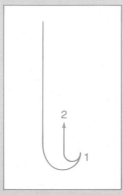

. Listen to two contrasting selections in compound meter. In which
  selection does the six-beat conducting pattern fit? In which
  selection does the two-beat conducting pattern fit? Describe the
  tempo of each selection. second; first; first: fast; second: slow

. Listen to the following musical selections and decide which
  ones contain polyrhythms. Examples 1 and 3

. Listen to the following musical selections and decide if they are
  examples of simple or compound meter. simple: Examples 1 and 3; compound:
  Examples 2 and 4

75

GIVING THE EVALUATION

Evaluation Unit 3 Copying Master can be
found in the *Teacher's Copying Masters* book
along with full directions for giving the
evaluation and checking the answers.

UNIT 4 • OVERVIEW

ELEMENTS OF MUSIC	UNIT 4 OBJECTIVES	Lesson 1 Focus: Major Scale, Creating Harmony	Lesson 2 Focus: Repetition of a Musical Idea, Texture
Dynamics			
Tone Color	Perform retrograde on percussion instruments Perform a song on bells or keyboard and classroom instruments	Identify number of singers and accompanying instruments (flute, guitar, hammered dulcimer) Perform accompaniments on keyboard or bells	
Tempo			
Duration/ Rhythm	Clap the rhythm of the melody as a canon Perform rhythms containing meter changes		Clap the rhythm of the melody as a canon Perform a canon with rhythmic accuracy
Pitch	**Learn pitch organization** **Define twelve-tone music** **Perform a tone row and its retrograde**	Identify a D major scale Learn about tonality Develop melodic reading skills Sing a song with a range of A-a	Perform a canon with pitch accuracy Sing a song with a range of d-d¹
Texture	Define harmony and consonance **Identify and define polyphonic, monophonic, and homophonic texture** **Perform melodic accompaniment**	Define harmony and consonance Play an accompaniment to a melody Identify consonant harmony Play a melodic accompaniment Perform a melodic accompaniment	Define and perform canon Perform a song in unison and as a two-part round Identify and define polyphonic, monophonic, and homophonic texture Analyze the musical texture of a composition Discuss and identify the three textures used in the "Hallelujah" Chorus
Form	Analyze phrase length	Identify and discuss a canon	Identify and discuss an oratorio
Style	Discuss a composer from the baroque period Discuss music of Schoenberg **Identify atonal music composition**		Discuss the composer, George Frederick Handel, from the baroque period Discuss and perform a Korean folk song canon
Reading	Follow listening map using ♪♪, ♩. ♪♪, ♩. ♩. ♪	Sing and play in ¾ using tie	Follow listening map using ♪♪, ♩. ♪♪, ♩. ♩. ♪

PURPOSE Unit 4: MELODY

In this unit the students will focus their attention on melody. They will review the major scale and investigate the concept of texture in music. They will be introduced to the twelve-tone row and investigate retrograde as a technique for organizing and developing a melodic pattern.

SUGGESTED TIME FRAME

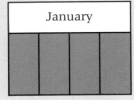

January

FOCUS

- Major Scale, Creating Harmony
- Repetition of a Musical Idea, Texture
- Retrograde Melodies
- Twelve-Tone Music

Lesson 3 Focus: Retrograde Melodies	**Lesson 4** Focus: Twelve-Tone Music
Perform a melody and its retrograde on bells, recorder, or keyboard Perform retrograde on percussion instruments	Perform a tone row on bells or keyboard Perform a song on bells or keyboard with instrumental parts (triangle, finger cymbals, tambourine, or maracas)
	Read and perform rhythms in an atonal composition containing meter changes between $\frac{6}{8}$ and $\frac{9}{8}$ Perform a rhythmic ostinato or body accompaniment to a melody
Read about pitch organization Identify and define retrograde Analyze the pitch organization of a composition	Identify, define, and discuss twelve-tone music Read and perform a twelve-tone row and its retrograde Listen to and perform a song with a range of b-d♭¹
Perform two retrograde sound pieces together	
Analyze phrase length Create and perform a retrograde sound piece	
	Discuss expressionism and the musical style of Arnold Schoenberg Create and perform an atonal composition and play in retrograde
Read score using ♪♩ , ♩ , ♩ , ♩ , $\frac{4}{4}$	Read rhythms in $\frac{6}{8}$, $\frac{9}{8}$

TECHNOLOGY

MUSIC WITH *MIDI*

MIDI technology allows students to manipulate musical elements and make musical decisions.

- Lesson 3, page 87: Create Using Elements of **Twelve-Tone and Chance Music**
- Lesson 4, page 90: Create Using Elements of **Twelve-Tone and Chance Music**

VIDEO RESOURCES

Use video resources to reinforce, extend, and enrich learning in this unit.

LESSON 1

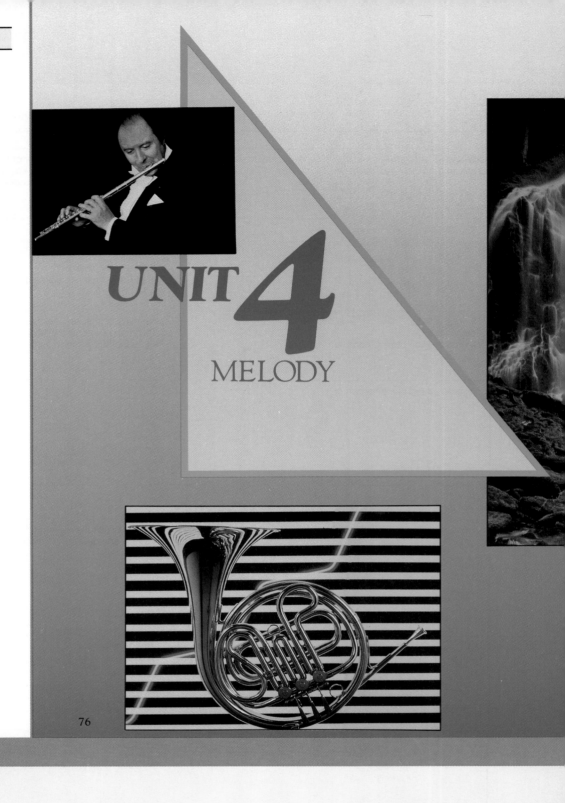

UNIT 4

MELODY

76

LESSON 1

Focus: Major Scale, Creating Harmony

Objectives
To identify the major scale and its use as a basis for melodies
To identify a tonal center
To read and perform a melodic accompaniment with accuracy

Materials
Recordings: "River"
　　　　　　Pachelbel, Canon
Keyboard or bells
Copying Master 4-1 (optional)

Vocabulary
Home tone, tone center, tonal music, tonality, harmony, consonance

1 **SETTING THE STAGE**
Tell the students they will play a melodic accompaniment to a song.

77

MELODY AND HARMONY

Key: D major   **Starting Pitch: D**   **Scale Tones:** *so, la, do re mi fa so*

A Song in D Major

- Listen to "River" and decide how many singers and which instruments you hear. 2 singers, steel-string guitar, hammered dulcimer, flute

 "River," by Bill Staines

LESSON 1

2 | TEACHING THE LESSON

1. Introduce "River." Have the students:

- Listen to the recording of the song and identify the number of singers (two) and the accompanying instruments. (hammered dulcimer, guitar, flute)

- Sing the song.

River

Words and music by Bill Staines

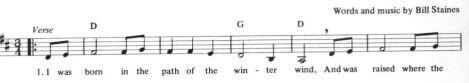

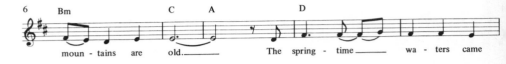

1. I was born in the path of the win-ter wind, And was raised where the

moun-tains are old.____ The spring-time____ wa-ters came

danc-ing down, I re-mem-ber the tales they told.____ The

whis-tling____ ways of my young-er days, Too quick-ly have

fad-ed on by.____ But all of the mem-o-ries

lin-ger still, Like the light in a fad-ing sky.____

78

EXTENSION

SIGNING FOR "RIVER"

It is important to express the mood and fluid qualities of this song with the body, face, and signs. The phrases should be smoothly connected; movement should continue with the sound.

River   Make a "W" for wa-ter close to the mouth then with palms down, left hand behind the right, wiggle the fingers as the hands move to the right. Roll the arms on "rolling old river."

Take Me (Bring [Me])

   With open palms up, move from left to right in an arc. Hands are not touching.

Sunshine   Outline a circle above the head.

Fingers are all touching.

Drop down and open as if rays of the sun.

Sing

   Move the hands away from the corners of the mouth in a gesture of singing.

Song (Music)   Extend left arm. The right hand points to the palm of the left hand and makes a series of wavy motions such as a conductor would make.

Refrain

Riv - er, take me a - long, In your sun - shine

sing me your song. Ev - er mov - ing and wind - ing and__

free. You roll - ing old riv - er, You chang - ing old riv - er, Let's

you and me, riv - er, Run down to the sea._____

sea._____ Let's you and me, riv - er, Run down to the sea.

2. I've been to the city and back again;
   I've been touched by some things that I've learned,
   Met a lot of good people, and I've called them friends,
   Felt the change when the seasons turned.
   I've heard all the songs that the children sing
   And I've listened to love's melodies;
   I've felt my own music within me rise
   Like the wind in the autumn trees.

   Refrain

3. Someday when the flowers are blooming still,
   Someday when the grass is still green,
   My rolling river will round the bend
   And flow into the open sea.
   So here's to the rainbow that's followed me here,
   And here's to the friends that I know,
   And here's to the song that's within me now;
   I will sing it where'er I go.

   Refrain

79

Winding (Rolling, Moving)

With palms facing and fingers pointing away from the body, the open hands move forward together in a series of curves.

Free

The "F" position hands are crossed at the wrists then un-crossed and opened, moving up and out in an arc.

Changing

With hands in modi-fied "A" position, palms face each other. Twist hands so they reverse posi-tions.

Let

Open hands, palms facing each other move down and up in a scooping motion.

You

Palms up, hands start together then move apart in a sweeping gesture.

Me

Point to the chest with the index finger.

Down to the Sea

Make a gesture of the river flowing to the sea.

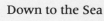

UNIT 4   **79**

LESSON 1

2. Introduce the D major scale. Have the students:
• Identify the D major scale.
• Give the letter names of the pitches in "River" that begin and end the song.
• Identify the measures which contain the chord symbol D (shown in score).
• Discuss the information on tonality, harmony, and consonance.

The melody of "River" contains the pitches of the **D major scale.**

D E F# G A B C# D   D C# B A G F# E D
1 2 3   4 5 6 7   8   8 7   6 5 4 3   2 1

• Give the letter names of the pitches that begin and end the song. D and D
• Which measures contain the chord symbol D? shown in score

The **home tone** D is the focus or **tone center** for "River." When music has a strong tonal center or pitch focus, it is called **tonal music.** It is said to have **tonality.**

When you play or sing two or more pitches together, you are creating **harmony.** Harmonic **consonance** results when the combination of pitches blends.

Right, the North Platte River, Nebraska. Below, the Firth River, Yukon Territory, Canada

80

- Play this melodic accompaniment on keyboard or bells with "River." Since it is based on the D major scale, this folklike harmonic accompaniment is **consonant**.

CD2:50

Melodic Accompaniment to "River"

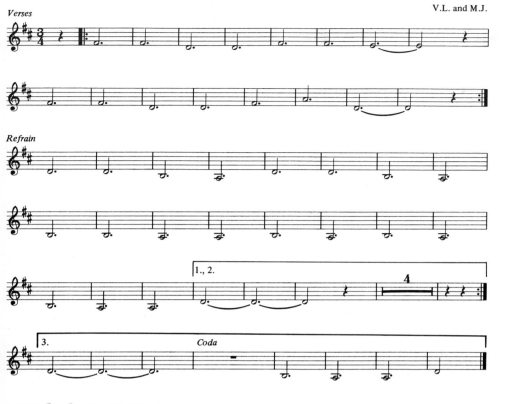

V.L. and M.J.

Verses

Refrain

A Melody in D Major

Johann Pachelbel (yō′ hän päKH′ əl-bel) used pitches from the D major scale in his Canon. You may have heard it in commercials and films. The melodies follow one another and, when combined, create harmony.

- Listen to the Canon to hear how Pachelbel used a major scale as a basis for the melodies.

 Canon, by Johann Pachelbel

81

- Play the melodic accompaniment to "River" on keyboard or bells as they listen to the recording.

3. Introduce creating harmony with scale tones. Have the students listen to Pachelbel's Canon to hear how he used a major scale as a basis for the melodies. (You may wish to use Copying Master 4-1 at this time.)

Reinforcing the Lesson
Review tonic and dominant chords on page 11.

3 APPRAISAL
The students should be able to:
1. Identify the major scale of D and its use as a basis for melodies.
2. Identify the tonal center of D major.
3. Read and perform a melodic accompaniment with accuracy.

MORE MUSIC TEACHING IDEAS
Have the students perform melodies to the Canon on keyboard, bells, or other C instruments.

SPECIAL LEARNERS
Students who have reading disabilities may experience difficulty following an overhead transparency of pupil page 81 and playing the melodic accompaniment on bells or recorders. Point out each measure or indicate the beginning of each line.

If the lesson includes Copying Master 4-1, students who have reading disabilities or difficulty tracking may need extra help following and playing the melodies. Point out the beginning of each line on an overhead transparency as it repeats or indicate each measure.

THE COMPOSER
Johann Pachelbel (1653–1706)—was a great German composer and organist. He studied composition, piano, and organ at Nuremberg. Throughout his life he held several important positions as organist, composer, and teacher. Pachelbel was one of the first composers to use major keys to convey happy moods and minor for sad moods in his compositions. Pachelbel was a close friend of the Bach family and taught several members. His keyboard compositions greatly influenced the young Johann Sebastian Bach.

LESSON 2

Focus: Repetition of a Musical Idea, Texture

Objectives
To read and perform a melody as a canon
To identify and describe monophonic, polyphonic, and homophonic texture

Materials
Recordings: Canon
"Ahrirang"
"Hallelujah" Chorus
"Memory"
"Joyfully Sing"
"Goin' Trav'lin'"
Rhythm instruments
Copying Master 4-2: Listening Map (optional)

Vocabulary
Canon, texture, monophonic, polyphonic, homophonic, oratorio

1 SETTING THE STAGE
Have the students review Pachelbel's Canon on page 81 as an example of this form.

2 TEACHING THE LESSON

1. Introduce performing a canon.
Have the students:
• Read the information and define canon.
• Learn to sing "Ahrirang" as a canon.
• Attempt the Challenge! and try to perform "Ahrirang" as a canon by clapping the rhythm of the melody without singing it.

TEXTURE IN MUSIC

Key: G major   Starting Pitch: D   Scale Tones: *so, la, do re mi so*

Performing a Canon

CD2:51 A **canon** is a musical composition in two or more voice parts. A musical phrase is started by one voice and repeated exactly by successive voices, which begin before the first voice has ended. The combination of voices produces harmony.

"Ahrirang" is a Korean folk song about the Ahrirang Pass in the mountains near the city of Seoul.

• Learn to sing "Ahrirang" as a canon.

Ahrirang

Korean folk song
English words by M.S

 CHALLENGE Try to perform "Ahrirang" as a canon by clapping the rhythm of the melody without singing it.

82

EXTENSION

SPECIAL LEARNERS
If the lesson includes the rhythm clapping Challenge! plan an alternative activity for those students with physical handicaps or motor disabilities. Have the students use rhythm instruments to either keep the steady beat or to play the first beat of each measure. Introduce the necessity for these instruments as a means of insuring success for the class activity.

VOCAL DEVELOPMENT
Strive to have the students experience the sustained quality of "Ahrirang" by emphasizing breath support and the use of sustained vowels. Have the students sing the following at different pitch levels to encourage the expansion of vocal range.

Musical Texture

Texture in music refers to the way layers of sound are combined. When you sang "Ahrirang" the first time without accompaniment, you sang in unison. Unison singing creates a texture known as **monophonic**, meaning one sound.

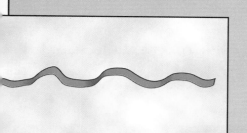

When you sang "Ahrirang" as a canon, you created a texture know as **polyphonic** (po-lē-fo'nik), meaning many voices sounding together.

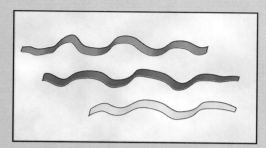

When you sang "River," the melody was in the foreground with accompaniment in the background. This texture is called **homophonic**.

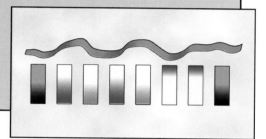

An **oratorio** is a large musical work for solo voices, chorus, and orchestra performed without special costumes or scenery. The "Hallelujah" Chorus from George Frederick Handel's oratorio *Messiah* is one of the most famous choral works in the English language. Handel creates harmonic interest by setting the text in monophonic, polyphonic, and homophonic textures.

The word *hallelujah* is stated and restated by different sections of the chorus almost like a cheering section. Other lines of the text are sung solemnly to emphasize their serious message, and for contrast. The festive quality of the piece is made even more brilliant by the trumpets and timpani. The story is told that at one of the first performances, the English king, George II, was so moved by the music that he stood up to show his approval.

83

2. Prepare analysis of musical texture. Have the students:
• Discuss the information on monophonic, polyphonic, and homophonic texture.
• Discuss the information on the use of musical texture in the "Hallelujah" Chorus.

COOPERATIVE LEARNING

Using the examples of musical texture found on pupil page 83, have the students work in cooperative groups of three to find examples of monophonic, polyphonic, and homophonic textures in the preceding 82 pages. Within each group, assign a specific category to each student. The student should find an example within the first 83 pages of the text to validate the specific category. Each member of the group will then present his or her example, providing documentation as to how it fits the assigned category. The validated examples for the entire group should be listed on a sheet of paper, which is signed by all the members of the group.

LESSON 2

• Follow the description as they listen to the ''Hallelujah'' Chorus. When each number is called, write on a sheet of paper the word that best describes the texture they hear. (You may wish to use Copying Master 4-2: Listening Map at this time.)

• Summarize Handel's use of three different textures in this selection.

 ''Hallelujah'' Chorus from *Messiah*, by George Frederick Handel

Versailles (vair·sī') Cathedral, France, is in the baroque style.

1. Introduction

2. Theme **A**

Hal - le - lu - jah, Hal - le - lu - jah, Hal - le - lu - jah, Hal - le - lu - jah, Hal -

- le - lu - jah,

84

SPECIAL LEARNERS

Students with visual or tracking disabilities may have difficulty following the Listening Map to the ''Hallelujah'' Chorus. Use an overhead transparency of pupil pages 84–85 and point to each section as it comes up in the recording. This will enable the students to hear the beginning of each theme. Students who have difficulties with aural and visual coordination will benefit from an overhead transparency of Copying Master 4-2. After each number is called, pause to allow the students to choose their response. Then fill in the correct response on the transparency. This will help strengthen aural and visual skills.

3. Theme B

for the Lord God Om-nip - o - tent reign - eth. Hal-le-

-lu - jah, Hal - le - lu - jah, Hal - le - lu - jah, Hal - le - lu - jah,

4. Theme B repeated higher

for the Lord God Om-nip - po - tent reign - eth. Hal-le-

lu - jah! Hal-le-lu - jah! Hal-le-lu - jah! Hal-le-lu - jah!

5. Theme C

The king - dom of this world is be - come

6. Theme D

And He shall reign for ev - er and ev - er

7. "King of Kings and Lord of Lords" is heard in long note values; "forever and ever" is added in shorter note values. Gradually, this moves higher and higher.

8. Theme D repeated

And He shall reign for ev - er and ev - er,

9. "King of Kings and Lord of Lords" is heard in long note values; "forever and ever" is added in shorter note values.

0. The coda ends with four "hallelujahs" followed by a dramatic pause and a final "hallelujah" in very long note values.

85

LESSON 2

LESSON 2

3. Introduce George Frederick Handel. Have the students discuss the information on Handel and the *Messiah*.

Reinforcing the Lesson

Review "Memory" (page 64), "Joyfully Sing" (page 66), and "Goin' Trav'lin'" (page 49) and identify the texture of each melody. (homophonic, polyphonic, homophonic)

3 APPRAISAL

The students should be able to:
1. Read and perform a canon with pitch and rhythmic accuracy.
2. Analyze the musical texture of the "Hallelujah" Chorus.

George Frederick Handel, Thomas Hudson, By courtesy of the NATIONAL PORTRAIT GALLERY, London

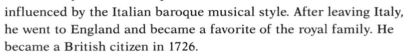

GEORGE FREDERICK HANDEL

George Frederick Handel (1685–1759) is one of the two most respected and revered musicians of the baroque period. He and Johann Sebastian Bach created musical compositions that brought the baroque period to its peak.

Handel was born in Germany in 1685, and began his formal musical training at the age of eight. In his early twenties he visited Italy and was impressed and influenced by the Italian baroque musical style. After leaving Italy, he went to England and became a favorite of the royal family. He became a British citizen in 1726.

Handel is remembered today for the English oratorios he wrote later in his life. However, he was probably more well known in his day for the fine Italian-style operas he wrote and produced. His most famous oratorio, *Messiah*, was composed in 1741 in less than three weeks and was an immediate success. On April 6, 1759, when completely blind, Handel conducted a performance of *Messiah* in London. Eight days later he died and was buried in Westminster Abbey.

86

EXTENSION

CURRICULUM CONNECTION: SOCIAL STUDIES

Westminster Abbey—officially called the Collegiate Church of St. Peter, is located in Westminster, a borough of London. Originally a monastery, it was rebuilt by Edward the Confessor and dedicated as a church in 1065. In 1245, Henry III tore down most of the church, replacing it with one in the Gothic style. Later monarchs added to the building. All the English kings and queens since William the Conqueror were crowned in the abbey, and eighteen monarchs are buried there. The abbey also houses the tombs and memorials of famous British subjects, including Chaucer, Shakespeare, Handel, T. S. Eliot, and many other authors, musicians, and statesmen.

A NEW WAY TO ORGANIZE A MELODY

mposers use different techniques to create and develop melodies.

Read "Backward Bill." What repeated word in the poem suggests
how a composer might work with a melody? backward

ackward Bill

ckward Bill, Backward Bill,
lives way up on Backward Hill,
hich is really a hole in the sandy ground
ut that's a hill turned upside down).

ckward Bill's got a backward shack
th a big front porch that's built out back.
u walk through the window and look out the door
d the cellar is up on the very top floor.

ckward Bill he rides like the wind
n't know where he's going but sees where he's been.
s spurs they go "neigh" and his horse it goes "clang."
d his six-gun goes "gnab," it never goes "bang."

ckward Bill's got a backward pup,
ey eat their supper when the sun comes up,
d he's got a wife named Backward Lil,
e's my own true hate," says Backward Bill.

ckward Bill wears his hat on his toes
d puts on his underwear over his clothes.
d come every payday he pays his boss,
d rides off a-smilin' a-carryin' his hoss.

hel Silverstein

LESSON 3

Focus: Retrograde Melodies

Objectives
To identify and define retrograde
To perform a retrograde melody with me-
lodic and rhythmic accuracy

Materials
Recordings: "Rhythms in Retrogade"
                   "Sounds in Retrograde"
                   "The Web"
Keyboard, bells, or recorder
Percussion instruments

Vocabulary
Retrograde

1 SETTING THE STAGE

Have the students read the words to "Backward Bill" and decide which repeated
word suggests how a composer might organize the pitches in a melody.

LESSON 3

1. Introduce retrograde. Have the students:

• Perform "Retrograde in D" on keyboard, recorder or bells.

• Discuss the relationship between measures 1–8 and 9–16.

• Identify and define retrograde.

Day and Night is by the Dutch artist M. C. Escher. Each side of this woodcut is the reverse of the other.

• Perform "Retrograde in D Major" on keyboard, recorder, or bells. The melody in measures 9–16 is a backward version of measures 1–8. The last tone in measure 8 becomes the first tone in measure 9. When a melodic pattern is reversed so that its beginning becomes its end, it is called a *retrograde*.

Retrograde in D major

88

SPECIAL LEARNERS

Mainstreamed students who have reading disabilities or tracking difficulties will benefit from an overhead transparency of pupil page 88. Point to each line or measure as the students play "Retrograde in D" on keyboard, recorder, or bells.

Compare the pitches of the melody in measures 1–8 with measures 9–16. Are the phrases of equal length? Are the same pitches used in both sections? yes; yes, but in reverse

• Perform "Rhythms in Retrograde."

Rhythms in Retrograde

V.L. and M.J.

• Choose percussion instruments and perform "Rhythms in Retrograde."
• Perform "Sounds in Retrograde."

Sounds in Retrograde

V.L.

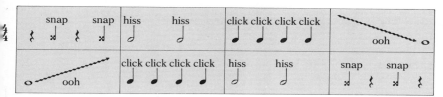

• Perform "Rhythms in Retrograde" and "Sounds in Retrograde" in combination.

 CHALLENGE Create, notate, and perform your own retrograde sound piece.

89

LESSON 3

• Compare the pitches of measures 1–8 with 9–16 and answer the questions.
2. Introduce rhythms and sounds in retrograde. Have the students:
• Perform "Rhythms in Retrograde" with hand motions and with percussion instruments.
• Perform "Sounds in Retrograde."
• Perform "Rhythms in Retrograde" and "Sounds in Retrograde" in combination.
• Attempt the Challenge! by creating, notating and performing original retrograde sound compositions.

Reinforcing the Lesson
Preview "The Web" on page 91 to experience a musical composition that uses retrograde.

3 APPRAISAL
The students should be able to:
1. Identify and define retrograde
2. Perform a retrograde melody with melodic and rhythmic accuracy.

CURRICULUM CONNECTION: LANGUAGE ARTS

Palindromes—"Retrograde in D" is a musical palindrome—a word, phrase or sentence that reads the same forward or backward. Examples of single-word palindromes, including names, are *pop, refer, Otto,* and *Anna.* One of the best-known palindromes is "Madam, I'm Adam."

Ask students to name a palindrome for each of the following definitions:
1. twelve o'clock (noon)
2. baby dog (pup)
3. part of the face (eye)
4. songs for one singer (solos)
5. signal sent to get help (SOS)
6. highest point (*two words*) (top spot)
Challenge students to think up their own palindromes.

LESSON 4

Focus: Twelve-Tone Music

Objectives
To identify tone row as a kind of pitch organization
To perform a song based on a tone row and its retrograde

Materials
Recordings: "The Web"
Begleitungsmusik zu einer Lichtspielscene (excerpt), Op. 34
Keyboard or bells
Percussion instruments

Vocabulary
Twelve-tone, serial, tone row, atonal, expressionism

1 SETTING THE STAGE

Tell the students they will be learning about a new method of pitch organization used by twentieth-century composers called twelve-tone or serial music.

2 TEACHING THE LESSON

1. Introduce "The Web." Have the students:
• Count all the black and white keys to determine the number of different notes from C to B on the keyboard.
• Discuss information on twelve-tone or serial music.
• Play the original tone row for "The Web" on keyboard or bells.
• Play the retrograde version of the tone row on keyboard or bells.
• Follow the score as they listen and identify the word in the song where the retrograde begins.

A NEW KIND OF PITCH ORGANIZATION

Twelve-Tone Music

• Count all the black and white keys to determine the number of different pitches from C to B on the keyboard.   7 white keys, 5 black keys, 12 in all

One kind of twentieth-century music is **twelve-tone,** or **serial,** music. In this musical style, the composer organizes all twelve tones in a **row.**

The song "The Web" is based on a twelve-tone row. It also makes use of retrograde. Here is the original tone row upon which "The Web" is based.

• Play this tone row on bells or keyboard.

• Play the retrograde on bells or keyboard.

• Follow the score as you listen to "The Web." Identify the words where the retrograde begins. "The front is the back."

90

E X T E N S I O N

SPECIAL LEARNERS

Mainstreamed students with visual or tracking disabilities may encounter difficulties in following the score to "The Web" as printed in the student text. Prepare an overhead transparency of "The Web" and point to each specific accompaniment line.

The Web

Piano Accompaniment on page PA 19

Words by Susan Lucas
Music by David Ward-Steinman

Sing "The Web" or play it on bells or keyboard with the
instrumental parts.

LESSON 4

- Notice the letter *O* in measure 3 and the bracket enclosing measures 3–8. (Tell the students that the bracket encloses the *original* organization of twelve tones in the tone row.)
- Notice the letter *R* at the end of measure 8. (Tell the students that this indicates where the original tone row starts being notated in *retrograde*.)
- Point to the places in the retrograde where the notes are written in different rhythms or a different octave than the original, though they remain in the exact reverse order.
- Sing "The Web" or play it on keyboard or bells with the instrumental parts.

CURRICULUM CONNECTION: SCIENCE

Spiderwebs—The spider secretes silk from glands in its abdomen. It begins a web by spinning a single silk thread, which is carried by a breeze until the end catches on a nearby object. The spider then attaches other strands to form an outside frame with connecting "spokes," which meet at the center. Next the spider constructs a loose, temporary spiral, starting at the center and going around to the outside frame. At this point, the spider begins to produce a sticky thread and constructs a final spiral, starting this time at the center and following and removing the earlier spiral. This sticky web traps the insects that the spider uses for food.

LESSON 4

2. Introduce atonal music. Have the students:

• Read and discuss information on atonal music.

• Suggest a reason why the composer of "The Web" chose to use a tone row organization and retrograde techniques. (Because the text is about a web that appears to have no beginning or ending like a tone row. The retrograde reflects the meaning of the words "the front is the back.")

• Create an atonal composition by playing each of the twelve tones without repetition of any tone. Decide on a meter and rhythmic pattern for the melody and reverse its order by playing in retrograde.

• Attempt the Challenge! by adding an instrumental steady beat, a rhythmic ostinato or a body percussion accompaniment to the created melody. Find a way to notate the composition.

In twelve-tone music, all twelve tones are played in the order the composer has chosen until each tone has been used once. The row is deliberately organized so that the melody has no tonal center. When a melody has no tonal center or tonic pitch to which all other tones relate, it is called **atonal**.

• The composer of "The Web" decided to use a tone row to organize the pitches of this song. He also chose to use retrograde. Suggest a reason why he might have done it. to fit the words

• Create your own atonal composition by:

1. Choosing an order in which to play each of the twelve tones without repetition of any tone to create an atonal melody
2. Deciding on a meter and a rhythmic pattern for your melody
3. Reversing the order of the melody, playing it backward, in retrograde

 CHALLENGE Add an instrumental steady beat, a rhythmic ostinato, or a body percussion accompaniment to your melody. Find a way to notate your composition.

Wassily Kandinsky painted *Improvisation XIV* in 1910, about ten years before Arnold Schoenberg introduced twelve-tone music.

THE ARTISTS

Wassily Kandinsky (vä-si-lē kan-din' skē) (1866–1944)—was a Russian painter who also lived in Germany. He thought of painting as a form of personal expression and said that color and line, rather than realistic subjects, were most emotional and inspiring. In *Improvisation XIV* he used vibrant colors and free brush strokes to give the painting its spontaneous, bold style.

Edvard Munch (ed' värd mōōnk) (1863–1944)—was a Norwegian artist whose works often show people expressing strong emotions, such as helplessness, isolation, fear, and jealousy. He painted portraits of girls as well as figures in landscapes, and he used intense colors to convey emotions. In *Girls on the Bridge* the deep blues, browns, and grays make the scene sombre and gloomy rather than peaceful or cheery.

Expressionism in Music

Arnold Schoenberg (shən' berg) (1874–1951) is known as one of the leaders of *expressionism* in music. The **expressionist** movement became popular in the early twentieth century. It was a movement in which artists—painters, composers, or authors—tried to produce works that expressed their own feelings about an object or event, rather than depicting the object itself in a realistic manner.

In music this type of creative activity required some new method of dealing with notes, chords, tone colors, and rhythms. Schoenberg first introduced twelve-tone, or serial, music around 1920. His new approach to composing often shocked people. He took away things they expected to hear. Melodies did not always sound "pretty." There were no major or minor harmonies.

Listen to this example of Schoenberg's work.

Begleitungsmusik zu einer Lichtspielscene (excerpt), Op. 34, by Arnold Schoenberg

Expressionist styles developed in art as well as in music. The painting on the right is a portrait of Arnold Schoenberg, done in 1917. Below, an expressionist painting by the Norwegian artist Edvard Munch.

Girls on the Bridge, Edvard Munch. NATIONAL GALLERY, Oslo

Portrait of Arnold Schoenberg, Egon Schiele

93

LESSON 4

3. Introduce expressionism in music.
Have the students:
• Discuss the information on Arnold Schoenberg and expressionism in music.
• Listen to the recording, which is a twelve-tone example of expressionism in music.

Reinforcing the Lesson

Have the students review "Retrograde in D" on page 88 as an example of retrograde motion in a melody.

3 APPRAISAL

The students should be able to:
1. Identify and define the use of tone row in "The Web."
2. Perform a tone row and its retrograde.
3. Create their own tone rows including a retrograde version and perform it with rhythmic and melodic accuracy.

COOPERATIVE LEARNING

Assign the students to cooperative groups of four. Have each group divide into two pairs. One pair will read and discuss the information on page 86, and the other pair will read and discuss the information on page 93. Then both pairs return to the group and teach the information they have learned to the other pair comparing and contrasting the two selections. They may wish to create one question from each page to quiz another group. If the other group can answer the question, that group wins the right to ask a question. If the answer is given by a student in the other group chosen at random, the whole group is rewarded or not depending on whether the answer is correct or incorrect. This encourages group members to be sure everyone knows all the information. The reward could be tangible, such as a snack or extra instrument playing time, or listening to a favorite recording. Another possibility might be listing the names of members of successful groups on a weekly honor roll to be displayed in the classroom.

THE ARTIST

Egon Schiele (ā' gon shē' lə) (1890–1918) —was an Austrian painter who concentrated on conveying emotions rather than portraying things naturally or realistically. In the *Portrait of Arnold Schoenberg*, with its distorted face, harsh brushstrokes, and flat colors, Schiele might have been trying to show Schoenberg's dissonant, unexpected approach to music.

REVIEW AND EVALUATION

JUST CHECKING

Objective
To review and test the skills and concepts taught in Unit 4

Materials
Recordings: Just Checking Unit 4 (questions 1–7)
Unit 4 Evaluation (questions 3, 4)
For Extra Credit recordings (optional)
Bells or keyboard
Copying Master 4-3 (optional)
Evaluation Unit 4 Copying Master

TEACHING THE LESSON

Review the skills and concepts taught in Unit 4. Have the students:
• Perform the activities and answer the questions on pages 94–95. (For this review, examples for questions 1 through 7 are included in the ''Just Checking Unit 4'' recording. Have the students answer these questions first. Then have them answer the other questions in the review.)
• Review their answers.
(You may wish to use Copying Master 4-3 at this time.)

JUST CHECKING

See how much you remember. Listen to the recording.

1. Listen to the recording and perform these melodies by singing or playing the bells or keyboard. The recording has a four-measure introduction.

2. The harmony you just performed could best be described as:
   atonal and dissonant   tonal and consonant

   tonal and consonant

3. Perform or listen to "Ahrirang" as a canon.

4. Listen to the last part of "River" and identify the home tone by humming it or playing it on keyboard, recorder, or bells.

. Listen to a portion of the "Hallelujah" Chorus and determine whether the texture is monophonic, polyphonic, or homophonic. Show your answer by pointing to the diagram that shows the texture as each number is called.

onophonic   polyphonic   homophonic

. Perform the following body percussion to review *retrograde*.

Rhythms in Retrograde

V.L. and M.J.

. Listen to "The Web" to review melodic retrograde. In which measures is the melodic pattern reversed so that its end becomes its beginning?

. On keyboard or bells play the following pitches that make up the twelve-tone row on which the melody of "The Web" is based.

. Play the retrograde of this tone row on keyboard or bells.

95

GIVING THE EVALUATION

Evaluation Unit 4 Copying Master can be found in the *Teacher's Copying Masters* book along with full directions for giving the evaluation and checking the answers.

FOR EXTRA CREDIT

You may want to have the students respond to the following:

Texture in music refers to the way sounds are combined. List one song or other composition you have studied for each of the following textures:

monophonic ("Ahrirang" in unison)
polyphonic ("Ahrirang" as a canon; "Hallelujah" Chorus)
homophonic ("River")

(You may wish to play these recordings to refresh students' memories.)

UNIT 5 • OVERVIEW

ELEMENTS OF MUSIC	UNIT 5 OBJECTIVES	Lesson 1 Focus: Modulation	Lesson 2 Focus: Use of the Blues Scale in Symphonic Music
Dynamics	Identify dynamic changes Determine how dynamics create a mood in the music	Discuss how dynamics affect the music	
Tone Color	Identify bright and dark tone colors Determine appropriate tone colors for a composition	Listen to a composition for flute and orchestra	Listen to and identify instruments Play chord progression on keyboard or bells
Tempo	Determine appropriate tempo for the composition		
Duration/ Rhythm		Create a rhythmic accompaniment	
Pitch	**Listen to and identify key changes** **Define register and modulation** **Identify bitonality**	Listen to and identify key changes Sing two songs with a range of G-d¹ and c♯-b♭¹ Define modulation Follow a score Experience changes of key signature in a score Define register	Create a melody in blues style
Texture	Perform accompaniments in minor tonality **Identify play tonic, subdominant, and dominant chords in C major**	Perform accompaniments in minor Perform a harmonic accompaniment	Identify and define tonic, subdominant, and dominant Identify chord changes in the twelve-bar blues
Form	**Perform the twelve-bar blues progression** Listen to, discuss, and create variations		Perform the twelve-bar blues progression
Style	Sing a song in Spanish Discuss the blues and music by an African American composer **Identify and discuss bitonal music** **Discuss and identify the art song**	Discuss gospel music Sing a Spanish song Read about word painting in music Identify modulation in 3 compositions of contrasting style Discuss the composer Cécile Chaminade	Identify and discuss the blues Discuss the African American composer William Grant Still Discuss and listen to *Afro-American Symphony*, Movement 1
Reading	Read and play ♩. on g, a, b♭, b♮, c	Sing songs in ¾ , 4/4 Read melodic notation g, a, b♭, b♮, c using ♩.	Read chord symbols I IV V Read and play twelve-bar blues

PURPOSE Unit 5: HARMONY

In this unit the students will review and/or experience some techniques composers use to develop melodies and harmonies in their compositions. They will be introduced to the concepts of consonance and dissonance, and will see how composers use changes from major to minor to create shifting moods in their works.

SUGGESTED TIME FRAME

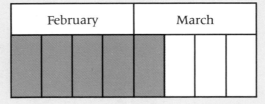

February					March		

FOCUS
• Modulation
• Use of the Blues Scale in Symphonic Music
• Harmony—Consonance and Dissonance
• Melody and Harmony

Lesson 3 Focus: Harmony—Consonance and Dissonance	**Lesson 4** Focus: Melody and Harmony
Listen to and identify dynamic changes	Determine the proper dynamics for a composition Identify how dynamics can create a mood
	Determine appropriate tone colors for a composition
	Determine the appropriate tempo for a composition
Listen to and discuss bitonal music	Identify the relationship between text, pitch register, and harmony Create a visual design that reflects musical ideas Discuss the contrasts in major and minor tonality and how they create the mood Identify characteristic themes in popular music
Define, identify, and discuss harmony that is consonant and dissonant	
Listen to, discuss, and create variations Create a variation by changing rhythm, tempo, or style	
Identify and discuss bitonal music Discuss the American composer Charles Ives	Discuss the art song of the romantic period Discuss the musical style of Franz Schubert Listen to determine the mood of a composition
Read melody in $\frac{3}{4}$ Read melodic notation d♭ - f¹ Read score	Read and follow the English translation of the original German text of a song

 TECHNOLOGY

MUSIC WITH *MIDI*

MIDI technology allows students to manipulate musical elements and make musical decisions.
- Lesson 1, page 98: *"Follow the Drinkin' Gourd"*
- Lesson 1, page 98: *"Goin' Down to Cairo"*
- Lesson 2, page 104 *"Mama Don't `Low"*
- Lesson 2, page 104: *"The Wabash Cannonball"*

VIDEO RESOURCES

Use video resources to reinforce, extend, and enrich learning in this unit.

LESSON 1

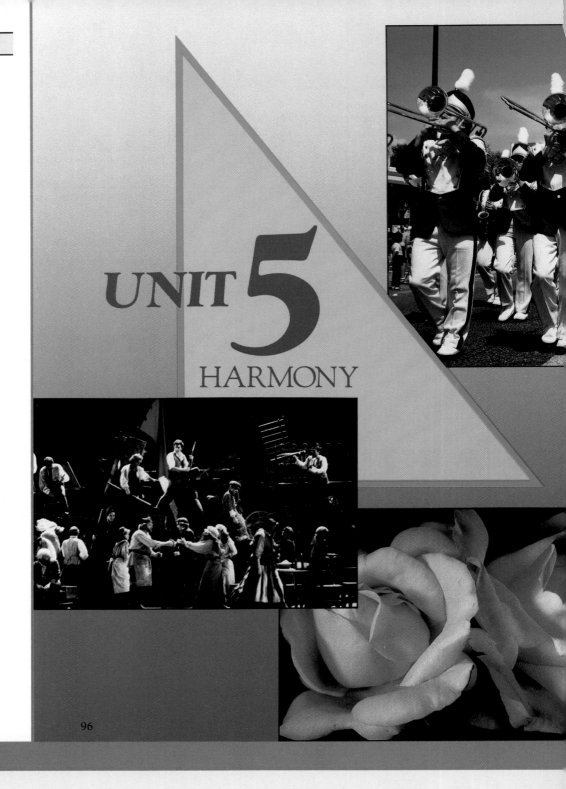

UNIT **5**

HARMONY

LESSON 1

Focus: Modulation

Objectives
To identify and perform modulation
To perform a melodic accompaniment

Materials
Recordings: "Climbing Up to Zion"
"Mi Caballo Blanco"
"Mi Caballo Blanco"
(performance mix)
Concertino for Flute and
Orchestra
"Run Joe"
"Our World"

Bells or guitar
Percussion instruments
Copying Master 5-1 (optional)

Vocabulary
Gospel, key, modulation, register

1 SETTING THE STAGE

Tell the students they will be learning
about how composers provide musical
interest and variety through changing keys.

97

LESSON 1

Key: C major   Starting Pitch: G   Scale Tones: *so, la, do re mi fa so la do' re*

2 TEACHING THE LESSON

1. Introduce word painting through melody. Have the students:
- Discuss the information on "Climbing Up to Zion" and word painting.
- Follow the different presentations of the melody as they listen to the recording.
- Identify whether the melody sounds higher or lower each time it repeats.
- Sing the melody with the recording.

Pictures Through Music

CD3:14 The music of the gospel song "Climbing Up to Zion" reflects the meaning of the words.

- Follow the different ways the melody is presented as you listen to the song. Decide whether the melody sounds higher or lower each time it repeats. higher.

🎵 "Climbing Up to Zion," by Wintley Phipps

- Sing the melody.

Climbing Up to Zion

Words and music by Wintley Phipps

98

EXTENSION

SIGNING FOR "CLIMBING UP TO ZION"

In the opening phrase, "I'm climbing up," move the hands four times as if moving up the rungs of a ladder. Move on the beat on climb/up/rest/rest. Even though the sound stops, the climbing continues throughout the two rests.

Climbing

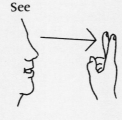

Curved "V" hands with palms facing each other, moving alternately upward.

Mountain/Zion

The right hand "A" strikes the back of the left hand "S." Both hands extend upward to show the side of the mountain.

See

The "V" position moves away from the eyes.

Lord

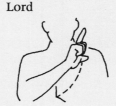

Right hand "L" moves from the left shoulder to the right hip.

WINTLEY PHIPPS

Wintley Phipps has traveled an unusual path to his career in religious music. He was born in Trinidad, West Indies, but raised in Montréal, Canada. Although familiar with hymns and church music from his early childhood, he did not come into contact with African American gospel music until his college days in Alabama. It was there that he started composing.

After earning a master's degree in divinity, Reverend Phipps knew that he would be devoting his life to church work. His love of music, however, continued. Today, Reverend Phipps both composes and performs his unique multicultural music.

Gospel Music

Gospel music is a type of religious music that originated in the South. It developed in African American Baptist churches during the 1930s, and quickly became more widely known. By the 1940s and 1950s radio stations all over the country played songs by such gospel singers as Rosetta Tharpe and Mahalia Jackson.

Gospel is different from other forms of African American religious music. The composer is usually known. The songs have instrumental accompaniments with complex harmonies, and the melodies are often quite elaborate. Gospel music, like jazz, has many polyrhythms. Early lyrics were based on the gospels but later became expressions of personal experience as well. In the 1990s, Kirk Franklin had an enormous impact on gospel music.

Gospel music has influenced rhythm and blues and soul music. The foot-stomping frenzy of gospel blended naturally into the intensely expressive soul music of James Brown, Otis Redding, and Ray Charles. A great number of rhythm and blues singers got their start by singing gospel music in church, including Aretha Franklin and Dionne Warwick.

99

LESSON 1

2. Introduce the composer and singer. Have the students discuss information on Wintley Phipps.

3. Introduce gospel music. Have the students discuss the information on the history of gospel music.

Brother

The root sign for male is made by outlining the brim of a hat. Bring index fingers together to indicate "same" or "boy-same," meaning two boys or brothers.

Listen (Hear)

The natural gesture of hearing—open palm behind ear.

Yes

The fist, palm down, nods up and down like a head. Nod once for "Oh," and again for "yes."

Sister

The root sign for female is signed by brushing the cheek toward chin to indicate the bonnet strings of a girl. The index fingers are brought together to show "same" or "girl-same," meaning sister.

Changing the Key for Effect

Key: D minor   **Starting Pitches:** A and
Scale Tones: *si, la, ti, do di re mi fa*

LESSON 1

4. Introduce "Mi Caballo Blanco."
Have the students:
• Listen to the song and decide if it moves
to a higher or lower key.
• Review the Spanish text.
• Identify and define modulation.

"Mi Caballo Blanco" is a popular song by Francisco Flores del
Campo (frän-sēs' kō flō' res del käm' pō) that describes the devotion
of the South American ranchers for their horses. As in "Climbing Up
to Zion," the composer moves the melody into different scales, or
keys, to create an effect.

• Listen and decide if the song moves to higher or lower keys. higher

 "Mi Caballo Blanco," by Francisco Flores del Campo

Mi Caballo Blanco

Words and music by
Francisco Flores del Campo

2. En alas de una dicha
Mi caballo corrió
En alas de una pena
El también me llevó.

3. Al Taita Dios le pido
Y él lo sabe muy bien
Si a su lado me llama
En mi caballo iré.

Each section of "Mi Caballo Blanco" is based in a minor key and
starts on a different pitch. The change from a section of music
based on one scale to a section of music based on another scale is
called **modulation.**

100

E X T E N S I O N

CURRICULUM CONNECTION: SOCIAL STUDIES

Ranching—an important industry in
Chile, makes up about one-sixth of all Chilean agricultural production. Ranching is
located primarily in the Southern Central
Valley and has been an important part of
Chilean life since the Spanish conquest.
Approximately one-fifth of Chile's population lives on ranches. Cowboys in Chile
are called *huasos.* They wear wide-
brimmed, flat-topped, brown or black hats;
short capes called *mantas*; leggings with
leather fringes; and high-heeled boots.

MORE MUSIC TEACHING IDEAS

Have the students:
1. Make a list of several "Top 40" popular
songs that make use of modulation.
2. Perform a harmonic accompaniment to
the first verse of "Mi Caballo Blanco" on
bells or guitar.
3. Create a rhythmic accompaniment to
"Mi Caballo Blanco."

PRONUNCIATION

1. Es mi caballo blanco
es mē kä-bä' yō blän' kō
My horse is white

Como un amanecer
kō' mō ōōn ä-mä-nä-sär'
as the dawn,

Siempre   juntitos   vamos,
s'yem'prä hōōn-tē'tōs vä'mōs
Always do we ride together,

Es mi amigo   más fiel.
es mē a-mē' gō mäs f'yel'
he is my most faithful friend.

Mi caballo,   mi caballo,
mē kä-bä' yō mē kä-bä' yō
My horse, my horse,

galopando va.
gä-lō-pän'dō vä
goes galloping.

Mi caballo,   mi caballo,
mē kä-bä' yō mē kä-bä' yō
My horse, my horse,

• Perform these three melodic accompaniments to "Mi Caballo Blanco." They are based on the D minor, E minor, and F minor scales.

Melodic Accompaniment to "Mi Caballo Blanco"

• Sing the song and perform the accompaniments.

• Perform the three melodic accompaniments (to be played in succession with the recording).
• Sing the song with the recording and perform the accompaniments.

se va y se va.
sā vä ē sā vä
just rides and rides.

2. En alas de una dicha
en ä' läs dä ōō' nä dē' chä
On the wings of joy

Mi caballo corrió
mē kä-bä' yō kōr-rē-ō'
my horse ran

En alas de una pena
en ä' läs dä ōō' nä pä' nä
on the wings of grief

El también me llevó
el täm-byen' mä yä-vō'
he carried me too.

3. Al Taita Dios le pido
äl täi' tä dē-ōs' lä pē' thō
I ask my beloved God

Y él lo sabe muy bien
ē el lō sä' bä mōō' ē byen
and he knows it very well

Si a su lado me llama
sē ä sōō lä' thō mä yä' mä
If he calls me to his side

En mi caballo iré.
en mē kä-bä' yō ē-rä'
on my horse I will go.

SPECIAL LEARNERS

Prepare an overhead transparency of pupil page 101 to use when the class sings the song in Spanish and plays the accompaniment. Assign the playing activity to any mainstreamed students who are having difficulty following the Spanish text. Split the class into two groups, assigning one group the singing and the other the playing. Point to the beginning of each line of the melodic accompaniments.

LESSON 1

5. Introduce creating harmonic interest and variety. Have the students:
• Follow the music as they listen to the opening section of the Concertino for Flute and Orchestra.
• Listen again to the recording and decide how the composer uses dynamics and register to create interest and variety.

Creating Variety in Music

Composers use modulation to create interest and variety in their compositions.

• Follow the chart as you listen to the opening section of Concertino for Flute and Orchestra by Cécile Chaminade (se-sēl′ sha-mē-näd′). The theme is stated several times.

 Concertino for Flute and Orchestra, by Cécile Chaminade

1. Statement of theme (key of D major)

2. Statement of theme (key of A major)

3. Statement of theme (key of B♭ major)

4. Statement of theme (key of D major)

• Listen again and decide how the composer uses dynamics and **register,** the high to low range of a voice or instrument, to create interest and variety. soft and loud dynamics; high and low register

102

CÉCILE CHAMINADE

Cécile Chaminade (1857–1944) made her first appearance as a concert pianist at the age of eighteen in her native Paris. She was an illustrious piano soloist and conductor, and traveled widely in France, England, and the United States from 1892 until well into the twentieth century. An active composer as well as performer, Cécile Chaminade is remembered mainly for her elegant piano compositions, many of which she performed in concert.

103

LESSON 1

• Discuss the information on the composer Cécile Chaminade.

Reinforcing the Lesson

Have the students review either "Run Joe" on page 10 to identify tonic and dominant chord changes, "Our World" on page 28 to identify contrasts between major and minor, or *Hiryu Sandan Gaeshi* on page 12 to identify changes in dynamics. (You may wish to have students do the activity on Copying Master 5-1, to review the major scale.)

3 APPRAISAL

The students should be able to:
1. Verbally define modulation and describe how it is used as a compositional device in general, and specifically in at least one composition.
2. Identify modulation in three compositions in contrasting styles.
3. Perform a melodic accompaniment to "Mi Caballo Blanco" with rhythmic and melodic accuracy.

LESSON 2

Focus: Use of the Blues Scale in Symphonic Music

Objectives
To perform a twelve-bar blues pattern
To identify the use of the blues scale in a symphonic composition
To identify orchestral tone color

Materials
Recordings: "Hear Me Talking to You"
    Afro-American Symphony,
    first movement
    Variations on "America"
Keyboard or bells

Vocabulary
Blues, twelve-bar blues, subdominant, pizzicato

1 SETTING THE STAGE

Tell the students they will be learning about the style of music called the blues, which was created by African Americans around the turn of the century.

2 TEACHING THE LESSON

1. Review the twelve-bar blues and the blues scale. Have the students:
• Discuss information on the blues.
• Listen to the recording of "Hear Me Talking to You" and identify the instruments that accompany the performance.
• Discuss the information on blues harmony, the subdominant chord, and a twelve-bar blues pattern. (Some twelve-bar blues patterns use a IV chord in the tenth measure.)

Playing the Twelve-Bar Blues

The **blues** is a style of music that was created by African Americans around the turn of the century. The words to blues songs are usually about loneliness, sadness, or lost love. The blues has its own scale and chord pattern called the **twelve-bar blues.**

• Listen to early blues singer Gertrude "Ma" Rainey sing "Hear Me Talking to You." Identify the instruments that accompany the performance.
piano, banjo, trumpet, trombone, tuba

 "Hear Me Talking to You," by Gertrude "Ma" Rainey

Blues harmony is based on three chords of the major scale: the tonic (I) chord, the dominant (V) chord, and the chord based on the fourth pitch of the scale called the **subdominant** or **IV chord.** You can play an accompaniment for all traditional blues songs once you learn these three chords.

C   D   E   F   G   A   B   C
I   IV   V

This twelve-bar accompaniment to "Hear Me Talking to You" shows a twelve-bar blues pattern.

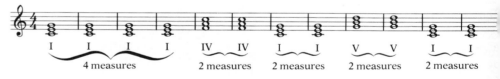

I   I   I   I   IV   IV   I   I   V   V   I   I
   4 measures   2 measures   2 measures   2 measures   2 measures

104

EXTENSION

THE COMPOSER

Gertrude "Ma" Rainey (1886–1939)— was one of the most significant early female blues singers. Her first public appearance was at age twelve in a talent show in her hometown of Columbus, Georgia. Soon after, she became a cabaret singer and toured with Tolliver's Circus and the Rabbit Foot Minstrels. During the 1920s she organized and toured throughout the South and Mexico with her Georgia Jazz Band. Ma Rainey made her first recording in 1923. Within five years she had made over one hundred recordings with many jazz greats including Louis Armstrong. Rainey is best known for her powerful voice, "moaning" style, and sensitive phrasing. She is also remembered for her lasting influence on Bessie Smith.

- Learn to play the chords in the twelve-bar blues. Then play them with the song.
- Create your own melody and words to go with the twelve-bar blues.

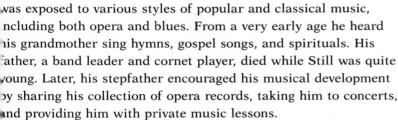

WILLIAM GRANT STILL

William Grant Still (1895–1978) is often referred to as the dean of African American composers. Best known for his music using African American and other American folk songs, he received many awards and honors as the result of his outstanding work.

Still grew up in a middle-class family in Mississippi and Arkansas and was exposed to various styles of popular and classical music, including both opera and blues. From a very early age he heard his grandmother sing hymns, gospel songs, and spirituals. His father, a band leader and cornet player, died while Still was quite young. Later, his stepfather encouraged his musical development by sharing his collection of opera records, taking him to concerts, and providing him with private music lessons.

Still arranged and composed music and directed the band at his college. In 1916 he studied with the French composer Edgar Varèse, further developing his composing skills.

The 1931 premiere of Still's *Afro-American Symphony* by the Rochester Symphony under Howard Hanson was the first performance by a major symphony orchestra of a symphonic work by an African American composer. Later, Still became the first African American to conduct a major American orchestra, the Los Angeles Philharmonic. In 1949 his opera *Troubled Island* was the first composed by an African American to be performed by a major opera company, the New York City Opera. He was also one of the first African American composers to write music for radio, films, and television.

105

LESSON 2

- Learn to play the chord progression of the traditional twelve-bar blues pattern on bells or keyboard. Then play it with the recording. (You may wish to use the keyboard section that begins on pupil page 232 for instruction on the playing of chords.)
- Create their own melody and words to go with the twelve-bar blues.

2. Introduce William Grant Still. Have the students discuss the information on the composer.

CURRICULUM CONNECTION: SOCIAL STUDIES

The blues—is a type of music that was created by African Americans. It grew mainly from work songs and spirituals. Most blues songs are sad, but sometimes express a defiant or humorous reaction to trouble.

The blues became popular in the early part of the twentieth century. W. C. Handy and Ferdinand "Jelly Roll" Morton were among the first blues composers. During the 1920s phonograph records helped make the blues more widely known. Two of the best-known blues composer-performers of this period were "Ma" Rainey and her protégée Bessie Smith (c. 1894–1937), the Empress of the Blues."

LESSON 2

3. Introduce the use of blues in the *Afro-American Symphony*. Have the students:

• Define as a blues melody Theme A of the *Afro-American Symphony*, first movement.

• Discuss the poem that serves as a program for the first movement of *Afro-American Symphony*.

• Identify and name the content of each picture, focusing on the order of the themes and tone color.

• Follow the map as you listen to the recording of Movement I.

• Discuss how the composer achieves unity and variety. (Unity is provided by the repetition of Theme A. Variety is provided through the use of a second theme and changes of tone colors, dynamics and tempo.)

Reinforcing the Lesson

Have the students preview Ives' *Variations on "America,"* page 109, for a very different use of a familiar theme in "classical" music.

3 APPRAISAL

The students should be able to:

1. Perform a twelve-bar blues accompaniment on bells or keyboard, with accuracy, to "Hear Me Talking To You."

2. Identify the composition *Afro-American Symphony* by Still as a composition using the blues scale.

3. Listen to sections or themes from *Afro-American Symphony* that have contrasting tone color and describe the tone color differences.

The Blues in a Symphony

Theme A of the first movement of William Grant Still's *Afro-American Symphony* is based on the twelve-bar blues. The overall mood of the music is one of longing, and is related to this verse of Paul Laurence Dunbar that was later applied to the music.

> All my life long twell de night has pas'
> Let de wo'k come es it will,
> So dat I fin' you, my honey, at last,
> Somewaih des ovah de hill.

• Follow the map as you listen to the first movement of *Afro-American Symphony*. The term **pizzicato** (pit-zi-kä' tō) in boxes 2 and 9 tells the string players to pluck the strings instead of using the bow.

 Afro-American Symphony, First Movement, by William Grant Still

INTRODUCTION

1 THEME A

SOLO

2 THEME A

SOLO

PIZZICATO

3

FULL ORCHESTRA

AND FASTER

THEN

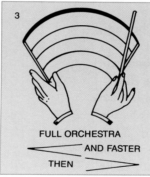

4 THEME B

SOLO

WITH OTHER STRINGS

EXTENSION

SPECIAL LEARNERS

Students with visual or tracking disabilities may have difficulty following the Listening Map to *Afro-American Symphony*. Prepare an overhead transparency of pupil pages 106 and 107 and point to each section as it comes up in the recording.

LISTENING

You may wish to use the Listening Map overhead transparency to help guide the students through the listening selection.

5 THEME B

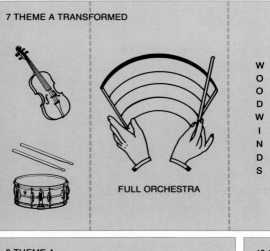

WITH OTHER STRINGS

6 THEME B (IN MINOR)

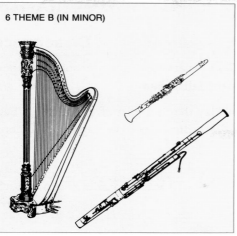

7 THEME A TRANSFORMED

FULL ORCHESTRA

WOODWINDS

8 THEME B (IN MINOR)

9 THEME A

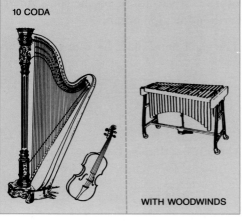

PIZZICATO

WITH WOODWINDS

10 CODA

WITH WOODWINDS

107

MORE MUSIC TEACHING IDEAS

Have the students improvise a melody using C, D, E, F, and G with the twelve-bar blues pattern in the key of C.

CURRICULUM CONNECTION: READING

Paul Laurence Dunbar (1872–1906)— African American poet, was best known for his poems on African American life. Dunbar grew up in Dayton, Ohio. After he graduated from high school he compiled a booklet of his verses called *Oak and Ivy* and sold it to passengers riding the elevator he operated. His next book of poems, called *Majors and Minors,* brought him instant recognition. Dunbar's best known collection is called *Lyrics of Lowly Life* which was published in 1896. Dunbar served as an assistant at the Library of Congress for a short period of time. He also appeared as a lecturer at colleges across the country.

LESSON 3

Focus: Harmony—Consonance and Dissonance

Objectives
To identify and perform consonance and dissonance
To identify bitonality

Materials
Recordings: "River"
　　　　　 "America," Version 1
　　　　　 "America," Version 2
　　　　　 Variations on "America"
Keyboard, recorder, bells, or guitar

Vocabulary
Dissonance, bitonal

1 SETTING THE STAGE
Have the students review "River" on page 78 as an example of consonant harmony.

2 TEACHING THE LESSON

1. Introduce consonance and dissonance. Have the students:
• Review the information on consonance on page 80.
• Discuss the information on dissonance.
• Play the first part of "America" on keyboard or bells with the recording of Version 1. (The recording has a four-measure introduction.)
• Identify the harmony in Version 1 as being consonant because there is little or no tension.
• Play the first part of "America" on keyboard or bells with the recording of Version 2. (The recording has a four-measure introduction.) Identify the harmony as dissonant because there is tension or clashing among the pitches.

2. Introduce bitonality. Have the students discuss the information on bitonality.

E X T E N S I O N

TYPES OF HARMONY

Consonance and Dissonance

Tones that do not seem to sound as though they go together are called **dissonant**.

• Play the first part of "America" on bells or keyboard with this recording. Does the music sound consonant or dissonant? Why?
consonant; answers will vary

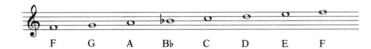
"America," Version 1

• Play the first part of "America" again with the recording of Version 2. Does the music sound consonant or dissonant? Why? dissonant; answers will vary

"America," Version 2

The dissonance in harmony in Version 2 of "America" was created by using two different tonal centers or scales at the same time. When music has two tonal centers at the same time, it is called **bitonal**. The bitonal harmony in Version 2 of "America" was written by the twentieth-century American composer Charles Ives as part of a set of variations on the song "America." The variations were written for pipe organ.

The right hand plays harmony based on the F major scale.

F G A B♭ C D E F

The left hand plays harmony based on the D♭ major scale.

D♭ E♭ F G♭ A♭ B♭ C D♭

108

• Listen to *Variations on "America"* to determine how the composer used different types of harmony, dynamics, and rhythm to create interest and variety.

CD3:22

Variations on "America," by Charles Ives

1. Introduction: Based on the beginning of the song; phrase "My country, 'tis of thee" most prominent; *ff*

2. "America": Presented in a traditional style; harmony consonant; *pp*

3. First Variation: Melody in bass with continually moving sixteenth notes above melody; *pp*

4. Second Variation: New harmonization of the theme much like the close harmony of a barbershop quartet

5. Interlude: Theme played as a canon; in bitonal harmony

6. Third Variation: Change of rhythm, which produces an effect similar to a calliope; *f*

7. Fourth Variation: Rhythm for theme based in the style of a polonaise, a dance of Poland; now based on a minor scale

8. Interlude: Again uses dissonant bitonal harmony

9. Fifth Variation: Melody played on the keyboard; contrasting line in the pedal part (the lowest part); directions to organists say to play the pedal part as fast as the feet can go

10. Coda: Described by Ives as "in a way a kind of take-off on the Bunker Hill fight."

This work is typical of Ives's strongly original style of music. He takes a recognized melody and treats it in a very creative way.

CHALLENGE

Create your own variations on "America." Change the rhythm, the tempo, or the style.

109

LESSON 3

3. Introduce *Variations on "America."* Have the students:
• Discuss information in preparation for listening to *Variations on "America."*
• Listen to *Variations on "America"* by following the descriptions as each number is called.
• Summarize how Ives used contrasts of harmony, dynamics and rhythm to create interest and variety.
4. Introduce the Challenge! activity. Have the students create original variations on "America" by changing the rhythm, tempo or style.

COOPERATIVE LEARNING

Have the students turn to page 16 in the text and perform "Ode to Joy" on keyboard, recorder, bells, or guitar. Assign the students to cooperative groups of four to explore the concept of variation, using "Ode to Joy" as the theme. The following variation techniques may provide the students with some models to begin the project:

1. changing from major to minor
2. varying the rhythm
3. changing the tempo
4. varying the dynamics
5. adding a bitonal harmonic accompaniment

Each group should rehearse its variations on "Ode to Joy." Select a conductor to help order the variations and a recorder to develop a simple graph score. Have each group perform its variation for the class.

UNIT 5   **109**

LESSON 3

5. Introduce the composer. Have the students discuss the information on Charles Ives.

Reinforcing the Lesson

Have the students take a familiar melody such as the "Ode to Joy" and create a bitonal accompaniment by using more than one tonality.

3 APPRAISAL

The students should be able to:

1. Verbally define the terms bitonality, consonant harmony and dissonant harmony.

2. Listen to several excerpts from *Variations on "America"* that are clear examples of either consonance or dissonance and accurately match the term to the example.

3. Perform the first six measures of "America" on bells or keyboard as written, while an accompaniment is played that results in either a version that is consonant or dissonant. Identify each with the correct label.

CHARLES IVES

Charles Ives (1874–1954) grew up in a small town in Connecticut where his father was the local bandmaster. He received his early musical training from his father, who encouraged him to experiment with all sorts of sound combinations to "stretch his ears." Ives liked the harsh dissonance created by playing "America" in one key with the right hand at the keyboard and in another key with the left. Doing this at the same time created bitonality.

As a teenager Ives became a church organist, and one can imagine that he enjoyed shocking the congregation by changing the harmonies of familiar songs like "America."

Because he thought his unconventional music was not going to be popular, Ives went into the insurance business. Eventually he founded a successful insurance agency and became very wealthy. However, music remained his first love, and he continued to compose evenings and weekends.

Ives found ideas for his music in the folk and popular music he knew as a boy: hymns, ragtime, village band concerts, church choir music, patriotic songs, and dances. Perhaps it was these sounds that gave him the idea for his *Variations on "America,"* written for pipe organ.

110

Franz Schubert's "The Erlking" is one of the finest examples of *art song* romanticism. An **art song** is a composition for solo voice and instrumental accompaniment, usually keyboard. The term *art song* is used to distinguish such songs from folk songs and popular songs. In the text to "The Erlking" the German poet Johann Wolfgang von Goethe (gə(r)' tə) tells of a father riding on horseback through a storm with his child in his arms. The boy, who is very sick with a high fever, remembers the legend that whoever is touched by the king of the elves, the Erlking, must die.

"The Erlking" has four separate characters. Usually all are sung by one person. Schubert uses a wide range of pitches and contrasts in vocal registers to depict each of the four characters. Contrasts of major and minor tonality also help to identify the characters.

- Listen to the beginning of "The Erlking," and choose one word to describe the mood. Which of these musical characteristics do you think help to express that mood? Answers may vary; minor, loud, fast

    major/minor   soft/loud   fast/slow

    "The Erlking," by Franz Schubert

- Listen to "The Erlking" and follow the translation of the German text.

111

LESSON 4

Focus: Melody and Harmony

Objectives
To identify the relationship between word painting, pitch register and harmony

Materials
Recordings: "The Erlking"
            "Climbing Up to Zion"

Vocabulary
Art song

1 SETTING THE STAGE
Review the romantic period on page 26.

2 TEACHING THE LESSON
1. Introduce the "The Erlking." Have the students:
- Discuss the information on the romantic period and "The Erlking."
- Listen to the beginning of "The Erlking" and decide on one word to describe the mood (anxious, scared, troubled, etc.). Decide which musical characteristics help to express that mood.
- Listen to "The Erlking" and follow the translation of the German text.

E X T E N S I O N

CURRICULUM CONNECTION: ART

Have one of the students write the names of the four characters found in Goethe's poem "The Erlking."

    Narrator   Father   Son   Erlking

Review the lesson on "The Erlking," focusing on the musical ideas Schubert used to depict each character. Have the students work in pairs to create a visual design that could be used for the cover of a record jacket for a recording of "The Erlking." Have each cooperative pair share its visual design with the class. Provide an opportunity to render constructive suggestions. Select several of the best designs and display them.

LESSON 4

The Erlking

Narrator

1. Who is that riding like the wind through the night?
   It is a father, holding his child.
   He holds him safely in his arms,
   He holds him tightly and keeps him warm.

Father

2. "My son, why do you hide your face so anxiously?"

Son

3. "Father, don't you see the Erlking?
   The Erlking with his crown and his train?"

Father

4. "My son, it is a streak of mist."

Erlking

5. "Ah, small boy, come away with me.
   We'll play the greatest games with you.
   We'll walk by the river, see beautiful flowers.
   My mother has fantastic clothes for you."

Son

6. "My father, my father, don't you hear
   the Erlking whispering promises to me?"

Father

7. "Be quiet, stay quiet, my child;
   the wind is rustling in the dead leaves."

112

EXTENSION

CURRICULUM CONNECTION: LITERATURE

Johann Wolfgang von Goethe (1749–1832)—German author, was one of the most important and influential writers of modern literature. Goethe was born in Frankfurt am Main to a wealthy family. From an early age he was encouraged to study foreign languages, literature, and the fine arts. While studying in Strasbourg, Goethe met philospher Johann Herder. Herder stimulated Goethe's interest in Homer, Shakespeare, ballads, and folk songs. During this time Goethe wrote many poems in a folk-song style, one of which was "The Erlking." Goethe wrote works in every genre. He spent many years writing his masterpiece, *Faust*. He completed it a few months before his death.

Erlking

8. "Ah, fine boy, are you sure you won't come with me?
My daughters will take good care of you.
There'll be parties every night—singing, dancing.
They'll cradle and dance you, and sing you a lullaby."

Son

9. "My father, my father, and don't you see there
the Erlking's daughters in the shadows?"

Father

10. "My son, my son, I see it clearly;
the old willows look so gray."

Erlking

11. "I must have you with me.
If you won't come, then I will use force!"

Son

12. "My father, my father, now he is taking hold of me!
The Erlking has hurt me!"

Narrator

13. The father shudders, he rides swiftly on,
he holds in his arms the groaning child,
he reaches the courtyard weary and anxious;
in his arms the child was dead.

113

LESSON 4

- Listen again to "The Erlking" and respond to the questions.
- Perform the Challenge! activity.

- Listen again to "The Erlking," and answer these questions.

How do dynamics create the mood? Erlking sings softly; other characters more loudly

How does the piano accompaniment set the mood of the story? It conveys the father's urgency, the son's panic, and the Erlking's persuasiveness.

Which character sings in major? Erlking

Why is the remainder of the song in minor? tragic subject

 "The Erlking," by Franz Schubert

 CHALLENGE Think of your favorite songs. Which song seems to use dynamics, accompaniment, and major or minor most effectively to set a mood? Compare this to how Schubert set the mood in "The Erlking." Share your song with your classmates.

Schubert Playing the Piano is by the Austrian artist Gustav Klimt (1872–1918). Klimt chose to paint the scene in a romantic style.

114

EXTENSION

THE ARTIST

Gustav Klimt (gōōs′ täf klēmt) (1862–1918)—was an Austrian painter. A patron commissioned two scenes, one of them *Schubert at the Piano,* for a place above the doors of the palace music room. The soft, golden light and the delicacy of the figures are romantic in style.

A view of Vienna in Schubert's time

FRANZ SCHUBERT

Franz Schubert, drawing after a water-color by W.A. Rieder

The music of every important composer has something special to offer. In the case of Franz Schubert (1797–1828), it is outstanding melodies, easily remembered for their beauty and simplicity.

Growing up in Austria as the son of a schoolmaster, Schubert received his musical training as a choirboy in the Royal Chapel. Schubert also began a teaching career, but soon abandoned this to devote himself entirely to music.

Schubert composed over six hundred songs for voice and piano, and once composed eight songs in one day. Besides songs, he composed instrumental music including symphonies, chamber music, and solo piano music. Schubert's world-famous "Unfinished" Symphony (so called because it has only two movements instead of the usual four) contains many beautiful melodies. Occasionally Schubert used melodies from his own songs as themes for his instrumental pieces as in the "Trout" Quintet for Piano and Strings and the String Quartet No. 14 in D Minor, known as the "Death and the Maiden" Quartet. Schubert's music also is important in that his style bridges the classical and romantic periods.

115

2. Introduce Franz Schubert. Have the students discuss the information on Schubert. You may wish to use the following item as a basis for extended discussion.

Name other compositions (folk songs, ballads, etc.) that tell a story through the music, and use expressive devices the way Schubert's music does.

Reinforcing the Lesson

Review "Climbing Up to Zion" on page 98 for examples of word painting as an expressive device.

3 APPRAISAL

The students should be able to listen to "The Erlking" and identify the relationship between word painting, pitch register, and harmony.

MORE MUSIC TEACHING IDEAS

Have the students name several cartoon characters and list the characteristics of the music that are used as their themes.

REVIEW AND EVALUATION

JUST CHECKING

Objective
To review and test the skills and concepts taught in Unit 5

Materials
Recordings: Just Checking Unit 5
(questions 3–10)
Unit 5 Evaluation (question 3)
For Extra Credit recordings
(optional)
Recorder, bells or keyboard
Copying Master 5-2 (optional)
Evaluation Unit 5 Copying Master

TEACHING THE LESSON

Review the skills and concepts taught in Unit 5. Have the students:
• Perform the activities and answer the questions on pages 116–117. (For this review, examples for questions 3 through 10 are included in the ''Just Checking Unit 5'' recording. Have the students answer these questions first. Then have them answer the other questions in the review.)
• Review their answers.
(You may wish to use Copying Master 5-2 at this time.)

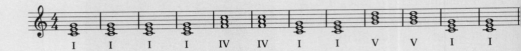

JUST CHECKING

See how much you remember.

1. Perform this melodic pattern on recorder, bells, or keyboard.

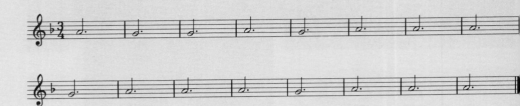

2. Perform this twelve bar blues harmonic progression on bells or keyboard.

3. Listen to part of "Climbing Up to Zion" to review modulation.
   Decide if the melody sounds higher or lower each time it repeats. higher

4. Listen to a section of the Concertino for Flute and Orchestra and decide how the composer uses dynamics and register to create interest and variety. soft and loud dynamics; high and low register

5. Listen and determine whether the style period for each of these examples is romantic, twentieth century, blues, or gospel.
   blues, romantic, gospel, twentieth century

6. Listen and determine whether the harmony in each example sounds more consonant or dissonant. consonant, dissonant, consonant, dissonant

116

7. Listen to a section of "Mi Caballo Blanco" and raise your hand when you hear the music modulate.

8. Listen to a section of "Mi Caballo Blanco" and decide if the music modulates to a higher or lower key. *a higher key*

9. As you listen to these examples from "The Erlking," decide which character is singing, based on whether you hear major or minor and the register of the melody. *Erlking,* major, high register; *father,* minor, low register; *son,* minor, high register

10. Listen to Theme A of the *Afro-American Symphony*. Identify the instrumental tone color by naming the picture that best describes what you are hearing. *picture 3*

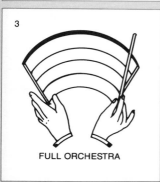

INTRODUCTION

1 THEME A

SOLO

2 THEME A

SOLO

PIZZICATO

3

FULL ORCHESTRA

4 THEME B

SOLO

WITH OTHER STRINGS

117

GIVING THE EVALUATION

Evaluation Unit 5 Copying Master can be found in the *Teacher's Copying Masters* book along with full directions for giving the evaluation and checking the answers.

FOR EXTRA CREDIT

You may want to have the students respond to the following in a paragraph:

Describe how tone color, melodic register, and major and minor tonalities are used to express the feelings and emotions of the text in "The Erlking." (The music setting of "The Erlking" has four separate characters sung by one voice. Each character has been assigned a specific vocal register—the father is in low register, the Erlking in high register, and so on. The father's voice is assigned a dark tone color while the Erlking is assigned a bright tone color. Only the part of the Erlking is set in major mode. All of the other parts are set in minor mode.) (You may wish to play this recording to refresh students' memories.)

ELEMENTS OF MUSIC	UNIT 6 OBJECTIVES	Lesson 1 Focus: Phrases of Equal Length	Lesson 2 Focus: Phrases of Unequal Length
Dynamics	**Discuss ways in which dynamics affect mood in music** Listen to, identify, and perform contrasting dynamics		Perform a song using contrasting dynamics
Tone Color	Creatively explore tone colors **Perform melodic accompaniment on bells, keyboard, or recorder**	Analyze compositions performed by jazz combo	
Tempo	**Discuss ways in which tempo affects mood in music** Identify tempo of a composition		
Duration/ Rhythm	**Perform a rhythmic motive** Perform steady beat Perform music with changing meters	Clap, snap, and step steady beat Identify phrase lengths in popular music	Perform a song with changing meters
Pitch	**Discuss how mode can express the mood of music**		Sing a song with a range of F#-d'
Texture	Perform melodic accompaniments	Perform a melodic and harmonic accompaniment on bells, keyboard, or guitar	
Form	**Listen to and identify phrases of different lengths** Identify, create, and perform rhythmic and melodic motives **Identify motive**	Define phrase Listen to, identify, and perform phrases of equal and unequal length	Listen to and identify phrases of different lengths
Style	Discuss musical characteristics of the romantic period and 20th century	Discuss the alternative rock movement, and the group R.E.M.	Listen to and perform songs by popular composers
Reading	Read and play melodic accompaniments using pitches g_1 b_1 c_1 d_1 e_1 f#$_1$ g, a, b,c,d,e Read and play Em, D, G, and C chords Use rhythms ♩ , ♩ , ♩. , ♪♪	Play from melodic notation c-e Read chord symbols Em, D, G, C	Sing song with changing meters: $\frac{4}{4}$, $\frac{2}{4}$, $\frac{3}{8}$, and *D.S. al Coda*

PURPOSE Unit 6: FORM AND STYLE

In this unit the students will review and extend their knowledge of form. They will explore phrases of equal and unequal length, investigate motives in art and music, discuss strophic form, and experience ballads and art songs.

SUGGESTED TIME FRAME

March				April		

FOCUS

Phrases of Equal Length
Phrases of Unequal Length
Repetition of Motives
Repetition of Sections

Lesson 3 Focus: Repetition of Motives	Lesson 4 Focus: Repetition of Sections
	Discuss ways in which dynamics can express the mood of a song Listen to and identify dynamics of a song
	Perform accompaniments on bells, recorder, guitar, or keyboard
	Discuss ways in which tempo can influence the mood of a song Listen to and identify the tempo of a song
Perform a rhythmic motive	Create a rhythmic accompaniment
Perform melodic motives on bells, recorder, keyboard, or guitar	Sing a ballad with pitch accuracy Discuss how mode can express the mood of a song Sing a song with a range of g_I-a
	Perform melodic and harmonic accompaniments on bells, recorder, guitar, or keyboard
Identify, define, and perform rhythmic and melodic motives Discuss repetition in paintings and architecture	Define strophic form Listen to, identify and perform a ballad
Discuss the contemporary musical style of Philip Glass Discuss 20th century musical characteristics Define and discuss minimalist music	Identify art song Discuss the art song and Fanny Mendelssohn Hensel Analyze a German art song Discuss characteristics of the romantic period
Read motives in $\frac{3}{4}$	Read and play melodic accompaniment using pitches g_I b_I c_I d_I e_I $f\sharp_I$ g, a Read and play challenge accompaniment using pitches e, f♯, g, a, b, c, d, e Read and play rhythms ♩ , ♩ , ♩. , ♫

TECHNOLOGY

MUSIC WITH *MIDI*

MIDI technology allows students to manipulate musical elements and make musical decisions.

- Lesson 3, page 126: Create Using Elements of **Minimalism**
- Lesson 3, page 126: Perform/Improvise Using Elements of **North Indian Music**
- Lesson 4, page 130: *"Red Iron Ore"*

VIDEO RESOURCES

Use video resources to reinforce, extend, and enrich learning in this unit.

LESSON 1

UNIT **6**

FORM
AND
STYLE

Dolmen in the Snow, Johann Christian Clausen Dahl, MUSEUM DER BILDENDEN KÜNSTE, Leipzig

118

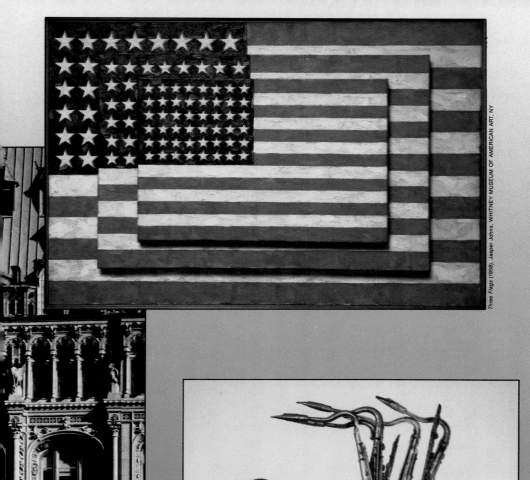

Three Flags (1959), Jasper Johns, WHITNEY MUSEUM OF AMERICAN ART, NY

Birds of Paradise, Arman, MARISA DEL RE GALLERY, NY

119

LESSON 1

Focus: Phrases of Equal Length

Objectives
To identify and perform phrases of equal length
To perform melodic and harmonic accompaniments

Materials
Recordings: "Magenta"
            "Patterns"
            "The One I Love"
            "River"
Keyboard, bells, or guitar

Vocabulary
Phrase

HE ARTIST

asper Johns (b. 1930)—is an American ainter and sculptor. Some of his paintings re of numbers, maps, targets, or American flags, because he believes that flat bjects are good subjects for paintings, vhich are also flat. He has made sculptures that are such accurate copies of light ulbs and flashlights that it is very difficult to tell they are not the real thing. In eneral he is interested in pointing out the nost common, popular objects of modern merican culture.

LESSON 1

1 SETTING THE STAGE

Discuss the information on phrases, and ask students why a musical phrase might be compared to a sentence. (A sentence and a musical phrase both express complete thoughts or ideas.)

2 TEACHING THE LESSON

1. Introduce phrases of equal length. Have the students:
• Listen to "Magenta."
• Clap and snap the eight-beat phrases as indicated.
• Move their hands in an arc to show the length of the phrases.
• Step, stand still, and move their hands in an arc for the phrases while listening again.
• Listen to "Patterns" and change movement patterns as they step each phrase. (Observe students' ability to follow the phrase structure as they listen.)
2. Accompany a song that has phrases of equal length. Have the students:
• Listen to "The One I Love." Move hands in an arc from left to right to show the phrase lengths.
• Answer the questions at the bottom of the pupil page. (The phrases are sixteen beats long; two distinct melodies are heard.)
• Determine whether the phrases are of equal or unequal length. (equal)

BUILDING BLOCKS OF FORM

When you create a story, you put words and thoughts into sentences. When you create music, you put musical thoughts into musical sentences called phrases. A **phrase** expresses a complete musical idea. Phrases of equal length contain the same number of beats. Phrases can be described as the building blocks of form.

As you listen to "Magenta":

• Clap the beat to show the length of the first phrase.
• Snap the beat to show the length of the next phrase.
• Move your hands in an arc to show the lengths of the phrases.

clap   snap

 "Magenta" by Greg Hansen

As you listen to "Magenta" again:

• Step the beat to show the length of the first phrase.
• Stand still and move your hands in an arc to show the length of the next phrase.

 "Patterns" by Greg Hansen

• Listen to "Patterns," and change your movement patterns as you step each phrase.

 "The One I Love" by Berry/Buck/Mills/Stipe

• Listen to "The One I Love" by R.E.M. How many beats are in each phrase? How many different melodies do you hear?

120

E X T E N S I O N

MORE MUSIC TEACHING IDEAS

Have the students listen to selected recordings of popular music that use regular phrase structures to determine the number of beats in each phrase.

Play this melodic accompaniment on bells or a keyboard instrument with "The One I Love."

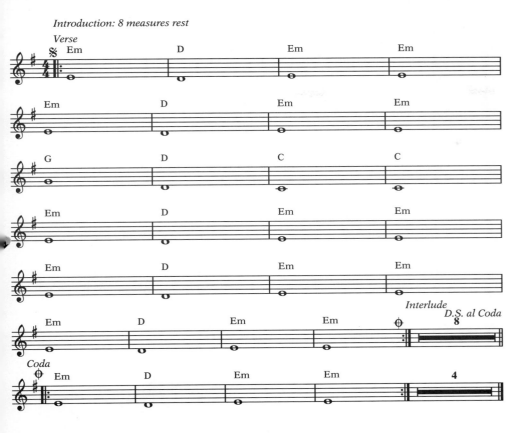

Introduction: 8 measures rest

Practice this chord progression on a keyboard.

Then, as you listen again, play the chordal accompaniment shown by the chord symbols on a keyboard instrument.

LESSON 1

• Look at the score of the melodic accompaniment and notice the indications for Introduction, Interlude, D.S. al Coda, and Coda.
• Practice the melodic accompaniment on keyboard, bells, or guitar.
• Play the melodic accompaniment on keyboard, bells, or guitar while listening to "The One I Love."
• Practice the chords given at the bottom of the pupil page.
• Note the order of the chord indications written above the melodic accompaniment, and practice the chords. (Students should note that the chords change at the same point that the contrasting melody is heard.)
• Play the chords indicated as they listen to "The One I Love" again.

SPECIAL LEARNERS

You may wish to use an overhead transparency of pupil page 121 the second time you play "The One I Love" for students who have difficulty reading notation. These students can play the melodic accompaniment at the top of the page while the others are playing the harmonic accompaniment at the bottom.

COOPERATIVE LEARNING

Review the lesson on "The One I Love," this time focusing on the overall phrase structure: a a b a a a. Then have the students work in cooperative groups of four to create a movement routine showing the phrase structure. (You may prefer to limit the routines to movement of the hands, arms, or feet, or a combination.) They might also want to use props. Remind the students to be sure that everyone gets a chance to contribute a movement idea. Each group should take into account the abilities of all group members; the movement plan should reflect those abilities. Group members should agree that the final product is appropriate in showing phrase structure. Have the groups practice their routines and perform them for the class.

LESSON 8

3. Introduce R.E.M. Have the students:
• Read and discuss the information on R.E.M. on page 122.
• Discuss the following questions: What styles were the alternative rock bands reacting against? What elements do you hear in "The One I Love" that might identify it as an alternative rock song? (The simple, rather repetitious melody; the predominance of guitar sounds over highly synthesized effects.) What other style are you familiar with that drew elements from two different pop styles? (folk rock)

Reinforcing the Lesson

Review "River" on page 78 and identify phrases of equal length.

3 APPRAISAL

The students should be able to:
1. Show through movement their understanding of regular phrase structures.
2. Perform melodic and harmonic accompaniments to "The One I Love" with accuracy.

R.E.M

In the early 1980s a movement called alternative rock began in the world of popular music. Reacting to the glossy, synthesized style of American and British popular music of the time, alternative rock bands returned to the roots of American rock in search for a less contrived sound. R.E.M., a four-man band out of Athens, Georgia, represents one of these alternative bands.

The original band members—Michael Stipe, Peter Buck, Mike Mills, and Bill Berry—formed the band R.E.M. in 1980. They combined elements from American folk, British punk, and rock and roll to create their own unique sound. R.E.M. was one of the first alternative bands to achieve a large national following. They helped pave the way for a number of other alternative rock bands. R.E.M.'s innovative albums incorporate a variety of styles. Examples include "Out of Time," which uses folk instruments such as the mandolin, and "Monster," which has a rougher, more punk-influenced rock and roll sound. R.E.M. is known for having melodies that are well crafted and lyrics that are thought provoking. "The One I Love," released in 1987, was R.E.M.'s first Top-Forty hit single.

122

PHRASES OF DIFFERENT LENGTHS

Composers can organize their phrases in many ways. Each phrase in "The One I Love" is four measures long. The melodic accompaniment on page 121 follows this four-measure-phrase structure. In "(Life Is a) Celebration," Rick Springfield uses another technique with phrases to create interest and variety.

- As you listen to "(Life Is a) Celebration," decide if the phrases are all the same length.

 "(Life Is a) Celebration" by Rick Springfield

- Listen again and move your hand in an arc on each phrase.

- Sing the song.

"(Life Is a) Celebration"

Words and music by
Rick Springfield

I was lost on a wind-ing road,

I thought that life had no-thing left to give.

And you came and showed me that just to live

was the great-est gift of all. And you showed me

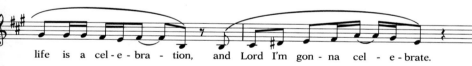
life is a cel-e-bra-tion, and Lord I'm gon-na cel-e-brate.

123

LESSON 2

Focus: Phrases of Unequal Length

Objective
To identify phrases of unequal length

Materials
Recordings: "(Life is a) Celebration"
"(Life is a) Celebration" (performance mix)
"Love Song"
"Love Song" (performance mix)

1 SETTING THE STAGE

Have the students listen to "(Life is a) Celebration" to determine the length of the phrases.

2 TEACHING THE LESSON

1. Introduce phrases of unequal length. Have the students:
- Listen to "(Life is a) Celebration" again and move their hands in an arc for each phrase.
- Sing the song.

Reinforcing the Lesson

Review "Love Song" on page 46 and identify phrases of unequal length.

3 APPRAISAL

The students should be able to identify irregular phrase structures.

EXTENSION

VOCAL DEVELOPMENT

Rhythmic precision is an important part of the style of "Life is a Celebration." Have the students carefully observe the phrasing markings, and strive for quick, crisp, and clean articulation of vowels and consonants to help capture the performance style of this composition.

THE COMPOSER

Rick Springfield—was born in Sydney, Australia, in 1948. He grew up on army bases in Australia and England. At thirteen Springfield received his first instrument, a guitar. By age sixteen he had organized his first band. In 1972, Springfield moved to the United States to establish a solo career. He appeared as an actor on several major television shows. While he was in the serial "General Hospital," his album *Working Class Dog* became a hit. His eight solo albums have received numerous awards. Springfield wrote "(Life Is a) Celebration" for an episode of the television show "Fame."

LESSON 2

124

SIGNING FOR "(LIFE IS A) CELEBRATION"

Life/Live — Both hands in an "L" position move in unison up the body

Celebration — Both hands hold imaginary flags. Wave them in small circles.

Come — Natural beckoning gesture.

Now 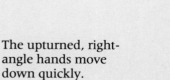 — The upturned, right-angle hands move down quickly.

Look  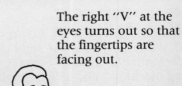 — The right "V" at the eyes turns out so that the fingertips are facing out.

Lord, I'm gon-na cel-e-brate. Life is a cel-e-bra - tion,

I

Life is a cel-e-bra - tion,

II *cresc.*

come on now_ and cel-e-brate, cel-e-brate.

ff

look it's a rev-e-la - tion. So cel-e-brate now, cel-e - brate life.

Cel-e-brate now, cel-e - brate life.

To Coda

Cel-e-brate now, cel-e - brate life. Cel-e-brate now, cel-e - brate life.

Cel-e-brate now, cel-e - brate life. Cel-e-brate now, cel-e - brate life.

D.S. al Coda ⊕ *Coda*

Cel-e-brate now, cel-e -

Cel-e-brate now, cel-e -

ff

-brate life. Cel - e - brate, cel - e - brate, cel - e - brate, cel - e - brate,

ff

-brate life. Cel - e - brate, cel - e - brate, cel - e - brate, cel - e - brate,

cel - e - brate, cel - e - brate, cel - e - brate, cel - e - brate life!

cel - e - brate, cel - e - brate, cel - e - brate, cel - e - brate life!

Revelation
(Information)

The fingertips are on either side of the fore-head. Both hands move down and open into palm-up posi-tion.

LESSON 3

Focus: Repetition of Motives

Objective
To identify and perform rhythmic and melodic motives

Materials
Recording: "Floe" from *Glassworks*
Keyboard, recorder, bells, or guitar

Vocabulary
Motives, minimalism

1 SETTING THE STAGE

Discuss the information on repetition in architecture and relate it to repetition of motives in music.

Motives in Architecture

When architects design buildings they often repeat small units or shapes such as squares, rectangles, circles, or triangles to create a much larger form. Identify some of the small units used to create the buildings pictured here. Answers will vary.

Below, the chapel at the Air Force Academy in Colorado Springs. Right, the Flatiron Building in New York City. Bottom, Habitat, in Montréal, Canada.

126

E X T E N S I O N

Motives in Music

Composers often use repetitions of short musical ideas to develop the form of a composition. These ideas are called *motives*. **A motive** is a short, easily recognized musical unit that keeps its basic identity through many repetitions.

In "Floe" from *Glassworks* by Philip Glass, different motives are used to create a larger form.

- Perform these motives from "Floe" on keyboard, recorder, bells, or guitar.

Motives from "Floe"

(6 times)

(2 times)

(4 times)

(4 times)

- Listen to "Floe" and identify the order in which you hear each motive. 3, 1, 4, 2

 "Floe" from *Glassworks*, by Philip Glass

- Listen again and perform each motive, with the recording, on keyboard, recorder, bells, or guitar.

127

LESSON 3

2 TEACHING THE LESSON

1. Introduce and define *motive.* Have the students:
- Discuss information on motives.
- Perform the motives from "Floe" on keyboard, recorder, bells or guitar.
- Notice that each of these motives is based on the pitches F E D E.
- Listen to "Floe" and identify each new motive as it is introduced by raising their hand.
- Identify the order in which the four motives are introduced.
- Listen again and perform each motive with the recording.

SPECIAL LEARNERS

Use an overhead transparency of pupil page 127 if your class includes students who have difficulty reading notation. Point to the beginning of each line to help the students hear and play each new theme.

LESSON 3

2. Introduce motives in visual art.
Have the students:
• Discuss the use of motives in Piet Mondrian's *Broadway Boogie-Woogie.* (repeated square and rectangular shapes give the painting unity)
• Discuss which shape or form serves as a motive for the computer art. (a sphere)

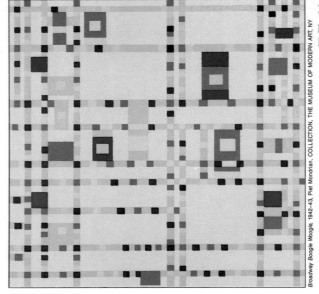

Broadway Boogie Woogie is by the Dutch artist Piet Mondrian.

Broadway Boogie Woogie, 1942–43, Piet Mondrian, COLLECTION, THE MUSEUM OF MODERN ART, NY

Motives in Art

The use of motives is found in many art forms. The two works shown on this page both use repetition of small forms to create a much larger form. The first, *Broadway Boogie Woogie*, by Piet Mondrian, was inspired by the artist's viewing of the traffic on Broadway from his studio in a nearby skyscraper. He compared the cars and trucks to the rhythms of boogie-woogie. The second work is a piece of computer art. What shape or form serves as a motive for this work? a sphere

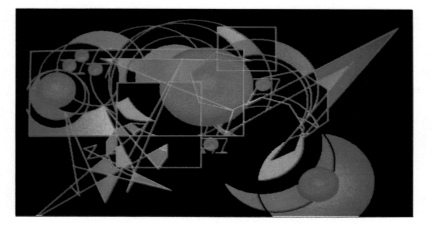

128

THE ARTIST

Piet Mondrian (1872–1944) – Dutch painter, is best known for his geometric style. In his paintings he stressed the principle of reducing to horizontal and vertical lines and planes through the use of only white, black, and the primary colors. His art has deeply influenced modern architecture and commercial design. *Broadway Boogie-Woogie* was one of Mondrian's last works. It was inspired by the view of the streets from his New York City studio. His use of small squares creates a playful atmosphere.

Philip Glass and Minimalism

The contemporary composer Philip Glass was born in Baltimore in 1937. Like many composers, he had a traditional musical education. However, he is most noted for his music in the twentieth-century style called **minimalism.**

While studying music in Europe, Glass met the great Indian sitar player Ravi Shankar, who introduced him to Indian classical music. Later, Glass traveled to Morocco and India to study Eastern music first hand. The influence of Eastern music ultimately was reflected in his own music. While he worked to perfect his style back in the United States, Glass took a variety of jobs, including moving furniture, doing carpentry, and driving a cab. About the same time, he met several painters and sculptors who influenced his work. Their method was to emphasize one aspect of visual art (for example, color or texture) to create the greatest possible effect with the least possible means. Glass adapted this method to his music, in combination with characteristics of the Eastern music he had studied.

Minimalist music does not imitate the sound of Eastern music. However, it does contain some of the same techniques, such as repetition of short rhythmic and melodic patterns. This emphasis on repetition is the basis of all minimalist music. In contrast, other Western musical styles emphasize melody or harmony. Young audiences in particular have found Glass's blend of rock realism and Eastern mysticism appealing.

"Floe" is a typical example of the minimalist style. In it, Glass achieves his effects with only a few repeated rhythmic and melodic ideas. By using orchestral instruments—especially the brasses—in unusual ways, Glass creates the tone qualities that are characteristic of minimalist music.

LESSON 3

3. Introduce Philip Glass and minimalism. Have the students discuss the information on Philip Glass and minimalism. You may wish to use the following item as a basis for extended discussion.

Philip Glass has composed some of the most exciting contemporary music in the world. After he demonstrated that his new musical ideas were worthwhile, his audiences grew and he again began to receive financial grants and commissions. One of his commissioned works was the music that accompanied the lighting of the torch at the 1984 Olympics. Discuss the meaning of *commissioned*. ("made to order") What are the benefits of this type of an assignment? (The composer knows he/she will be paid for work done.) What are some of the hazards? (The commissioner may not like the finished product; the work may not be exactly to the composer's liking.) (answers will vary)

Reinforcing the Lesson

Have the students create new motives on the pitches used in the "Floe" examples (D, E, F and A) and perform them on keyboard, recorder, bells, or guitar with the recording.

3 APPRAISAL

The students should be able to:
1. Identify repetition in architecture and paintings.
2. Identify and perform motives found in "Floe."
3. Identify the use of motives in minimalist music and certain art forms.

LESSON 4

Focus: Repetition of Sections

Objectives
To identify and perform a composition in strophic form
To identify the characteristics of a ballad
To identify the musical characteristics of art song

Materials
Recordings: "The Golden Vanity"
"The Golden Vanity" (performance mix)
"Schwanenlied"
"The Erlking"
Keyboard, recorder, or bells

Vocabulary
Ballad, strophic form

1 SETTING THE STAGE

Have the students review the definition of art song on page 111.

2 TEACHING THE LESSON

1. Introduce repetition of sections.
Have the students:
• Discuss the information on ballad and strophic form.
• Listen to "The Golden Vanity" and follow the story.
• Perform the melodic accompaniment to "The Golden Vanity" on keyboard, recorder, or bells.

The Ballad

A **ballad** is a narrative poem or song. The ballad is one of the oldest forms of poetry and one of the oldest kinds of music. Its beginnings are almost impossible to trace, partly because the earliest composers of ballads probably could not read or write. The ballad form apparently was established by 1400. Ballads were passed down by word of mouth from generation to generation. European settlers brought their ballads to the New World, besides composing new ones. Some surviving ballads from the 1500s and 1600s were sung in much the same way as we sing them now.

In the ballad "The Golden Vanity," we learn the story of a captain and his clever cabin boy. Eight different verses, all set to repetitions of the same melody and harmony, describe an adventure of trickery and wit.

"The Golden Vanity" is a folk song ballad set in strophic form. **Strophic form** repeats the same melody or section of music with each new verse or stanza of text.

• Listen to "The Golden Vanity" and follow the story.

 "The Golden Vanity"

• Perform the melodic accompaniment to "The Golden Vanity" on keyboard, recorder, or bells.

130

EXTENSION

SPECIAL LEARNERS

Use an overhead transparency of pupil page 131 if there are any students who have difficulty reading notation. Point to the beginning of each line as the students play the melodic accompaniment to "The Golden Vanity."

MORE MUSIC TEACHING IDEAS

Have the student create a stylistically appropriate rhythmic accompaniment to "The Golden Vanity."

The Golden Vanity
Piano Accompaniment on page PA 26

English Folk Song

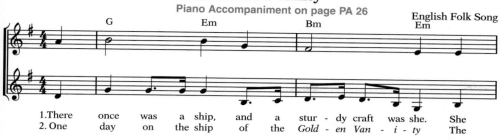

1.There once was a ship, and a stur - dy craft was she. She
2. One day on the ship of the *Gold - en Van - i - ty* The

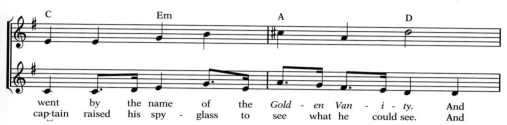

went by the name of the *Gold - en Van - i - ty.* And
cap-tain raised his spy - glass to see what he could see. And

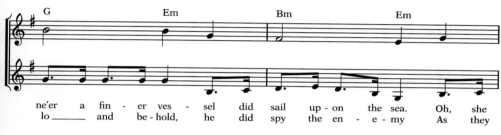

ne'er a fin - er ves - sel did sail up - on the sea. Oh, she
lo ____ and be - hold, he did spy the en - e - my As they

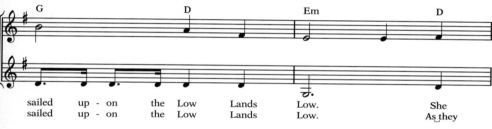

sailed up - on the Low Lands Low. She
sailed up - on the Low Lands Low. As they

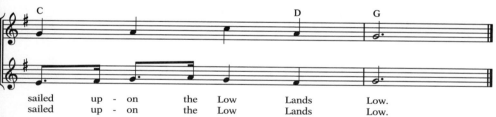

sailed up - on the Low Lands Low.
sailed up - on the Low Lands Low.

131

LESSON 4

3. ≈≈≈

The captain was pond'ring the course he would pursue,
When up spoke the cabin boy, the youngest of the crew.
"Pray, sir, what will you give me to rout the foe for you
As they sail upon the Low Lands Low?" *(two times)*

4. ≈≈≈

The captain was amazed and a little bit annoyed
To think he must depend on a lowly cabin boy,
But he said he'd give his daughter, his very pride and joy,
If he'd sink them in the Low Lands Low. *(two times)*

5. ≈≈≈

The boy spread his arms and into the sea he dived.
He swam and he swam, it's a wonder he survived!
He bored some tiny holes in the other vessel's side
And he sank it in the Low Lands Low. *(two times)*

6. ≈≈≈

Then back once again to the Vanity he sped.
He thought as he swam of the pretty girl he'd wed,
For, "You shall have my daughter," the captain'd plainly said,
"And you'll sail upon the Low Lands Low. *(two times)*

7. ≈≈≈

And when he reached the ship and was safely at her side,
"Good captain, help me come aboard!" the cabin boy did cry.
The captain, though ignored him, and merely breathed a sigh
As he sailed upon the Low Lands Low. *(two times)*

8. ≈≈≈

"Good captain, help me up," cried the cabin boy once more,
"Or else I'll bore your ship and send it to the ocean floor."
The captain then moved quickly and pulled the lad aboard
And they sailed upon the Low Lands Low. *(two times)*

Both England and the United States sailed
ships such as this during the 1700s and 1800s.

132

• After you have become familiar with the rhythm of the song, learn this melodic accompaniment.

The Golden Vanity
Challenge Melodic Accompaniment

CURRICULUM CONNECTION: SOCIAL STUDIES

Ballads—The ballad is one of the oldest surviving forms of poetry and music. The earliest ballad composers were professional musicians, as well as poets, clergymen, and nobles. Gradually the lower classes became familiar with ballads and began to use them for telling stories and news. These ballads were passed orally from generation to generation. Sixteenth-century ballads were simple compositions; nineteenth-century ballads were complex romantic songs. Appalachia and the Midwest have produced hundreds of mountain and cowboy ballads. The ballad reemerged in popular culture in the 1950s and 1960s with such singers as the Weavers, Bob Dylan, and Joan Baez composing and performing songs of social protest.

LESSON 4

3. Introduce art song. Have the students:
• Discuss the information on art song.
• Listen to *"Schwanenlied"* and read the English translation of the German text as each number is called, and answer the question.
• Decide which musical characteristics help to express the mood of the song.

4. Introduce the composer. Have the students discuss the information on Fanny Mendelssohn Hensel.
You may wish to use the following item as a basis for extended discussion.

During the nineteenth century women were not expected to follow the same kinds of careers they do today. How might this have affected Fanny Mendelssohn's pursuit of a career in music?

Reinforcing the Lesson

Have the students review "The Erlking" on page 111 as another example of art song. Compare the way the texts, harmonies, dynamics, and pitches create contrast and variety.

3 APPRAISAL

The students should be able to:
1. Identify a song in strophic form.
2. Identify and perform a ballad by singing and accompanying "The Golden Vanity."
3. Identify the musical characteristics used to create mood in *"Schwanenlied."*

An Art Song

The art song was one of the most important forms of the romantic period. These songs usually combine a solo voice with piano accompaniment. Through poetry and music, art songs express a particular mood or idea, often with deep emotion. Like "The Golden Vanity," *"Schwanenlied"* (shvän´ en lēd) is in strophic form. *"Schwanenlied"* was composed by Fanny Mendelssohn Hensel. The text was written by Heinrich Heine (hīn´ riKH hī´nə) (1797–1856), one of the greatest German poets.

• Listen to *"Schwanenlied,"* and read the English translation of the German text on page 135. Decide on a word to describe the mood of the text. sorrowful

 "Schwanenlied," by Fanny Mendelssohn Hensel

Fanny Mendelssohn Hensel (1805–1847), German composer and pianist, was the oldest of four children in an extremely talented family. Her grandfather was a well-known philosopher, and her brother Felix also became a renowned composer and pianist. Fanny displayed great musical talent at an early age. Felix often remarked that she was a better pianist than he was. He always asked her advice on his musical ideas before writing them down.

Fanny published only five collections of songs and a piano trio during her lifetime. In fact, her early works were published under Felix's name. Queen Victoria's favorite Mendelssohn song, *"Italien,"* actually was written by Fanny. Her art songs, such as *"Schwanenlied,"* reveal many characteristics of the romantic period, such as direct expression of emotions and long, complex melodies.

134

EXTENSION

CURRICULUM CONNECTION: LITERATURE

Heinrich Heine (1797–1856)—was one of the most popular writers of German literature. He was born in Düsseldorf, the eldest son of Jewish parents. He was mainly taught by French priests, and he became deeply influenced by French liberalism. In 1831 he moved to Paris and lived there for the rest of his life. In his writings, Heine tried to bring about greater understanding between the French and German people. One of his poetry collections, *Buch der Lieder* ("Songbook") was set to music by Schubert and Schumann.

MORE MUSIC TEACHING IDEAS

Have the students list important twentieth-century women composers. (Answers will vary; encourage students to name popular music performers and groups.)

Schwanenlied (Swan's Song)

Verse 1

Es fällt ein Stern herunter aus seiner funkelnden Höh,
A star falls down from its sparkling heights.

das ist der Stern der Liebe, den ich dort fallen seh.
That is the star of love that I see falling.

Es fallen von Apfelbaume, der weissen Blätter so viel,
So many white leaves fall from the apple tree

es kommen die neckenden Lüfte, und treiben damit ihr spiel.
The teasing breezes come and playfully use them for their games.

Verse 2

Es singt der Schwan im Weiher, und rudert auf und ab,
The swan sings in the pond and glides back and forth,

und immer leiser singend, taucht er ins Fluthengrab.
And ever so softly singing he dips into the deep watery grave.

Es ist so still und dunkel, verweht ist Blatt und Blüth,
It is so still and dark, leaves and blossoms have disappeared.

der Stern ist knisternd zerstoben, Verklungen das Schwanenlied.
The star's brilliance is gone. The swan's song has died away.

Which of these musical characteristics express the mood of
"Schwanenlied"? slow; minor; mostly soft

slow or fast   major or minor   mostly loud or mostly soft

135

REVIEW AND EVALUATION

JUST CHECKING

Objective
To review and test the skills and concepts taught in Unit 6

Materials
Recordings: "Floe"
            "The Golden Vanity"
            "The One I Love"
            Just Checking Unit 6
            (questions 4–9)
            Unit 6 Evaluation (question 2)
            For Extra Credit recordings
            (optional)
Keyboard, recorder, bells, or guitar
Copying Master 6-1 (optional)
Evaluation Unit 6 Copying Master

TEACHING THE LESSON

Review the skills and concepts taught in Unit 6. Have the students:
• Perform the activities and answer the questions on pages 136–137. (For this review, examples for questions 4 through 9 are included in the "Just Checking Unit 6" recording. Have students answer these questions first. Then have them answer the other questions in the review, using the recordings in the unit where necessary.)
• Review their answers.
(You may wish to use Copying Master 6-1 at this time.)

JUST CHECKING

See how much you remember. Listen to the recording.

1. Listen to the steady beat and perform these motives on keyboard, recorder, bells, or guitar.

2. Perform this melodic accompaniment on bells, recorder or keyboard.

3. Perform this melodic accompaniment on keyboard, bells, or recorder with the first 8 measures after the introduction of "The One I Love."

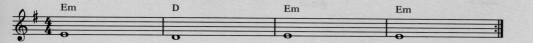

4. Listen to a portion of "The Golden Vanity" and determine if the form is strophic or ternary. strophic

5. Listen to a portion of "(Life Is a) Celebration" and show the regular and irregular phrase structure by moving your hand in an arc.

6. Listen to "Schwanenlied" and decide whether the composition is in major or minor. minor

7. Perform a body percussion movement to show the equal eight-beat phrase lengths in "The One I Love."

8. Name some musical characteristics that express the mood of "Schwanenlied." slow and mostly soft, minor

GIVING THE EVALUATION

Evaluation Unit 6 Copying Master can be found in the *Teacher's Copying Masters* book along with full directions for giving the evaluation and checking the answers.

FOR EXTRA CREDIT

You may want to have the students respond to the following:

Discuss some of the techniques composers use to develop a theme. (repetition of motives, rhythmic alteration, melodic alteration, change of textures, change of tone color, change of register)

(You may wish to play recordings to refresh the students' memories.)

137

ELEMENTS OF MUSIC	UNIT 7 OBJECTIVES	Lesson 1 Focus: Classical Symphony	Lesson 2 Focus: Development of a Musical Idea
Dynamics	Follow dynamics from a listening map Listen to and identify contrasting dynamics		Follow dynamics of a symphony from a listening map
Tone Color	Listen to and identify the orchestra	Listen to a symphony orchestra	Listen to a symphony orchestra
Tempo	Perform a free form composition keeping a steady tempo		
Duration/ Rhythm	**Identify rhythmic motives** **Define *legato* and *staccato* articulation**	Locate, identify and perform rhythmic motives following a listening map Perform rhythmic motives by using body movement Define *legato* and *staccato* articulation	Identify, perform, and create rhythmic motives
Pitch	Follow a melodic listening map Create a melodic motive Identify pitch levels and major/ minor tonality Read and perform spoken music		Sing a song with a range of e-d' Perform a melody on bells, recorder, and keyboard Perform and create a melodic motive Listen to and identify levels of pitch
Texture			
Form	**Discuss and identify motives** **Discuss sonata allegro form** **Listen to and identify free form** Discuss, create, and perform a composition in free form	Identify rhythmic and melodic motives Analyze and discuss repeated motives as a unifying device	Define development Define and discuss sonata allegro form Discuss the symphony
Style	**Identify musical characteristics of the classical and neoclassical style period** **Identify program music**	Discuss characteristics of the classical period Identify composers of the classical period	Discuss neoclassical style
Reading	Read *staccato* and *legato* patterns:	Read rhythms in $\frac{2}{4}$ Recognize *staccato* and *legato* Read score Follow listening map	Follow listening map

PURPOSE Unit 7: ELEMENTS OF FORM

In this unit the students will extend their concept of form. They will develop an awareness of the use of motives and will investigate the classical aesthetic principles of unity, variety, and clarity. They will define and experience sonata allegro form, be introduced to program music, and investigate free form.

SUGGESTED TIME FRAME

April	May

FOCUS

Classical Symphony
Development of a Musical Idea
Program Music
Free Form

Lesson 3 Focus: Program Music	**Lesson 4** Focus: Free Form
Identify the contrasting dynamics of a composition	
	Read and perform a composition for spoken chorus
Identify major/minor tonality	
Listen to and identify themes in a composition	Identify, listen to, define, discuss, create, and perform a composition in free form
Identify, define, and listen to program music Define absolute music Create program music	Discuss creative developments in 20th century art
Follow listening map	Read contemporary score in $\frac{6}{8}$

 **TECHNOLOGY**

MUSIC WITH *MIDI*

MIDI technology allows students to manipulate musical elements and make musical decisions.

- Lesson 4, page 156: Create Using Elements of **Twelve-Tone and Chance Music**

VIDEO RESOURCES

Use video resources to reinforce, extend, and enrich learning in this unit.

UNIT 7

ELEMENTS
OF FORM

138

Still Life with Fruit Bowls, Carafe, and Fruit, Paul Cézanne, LOUVRE, Paris

View from Wind River Mountains, Wyoming, Albert Bierstadt, THE MUSEUM OF FINE ARTS, Boston

139

LESSON 1

Focus: Classical Symphony

Objectives
To develop awareness of the use of a motive
To identify legato and staccato
To explore aspects of the classical period and its aesthetic principles of unity, variety and clarity
To listen to a complete movement of a symphony

Materials
Recordings: "Beethoven Seventh Motive Montage"
Beethoven, Symphony No. 7, Second Movement
Mozart, Quintet for Clarinet and Strings in A Major, Fourth Movement (optional)

Vocabulary
Legato, staccato

1 **SETTING THE STAGE**

Tell the students they will learn about new ways to use themes and motives in music.

THE ARTISTS

Albert Bierstadt (bēr' stät) (1830–1902)—was born in Germany and grew up in the United States. He painted romanticized panoramas of the American West, such as the *View from Wind River Mountains.* He was very successful because many people of his time had not seen the scenery of the West, and he was considered one of the greatest American landscape painters of the time.

Paul Cézanne (se' zän) (1839–1906)—was a French painter who aimed to see objects as spheres, cylinders, cones, and other basic forms. He painted very slowly, so he liked to paint apples because they did not move or rot quickly.

LESSON 1

2 TEACHING THE LESSON

1. Introduce the motives in the second movement of Beethoven's Seventh Symphony. Have the students:
• Perform each of the rhythmic motives from Symphony No. 7 using pats, claps, and snaps.
• Analyze melodies a, b, and c and identify which of the rhythm motives 1, 2, and 3 goes with each melody, (1, b; 2, a; 3, c)

Identifying Motives

The second movement of Ludwig van Beethoven's Symphony No. 7 is based on repetition of rhythmic and melodic motives.

• Perform these rhythmic motives by patting the quarter notes, pat-sliding the tied notes, clapping the eighth notes, and snapping the triplets with alternating hands.

Each of the following melodies uses one of the rhythmic motives you have performed.

• Identify the melody that uses rhythmic motive 1, motive 2, and motive 3. 1,b; 2,a; 3,c

140

SPECIAL LEARNERS

Prepare an overhead transparency of pupil page 140 if there are students in the class who have difficulty reading notation. Point to each beat when the students play motives 2 and 3 together. This will enable the students to coordinate the two rhythm patterns. You may also wish to split the class into two groups, assigning a line to each.

Listen and match the rhythmic motives 1, 2, or 3 with recorded examples a, b, and c from the second movement of the Seventh Symphony. 1, b; 2, a; 3, c

 Beethoven Seventh Motive Montage

Which of the melodies in the Beethoven Seventh Motive Montage sounded smooth and connected? a

Which of the melodies sounded detached and crisp? b and c

Music that sounds smooth is said to be performed **legato** (le-gä' tō).
Music that sounds detached and crisp is said to be performed
staccato (stä-kä' tō). Notes to be played or sung staccato are written
this way: ♩ or ♩ .

Symphony orchestras often consist of over a hundred musicians. These two photos show the Boston Symphony Orchestra in performance.

LESSON 1

- Listen to the Beethoven Seventh Motive Montage and match rhythmic motives 1, 2, or 3 with recorded examples a, b, and c. (1, b; 2, a; 3, c)

2. Introduce legato and staccato. Have the students:
- Identify which term is appropriate for the melodies in the Beethoven Seventh Motive Montage.
- Discuss the differences between the terms legato and staccato, with emphasis on using the terms in the discussion.
- Identify examples of legato and staccato in popular tunes of today. (answers will vary)

COOPERATIVE LEARNING

Place the following articulation markings on the board:

⌒ ....

After identifying and reviewing legato and staccato, have the students work in cooperative groups to find examples with the first six units of the text of melodies that contain legato and staccato. Each student in the cooperative groups should find an example within the designated portion of the text to validate the specific category. Each member of the group will then present his or her example, providing documentation as to how it fits the assigned category. The validated examples for the entire group should be listed on a sheet of paper, which is then signed by all of the group members.

SPECIAL LEARNERS

You may wish to use an overhead transparency of pupil pages 140 and 141 if there are students in the class who have difficulty coordinating visual and audio skills. After each melody, pause to allow the students to choose the correct response. Then mark the correct response on the overhead transparency.

3. Introduce identifying motives in a listening map. Have the students:
• Listen to the first portion of the second movement of Beethoven's Symphony No. 7 and point to each repetition of the motive on the map.
• Locate rhythmic motives 2 and 3.
• Listen to the entire second movement and point to the rhythmic motives as they follow the map.

Identifying Motives in a Listening Map

CD4:2 • Listen to the first portion of the second movement of Beethoven's Symphony No. 7. When you hear rhythmic motive 1 (♩ ♫ | ♩ ♩), find it on the map.

 Symphony No. 7, Second Movement, by Ludwig van Beethoven

• Examine the map. Find rhythmic motive 2 (♩ | ♩ ♩) and rhythmic motive 3 (♪♪♪ ♪♪♪).
• Follow the map as you listen to the second movement of Beethoven's Symphony No. 7.

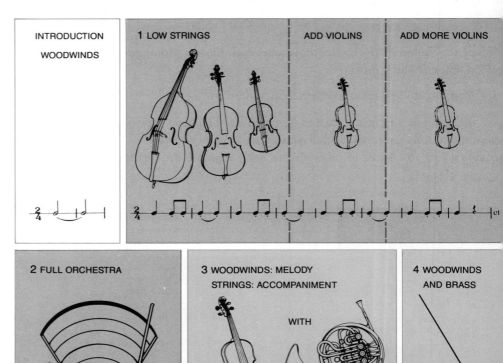

142

SPECIAL LEARNERS

Use an overhead transparency of pupil pages 142 and 143 if the class includes students who have difficulty reading abstract musical notation or who have visual tracking disabilities. Pause after each call number and have the students indicate the correct rhythmic motive. Then point to the correct notation.

LISTENING

You may wish to use the Listening Map overhead transparency to help guide the students through the listening selection.

5 STRING BASSES: MELODY (PIZZICATO)

WOODWINDS AND STRINGS: ACCOMPANIMENT

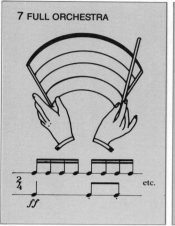

6 POLYPHONY

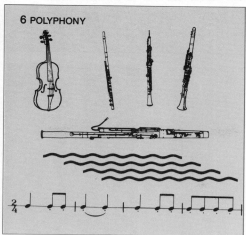

7 FULL ORCHESTRA

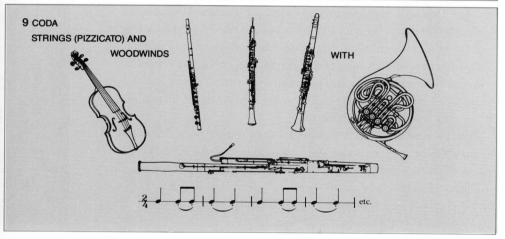

8 WOODWINDS: MELODY

STRINGS: ACCOMPANIMENT

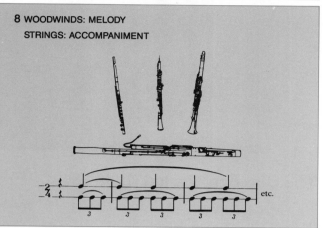

9 CODA

STRINGS (PIZZICATO) AND WOODWINDS   WITH

THE COMPOSER

Ludwig van Beethoven (1770–1827)—great German composer, was born in Bonn. He showed great promise on both the violin and piano at an early age. By age twelve he was publishing his keyboard compositions. In 1792 Beethoven moved to Vienna, where he studied composition with Haydn and Salieri. Beethoven began to lose his hearing by the late 1790s. As he lost his hearing, he began to withdraw from his friends and became extremely suspicious and sensitive. Many of his greatest works, such as the Ninth Symphony, were written when he was almost completely deaf. The Seventh Symphony was also written during this period. The first performance was at a benefit concert for wounded Austrian soldiers on December 8, 1813.

LESSON 1

4. Review the classical period. Have the students:
• Discuss the characteristics of the classical period.
• Examine the pictures from the period.
• Define and identify Beethoven as being a bridge composer. Evidence used to support this should be his life dates (1770–1827) and a combination of both classical and romantic characteristics present in the ABA structure of the second movement. (romantic: drama, intense expression; classical: repetition, variety, balance and unity)

Reinforcing the Lesson

Review motives in music (pages 127–129) and compare the ways Beethoven and Glass incorporate motives in their compositions.

3 APPRAISAL

The students should be able to:
1. Find, identify, and perform motives found in the second movement of Beethoven's Seventh Symphony.
2. Analyze and discuss repeated motives as a unifying device.
3. Identify and define the expressive markings of legato and staccato as contained in the second movement of Beethoven's Seventh Symphony.
4. Define and discuss the artistic principles of unity, variety, balance, and clarity as found in the classical period.

Artists of the classical period often depicted scenes of ancient Greece and Rome.

Countryside of Arcadia, Nicolas Poussin. LOUVRE, Paris

The Classical Period (1750-1830)

The characteristics of music from the classical period are charm, delicacy, and gracefulness. Melodies generally are short and tuneful. Beneath this seeming simplicity there are often deeper feelings; however, these feelings are usually understated. A single section of a classical work can have contrasting moods, and dynamic changes include crescendo and decrescendo. Classical composers wrote operas and concertos, as did the earlier baroque composers. They also established some new musical forms, the symphony and the string quartet.

The orchestra of today developed during this period in musical history. Great composers of the classical period include Haydn (hī' dən) and Mozart (mōt' särt). Early works of Beethoven are often considered to be classical in style. However, Beethoven is credited by most musicians with ushering in the next great period in musical history, the romantic period.

144

The Pantheon, Paris

Characteristics of Classical Period Music

Changes of mood within sections of a composition
Dynamic changes including crescendo and decrescendo
Short, tuneful melodies
Controlled feelings or emotions
Emphasis on unity and balance

Hippocrates Refusing the Presents of Artaxerxes, Anne-Louis Girodet-Trioson, FACULTÉ DE MEDECINE, Paris

Above, architects of the classical period often were influenced by Greek and Roman styles. Left, this painting illustrates a scene from the life of Hippocrates, the ancient Greek "father of medicine."

145

MORE MUSIC TEACHING IDEAS

Have the students listen to the fourth movement of Mozart's Quintet for Clarinet and Strings in A Major, K. 581 (page 194), an example of the classical style.

LESSON 2

Focus: Development of a Musical Idea

Objectives
To identify and perform techniques of development
To identify and define sonata allegro form

Materials
Recordings: Beethoven, Symphony No. 7, Second Movement
Prokofiev, *Classical Symphony*, First Movement
Keyboard, recorder, or bells

Vocabulary
Development, rhythmic motive, melodic motive, symphony, sonata allegro form, introduction, exposition, recapitulation, neoclassical

1 SETTING THE STAGE

Review the repetition of rhythmic and melodic motives in the second movement of Beethoven's Symphony No. 7, pages 142–143.

2 TEACHING THE LESSON

1. Introduce repetition in visual art.
Have the students compare the different shapes and forms in Arthur Dove's painting *Clouds and Water*.

Repetition in Art

Arthur Dove's painting *Clouds and Water* is made up of simple curved shapes that are repeated and contrasted. The waves in the water are repeated in the shapes of the mountains and clouds. Contrast is provided by the different colors of the water, land, and sky. The sails on the three boats provide additional contrasts of color and movement. Each area of the painting is an adaptation, expansion, contraction, alteration, or elaboration of a basic curved shape.

• Compare the different shapes and forms in the painting.

Clouds and Water, Arthur G. Dove. THE METROPOLITAN MUSEUM OF ART, NY

146

Transforming a Musical Idea

Key: F major   Starting Pitch: F
Scale Tones: *ti do re mi fa so la*

Like the artist who painted *Clouds and Water,* a composer may decide to adapt, expand, contract, alter, or elaborate a musical idea. This transformation of a musical idea is known as **development.**

Because the melody of "America" is well known, you can probably remember how different parts of the song sound. This should enable you to explore some of the techniques composers use to develop a musical idea.

• Sing through one verse of "America." Use the lyrics to help you keep track of each measure while you are singing.

America

Words by Samuel F. Smith
Music by Henry Carey

How many times does the rhythmic pattern ♩ ♩ ♩ | ♩. ♪ ♪ ♩ appear in the song? 4

The rhythmic pattern you just identified is called a **rhythmic motive.**

• Perform the beginning of "America."

• Create your own rhythmic motives by changing the rhythm of one measure.

You have just altered the rhythm of the melody.

147

2. Introduce transformation of a musical idea. Have the students:
• Discuss the information on development, or transformation, of a musical idea.
• Sing through one verse of "America."
• Count the number of times the rhythmic motive of measures 1 and 2 appears in the song.
• Perform the beginning of "America."
• Create their own rhythmic motives by changing the rhythm of one measure.

LESSON 2

- Perform "America" on keyboard, re-corder or bells.
- Create a new melodic motive by performing measures 1 and 11 together.
- Create further motives by combining other measures of the song.
- Perform measures 7 and 8, then 9 and 10, and decide if the latter two measures are higher or lower than the former. Decide if they have the same or different rhythm patterns.
- Discuss the different techniques which can be used to develop a musical idea.

- Perform "America" on keyboard, recorder, or bells.
- Perform measure 1 and then measure 11.

My coun-try from ev -'ry____

You have just created a **melodic motive** from portions of "America."

- Create your own melodic motives by combining other measures of the song.
- Perform measures 7 and 8, then perform measures 9 and 10.

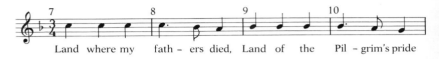

Land where my fath – ers died, Land of the Pil – grim's pride

Do measures 9 and 10 sound higher or lower than measures 7 and 8?

Do they have the same or different rhythm patterns?

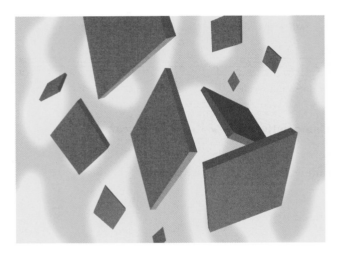

Although the diamond shapes in this computer art are turned at different angles, you can still recognize their basic form.

You can use any of these techniques, along with many others, to develop a musical idea:

        Altering rhythms
        Altering melodies
        Creating rhythmic and melodic motives

148

Organization in the First Movement of a Symphony

The symphony as a musical art form emerged during the classical period. A **symphony** is a long orchestral work organized into four movements. The first movement is almost always in what is called *sonata allegro form*. **Sonata allegro form** consists of three sections much like ABA form.

The A section sometimes begins with a foreshadowing of the musical ideas to come. This is called the *introduction* and is followed by the presentation of two or more musical ideas or themes. These themes are often contrasting in nature. The presentation of the themes is called the *exposition*. The B section is developmental. Here the themes presented in the exposition are adapted, expanded, contracted, altered, and elaborated. The composer uses a variety of techniques to transform the original musical ideas. The last section of sonata allegro form is the *recapitulation* in which the composer restates each of the themes. This section sometimes ends with a summary called the *coda*.

The following diagram depicts sonata allegro form graphically.

A	B	A
Exposition	Development	Recapitulation
(Ideas stated)	(Ideas transformed)	(Ideas restated)
Themes A and B introduced	Themes A and B developed	Themes A and B restated

Twentieth-century composer Sergei Prokofiev (ser-gā′ prō-kof′ yəf) (1891–1953) wrote his first symphony in the style of the classical period. The symphony is referred to as **neoclassical** since it exhibits all the characteristics of a classical symphony but was written almost a century after the close of that musical period.

The first movement of Prokofiev's Symphony No. 1 in D Major, or *Classical Symphony*, is an excellent example of sonata allegro form.

149

LESSON 2

3. Introduce development in the first movement of a symphony. Have the students:
• Discuss the information on the symphony and sonata allegro form.
• Discuss the information on Sergei Prokofiev.
You may wish to use the following as a basis for extended discussion.

Prokofiev is famous for his use of humor in music. How does he use this talent in the first movement of his *Classical Symphony*? (He uses twentieth-century techniques to exaggerate the eighteenth-century forms.) Describe some other ways to show humor in music. (surprises, abrupt changes in pace, use of unusual instruments and unusual combinations of instruments, and so on)

THE COMPOSER

Sergei Prokofiev (1891–1953)—was a leading Soviet composer. Prokofiev was born in the Ukraine and received his first musical training from his mother, an amateur pianist. At thirteen he entered the St. Petersburg Conservatory where he studied composition with Rimsky-Korsakov. He graduated in 1914, receiving the Anton Rubinstein Prize—a grand piano. In 1918 he left Russia and spent sixteen years in France, Germany, and the United States. In 1934 Prokofiev returned to Russia, where he composed most of his major works. The *Classical Symphony* was written early in his career and was first performed in the spring of 1918. In this work he re-created the formal style popular in the eighteenth century while using many twentieth-century techniques.

LESSON 2

4. Introduce the listening map. Have the students follow the listening map of the first movement of Prokofiev's *Classical Symphony* while listening to the music.

Reinforcing the Lesson

Have the students take familiar melodies and experiment with creating techniques for developing a musical idea. (change of rhythm, change of register)

3 APPRAISAL

The students should be able to:
1. Identify and perform examples of developmental techniques on keyboard, recorder or bells.
2. Identify and define sonata allegro form.
3. Accurately follow a listening map of the *Classical Symphony*.

CD4:3 • Follow the listening map of the first movement of Prokofiev's *Classical Symphony,* as you listen to the music.

 Classical Symphony, First Movement, by Sergei Prokofiev

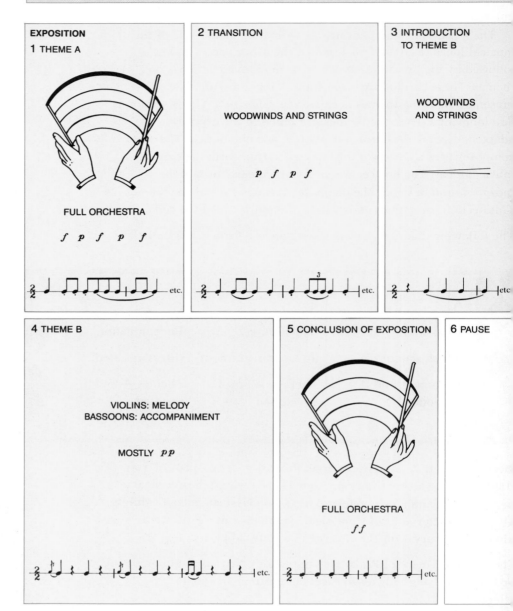

150

E X T E N S I O N

SPECIAL LEARNERS

Prepare an overhead transparency of pupil pages 150 and 151 if the class includes students who have difficulty with abstract musical notation or have visual tracking disabilities. Pause after each call number and point to the different thematic motives. This will enable the students to better understand sonata allegro form.

LISTENING

You may wish to use the Listening Map overhead transparency to help guide the students through the listening selection.

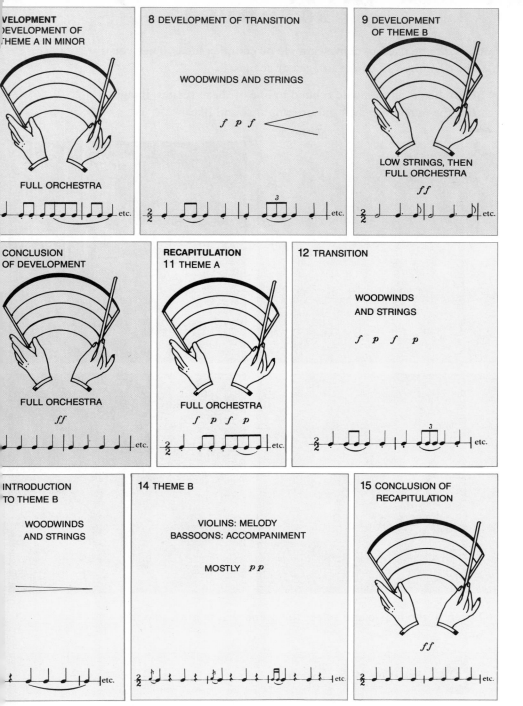

151

MORE MUSIC TEACHING IDEAS

Have the students examine other art forms
that are neoclassical in style. (for example,
the Lincoln Memorial in Washington, D.C.)

PROGRAM MUSIC

LESSON 3

Focus: Program Music

Objectives
To identify and define program music
To listen to a composition based on a story

Materials
Recordings: "The Erlking"
"Program Music Example"
("The Steel Foundry" by
Mossolov)
"Marche"
Wellington's Victory Theme
Montage
Wellington's Victory
"The Birth of Kijé" (optional)
"The Wedding of Kijé"
(optional)
Percussion instruments, keyboard,
recorder, guitar, and bells

Vocabulary
Absolute music, program music

 SETTING THE STAGE

Review "The Erlking" (page 111), which
represents pictures through music and is a
kind of program music

2 TEACHING THE LESSON

1. Introduce program music. Have the
students:
• Discuss the information on program
music.
• Examine the pictures and imagine what
the music might sound like for each.

Sounds can be used to convey simple or complex ideas. They can
also be organized to depict images or scenes.

• Before listening to music related to one of these scenes, imagine
what the music for each picture might sound like.

• Listen to the music and select the scene that is most like the
music. factory scene

🎵 Program Music Example

152

The terms below describe some of the musical characteristics of pitch, rhythm, and tone color that helped you select the scene. Which characteristics helped you make your choice?

fast	melody	no steady beat	common tone colors
slow	no melody	steady beat	unusual tone colors
loud		strong beat	repeated patterns
soft		weak beat	no repeated patterns

The term *program music* is often used to describe musical works that tell a story, describe an action or event, paint a picture, or create an impression. The term is used in contrast to **absolute music**, music which attempts to do none of those things.

Program music was a popular style of the nineteenth century. People were interested in poetry, prose, mythology, history, and current events. They especially enjoyed hearing musical interpretations of those interests. Composers often used literature or history as a guide for developing their music.

Wellington's Victory by Ludwig van Beethoven is an example of program music that depicts a dramatic battle in 1813 between the French and British armies.

You may recognize three of the main themes in *Wellington's Victory*. The first theme, representing the British army, is "Rule Britannia." This theme is often used in films or on television to represent the British people. The second theme, "Marlborough," represents the French army and is best known to small children as "The Bear Went Over the Mountain." The last popular theme heard is "God Save the King," which uses the same melody as our own patriotic song "America."

- Listen to the three main themes used by Beethoven in *Wellington's Victory*.

 Wellington's Victory Theme Montage

- Listen to "Program Music Example" and select the scene which is most like the music.
- Discuss the terms used to describe musical characteristics.

2. Introduce *Wellington's Victory*. Have the students:

- Discuss information on program and absolute music. Compare examples of the two. (e.g., "Marche" by Lully, "The Erlking" by Schubert)
- Discuss the information on *Wellington's Victory*.
- Listen to the three main themes used by Beethoven in *Wellington's Victory*.

CURRICULUM CONNECTION: SOCIAL STUDIES

History—*Wellington's Victory* was written to celebrate the Duke of Wellington's victory over Napoleon's armies at Vittoria in 1813. Beethoven was ask to write a composition to celebrate the victory by Johann Mälzel, the inventor of the modern metronome. Mälzel thought that the piece with such easily recognizable themes as "Rule Britannia" and "God Save the King" would be well received in both Vienna and England. The piece, also known as the "Battle Symphony," was originally written for the Panharmonicon, a mechanical instrument intended to reproduce the sound of an entire orchestra. The first performance of the piece took place on December 8, 1813, at a benefit for wounded Austrian soldiers.

LESSON 3

3. Introduce the listening map to Wellington's Victory. Have the students follow the listening map as they listen to the recording of *Wellington's Victory*.

Reinforcing the Lesson

Identify examples of program music from popular music of today. (answers will vary)

3 APPRAISAL

The students should be able to:
1. Identify and define program music.
2. Follow a listening guide to *Wellington's Victory*.

• As you listen to *Wellington's Victory*, follow the listening map. You can determine the losers because the theme representing the defeated army is played in minor and at a soft dynamic level.

 Wellington's Victory, by Ludwig van Beethoven

Listening Map to *Wellington's Victory*

1 TRUMPETS / DRUM

2

3 TRUMPETS / DRUM

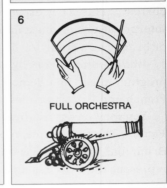

4

5 TRUMPETS SOLO

6 FULL ORCHESTRA

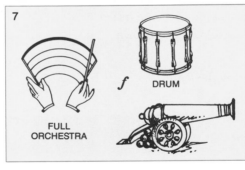

7 FULL ORCHESTRA / *f* DRUM

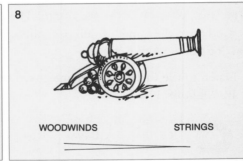

8 WOODWINDS STRINGS

154

E X T E N S I O N

SPECIAL LEARNERS

Prepare an overhead transparency of pupil pages 154 and 155 if there are students in the class who have difficulty coordinating visual and audio skills. Point to each call number to help the students clearly identify each theme. This will enable the students to better understand the concept of program music.

MORE MUSIC TEACHING IDEAS

Have the students listen to "The Birth of Kijé" and "The Wedding of Kijé" from Prokofiev's *Lieutenant Kijé Suite* (page 204), another example of program music.

LISTENING

You may wish to use the Listening Map overhead transparency to help guide the students through the listening selection.

9

WOODWINDS   STRINGS

10

VICTORY!

TIMPANI

f

11

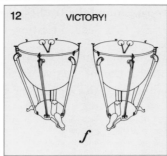

"GOD SAVE THE KING"

p

12

VICTORY!

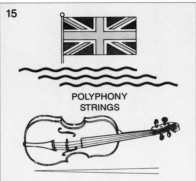

f

13

"GOD SAVE THE KING"

p f p f p f p f p f p f

14

STRINGS

FRENCH HORN

OBOE

so

‖: mi   fa   :‖

15

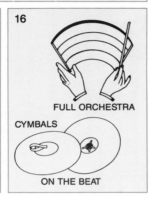

POLYPHONY STRINGS

16

FULL ORCHESTRA

CYMBALS

ON THE BEAT

17

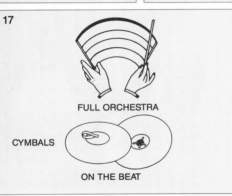

FULL ORCHESTRA

CYMBALS

ON THE BEAT

18

STRINGS, THEN

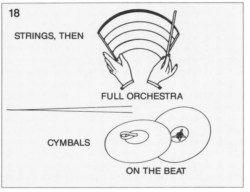

FULL ORCHESTRA

CYMBALS

ON THE BEAT

155

MORE MUSIC TEACHING IDEAS

Have the students read "April Rain Song" by Langston Hughes. Create a composition using classroom instruments to depict the images in the poem.

April Rain Song

Let the rain kiss you.
Let the rain beat upon your head with
 silver liquid drops.
Let the rain sing you a lullaby.
The rain makes still pools on the sidewalk.
The rain makes running pools in the gutter.
The rain plays a little sleep-song on our
 roof at night—and I love the rain.

—Langston Hughes

LESSON 4

Focus: Free Form

Objectives
To identify and define free form
To perform a composition in free form
To create a composition in free form

Materials
Recording: "A Marvelous Place"
Percussion instruments, keyboard, recorder, guitar, bells
Ice cream or other sticks (at least eight)

Vocabulary
Free form

1 SETTING THE STAGE

Discuss the art shown and look for characteristics of twentieth-century style.

2 TEACHING THE LESSON

1. Introduce twentieth-century styles in music. Have the students discuss the information on creative developments in the twentieth century.

CREATIVITY IN THE TWENTIETH CENTURY

Creativity in Art

The creative principles of balance, unity, control, and variety were extremely important during the baroque, classical, and romantic periods. Some artists of the twentieth century have continued the traditions of the past. To others creativity has been characterized by a search for new ideas and new sounds.

• Examine the contemporary works of art pictured on these pages. Which works illustrate the experimentation of the twentieth century? Which works illustrate the principles emphasized during earlier style periods?
  Moore, Picasso, Cornell; Valerio

Street View, James Valerio, FRUMKIN/ADAMS GALLERY, NY, Collection of Dr. Larry and Marlene Milner

Artists of the twentieth century have created art in many styles. The painting above is by the American artist James Valerio. The sculpture at right is by the English artist Henry Moore.

Family Group, Henry Moore, THE TATE GALLERY, London

156

EXTENSION

THE ARTIST

Henry Moore (1898–1986)—was an English sculptor whose works are large stone figures. He used holes or openings in the stone to create a sense of mass. Many of Moore's sculptures are designed to stand outdoors.

Pablo Picasso painted *Three Musicians* (left) in 1921. Joseph Cornell created his "pantry ballet" just for fun.

Pantry Ballet (for Jacques Offenbach). Joseph Cornell. THE NELSON-ATKINS MUSEUM OF ART. Kansas City, MO

157

THE ARTIST

Pablo Picasso (pä′blō pē-käs′ sō) (1881– 1973)—was born in Spain and worked in France. He was a pioneer in many styles of painting during his lifetime, and was one of the most famous painters of the twentieth century. In one of his styles, Picasso painted more than one side of his subject and put pieces of the many views together in overlapping geometric shapes. In the *Three Musicians,* for example, three musicians are visible and are portrayed in an original combination of shapes.

2. Introduce a composition in free form. Have the students:
• Discuss the information on the structure of "A Marvelous Place."
• Examine the score and identify the six events whose order can change in each performance. (all lines except the beginning and the ending)
• Listen to the music and follow the score in preparation for performing this composition.

CD4:7 **A Composition in Free Form**

"A Marvelous Place" is a composition for speaking chorus. The score for this composition looks unusual because it is in *free form*. A composition is in **free form** when the order of the individual sections of the piece can change from one performance to the next. "A Marvelous Place" contains six events that can be performed in any order.

• Examine the score and identify the six events which can change.
• Listen to the recording and follow the score to get ready to perform this composition.

 "A Marvelous Place"

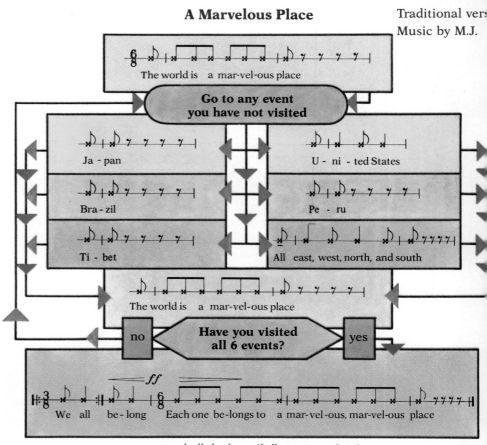

A Marvelous Place

Traditional vers:
Music by M.J.

158

repeat gradually louder until all parts are performing

SPECIAL LEARNERS

Use an overhead transparency of pupil page 158 if the class includes different learners. Count or loudly clap each beat. This will help the students to keep in time and in place. You may also wish to pause after each section and to point to the next general area. This will help different learners to find their next location on the listening map.

Creating Free Compositions

Free composition is not new. Composers in different style periods have experimented with giving up their power to make decisions about melody, harmony, tone color, and form. In 1751, William Hayes, an English composer, wrote *The Art of Composing Music by a Method Entirely New, Suited to the Meanest Capacity.* He described a method in which a small paint brush is dipped in ink. The brush then is shaken over music paper so that the ink falls on the staff lines. The ink splatterings then become the note heads. The classical composer Wolfgang Amadeus Mozart created music in which melodies were to be played in an order determined by a spinning dial, such as you see at carnivals.

Here are several suggestions to help you create free compositions. What is free about each of these compositional techniques? Answers will vary.

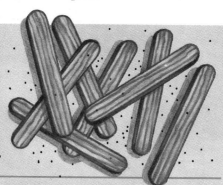

Stick Melody
1. Choose eight pitches.
2. Assign each pitch a number.
3. Number eight sticks.
4. Drop the sticks and read from left to right to determine the order of pitches to be performed.

Telephone Harmony

A	0
B	1
C	2
:	:
B'	8
C'	9

1. Choose ten pitches
2. Assign each pitch a number. (0–9)
3. Select 3 ten-digit phone numbers.
4. Write each as a pitch pattern.
   212-702-7 8 9 6
   CBC-A'AC-A'B'C'G
5. Perform the three patterns at the same time to produce harmony.

Combine aspects of both of these free compositional techniques to create music with melody and harmony. Think of other free techniques that can be used to create music.

3. Prepare creating free-form compositions. Have the students:
• Discuss the information on creating free-form compositions.
• Create musical compositions using the free compositional procedures indicated.

Reinforcing the Lesson
Have the students think of other free techniques which can be used to create music. (telephone numbers, license plates, addresses, letters of a name)

3 APPRAISAL
The students should be able to:
1. Identify and define free forms as used in twentieth-century compositions.
2. Read and perform the free-form composition "A Marvelous Place."
3. Create and perform a composition in free form.

SPECIAL LEARNERS
If the class includes different learners, split the class into small groups. Make sure each group is a mixture of exceptional and regular learners. Clarify the expectations and directions for creating a free composition.

REVIEW AND EVALUATION

JUST CHECKING

Objective
To review and test the skills and concepts taught in Unit 7

Materials
Recordings: Just Checking Unit 7 (questions 1, 3, 5, 6)
Unit 7 Evaluation (question 2)
For Extra Credit recordings (optional)
Copying Master 7-1 (optional)
Evaluation Unit 7 Copying Master

TEACHING THE LESSON

Review the skills and concepts taught in Unit 7. Have the students:

• Perform the activities and answer the questions on pages 160–161. (For this review, examples for questions 1, 3, 5, and 6 are included in the ''Just Checking Unit 7'' recording. Have the students answer these questions first. Then have them answer the other questions in the review.)

• Review their answers.
(You may wish to use Copying Master 7-1 at this time.)

JUST CHECKING

See how much you remember. Listen to the recording.

1. Listen to the steady beat and perform these rhythm motives by patting the quarter notes, pat-sliding the tied notes, clapping the eighth notes, and snapping the triplets with alternating hands.

2. Identify the melody below that uses rhythm motive 1, motive 2, or motive 3 above. 1,b: 2,c; 3,a

3. Listen to this section of the second movement of Beethoven's Symphony No. 7 and decide whether the articulation is legato or staccato. staccato

160

4. Which of the following defines legato? Which defines staccato? a, staccato; b, legato

   a. detached and crisp
   b. smooth and connected

5. Listen to this section of the *Classical Symphony,* by Sergei Prokofiev. Identify the different sections of the exposition section by pointing to the descriptions on the listening map.

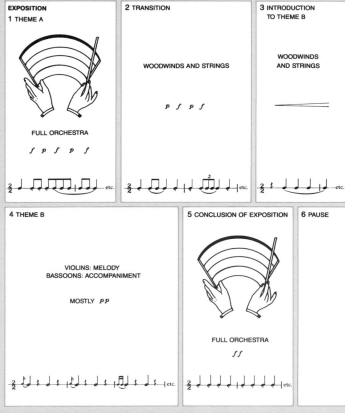

6. Listen to this version of the "America" melody. It is an example of: alteration of rhythm

   alteration of rhythm   creating a motive

7. Which of the following describes free form? a

   a. order of sections can change b. order stays the same

161

GIVING THE EVALUATION

Evaluation Unit 7 Copying Master can be found in the *Teacher's Copying Masters* book along with full directions for giving the evaluation and checking the answers.

FOR EXTRA CREDIT

You may want to have the students respond to the following:

Describe how Beethoven used tone color, legato, staccato, and rhythmic motives to create unity and contrast in the second movement of his Symphony No. 7. (The work is in ABA form. The A sections have a basic string tone color. The B section features woodwinds and strings. The A sections and the B section have contrasting rhythmic motives. While the A section is *mostly* staccato, the B section is *mostly* legato.)

(You may wish to play recordings to refresh the students' memories.)

ELEMENTS OF MUSIC	UNIT 8 OBJECTIVES	Lesson 1 Focus: Traditional Instruments Used in Nontraditional Ways	Lesson 2 Focus: New Tone Colors
Dynamics	Listen to, identify, and perform contrasting dynamics		
Tone Color	**Discuss traditional and nontraditional tone colors Perform vocal tone colors Listen to prepared piano and steel band Identify new sounds from found objects Identify synthesizer**	Discuss information on percussion instruments Discuss ways in which composers experiment with new tone color Create new instruments	Follow a contemporary tone color score Experience new tone colors produced on traditional instruments Read and perform vocal tone colors Experiment with tone colors on piano Discuss ways to produce new sounds from voices and traditional instruments
Tempo	Read and perform sounds at different tempos		
Duration/ Rhythm	**Read and perform a rhythm score**	Read and perform a rhythmic accompaniment Read and perform a rhythm score with drumsticks	
Pitch	**Read and perform pitch sounds from a score**		Read and perform new pitch sounds from a score Read and perform pitches on Autoharp
Texture			
Form			
Style	**Discuss the pipe organ and synthesizer Identify composer Vangelis** Discuss composers **Discuss ways to produce new sounds from voices and traditional instruments** Discuss the electronic revolution	Discuss the fact that percussion instruments were used in ancient times	
Reading	Read and play rhythm scores for contemporary music using	Read sticking patterns (R, L) and rhythm scores Read contemporary score	Read contemporary score and contemporary voice notation

PURPOSE Unit 8: TONE COLOR IN DIFFERENT STYLES

In this unit the students will investigate twentieth-century musical innovations. They will experience traditional instruments used in nontraditional ways as well as new tone colors produced by recently developed electronic instruments. They will listen to a traditional romantic composition as it was originally composed for piano, as it was later orchestrated, and as it sounds performed on a synthesizer. They will hopefully extend their understanding and appreciation of many forms and styles of music of yesterday and today.

SUGGESTED TIME FRAME

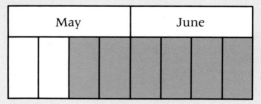

May			June			

FOCUS

Traditional Instruments Used in Nontraditional Ways
New Tone Colors
Comparing Traditional and Twentieth-Century Tone Colors
Prepared Piano
Electronic Tone Colors
Recycling Sound (Found Objects)

Lesson 3 Focus: Comparing Traditional and Twentieth-Century Tone Colors	Lesson 4 Focus: Prepared Piano	Lesson 5 Focus: Electronic Tone Colors	Lesson 6 Focus: Recycling Sound (Found Objects)
		Listen to and identify contrasts in dynamics	Perform dynamic contrasts in a composition using sound sources
Discuss the tone color of the pipe organ Listen to and describe traditional and nontraditional tone colors Compare the tone color of keyboard instruments from two style periods (synthesizers, pipe organ)	Listen to and identify instruments Listen to tone colors of prepared piano Discuss the parts of a piano and the types of tones produced Create new tone colors on piano	Listen to and identify contrasts in tone color Listen to and discuss music performed electronically on synthesizer	Identify the use of new sound sources from found objects Listen to and identify traditional and found objects used in composition Listen to and identify tone color of steel drums Create melodies on pitches of found objects
			Perform different tempos in a composition using source sounds
Discuss the pipe organ of the baroque period Listen to J.S. Bach's baroque organ music Discuss the synthesizer of the 20th century Perform movements to a 20th-century composition Discuss the 20th-century Greek composer Vangelis	Discuss the musical style of John Cage and use of the prepared piano Perform a composition on a prepared piano	Discuss the electronic revolution of the 20th century and its effect on music Discuss the Japanese composer Isao Tomita Listen to and discuss a work by Milton Babbitt	Listen to music performed by found objects Create a composition using found objects Discuss American composer Harry Partch
Follow contemporary music movement score	Read prepared piano score in $\frac{4}{4}$ using a *ritardando*		

 **TECHNOLOGY**

MUSIC WITH *MIDI*

MIDI technology allows students to manipulate musical elements and make musical decisions.

- Lesson 1, page 163: Create Using Elements of **Balinese Gamelan Music**
- Lesson 7, page 178: Analyze **Tone Color:** *"Promenade" from Pictures at an Exhibition by M. Mussorgsky*

VIDEO RESOURCES

Use video resources to reinforce, extend, and enrich learning in this unit.

UNIT 8

TONE COLOR IN DIFFERENT STYLES

Guitar, Paris (1912, early), Pablo Picasso, COLLECTION, THE MUSEUM OF MODERN ART, NY

162

Quartet, Ben Shahn, Private Collection

163

LESSON 1

Focus: Traditional Instruments Used in Nontraditional Ways

Objectives
To perform a rhythmic accompaniment
To play percussion instruments in non-traditional ways

Materials
Recordings: "Tone Color Montage"
            Heaven and Hell, Part 2
Drumsticks
Pitched and unpitched classroom instruments

1 **SETTING THE STAGE**

Tell the students they will be learning to identify new ways of creating sound developed by twentieth-century composers.

THE ARTIST

Ben Shahn (shän) (1898–1969)—was an American painter who often portrayed controversial subjects such as labor movements, race relations, and atomic warfare. He painted strong figures of common people, such as the musicians in *Quartet*. He wanted his figures and his direct style to communicate his interest in social justice to his viewers.

LESSON 1

2 TEACHING THE LESSON

1. Introduce creating sounds. Have the students:

• Read information about composers experimenting with new ways of creating sounds.

• Listen to "Tone Color Montage." As each number is called follow and listen as old instruments produce tone colors in new ways. (1, prepared piano; 2, electric bass guitar, slapped; 3, violin, struck with wood part of bow; 4, vocal sounds; 5, gong, played with a bow)

• Examine the pictures and examine how new tone colors were created.

Creating Sounds

CD4:16 Musicians have often explored new ways to create sound. Twentieth-century musicians have continued to experiment with tone color. They have developed new instruments. They have also experimented with unusual ways to play traditional instruments. The musicians in these pictures are creating new tone colors.

• Listen to these examples of traditional instruments producing musical sounds in new ways.

"Tone Color Montage"

164

Percussion Instruments

Percussion instruments are among the oldest musical instruments in the world. Ancient writings, drawings, carvings, and sculptures show percussion instruments in a variety of settings.

Percussion instruments are generally used to establish or maintain the beat. Many musical compositions feature strong, repeated rhythms on percussion instruments.

- Read and practice each pattern with your drumsticks using the matched grip. Use your right hand (R) and left hand (L) as indicated.

This Greek vase is about twenty-five hundred years old. The god of music, Apollo, is shown at left. The woman at right is playing an ancient percussion instrument.

Apollo and the Muses. Greek Attic lekythos. LOUVRE, Paris

2. Introduce percussion instruments.
Have the students:
- Discuss the information on percussion instruments.
- Practice the rhythmic patterns with drumsticks using the matched grip. Use right and left hands (R and L) as indicated.

165

3. Introduce performing a rhythmic accompaniment. Have the students:
• Listen to *Heaven and Hell,* Part 2.
• Read and perform the rhythmic accompaniment using the matched grip.

Performing a Rhythmic Accompaniment

CD4:17 Vangelis (van-je' lis), a Greek composer, created the theme music for the Academy Award-winning film *Chariots of Fire.* The rhythms you have performed can be played as an accompaniment to *Heaven and Hell,* Part 2, another of his compositions.

• Listen to the recording of *Heaven and Hell,* Part 2. Read and perform the rhythmic accompaniment with your drumsticks using the matched grip.

 Heaven and Hell, Part 2 by Vangelis

Accompaniment to *Heaven and Hell*, Part 2

166

R   R   R   L   R   R L R   R   L   R   L

Refrain

R   R   L   R   R L   R   R   L   R   L

Refrain

R   L   R   L   R   R L R   R L   R   L   R   L   R   R L R

Refrain

The Greek composer Vangelis was born in Athens in 1943. He is basically a self-taught musician. As a child he studied the piano and later the pipe organ. His interest in the variety of sounds that could be produced by the pipe organ led Vangelis to its modern equivalent, the synthesizer. The possibilities of producing both traditional and non-traditional sounds attracted him.

Vangelis performed with the Greek rock band Formynx. Political pressures led him to leave Greece and settle in Paris. He composed soundtracks for many European films and television documentaries.

The synthesizer has enabled Vangelis to use many new sounds. He finds this instrument the best means of expressing his musical ideas. He has composed, produced, and performed on over forty record albums.

167

4. Introduce the composer. Have the students discuss the information on the Greek composer Vangelis.

LESSON 1

5. Introduce new percussion sounds.
Have the students:
• Read the information about new ways percussionists use their drumsticks to produce new tone colors.
• Experiment with their drumsticks to produce new tone colors as indicated, observing the notation.
• Read and practice the patterns in the percussion score to *Heaven and Hell,* Part 2, and perform as indicated with the recording.

Reinforcing the Lesson

Have the students select a classroom instrument which they would like to investigate. List the many different ways sound can be produced on this instrument. Describe the type of sound produced. (Answers will vary.)

3 APPRAISAL

The students should be able to:
1. Perform a rhythmic accompaniment to *Heaven and Hell,* Part 2.
2. Read and perform traditional and non-traditional drumstick patterns with rhythmic accuracy.

New Percussion Sounds

Sometimes percussionists use their instruments in new or different ways. In this example, the drumsticks are used in different ways to create new tone colors. The symbol ⨳ means "hold the drumsticks in the air and tap them lightly together." The symbol ⊠→ means "hold the drumsticks in the air, tap them together, then slide one over the other as shown in this photograph."

• Read and practice these patterns with your drumsticks.

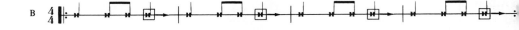

• Perform these patterns as you listen to *Heaven and Hell,* Part 2 again. Use this order:

A–B–C–D–E–D–E–D–C–D

168

EXTENSION

MORE MUSIC TEACHING IDEAS

Have the students create a new instrument. Use this instrument as an accompaniment to a familiar musical selection.

COOPERATIVE LEARNING

Have the students read "Dreams" on page 15. Review the information on using traditional instruments in new ways on pupil page 168. Assign the students to work in cooperative groups of four. Each group should create a sound composition to accompany a reading of the poem. The sound piece should use traditional classroom pitched and unpitched instruments in new and different ways. A second aspect of the project might be to create special notation to indicate the new sounds. Appoint one student to be the recorder to prepare a simple line score. Another student will be the conductor, one the reader, and one the discussion leader who will lead the evaluation process. Have each group practice its sound piece and perform for the entire class. On another day, you may want to have the groups exchange scores.

You may want to have the groups use different poems for this activity.

PERFORM WITH NEW TONE COLORS

Notation

The tone colors of "Misty, Moisty Morning" are produced by using traditional instruments in new ways. The composer used some special notation to indicate these new sounds.

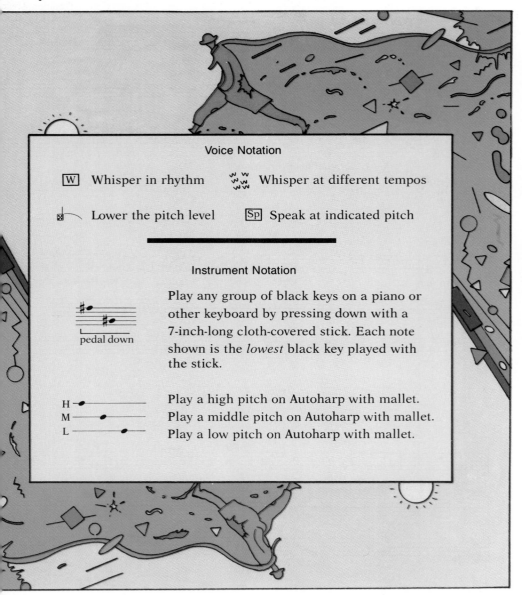

Voice Notation

W Whisper in rhythm   Whisper at different tempos

Lower the pitch level   Sp Speak at indicated pitch

Instrument Notation

pedal down
Play any group of black keys on a piano or other keyboard by pressing down with a 7-inch-long cloth-covered stick. Each note shown is the *lowest* black key played with the stick.

H Play a high pitch on Autoharp with mallet.
M Play a middle pitch on Autoharp with mallet.
L Play a low pitch on Autoharp with mallet.

169

LESSON 2

Focus: New Tone Colors

Objectives
To perform a vocal composition using non-traditional notation
To identify the use of new tone colors in a twentieth-century vocal composition

Materials
Recordings: "Our World"
"Misty, Moisty Morning"
Saint Luke Passion
Piano, Autoharp, recorder, bells, guitar, percussion instruments

1 SETTING THE STAGE

Have the students review "Our World" (page 28), which has traditional tone colors and notation.

2 TEACHING THE LESSON

1. Introduce performing with unusual tone colors. Have the students:
• Discuss information on the special notation used by the composer of "Misty, Moisty Morning" to designate unusual sounds.
• Focus on the notation and practice each example in preparation for performing the composition.

• Perform "Misty, Moisty Morning" to experience music with new tone colors.

LESSON 2

• Perform ''Misty, Moisty Morning'' to experience music with unusual vocal tone colors.

Misty, Moisty Morning

170

VOCAL DEVELOPMENT

Have the students expand the expressive qualities of the voice by encouraging the use of correct breathing, posture, vowels, and diction in performing ''Misty, Moisty Morning.'' Have them experience speaking, singing, and whispering portions of the text to assist in ''feeling'' the difference in the use of the vocal instrument.

CD4:19

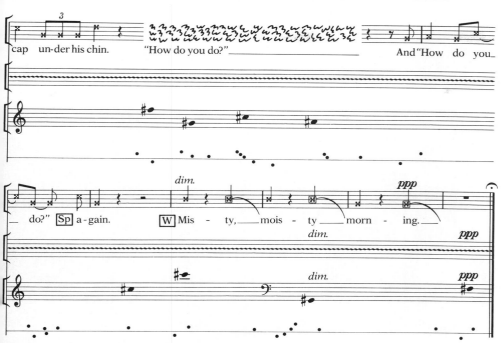

cap un-der his chin.   "How do you do?"_____   And "How do you_

do?" [Sp] a-gain.   [W] Mis - ty, mois - ty morn - ing.

dim.   *ppp*

Other New Tone Colors

Krzysztof Penderecki (kris' tof pen-de-re' skē) is a contemporary
Polish composer who draws novel sounds from voices and
traditional instruments. He also was one of the first composers to
experiment with sounds such as saws cutting wood and paper
rustling, as well as unusual vocal effects. His *Saint Luke Passion*
was an immediate success after its premiere in 1966.

• Listen to part of the *Saint Luke Passion*. Listen for singers
  hissing, shouting, and whispering, and for percussive effects
  produced by voices in the chorus.

 Saint Luke Passion by Krzysztof Penderecki

171

LESSON 2

2. Introduce other new tone colors.
Have the students:
• Discuss information on the composer
Krzysztof Penderecki.
• Listen to part of the *Saint Luke Passion*,
paying particular attention to the special
effects produced by voices in the chorus.

Reinforcing the Lesson

Have the students create a new accompaniment to a traditional song, for example,
"Our World" (page 28), using unusual
tone colors.

3 APPRAISAL

The students should be able to:
1. Read and perform "Misty, Moisty
Morning" with rhythmic, melodic and
vocal tone color accuracy.
2. Identify the use of new tone colors in a
twentieth-century vocal composition.

LESSON 3

Focus: Comparing Traditional and Twentieth-Century Tone Colors

Objectives
To compare the tone color of keyboard instruments from two contrasting style periods
To move to a twentieth-century electronic composition

Materials
Recordings: Toccata and Fugue in D Minor
"Alpha" from *Albedo 39*
Ensembles for Synthesizer
Composition for Synthesizer

1 SETTING THE STAGE

Tell the students they will be learning to identify the tone color of the electronic instruments known as synthesizers.

2 TEACHING THE LESSON

1. Introduce the pipe organ. Have the students:
• Discuss information on the pipe organ.
• Listen for the sound of the instrument in the Toccata and Fugue in D Minor.

FROM PIPE ORGAN TO SYNTHESIZER

Pipe Organ

During the baroque period (1600–1750) the pipe organ was a popular instrument. It could produce a wide variety of sounds.

• Listen for the sound of the pipe organ.

 Toccata and Fugue in D Minor, by Johann Sebastian Bach

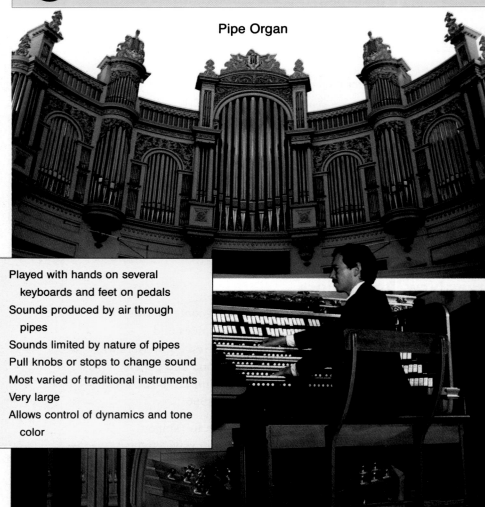

Pipe Organ

Played with hands on several keyboards and feet on pedals
Sounds produced by air through pipes
Sounds limited by nature of pipes
Pull knobs or stops to change sound
Most varied of traditional instruments
Very large
Allows control of dynamics and tone color

172

Synthesizer

The Greek composer Vangelis first composed for the pipe organ. He later became interested in the synthesizer because of its even greater tone color possibilities. He composed "Alpha," from his *Albedo 39,* for the synthesizer.

• Listen and describe the traditional and nontraditional sounds.

 "Alpha," from *Albedo 39,* by Vangelis

Ensembles for Synthesizer takes advantage of other tone color possibilities.

• Listen for the many sounds of the synthesizer.

 Ensembles for Synthesizer by Milton Babbitt

Usually played with hands on one or more keyboards

Sounds produced by electronic components

Sound limited only by composer's imagination

Buttons and knobs change sounds

Most flexible of nontraditional instruments

Generally small and compact

Allows almost total control of tone color, pitch, rhythm, and dynamics.

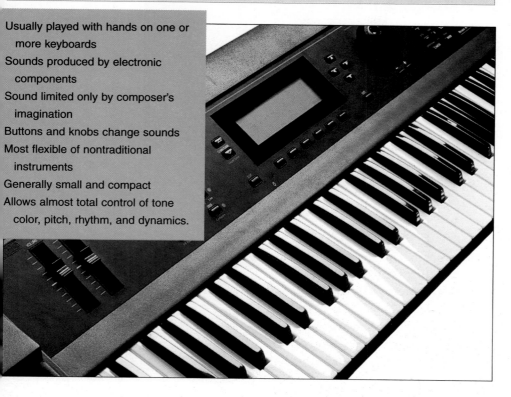

LESSON 3

2. Introduce the synthesizer. Have the students:
• Discuss information on the tone colors of "Alpha."
• Listen to the recording of "Alpha" and describe the traditional and nontraditional sounds.
• Identify the many sounds of the synthesizer as they listen to *Ensembles for Synthesizer.*
• Discuss similarities between the synthesizer of the twentieth-century and the pipe organ of the baroque period.

173

3. Introduce movement to sounds of the twentieth century. Have the students:
• Examine the pictures of dance movements.
• Describe the movements shown in each picture as short and choppy, long and sustained, or high and low.
• Practice each movement.
• Listen to "Alpha" again and perform each movement in order with the music.

Reinforcing the Lesson

Preview page 180 and listen to *Composition for Synthesizer* by Milton Babbitt as a further example of an electronically generated work by this composer.

3 APPRAISAL

The students should be able to:
1. Compare the tone color resources of the baroque pipe organ and the twentieth-century synthesizer.
2. Identify and perform movement gestures based on line drawings to "Alpha."

Moving to Sounds of the Twentieth Century

These pictures show contemporary dance movements.

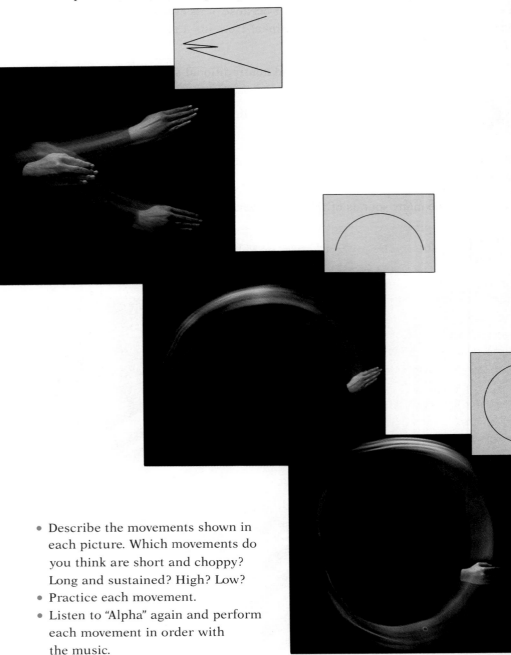

• Describe the movements shown in each picture. Which movements do you think are short and choppy? Long and sustained? High? Low?
• Practice each movement.
• Listen to "Alpha" again and perform each movement in order with the music.

174

What Is It?

Sometimes familiar instruments can produce new or different tone colors.

- Listen to this music. Try to identify the instrument or instruments you hear.

 The Perilous Night, by John Cage

The instrument you heard is a **prepared piano.** Pianos can be prepared in several ways. Items made of wood, metal, or rubber can be placed on or between the strings of the piano. Other piano sounds are produced when the performer strums the strings inside the piano or uses a mallet to hit the wood of the piano. It all depends what sounds the composer wants produced.

John Cage, an American composer, developed the idea of the prepared piano and used it in his compositions to produce different tone colors.

175

LESSON 4

Focus: Prepared Piano

Objective
To create a composition for prepared piano

Materials
Recordings: *The Perilous Night*
                    "Eraser Piano Tees"
                    Suite for Percussion
Piano, facing class with front panels off, both top and bottom. (If a grand piano, the lid should be raised so class can gather around.)
Two golf tees
Two rubber erasers (ink or pencil)

Vocabulary
Prepared piano

1 SETTING THE STAGE

Tell the students they will be introduced to compositions that develop new ways of creating sound from a piano.

2 TEACHING THE LESSON

1. Introduce new sounds from a familiar instrument. Have the students:
- Listen to *The Perilous Night* and identify the instrument they hear.
- Discuss the information on the prepared piano and the composer John Cage.

EXTENSION

THE COMPOSER

John Cage—American experimental composer, was born in Los Angeles in 1912. He studied composition with Adolph Weiss and Henry Cowell, and also attended Arnold Schoenberg's classes at the University of California. Cage's 1951 work *Music of Changes* for piano was the first well-known twentieth-century *aleatory,* or chance, music. Aleatory music contains elements of chance or unpredictability, with some or all choices in performance determined by the player. Cage also developed the "prepared piano." The preparation consists of placing screws, coins, rubber bands, and other objects on the piano strings to change the tone color of individual keys. Cage is a lecturer and performer, and encourages his audiences to participate in his presentations.

LESSON 4

2. Introduce the piano. Have the students:
- Move to the area around the piano. (You may wish to divide the class into two or more groups.)
- Experiment with the tone color options of the piano as indicated.

Inside the Piano

A piano has many parts: keyboard, pedals, hammers, strings. You can look inside a piano to see how the parts work together.

- Observe the hammers. What do they do? strike the strings

- Place your hand across a group of strings. Play the keys for these strings. What happens to the tone? becomes muffled

- The thickness of the strings and the number of strings related to each key affect the sound produced by the key. Locate the thickest strings. What kind of tone do their keys produce? low

- Locate the keys that use three strings; two strings; one string. What kind of tones do these keys produce? high, middle, low

- Find the pedals. What is the purpose of each? Left—softer tone, middle—sustains low tones, right—sustains all tones

176

**CURRICULUM CONNECTION:
SOCIAL STUDIES**

The piano—In about 1709, Bartolommeo Cristofori of Florence designed the first piano in an attempt to create an instrument that was capable of playing loud and soft. First described as a "harpsichord with soft and loud," the instrument later was called the pianoforte. During the late 1700s and the 1800s several instrument makers improved on Cristofori's invention. John Broadwood of London created a piano with a louder and richer tone. Sebastien Érard of Paris perfected the mechanics for rapid repetition of a note. Alpheus Babcock of Boston invented the cast-iron frame, which could stand the stress of thicker strings and greater tension. In 1855 Steinway and Sons incorporated all the many improvements to create the modern piano.

Performing on a Prepared Piano

"Eraser Piano Tees" is a prepared piano composition written for eight prepared notes.

CD4:24

- Prepare four low notes on the piano by using two large rubber erasers. Place each eraser between two sets of low strings.

- Prepare four middle range notes (near middle C) by using four golf tees. Place each tee between the two strings for each middle range note.

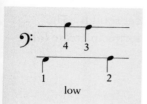

- Use your prepared piano notes to play this composition. The pitches are numbered from the lowest to highest.

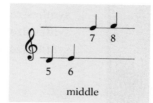

low

middle

Eraser Piano Tees

Dorothy Gail Elliott

177

---

3. Introduce performing a prepared piano composition. Have the students:
- Discuss the information in preparation for notating and performing "Eraser Piano Tees."
- Prepare the piano as indicated.
- Perform "Eraser Piano Tees" from the notation.

Reinforcing the Lesson

Preview page 181 and listen to *Suite for Percussion* as an example of both traditional and nontraditional instruments being used as sound sources.

3 APPRAISAL

The students should be able to:
1. Identify a prepared piano composition.
2. Create and perform a prepared piano composition from notation.

MORE MUSIC TEACHING IDEAS

Have the students experiment with the piano to produce new sounds.
1. Depress C E G without making any sound. Then strum the center section of piano strings with fingers or a pick. This was a technique Henry Cowell used in his *Aeolian Harp*.
2. Tap on the case of the piano at various spots. Use hard rubber-tipped mallets to protect the finish of the piano. Try to create at least five different sounds.

LESSON 5

Focus: Electronic Tone Colors

Objectives
To identify and define electronic tone colors used by twentieth-century composers
To listen to a composition performed with three different tone colors
To identify Milton Babbitt as a twentieth-century composer of electronic music

Materials
Recordings: "Alpha" from *Albedo 39*
"Promenade Montage"
Composition for Synthesizer

1 SETTING THE STAGE

Review the information on the synthesizer on page 173 and listen to "Alpha" from *Albedo 39*.

2 TEACHING THE LESSON

1. Introduce the electronic revolution. Have the students discuss the information on electronic musical instruments.

THE ELECTRONIC REVOLUTION

Electronic musical instruments were developed in the twentieth century. These instruments produce new sounds that were not possible on acoustic instruments such as the piano. In 1927 Leon Theremin (ther´ə min), a Russian scientist and musician, invented the first electronic musical instrument, the Theremin. To control the volume and the pitch of its eerie sound, the player moves his or her hands toward or away from the instrument's antennas. The Theremin detects these physical motions through disruptions of a magnetic field.

Maurice Martenot (mär te nô´), a French musician, invented the earliest form of the synthesizer in 1928. The invention of the synthesizer further expanded the range of musical sounds. The synthesizer combines different electronic wave forms to create (or synthesize) complex sounds.

178

With the invention of the transistor and then the integrated circuit, the technology to create and manipulate electronic sound became easier and less expensive to use.

The electronic revolution moved quickly in music. By the late 1950s many studios for electronic music were in operation. They increased the availability of new electronic sounds. The Moog and Bulcha synthesizers of the 1960s allowed musicians to create a diverse range of sounds. Sometimes these sounds are designed to imitate acoustic instruments such as a violin. Other times they create unusual and totally unique sounds.

Today personal computers are often used to create and manipulate complex sounds. Some allow you to record and play back any sound you choose. Many computers contain soundcards and options that allow you to access a variety of tone colors through **FM** or **wave synthesis**, **compact disc** (CD), and **General MIDI** technology. With the addition of a simple **tone generator** a computer will allow you to manipulate an even greater variety of interesting tone colors.

One Composition—Several Styles

Pictures at an Exhibition by Modest Mussorgsky was composed for the piano alone. The French composer Maurice Ravel arranged the work for full orchestra. In 1975 the Japanese composer Isao Tomita created an electronic version.

Listen to "Promenade" from *Pictures at an Exhibition* in piano, orchestral, and electronic versions. Compare them. In which version is the contrast of dynamics and tone color most obvious? Which version do you find most interesting? Why?

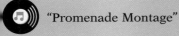

"Promenade Montage"

Isao Tomita

LESSON 5

2. Introduce one composition in several styles. Have the students:
• Discuss the information on the different versions of Mussorgsky's "Promenade."
• Listen to the "Promenade" in piano, orchestral and electronic versions.
• Compare and discuss which version displays the most obvious contrasts of dynamics and tone color, and decide which version they find most interesting. (answers will vary)

179

LESSON 5

3. Introduce other electronic music.
Have the students:
• Discuss the information on Milton Babbitt and his *Composition for Synthesizer*.
• Follow the description of the first part of the work as they listen to the recording.
You may wish to use the following items as a basis for extended discussion.
1. In the development of electronic musical instruments, is it a necessary prerequisite to be a musician? Why? (Yes; musical knowledge needed to create compositions on electronic instruments.)
2. How did the synthesizer get its name? Think of another name by which this instrument might have been called. Justify your choice. (The music is created by synthesis; sound processor: the instrument processes sound as a word processor does words.)

Reinforcing the Lesson

Have the students identify popular musicians of today who use synthesizers.

3 APPRAISAL

The students should be able to:
1. Identify and define electronic tone colors used by twentieth-century composers.
2. Listen and compare three tone color versions of "Promenade" from *Pictures at an Exhibition*.
3. Identify Milton Babbitt as a twentieth-century composer of electronic music.

More Electronic Music

CD5:1 Milton Babbitt has long been a composer of electronic music. His control of sound is evident in *Composition for Synthesizer*, composed in 1960–1961. The synthesizer produces pitches and rhythms from directions provided by the composer. This work presents sounds with an evenness and a speed only possible through electronics.

 Composition for Synthesizer, by Milton Babbitt

As you listen to this composition follow this description:
1. Two gonglike sustained chords. A staccato melody.
2. Two sustained chords. Two staccato melodies.
3. One sustained chord. Two high staccato melodies with a low, legato melody.

Milton Babbitt, distinguished contemporary American composer, was born in Philadelphia in 1916. He received his early musical training in Jackson, Mississippi, and went on to study at New York University and Princeton University. He later became a professor of music at Princeton, where he also taught mathematics.

Babbitt began a program of electronic music at Princeton and Columbia universities, working with the newly developed synthesizer. He helped create the Columbia–Princeton Electronic Music Center, which became a haven for experiments in electronic music. Babbitt has also written many books and articles on music and musicians. His theories about mathematics and music and his innovations with the synthesizer have influenced the musical thinking of many young American composers.

180

E X T E N S I O N

COOPERATIVE LEARNING

Have the students form cooperative groups of three members or pairs. Each member or pair should read either page 167, 171, or 180. Then the students should return to the group and teach the information they have learned to the rest of the group members. If each group member or pair writes down three main points about the composer, the group can use these facts to create test questions. This time, you may want to collect one question from each group, put all the questions together into a test, and give the test during the next class period. Each group's grades should be combined to give a group grade. Any group achieving above a certain percentage correct can be rewarded in the ways suggested on page 93.

Found Objects

CD5:2

Composers sometimes search for new sound sources when traditional musical instruments are not able to produce all the sounds that they want. *Suite for Percussion,* by Lou Harrison, uses both traditional percussion instruments and new sound sources. His new sources include **found objects,** or everyday objects.

• Listen for both traditional instruments and found objects you think were used.

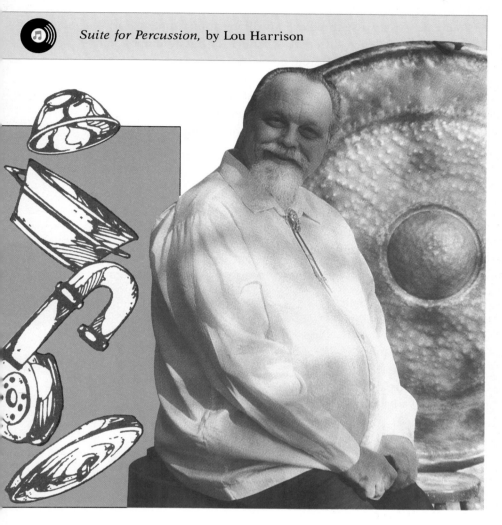

Suite for Percussion, by Lou Harrison

181

EXTENSION

CD5

LESSON 6

Focus: Recycling Sound (Found Objects)

Objectives
To identify the use of new instruments from found objects
To create an improvisation using found objects
To identify the tone color of steel drums

Materials
Recordings: *Suite for Percussion*
Steel band music
Harry Partch on *Spoils of War*
Classroom objects suitable as sound sources

Vocabulary
Found objects

1 SETTING THE STAGE
Tell the students they will be learning to create sound from new sources found in the classroom.

2 TEACHING THE LESSON
1. Introduce found objects. Have the students:
• Discuss the information on found objects as new sources of sound.
• Listen to *Suite for Percussion,* by Lou Harrison, and identify both the traditional instruments and the found objects they think were used in the composition. (Answers may vary. *Suite for Percussion* uses the following: traditional instruments—bells, timpani, snare drum, gong, tom-tom, chimes, triangle, bass drum; found objects—automobile brake drums, lengths of plumbers' pipes, galvanized washtubs, glass bowls.)

THE COMPOSER

Lou Harrison—American avante-garde composer, was born in Oregon in 1917. Like John Cage, he studied with Henry Cowell and attended Arnold Schoenberg's classes at the University of California. In 1943 he moved to New York City, where he became a music critic for the *New York Herald-Tribune.* He has also taught at Black Mountain College and San José State College. In 1961 he went to the Orient to study Japanese and Korean rhythmic structures and modalities. Harrison also tried his luck as an instrument maker. He invented new principles for clavichord construction as well as a process for direct composing on a phonograph disc. Through his composing Harrison has sought new sources of sound production.

LESSON 6

2. Prepare to create a recycled sound composition. Have the students:
• Discuss the information on creating new sound compositions using found objects.
• Work in small groups to identify classroom objects that would be good sound sources.
• Experiment with the new instruments and discover one short sound and one sustained sound.
• Use the suggestions listed as they create their own compositions.
• Perform their compositions several different ways, and tape record different performances.
• Decide which performance demonstrates the most contrast, and which is the most interesting. (answer will vary)

3. Introduce unusual instruments. Have the students:
• Discuss the information on steel drums.
• Listen to the recording of steel band music.
• Listen for the tone color of the steel drums as they pat or clap the steady beat while listening to the recording.

Your Own Recycled Sound Composition

CD5:3 You and your classmates can create your own compositions using new sources for sound. It is more fun to work in small groups.
1. Work with your group to identify classroom objects (found objects) that would be good sound sources.
2. Experiment with your new instruments. Discover one short sound and one sustained sound.
3. To create unity, play one instrument continuously throughout the composition.
4. Plan a definite beginning and a definite ending.
5. Plan a definite order for different players.
6. To create variety, use three or four different instruments for contrast. Use silence, different dynamics, different tempos, and different pitches. Try different combinations.
7. Perform your composition several different ways.
8. Tape-record different performances of your composition.
9. Decide which of your performances demonstrates the most contrast. Which one is the most interesting?

Unusual Instruments

After World War II, the United States Navy left many large, empty oil containers in the West Indies. These fifty-gallon steel containers inspired the people of the West Indies to create their own special instruments. The oil containers were cut and hammered into steel drums. Groups of steel drum players formed bands with their own unique tone color.

• Listen for the tone color of the steel drums as you pat or clap the steady beat.

 Steel Band Music

182

**CURRICULUM CONNECTION:
SOCIAL STUDIES**

Steel band music—is created with a combination of homemade instruments. Some of the instruments used are steel drums of various sizes and timbres, "chit-chats" (maracas), scratch sticks, and "cutters" (brake drums from Model T Fords). The steel drums provide all the melody and have a range of four octaves. They are played by striking the hammered sides with the fingertips or a rubber-tipped mallet. This creates a marimbalike sound that is slightly flat or sharp. Steel band music has become popular in the United States. The 10th Naval District Steel Band is one of the more well-known bands.

Creating New Instruments

Harry Partch (1901-1973), an American experimental composer, inspired others with his creative ideas. He also invented original instruments for special effects.

Listen to learn about his composition *Spoils of War* and the unique instruments used in it.

Harry Partch on *Spoils of War*

Below is a list of "instruments" used in *Spoils of War*. Which ones are not familiar to you?

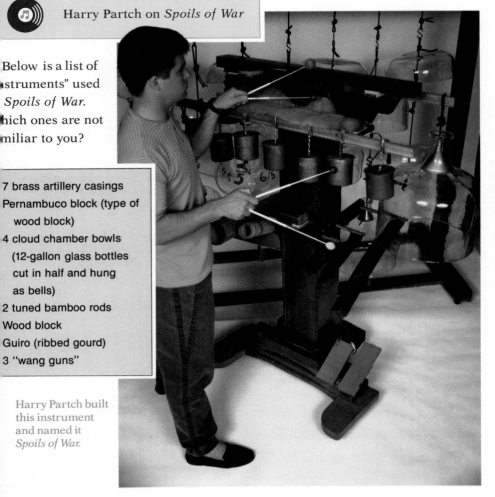

7 brass artillery casings

Pernambuco block (type of wood block)

4 cloud chamber bowls (12-gallon glass bottles cut in half and hung as bells)

2 tuned bamboo rods

Wood block

Guiro (ribbed gourd)

3 "wang guns"

Harry Partch built this instrument and named it *Spoils of War.*

Many modern composers feel free to use any sounds that have the qualities they like. What found instruments might you use to improvise music?

183

LESSON 6

4. Introduce inventing new instruments. Have the students:
• Discuss the information on the experimental composer Harry Partch.
• Listen to the composer discuss his *Spoils of War* and play the instruments.
• Identify the parts of *Spoils of War*.
• Decide what instruments they might use to improvise a music piece similar to the Partch composition.

Reinforcing the Lesson

Have the students create an original accompaniment to any folk or traditional song, using found objects as sound sources.

3 APPRAISAL

The students should be able to:
1. Identify the basic properties of the tone color of new instruments created from found objects.
2. Create an improvised composition using the basic properties of found objects.
3. Identify the tone color of steel drums.

MORE MUSIC TEACHING IDEAS

Have the students choose twelve pitched found objects that will give the twelve tones of a tone-row with different timbres and improvise a short composition. (Have some students play a few unpitched instruments to keep the beat.)

THE COMPOSER

Harry Partch (1901–1974)—was a remarkable self-taught American composer. He began his work by experimenting with instruments that could produce fractional intervals, and in the process devised a 43-tone scale. He published his findings in a book, *Genesis of a Music*. Partch invented and built his own instruments and trained musicians to play them. His *Spoils of War* was named for the military scrap it contains. Some of his other instruments are kitharas with 72 strings and harmonic canons with 44 strings. Partch also was interested in American folk life. He traveled across the country during the Depression, collecting folk expressions and graffiti, which he used as texts in his compositions.

REVIEW AND EVALUATION

JUST CHECKING

Objective
To review and test the skills and concepts taught in Unit 8

Materials
Recordings: Just Checking Unit 8 (questions 1–6, 9–11)
''Alpha''
Unit 8 Evaluation (question 3)
For Extra Credit recordings (optional)
Drumsticks
Copying Master 8-1 (optional)
Evaluation Unit 8 Copying Master

TEACHING THE LESSON

Review the skills and concepts taught in Unit 8. Have the students:
• Perform the activities and answer the questions on pages 184–185. (For this review, examples for questions 1 through 6 and 9 through 11 are included in the ''Just Checking Unit 8'' recording. Have the students answer these questions first. Then have them answer the other questions in the review, using the recordings in the unit where necessary.)
• Review their answers.
(You may wish to use Copying Master 8-1 at this time.)

JUST CHECKING

See how much you remember. Listen to the recording.

1. Listen to the steady beat and perform these rhythms on drumsticks using the matched grip.

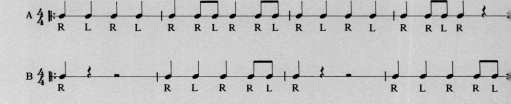

2. Listen to a portion of the *Saint Luke Passion* and identify the unusual vocal effects. hissing, shouting, chanting, speech

3. Listen to excerpts of three versions of "Promenade" and describe the contrasts of dynamics and tone color. answers will vary

4. The unique tone color of this ensemble is produced on homemade instruments. Name the instrument. steel drums

184

Perform these vocal sounds with the recording of "Misty, Moisty Morning."

♩ = 96 *(No Ritards)*   *p*

$\frac{4}{4}$

W One   Mis - ty,_____ mois - ty_____

Listen to this selection and tell whether the tone color is created by a pipe organ or a synthesizer. synthesizer

Listen to "Alpha" from *Albedo 39* by Vangelis. Use appropriate contemporary dance movements with this piece.

Name and describe two unusual instruments or familiar instruments used in unusual ways. Answers will vary.

Listen and identify the selection you hear. Choose from the titles below. c

a. Toccata and Fugue in D minor
b. "Alpha" from *Albedo 39*
c. *Heaven and Hell,* Part 2
d. "Promenade" from *Pictures at an Exhibition*
e. *The Perilous Night*

Listen to a portion of *The Perilous Night* and describe how the composer used a traditional instrument to produce different tone colors. John Cage prepared the piano by placing wood, metal, and rubber objects between the strings of the piano.

Listen to a portion of *Spoils of War* and describe several of the original instruments Harry Partch invented. cloud chamber bowls, tuned bamboo rods, brass artillery casings, "wang gun"

185

YEAR-END REVIEW

Objective
To review the skills and concepts taught throughout Grade 8

Materials
Recording: Year-End Review (questions 1–4, 7–10)
Keyboard or bells

TEACHING THE LESSON

Review the skills and concepts taught in Grade 8. Have the students:
• Perform the activities and answer the questions on pages 186–187. (For this review, examples for questions 1 through 4 and 7 through 10 are included in the "Year-End Review" recording. Have the students answer these questions first. Then have them answer the other questions in the review.)
• Review their answers.

YEAR-END REVIEW

CD5:20–31

1. Listen to determine whether the style of each example is African, rock and roll, Japanese, calypso, or reggae.
   reggae, Japanese, rock and roll, calypso

2. Listen to Bizet's "Farandole" and determine whether the form of the selection is AB or ABA. AB

3. Listen to this musical selection, which is an example of changing meters. Identify when the meter changes by conducting the appropriate pattern. The selection begins in duple meter.
   duple; triple; duple

4. Listen to this excerpt from "Caprice" from Claude Bolling's Suite for Violin and Jazz Piano. Determine if this section is in compound or quadruple meter. Demonstrate your answer by conducting the appropriate pattern. compound meter

5a. Play the following pitches on keyboard or bells that make up the twelve-tone row on which the melody of "The Web" is based.

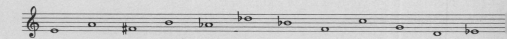

5b. Play the retrograde of this tone row on keyboard or bells.

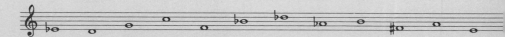

6. Perform this twelve-bar blues harmonic progression on bells or keyboard.

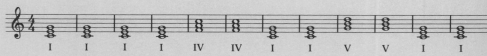

I   I   I   I   IV   IV   I   I   V   V   I   I

186

7a. Listen to a section of "Mi Caballo Blanco" and raise your hand when you hear the music modulate.

b. Listen to a section of "Mi Caballo Blanco" and decide if the music modulates to a higher or lower key. a higher key

8. Listen to *"Schwanenlied"* and decide whether the composition is in major or minor. minor

9. Listen to this section of Symphony No. 1 by Sergei Prokofiev. Identify the different parts of the exposition section by pointing to the descriptions on the listening map.

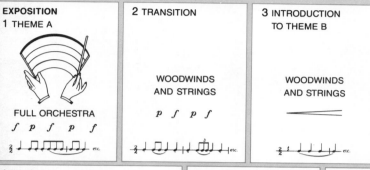

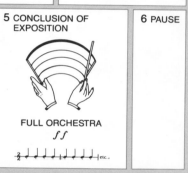

10. Listen and identify the selection you hear. Choose from the titles below. c

    a. Toccata and Fugue in D minor

    b. "Alpha"

    c. *Heaven and Hell,* Part 2

    d. "Promenade" *(Pictures at an Exhibition)*

    e. *The Perilous Night*

187

WESTERN MUSICAL STYLES

Francesco Veracini

188

...g the Piano in Prince Anton Radziwill's Salon at Berlin, Siemiradski

189

WESTERN MUSICAL STYLES

Renaissance: *O Care, thou wilt despatch me,* by Thomas Weelkes

Materials
Recording: *O Care, thou wilt despatch me*

TEACHING THE LESSON

Introduce Renaissance musical styles.
Have the students:
• Discuss the information on the madrigal.
• Discuss and define homophonic and polyphonic musical textures.
• Listen to *O Care, thou wilt despatch me* and identify the two moods the composer portrays. How does the music depict his unhappiness? How does it depict the joy he hopes to find in music? (long note values; short note values)
• Compare madrigals with today's popular music. What do both have in common? (short; performed by small groups; same music for each verse; lyrics can be about love or events of the day; can be performed by amateurs or professionals)

RENAISSANCE

O Care, thou wilt despatch me, by Thomas Weelkes

One of the most popular forms of vocal music in the Renaissance was the **madrigal** (mad′ ri-gǝl). Madrigals were written in polyphonic style, usually for five singers. They generally were short works, simple in structure. The lyrics were taken from both great literature and popular poetry. Like the popular songs of today, most madrigals were about love, happy or unhappy. Other topics included politics and issues of the day. Most madrigals were in **strophic** form, with each verse being sung to essentially the same music. This made madrigals easy to learn.

Vocal music was especially popular in the Renaissance, which is often called the "Golden Age of Singing." Church music was sung by professional, all-male choirs, but madrigals were sung by both men and women. Madrigals were performed at social gatherings and as home entertainment. Usually one performer sang each part, sometimes accompanied by recorders, lutes, or viols playing the same music.

In *O Care, thou wilt despatch me,* the English composer Thomas Weelkes looks to music to cheer him up.

> O Care, thou wilt despatch me,
> If music do not match thee.
> Fa la la la la la la.
> So deadly dost thou sting me,
> Mirth only help can bring me.
> Fa la la la la la,
> Fa la la la la la.

• Listen for the two moods the composer portrays. How does the music depict his unhappiness? How does it depict the joy he hopes to find in music? long note values; short note values

 O Care, thou wilt despatch me, by Thomas Weelkes

• Compare madrigals with today's pop music. What do both have in common? both short; performed by small groups; same music for each verse; lyrics could be about love, or events of the day; both

190

E X T E N S I O N

THE COMPOSER

Thomas Weelkes (1576?–1623)—was an English composer and organist. Little is known about his early life. He received a degree in music from Oxford University and was for a time organist at Chichester Cathedral. Weelkes wrote a great deal of church music and also instrumental works, but it is his madrigals for which he is best remembered. Besides showing a remarkable union of melody and text, many of these songs contain harmonies and chord progressions that were well ahead of their time. For this, Weelkes is considered one of the greatest English madrigalists.

MORE MUSIC TEACHING IDEAS

Have the students:
1. Compare the text of *O Care, thou wilt despatch me* with texts of songs from other periods and identify how different periods treat the same idea. (See pages 343, 357.)
2. Perform compositions containing homophonic and polyphonic sections. (See pages 330, 343.)
3. Listen to examples of unaccompanied choral singing and identify similarities and differences in vocal tone color. (See pages 340, 355.)
4. Create a text that has a similar meaning to that of *O Care, thou wilt despatch me.*

You may wish to use this selection in conjunction with:
European-Western Styles, pp. 16–17
Performing a Canon, p. 82

During the Renaissance, people enjoyed singing and playing music together. The instruments shown in these paintings include viols (early members of the violin family), lutes, recorder, and a type of portable harpsichord.

Hearing, Abraham Bosse

Group with Lute Player and Three Musicians on the Terrace of a House, unknown 16th-century artist

191

WESTERN MUSICAL STYLES

General Characteristics

1. Emphasis on unaccompanied polyphonic choral music sometimes based on Gregorian chant melodies
2. In polyphonic music, equal importance given to each voice
3. Carefully controlled consonance and dissonance
4. Rhythms often very complex and frequently changing
5. Dance music usually homophonic and instrumental (recorders and so on)
6. The beginning of music for solo instruments, such as the lute

Form Alternation of polyphonic and homophonic sections determined by the text in vocal music; dances usually in binary form

Tone Color Unaccompanied voices, instruments of the Renaissance

WESTERN MUSICAL STYLES

Baroque: "Spring" (First Movement) from *The Four Seasons*, by Antonio Vivaldi

Materials
Recordings: "Spring"
"Marche" (optional)

TEACHING THE LESSON

Review the baroque musical style. Have the students:
• Review the information about baroque style on pages 22–23.
• Discuss the information on "Spring" and the concerto.

"Spring" (First Movement) from *The Four Seasons*, by Antonio Vivaldi

The **concerto** (kôn-cher′tō) was one of the most important instrumental forms used in the baroque period. The term *concerto* comes from the Italian word *concertare* (kôn-cher-tä′ re), which suggests a friendly argument or contrasting forces. In a concerto, one instrument or group of instruments is set against the orchestra.

The Four Seasons is a group of violin concertos written around 1725 by the Italian baroque composer Antonio Vivaldi (än-tō′ nē-ō vi-väl′ dē) (1675-1741). Each concerto is accompanied by a poem, also written by Vivaldi, describing that season. This is a very early example of **program music,** music that tells a story or describes a scene.

One of the musical characteristics emphasized in the baroque concerto was *contrast*. In a style typical of the baroque, Vivaldi used two contrasting groups of instruments, contrasting melodies, and abrupt contrasts of loud and soft.

Vivaldi was born in Venice and lived most of his life there. This painting by the Italian artist Canaletto (1697–1768) shows Venice as it looked during Vivaldi's lifetime.

"Spring" begins with the main theme played by everyone. Sections of a concerto played by everyone are called **ritornello** (ri-tôr-ne′ lō). The contrasting sections, called **episodes,** are played by the solo players. The music played suggests musical descriptions of spring, such as birds singing, murmuring waters, lightning and thunder.

192

E X T E N S I O N

THE COMPOSER

Antonio Vivaldi (1678–1741)—was born in Venice. He studied violin with his father, who was a professional musician. When Vivaldi was fifteen he entered the priesthood, and was ordained in 1703. A year later he became the music director at the Ospedale della Pietà, a conservatory in Venice. Many of his vocal works were written for the students there. Vivaldi also composed many successful operas. But his chief fame rests on his instrumental music, in particular his violin concertos. *The Four Seasons,* early examples of program music, are the first four in a series of twelve violin concertos called *The Contest Between Harmony and Invention.* Each season's concerto is accompanied by a descriptive poem, also written by Vivaldi.

THE ARTIST

Canaletto (1697-1768)—was an Italian painter best known for his scenes of 18th-century Venice. His paintings are colorful and show the famous buildings that lined the main canals of Venice. Canaletto first worked as a painter of theater scenery in his father's studio. Many of his paintings of Venice were commissioned by English visitors.

ach picture represents musical sounds. The term *concertino* (kôn-cher-tē′ no) refers to the solo instrument or instruments. *Tutti* (too′ tē) refers to all the instruments together.

Which pictures are similar? Which are different? *like:* pictures 1, 3, 4, 5, 7, 9; pictures 2, 8; *different:* 6

Listen to "Spring" and notice the contrasts in tone color, themes, and dynamics. Follow the map as you listen.

Describe the sound of the baroque orchestra. What instruments are used? What keyboard instrument can you hear throughout the concerto? stringed instruments; harpsichord

"Spring" (First Movement), from *The Four Seasons*, by Antonio Vivaldi

Listening Map of "Spring" (First Movement) from *The Four Seasons*

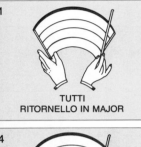 1 — TUTTI RITORNELLO IN MAJOR	 2 — SOLO AND CONCERTINO — BIRD CALLS	 3 — TUTTI RITORNELLO IN MAJOR
 4 — TUTTI A MURMURING STREAM	 5 — TUTTI RITORNELLO IN MAJOR	 6 — SOLO TUTTI LIGHTNING AND THUNDER
 7 — TUTTI RITORNELLO IN MINOR	8 — SOLO AND CONCERTINO BIRDS RETURN AFTER THE STORM	 9 — SOLO, CONCERTINO, AND TUTTI RITORNELLO IN MAJOR

193

WESTERN MUSICAL STYLES

• Prepare to listen by identifying the musical sounds represented by each picture. Which pictures are similar and which are different?
• Listen to the recording, following the map. Notice the contrasts in tone color, themes, and dynamics as they listen.
• Describe the sound of the baroque orchestra (small size with strings predominant).
• Determine what instruments were used in this recording. (strings, harpsichord)

General Characteristics
1. Development of instrumental music in the form of the concerto
2. Steady rhythms and repetition of rhythmic motives and patterns
3. Sudden changes in dynamics
4. Contrasts of solo and tutti
5. Contrasts of textures

Form Based on contrasts between solo and tutti, episode and ritornello

Tone Color Homogenous instrumental sound in string concertos; clearly defined individual lines or voices in polyphonic compositions

---

MORE MUSIC TEACHING IDEAS
Have the students:
1. Compare "Spring" with other compositions in baroque style. ("Marche" by Lully, page 18)
2. Perform compositions that use contrasts of dynamics and tone color. (instrumental accompaniment to "Marche")
3. Listen to examples of compositions in baroque style.
4. Create a sound composition that uses contrasts of tone color and dynamics.
5. Analyze popular music of today and identify characteristics similar to those of "Spring."

You may wish to use this selection in conjunction with:
European-Western Styles, pp. 16–17
Moving to Sounds of the Twentieth Century, p. 174

LISTENING
You may wish to use the Listening Map overhead transparency to help guide the students through the listening selection.

WESTERN MUSICAL STYLES

CD5

Classical: Quintet for Clarinet and Strings in A Major, K. 581 (Fourth Movement), by Wolfgang Amadeus Mozart

Materials
Recording: Quintet for Clarinet and Strings (fourth movement)

TEACHING THE LESSON

Review the classical style. Have the students:
• Read about classical style on pages 144–145.
• Discuss the information on Mozart's Quintet for Clarinet and Strings, focusing on the theme and variation form used in the fourth movement.
• Listen to the recording, reading the description for each section. Notice the contrast between staccato and legato.

General Characteristics
1. Strict use of form
2. Clarity, order, and refinement
3. Straightforward, predictable harmonies
4. More subtle phrasing, dynamics, and orchestration than baroque style
5. Short and tuneful melodies

Form ABA, sonata, theme and variations

Tone Color Development of the orchestra as we know it today

CD5:34 **Quintet for Clarinet and Strings in A Major, K. 581, Fourth Movement, by Wolfgang Amadeus Mozart**

Compositions for small groups of instruments are called **chamber music** because they are designed to be performed in rooms (chambers) rather than concert halls. Like **symphonies** (works for full orchestra), chamber works are in several movements.

For the fourth and final movement of his Clarinet Quintet, Wolfgang Amadeus Mozart (volf' gäng ä-mä-dā' ōōs mōt' särt) decided to write a theme with six variations and a **coda,** or conclusion. The theme itself is a very simple one, which Mozart varies in several ways. For example, he shows off the instruments' abilities to change from major to minor, or to play **legato** (lā-gä' tō, smoothly) or **staccato** (stä-kä' tō, detached). For contrasting tone color, Mozart even leaves out the clarinet entirely in one variation.

• Listen to the music and read the description on page 195. Notice the contrast between staccato and legato sections.

 Quintet for Clarinet and Strings in A Major, K. 581, Fourth Movement, by Wolfgang Amadeus Mozart

EXTENSION

THE COMPOSER

Wolfgang Amadeus Mozart (1756–1791)—was born in Salzburg, Austria. His great talent was evident very early; his father took him and his older sister Nannerl on tours all across Europe. Mozart's father, an excellent musician, gave Wolfgang solid musical training. Wolfgang also studied with Johann Christian Bach. In 1781 Mozart settled in Vienna. He wrote operas, symphonies, chamber music, piano music, sacred music, and many other works, all unsurpassed in melodic beauty and expressiveness.

MORE MUSIC TEACHING IDEAS

Have the students:
1. Compare the Quintet for Clarinet and Strings to other compositions in classical style ("Ode to Joy," page 16).
2. Perform compositions that use variations on a basic melodic idea.
3. Listen to other examples of theme and variations form in classical style.
4. Create a theme and variations as indicated on page 109.
5. Analyze popular music of today and identify characteristics similar to those of the Quintet for Clarinet and Strings (answers will vary).

You may wish to use this selection in conjunction with:
European-Western Styles, pp. 16–17
Repetition and Identifying Motives, pp. 140–141
Repetition and Development, pp. 146–151

1. *Theme:* Cheerful, staccato theme is played and immediately repeated. The second part of the theme, momentarily legato, leads right back to the first (staccato) part, and this is repeated.
2. *Variation 1:* Clarinet, legato, has a new tune as strings play the staccato basic theme. This continues into Part 2 of the theme.
3. *Variation 2:* Strings agitated, but melody soars when clarinet enters. In Part 2 the agitation continues.
4. *Variation 3:* A change to minor gives a melancholy quality to the theme. This entire variation is played by strings only.
5. *Variation 4:* Rapid passages in clarinet accompany a return to the jolly mood of the theme in the strings.
6. *Adagio (Variation 5):* Change to a slow tempo is introduced by a series of chords and descending passages on the clarinet. Strings play yet another variation on the theme, joined by a wistful song on the clarinet, and this segment is repeated. The second part of the theme has the clarinet dominating, then giving in to the strings, and this segment also is repeated. A short, legato passage leads to:
7. *Allegro (Variation 6):* Another treatment of the basic theme. A coda of four chords brings this music to a strong conclusion.

Below, a typical chamber music concert during Mozart's time. Right, the child Mozart (at the keyboard) with his father and sister.

The Concert, Augustin de Saint Aubin

Mozart as a Child, with his Father and Sister, Carmontelle, MUSÉE CONDÉ Chantilly

195

WESTERN MUSICAL STYLES

Romantic: "Un bel dì vedremo" from
Madama Butterfly, **by Giacomo Puccini**

Materials
Recordings: *"Un bel dì vedremo"*
"The Erlking" (optional)
"Schwanenlied" (optional)

TEACHING THE LESSON

Introduce the romantic style. Have the students:
• Discuss the information on the opera *Madama Butterfly.*
• Read the description and musical analysis of the aria *"Un bel dì vedremo."*

ROMANTIC

"Un bel dì vedremo," from *Madama Butterfly,* by Giacomo Puccini

Opera is one of the most exciting of all musical forms, for it offers not only music, but also dramatic action, scenery, costumes, interesting stories and, often, unusual lighting effects. An opera performance, therefore, is a special event.

Madama Butterfly, by the Italian composer Giacomo Puccini, is one of the most popular operas ever written. Puccini's characters are understandable and human.

Madama Butterfly is another name for Cio-Cio-San (chō' chō-sän), a young Japanese woman who marries an American naval officer, Lieutenant Pinkerton. She plans to devote her life to this marriage, but to Pinkerton, it is just a temporary fling until he meets and marries the American woman of his dreams. Butterfly remains true, but Pinkerton, while in America, marries someone else. When Butterfly realizes that Pinkerton has deserted her, she kills herself.

Butterfly sings the famous **aria** (ä' rē-ä, solo song) *"Un bel dì vedremo,"* while she still believes Pinkerton will come back to her. She tells her servant, Suzuki, that one beautiful day Pinkerton will return, and she describes everything she thinks will happen.

The powerful opening melody of this aria occurs again near the end of the song, making a kind of ABA form. Butterfly's belief that Pinkerton will return to her is reflected in the straightforward melody. Near the end of her song, the music becomes more insistent as she talks herself and her servant into believing that what she says actually will come to pass.

As you listen to this selection, you will notice that the composer has provided several changes of mood and tempo to illustrate the situations Butterfly describes. Puccini's melody is strong at the beginning when Pinkerton's return is described, but becomes gentler as Butterfly tells of her own reactions to the situation. She will stay where she is, waiting anxiously for Pinkerton to find her, almost unable to control her emotions. The first melody returns as she describes their first meeting. The aria reaches its peak near the end as Butterfly tries to assure Suzuki that Pinkerton will, indeed, return.

196

E X T E N S I O N

THE COMPOSER

Giacomo Puccini (1858–1924)—Italian composer, is considered one of the world's great operatic composers. As a child he showed no leaning or special talent for music, but entered music school at his mother's insistence. Indifference soon turned to enthusiasm. While Puccini was studying composition at the Milan Conservatory one of his teachers persuaded him to enter a one-act opera competition. Although his opera did not win, it attracted the attention of influential people, one of whom commissioned Puccini to write a second opera. This work was a failure, but his next effort, *Manon Lescaut,* was a success. The operas that followed won international fame. Among these, *La Bohème, Tosca, Madama Butterfly,* and *Turandot* remain very popular.

Right, poster advertising a 1906 production of *Madama Butterfly*. Below and page 198, Renata Scotto in the Metropolitan Opera production. Below is the wedding scene; on page 198, *"Un bel dì vedremo."*

197

WESTERN MUSICAL STYLES

• Listen to the recording, following the Italian words and the translation. Notice how Puccini's music reflects Butterfly's hopes and feelings.

General Characteristics of Romantic Music

1. Changes of mood within sections of a composition
2. Definite expressions of feelings and emotions
3. Melodies often long and complex
4. Extreme modulations
5. Program music as important as absolute music
6. Virtuosity emphasized and technique developed
7. New status of the artist as a creative personality, in contrast to formerly being regarded as an employee of the church or court

Characteristics of Romantic Operas

Form Through composed, often reflecting the feelings and emotions behind the words

Tone Color Larger orchestras, with newly improved instruments added

CD5:35 • Follow the Italian words and their translation as you hear them. Notice how Puccini's music reflects the hopes and feelings to which Butterfly refers.

Un bel dì, vedremo
Levarsi un fil di fumo
Sull'estremo confin del mare.
E poi la nave appare.
Poi la nave bianca
Entra nel porto,
Romba il suo saluto.
Vedi? È venuto!
Io non gli scendo incontro. Io no. Mi metto là sul ciglio del colle e aspetto, e aspetto gran tempo e non mi pesa la lunga attesa.
E uscito dalla folla cittadina un uomo, un picciol punto s'avvia per la collina.

Chi sarà? Chi sarà? E come sarà giunto che dirà? Che dirà? Chiamerà Butterfly dalla lontana. Io, senza dar risposta me ne starò nascosta un po' per celia, e un po' per non morire al primo incontro, ed egli alquanto in pena chiamerà, chiamerà: "Piccina mogliettina olezzo di verbena" i nomi che mi dava al suo venire.

Tutto questo avverrà, te lo prometto.

Tienti la tua paura, io con sicura fede l'aspetto.

One fine day, we shall see
A thread of smoke rising
Over the horizon
And then the ship will appear.
Then the white ship
Enters the harbor.
Her salute thunders out.
You see? He has come!
I don't go down to meet him. Not I. I stand on the brow of the hill and wait, and wait a long time and do not weary of the long watch.
Out of the city crowds there comes a man—a tiny speck—who makes his way toward the hill.
Who can it be? Who can it be? And when he arrives what will he say? What will he say? He will call Butterfly from the distance. I, without answering, will stay hidden partly for fun, and partly so as not to die at the first meeting. And he, a little troubled, will call, he will call: "My little wife, my sweet-scented flower"—the names he used to call me when he came.
All this will come to pass, I promise you.

Keep your fears: I, with unshakeable faith, will await him.

 "Un bel dì vedremo," from Madama Butterfly, by Giacomo Puccini

198

198   WESTERN MUSICAL STYLES

EXTENSION

MORE MUSIC TEACHING IDEAS

Have the students:
1. Compare "Un bel dì vedremo" with other compositions in romantic style ("The Erlking," p. 111; "Schwanenlied," p. 134).
2. Listen to other examples of romantic vocal music in which the music reflects the feelings and ideas of the words.
3. Analyze popular music of today and identify characteristics similar to those in "Un bel dì vedremo."

You may wish to use this selection in conjunction with:
European-Western Styles, pp. 16–17
Story Through Song, pp. 130–135
Telling a Story, pages 111–115

Étude in E Minor, Opus 25, No. 5, by Frédéric Chopin

Polish composer Frédéric Chopin specialized in writing music for the piano. Among his finest works, which include waltzes, sonatas, and many other pieces, are his **études**. *Étude* means "study," and an étude's purpose is to help students with technical playing problems. Chopin's études are more than just studies, however, because they are important musical selections in their own right. Chopin played several of them in his concerts, and many pianists do so today.

Of the more than two dozen études that Chopin composed, the Étude in E Minor, Opus 25, No. 5, is particularly impressive. Its opening section (A) is mainly staccato and is played at a fast tempo. The middle section (B) offers an expressive legato, in a slower tempo. When the A section returns, its staccato idea brings to mind the strong contrast that exists between the three sections of this work. Chopin includes a coda (ending section) with chords and a melodic trill at the close.

● Listen to the Étude in E Minor and raise your hand when you hear the contrasting B section.

● How does the étude show unity and variety? unity: A section repeated; variety: contrasting B section

🎵 Étude in E Minor, Opus 25, No. 5, by Frédéric Chopin

Frédéric Chopin. Eugène Delacroix. LOUVRE, Paris

Chopin often played private concerts in the homes of the nobility.

Chopin Playing the Piano in Prince Anton Radziwill's Salon at Berlin, Siemiradski

WESTERN MUSICAL STYLES

Étude in E Minor, Opus 25, No. 5, by Frédéric Chopin

Materials
Recordings: Étude in E Minor
                "Farandole" (optional)

TEACHING THE LESSON

Introduce piano music of the romantic era. Have the students:
• Discuss the information on Frédéric Chopin and the étude.
• Read the description and musical analysis of Étude No. 5.
• Listen to the recording and indicate the beginning of the contrasting B section by raising their hands.
• Identify how the Étude shows unity and variety. (unity: A section repeated; variety: contrasting B section)

Characteristics of Étude in E Minor

Form ABA; small forms and miniatures popular, especially for solo instruments

Tone Color Importance of the piano as a solo instrument

EXTENSION

MORE MUSIC TEACHING IDEAS
Have the students:
1. Compare the Étude in E Minor with other romantic compositions ("Farandole," p. 24).
2. Listen to other examples of romantic music in which there are changes of mood within a single composition.
3. Analyze popular music of today and identify characteristics similar to those in the Étude in E Minor.

You may wish to use this selection in conjunction with:
European-Western Styles, pp. 16–17
Characteristics of the Romantic Period, pp. 26–27

THE ARTIST
Eugene Delacroix (de-lä-krwä') (1798-1863)—was a French painter important in the Romantic movement. The subjects of many of his paintings were inspired by the writings of William Shakespeare, Dante, Lord Byron, and Sir Walter Scott. He particularly liked to paint exciting, violent, or exotic scenes, including battles and lion hunts. He was also known as a portrait painter, and among his subjects was Frédéric Chopin.

THE COMPOSER
Frédéric Chopin (1810–1849)—Polish composer and pianist. He began studying piano when he was six and gave his first public performance at the age of eight. By this time he had already begun to compose. After finishing his studies at the Warsaw Conservatory, Chopin left Poland and eventually settled in Paris. Chopin is one of the few composers who wrote almost exclusively for solo piano. In his use of the rhythms of Polish folk dances such as the mazurka and the polonaise, he was one of the first nationalistic composers. He was a master of small forms, such as the waltz, nocturne, and prelude. His études brought the study of technical problems to the level of great art. Today Chopin is regarded as one of the most influential composers of piano music.

WESTERN MUSICAL STYLES

Twentieth Century: "Infernal Dance," from *The Firebird*, by Igor Stravinsky

Materials

Recordings: "Infernal Dance"
"Misty, Moisty Morning" (optional)
Saint Luke Passion (optional)
Suite for Percussion (optional)
Steel Band Music (optional)
Harry Partch on *Spoils of War* (optional)

TEACHING THE LESSON

Introduce twentieth-century music.

Have the students:

• Discuss the information on *The Firebird* and the "Infernal Dance."

• Listen to the recording and read the description for each number.

General Characteristics of Twentieth-Century Music

1. Use of many different styles and types of music
2. Experimentation with new sounds and combinations of instruments (as in *Spoils of War*, by Harry Partch, on page 183)
3. Extreme dissonance (as in *Variations on "America,"* by Charles Ives, on page 108), extending to atonality
4. Abandonment of standard melodic formulas (as in *Saint Luke Passion*, by Krzysztof Penderecki, on page 171)
5. Development of new tonal systems, such as serialism (as in "The Web" on page 91)

Characteristics of "Infernal Dance"

Form Determined by the composer

Tone Color Large orchestra; use of persistent rhythms and dramatic effects

---

Infernal Dance, from *The Firebird*, by Igor Stravinsky

Through movement, ballet can express feelings that would be difficult or impossible to say in words. Some ballets are story ballets. Stravinsky's *The Firebird* is one of the finest story ballets of the twentieth century. Based on a Russian folk legend, it tells of Prince Ivan. He discovers a magic garden whose inhabitants are under the spell of an evil king named Kastchei (käs-chā′ē). With the help of the enchanted firebird, Ivan breaks the spell. This releases, among the others, the girl he marries, and all ends happily.

In the Infernal Dance, Stravinsky describes the King Kastchei's evil power through ominous-sounding themes, abrupt changes of instruments and dynamics, and strong rhythms. One can imagine, just by listening to this music, Kastchei's menacing gestures and his domination of the scene, even without seeing his actions on stage.

• Listen to the music and read the description below.

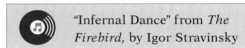
"Infernal Dance" from *The Firebird*, by Igor Stravinsky

1. Loud chord—brasses and bassoons present ominous theme; theme is repeated.
2. Xylophone joins the proceedings.
3. A flowing melody in the strings.
4. Xylophone alternates with other instruments.
5. Smoother melodic ideas in strings and other instruments, soft and loud.
6. Entire orchestra plays the smoother idea at a loud dynamic level.
7. Suddenly soft, though the scary mood continues.
8. Theme (soft) punctuated by xylophone.
9. Crescendo built with shorter, faster notes.
10. Brasses alternate with other instruments.
11. Faster tempo builds a peak; music ends with one loud chord, then a soft chord.

200

E X T E N S I O N

THE COMPOSER

Igor Stravinsky (1882–1972)—Russian-born composer. As a young man Stravinsky studied law, but eventually turned to music. Stravinsky first became famous when he composed three ballets in Paris between 1909 and 1913. The first two—*The Firebird* and *Petrushka*—were easy to listen to and quickly became popular. The third, *The Rite of Spring*, was so unconventional that the audience rioted at the first performance. In the 1920s Stravinsky wrote in a neoclassical style with a twentieth-century flavor (*Symphony of Psalms*). At the outbreak of World War II Stravinsky moved to the United States. Stravinsky's innovations and versatility have greatly influenced twentieth-century music.

MORE MUSIC TEACHING IDEAS

Have the students:

1. Compare the "Infernal Dance" with other twentieth-century compositions ("Misty, Moisty Morning," and *Saint Luke Passion*, pp. 169–171; Recycling for Sound, pp. 181–183).
2. Listen to compositions that use traditional instruments in experimental ways ("Misty, Moisty Morning," pp. 170–171).
3. Create compositions that use traditional instruments in experimental ways (Create a Sound Composition, p. 14)
4. Analyze popular music of today and identify characteristics similar to those in the "Infernal Dance."

You may wish to use this selection in conjunction with:
European-Western Styles, pp. 16–17
New Sounds from a Familiar Instrument, pp. 175–177

"Tonight," from *West Side Story*, by Leonard Bernstein and Stephen Sondheim

When *West Side Story* opened on Broadway in 1957, it was quite different from other musical plays of the time. In it, the story of Romeo and Juliet was transplanted to New York's West Side and given a contemporary flavor by the use of popular music styles.

The plot of *West Side Story* concerns two street gangs, the Jets and the Sharks, each of which wants to rule the neighborhood. At the beginning of the story Tony, formerly a member of the Jets, has quit the gang and taken a job in hopes of bettering his life. One night at a dance Tony meets Maria, a Puerto Rican girl. They fall in love. But Maria and Tony's romance is doomed from the start. Maria is the sister of Bernardo, the leader of the Sharks, and is engaged to Bernardo's friend Chino. Despite this the two lovers meet secretly. In a scene reminiscent of the famous balcony scene in *Romeo and Juliet* they sing the beautiful duet "Tonight" on the fire escape outside Maria's apartment.

The two rival gangs plan a rumble (fight) to determine who will rule the neighborhood. Tony tries unsuccessfully to stop the fight and make peace between the two gangs. Bernardo and Tony's best friend Riff fight as everyone else watches. The rules for the fight specify no weapons, but knives are drawn and Bernardo kills Riff. In a grief-stricken rage, Tony takes Riff's knife and kills Bernardo. The gang members scatter as the police arrive.

Anita, Bernardo's girlfriend, learns the outcome of the rumble and goes to Maria to break the news about Bernardo to her. Maria is only concerned about Tony. Angrily, Anita tells her that Tony killed Bernardo. Maria is sorrowful, but is determined to forgive Tony.

Tony and Maria make plans to go away together. When Maria is delayed she sends Anita with a message for Tony. Anita goes to the store where Tony works and encounters some of the Jets. They know she is Bernardo's girlfriend and taunt her. Enraged, Anita gives

201

WESTERN MUSICAL STYLES

"Tonight," from *West Side Story*, by Leonard Bernstein and Stephen Sondheim

Materials
Recordings: "Tonight"
"The Erlking" (optional)
"Schwanenlied" (optional)

TEACHING THE LESSON

Introduce twentieth-century styles.
Have the students:
• Discuss the information on *West Side Story* and "Tonight."

THE COMPOSER

Leonard Bernstein (1918-1990)—American composer and conductor, was born in Lawrence, Massachusetts. He studied at Harvard, the Curtis Institute in Philadelphia and Tanglewood. In 1943 he became an assistant conductor with the New York Philharmonic. Later that year he rose to fame when he substituted for Bruno Walter, who was ill. In 1958 Bernstein became the principal conductor of the New York Philharmonic, the first American ever to hold that post. Bernstein was an equally gifted composer of both classical and popular music. He wrote a series of successful musicals, including *On the Town* (1944), *Candide* (1956), and *West Side Story* (1957). Bernstein was also a fine lecturer on music, with his televised series of Young People's Concerts in the 1950s.

WESTERN MUSICAL STYLES

- Listen to the recording, focusing on the story line, and read the description for each number.
- Describe the different kinds of music the composer provides for each character or group, and how he may have decided on it. (answers will vary)

Characteristics of "Tonight"

Form Partner song

Tone Color Use of vocal tone color, range, and register to reflect mood and feelings

them a different message for Tony: Chino found out about Tony and Maria, and killed her.

Tony, numb with grief, goes looking for Chino. But Chino finds Tony first, and shoots him in revenge for Bernardo. Maria finds Tony lying in the street. She cradles him in her arms as he dies. United by tragedy, the rival gangs finally make an effort at peace and jointly carry Tony's body away as Maria follows.

West Side Story contains solos, duets, instrumental sections, and ensembles (music in which several people sing at the same time). If several actors were to talk at the same time, the audience would not be able to understand them. However, in music, two or more things can happen at once, and the results will still be understandable. This ensemble, entitled "Tonight," has several different ideas going on at the same time: Maria and Tony express their love for each other; Anita looks forward to an evening of fun; and the opposing gangs plot the rumble that is about to take place.

- Follow the story line in "Tonight" by reading the descriptions.

1. *Jets*: "The Jets are gonna have their day tonight."
   Sharks: "We're gonna hand them a surprise tonight."
   Brief, jazzy introduction, Jets and Sharks in a fast tempo, with a strong rhythmic accompaniment.

2. *Anita*: "Anita's gonna get her kicks tonight."
   Introduced by brief, jazzlike pattern; same melody that was sung by Jets and Sharks, but sung as a solo.

3. *Tony*: " Tonight, tonight."
   A new melody is introduced; rhythmic accompaniment here is more subdued for this soaring, smoother tune, which depicts Tony and Maria's love for each other.

4. *Maria* continues Tony's melody of "Tonight."

5. Comments from gang members.
   Strong accompaniment returns, illustrating the warlike mentality of the gangs.

6. *Maria* sings "Tonight" with short comments in the background by the *Jets*, the *Sharks*, *Tony*, and *Anita*. Each melody is different from the others, even though they are all sung at the same time. The quintet reaches an exciting conclusion.

- Decide how the composer provides different music for each character or group.

202

E X T E N S I O N

THE LYRICIST

Stephen Sondheim—American composer and lyricist, was born in New York City in 1930. He studied with the lyricist Oscar Hammerstein II and the composer Milton Babbitt. Sondheim's first major work was with Leonard Bernstein on *West Side Story*. The first musical for which he wrote both music and lyrics was *A Funny Thing Happened on the Way to the Forum* (1962), based on the comedies of the Roman author Plautus. Sondheim's shows are notable for their complex melodies, witty lyrics, and sophisticated plots. Other Sondheim shows include *Company* (1970), *Follies* (1971), *A Little Night Music* (1973), *Sweeney Todd* (1979), *Sunday in the Park with George* (1984), and *Into the Woods* (1987).

MORE MUSIC TEACHING IDEAS

Have the students:
1. Compare "Tonight" with other dramatic vocal compositions ("The Erlking," pp. 111–115; "Schwanenlied," pp. 134–135).
2. Perform selections in which the music reflects the feelings and mood of the words.
3. Create compositions in which the music reflects the feelings and mood of the text (Create a Sound Composition, page 14).
4. Analyze popular music of today and identify characteristics similar to those in "Tonight." (answers will vary)

You may wish to use this selection in conjunction with:
European-Western Styles, pp. 16–17
Story Through Song, pp. 130–135
Telling a Story, pp. 111–115

These scenes are from the film of *West Side Story*. Above, the rumble. Tony (Richard Beymer) is facing forward. Left, Anita (Rita Moreno) and some friends on the roof of their apartment building.

"Tonight," quintet from *West Side Story*, by Leonard Bernstein and Stephen Sondheim

Maria (Natalie Wood) and Tony declare their love in this "wedding" scene.

203

WESTERN MUSICAL STYLES

Lieutenant Kijé Suite, by Sergei Prokofiev

Materials
Recordings: "The Birth of Kijé"
　　　　　　Wellington's Victory (optional)
　　　　　　"The Wedding of Kijé"
Copying Master W1: Listening Map
(optional)

TEACHING THE LESSON

Introduce twentieth-century styles.
Have the students:
• Discuss the information on the *Lieutenant Kijé Suite.* (You may wish to review the information on Prokofiev on page 149 of the Teacher's Edition.)
• Identify the "Kijé" theme.
• Listen to the first movement of the suite and identify the instruments that Prokofiev uses to convey the idea of Kije's military service. (brass and percussion)
• Continue following the story line.
• Identify themes 2 and 3.

Lieutenant Kijé Suite, by Sergei Prokofiev

Lieutenant Kijé (kē′ jā) was a Russian film for which Sergei Prokofiev (ser′ gā prō-kō′ fē-ev) composed the score. The story of *Lieutenant Kijé* is a humorous one, set in the nineteenth century. One day the czar of Russia is looking at military reports and misreads the name *Kijé* in an account of a heroic deed. When the czar asks questions about Lieutenant Kijé, his advisors are afraid to tell him that he has made a mistake. Consequently they proceed to make up a life story for the imaginary Lieutenant Kijé.

In the first movement of the suite, "The Birth of Kijé," a solo cornet theme decribes Kijé's birth and some of his supposed military exploits. A separate theme is used to represent Kijé himself. This theme reappears in later movements of the suite whenever Kijé is present.

• Listen to the first movement of this suite and identify the instruments that Prokofiev uses to convey the idea of Kijé's military service. brass and percussion

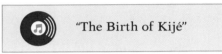
"The Birth of Kijé"

The advisors continue their story, and in the second movement of the suite, "Romance," Kijé falls in love. A "love song" theme is played by string bass, cello, and tenor saxophone. This is followed by themes from Kijé's wedding and the celebration afterward.

204

E X T E N S I O N

CURRICULUM CONNECTION: VISUAL ARTS

Motion Pictures—The 1934 film *Lieutenant Kijé* was the first film for which Sergei Prokofiev wrote the score. Later Prokofiev adapted an orchestral suite from this music. He conducted the first performance of the suite in Paris in 1937. Since then the *Lieutenant Kijé Suite* has become part of orchestra repertoires around the world. Other films for which Prokofiev wrote music include *Alexander Nevsky* (1938) and *Ivan the Terrible* (1942–1945).

MORE MUSIC TEACHING IDEAS

Have the students:
1. Compare the *Lieutenant Kijé Suite* with other programmatic selections. (*Wellington's Victory,* pp. 153–155)
2. Create compositions that are programmatic in nature. (Create a Sound Composition, p. 14)
3. Analyze film music of today and identify characteristics similar to those of *Lieutenant Kijé.* (program music)

A scene from
the 1934 film
Lieutenant Kijé

Prokofiev uses these two themes in the third movement, "The Wedding of Kijé," to describe the relationship between the stately ceremony (Theme 2) and the celebration (Theme 3). Kijé's theme (Theme 1) also is heard throughout.

- Listen and identify which theme you hear for each number. No. 1: Theme 2; No. 2: Theme 3; No. 3: Theme 1; No. 4: Theme 3; No. 5: Theme 2; No. 6: Theme 3; No. 7: Theme 2

 "The Wedding of Kijé"

The advisors describe more of Kijé's deeds to the czar. Their plan backfires when the czar is so interested that he asks to meet Kijé! The advisors must do something quickly. They tell the czar that Kijé has died and has been buried with full military honors.

In the fifth and last movement, "The Burial of Kijé," Prokofiev uses many of the themes from the earlier movements to remind the audience of Kijé's life. Then the solo cornet returns with the opening theme as the hero is laid to rest.

205

WESTERN MUSICAL STYLES

- Listen to the third movement and identify which theme is heard as each number is called. (You may wish to use Copying Master W-1: Listening Map at this time.)
- Discuss the end of the story.

Characteristics of *Lieutenant Kijé Suite*

Form Suite

Tone Color Use of unusual tone colors, range, and register to reflect mood and feelings

WESTERN MUSICAL STYLES

"Ev'ry Time I Feel the Spirit," an African American spiritual, arranged by William Dawson

Materials

Recordings: "Ev'ry Time I Feel the
            Spirit"
            "Run Joe" (optional)
Keyboard or bells

TEACHING THE LESSON

Introduce arrangement as a musical technique. Have the students:
• Discuss the information on arranging a melody.
• Discuss the information on William Dawson and "Ev'ry Time I Feel the Spirit."

An Arrangement by William Dawson

Some musicians arrange rather than compose music. In arranging, a musician takes an existing composition and resets it for a different combination of musical resources. For example, a work for two voices may be arranged for two clarinets.

One of the challenges an arranger faces is to keep the arrangement from overpowering the unique qualities of the original music. William Dawson illustrated his sensitivity and skill in preserving the characteristics of spirituals in his choral arrangement of "Ev'ry Time I Feel the Spirit."

William Dawson was born at the turn of the century. He arranged many African American spirituals. By creating arrangements, he

William Dawson, composer, arranger, and conductor

made it possible for choirs to perform this exciting and expressive music. As choir director at Tuskegee Institute in Alabama, Dawson shared his arrangements with people throughout the United States and Europe.

"Ev'ry Time I Feel the Spirit" is one of William Dawson's best-known choral arrangements. He used strongly syncopated rhythms, contrasts between group and solo singing, and the improvised quality of the choral parts to create an exciting musical setting.

Learn the melody before you listen to a performance of "Ev'ry Time I Feel the Spirit" by the Brazeal Dennard Chorale.

206

EXTENSION

THE ARRANGER

William Dawson (1898–1990)—African American composer, arranger, and trombonist, was born in Anniston, Alabama. He left home at thirteen to enter the Tuskeegee Institute. After graduation he continued his studies at the Horner Institute for Fine Arts in Kansas City, and at the American Conservatory in Chicago, where he received his master's degree. He played first trombone with the Chicago Civic Orchestra before returning to Tuskeegee as choir director. Dawson was well known as a composer and arranger. Among his own compositions is the three-movement *Negro Folk Symphony*.

Key: E♭ major   **Starting Pitch: E♭**   **Scale Tones:** *do re mi so la do¹*

Perform the melody by singing it or playing it on keyboard or bells.

05:41

Ev'ry Time I Feel the Spirit

African American Spiritual

Ev - 'ry time I___feel the spi - rit___Mov - in' in my heart. I will pray; Yes; ev-'ry

time I___feel the spi - rit___Mov - in' in my heart_ I will pray.___

Listen to the Brazeal Dennard Chorale perform "Ev'ry Time I Feel the Spirit."

"Ev'ry Time I Feel the Spirit"

The Brazeal Dennard Chorale of Detroit, Michigan, specializes in performing music by African American composers and arrangers. Named after its conductor, the group has performed many concerts in the Detroit area as well as in Michigan and Ohio.

the Brazeal Dennard Chorale. Mr. Dennard is at the lower right.

207

WESTERN MUSICAL STYLES

- Perform the melody of "Ev'ry Time I Feel the Spirit" by singing it or playing it on keyboard or bells.
- Listen to the recording.
- Discuss the information on the Brazeal Dennard Chorale.
- Summarize the information on arranging a melody.

General Characteristics

1. Folk style is characterized by simple melody, harmony, and phrasing
2. Rhythms sometimes very syncopated, as in "Ev'ry Time I Feel the Spirit"

Form Strophic (same music, different words)

Tone Color Choral ensemble of soprano, alto, tenor, and bass

MORE MUSIC TEACHING IDEAS

Have the students:
1. Compare "Ev'ry Time I Feel the Spirit" with other folk songs and spirituals ("Run Joe," p. 10).
2. Listen to other selections in a folk or spiritual style.
3. Analyze popular music of today and identify characteristics similar to those in "Ev'ry Time I Feel the Spirit." (answers will vary)

You may wish to use this selection in conjunction with:
European-Western Styles, pp. 16–17
Major and Minor in Two Styles, pp. 24–29

CURRICULUM CONNECTION: SOCIAL STUDIES

The spiritual—is a type of folk song that is usually religious. Developed by African American slaves, spirituals are songs of yearning. Spirituals are characterized by variations in meter and intonation, and sometimes by the use of call-and-response patterns. Some spirituals are sorrow songs ("Nobody Knows the Trouble I've Seen") or shouts ("Give me that Old-Time Religion). The first spiritual to be published was "Roll, Jordan, Roll" in 1867. However, it was not until the tour of the Fisk Jubilee Singers in 1871 that the world really became familiar with this music.

MUSIC OF THE WORLD'S CULTURES

MUSIC OF THE WORLD'S CULTURES

208

209

MUSIC OF THE WORLD'S CULTURES

Focus: Cultures of the World Interact

Objectives
To identify and define the combining of characteristics of different cultures
To identify the presence of different cultures in music and architecture
To play accompaniments to music combining the characteristics of different cultures

Materials
Recordings: *Kogoklaras*
"Come On Baby Dance with Me"
Guitar or keyboard
Drumsticks or other percussion instruments

1 SETTING THE STAGE
Discuss the text at the top of the page. (Emphasize that culture is the product of the people of a society.)

2 TEACHING THE LESSON
1. Identify characteristics of different cultures. Have the students examine and describe the Western and Egyptian influences in the architectural example. (Western: use of steel and glass; Egyptian: influence of the pyramid.)

THE INFLUENCE OF WORLD CULTURES

Musicians, dancers, authors, architects, and sculptors get their ideas from many different sources. They are often influenced by the cultural traditions of other countries.

Sometimes the characteristics of other cultures are obvious. At other times cultural influences may be more difficult to identify. The College Life Insurance headquarters buildings have characteristics of contemporary styles and the styles of ancient Egypt.

- Identify the contemporary characteristics of these buildings. use of steel and glass
- Identify the ancient Egyptian characteristics. pyramid shape

Left, the pyramids at Giza, Egypt. Below, the College Life Insurance Headquarters, Indianapolis, Indiana.

210

Mixing Musical Cultures

In this first section you will listen to music that mixes the characteristics of music of the United States with characteristics of the music of another culture. Some ways musicians do this are to combine instruments, rhythm, melodies, or harmonies of both cultures.

Kogoklaras (kō-gō-klä′ räs) is one example of this mix. It combines characteristics of Indonesian music and music of the United States.

Right and below, dancers from the island of Bali, Indonesia. The dancers must practice for years to master these difficult techniques.

Listen and identify musical characteristics of Indonesia and the United States. Indonesian instruments U.S.: prepared piano

 Kogoklaras, by Vincent McDermott

211

2. Introduce aspects of different musical cultures. Have the students discuss how musical compositions can also merge different ideas together to create something new.

3. Listen to identify aspects of different musical cultures. Have the students:
• Identify characteristics of the Indonesian and Western musical cultures while listening to *Kogoklaras*. (Indonesia: Indonesian instruments; U.S.: prepared piano)
• Discuss how effectively the musical traditions of these two cultures are merged: "Is the composition musically interesting?"

MUSIC OF THE WORLD'S CULTURES

4. Discuss the influence on Western music of other music. Have the students:
• Discuss the text at the top of the page.
• Listen for characteristics of Indian music and music of the United States in "Come On Baby Dance with Me."

5. Introduce the accompaniment to "Come On Baby Dance with Me." Have the students:
• Practice the rhythm on percussion instruments.
• Read and identify the notes of the chord.
• Practice the chords on guitar or keyboard.
• Form two groups and play the rhythm and chords with the recording.
• Respond to the Challenge! by playing the melody or the ostinati with the recording.

Reinforcing the Lesson

Discuss the fact that different cultures have different traditions in general, and different musical traditions in particular. Because of increased interactions between different cultures, musical compositions of one culture can be influenced by the music of other cultures.

3 APPRAISAL

The students should be able to:
1. Verbally define characteristics of architecture and music that combine elements from different cultures.
2. Identify non-Western influences on architecture and music of the United States.
3. Perform an accompaniment accurately on percussion, and keyboard or guitar.

American and Indian Cultures Interact

Other cultures, including that of India, have influenced the music of the United States. Shakti, a musical group from the United States, combines Indian traditional music and instruments with rock style instruments of the United States in "Come On Baby Dance With Me."

• Listen for characteristics of Indian music and music of the United States.

 "Come On Baby Dance With Me," performed by Shakti

You can learn these instrumental parts to perform accompaniments to "Come On Baby Dance With Me."

• Practice each part before performing with the recording.

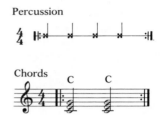

• Form groups. One group should play the percussion part with drumsticks or other percussion instruments. The other group should play the chords on guitar or keyboard.

CHALLENGE Try playing these melodic patterns to "Come On Baby Dance With Me."

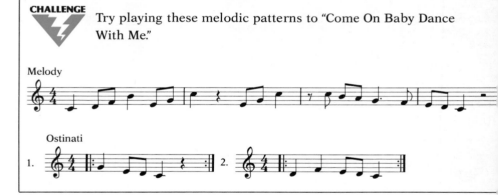

212

EXTENSION

MORE MUSIC TEACHING IDEAS

Have the students identify elements from other cultures, other than architecture, that exist in our environment. (Clothing and food are evident.)

THE MUSIC OF INDIA

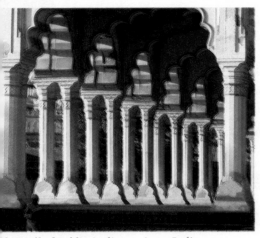

The Hall of Public Audience, Agra, India

"Come On Baby Dance With Me" is a combination of Indian music and music of the United States. Next you will hear Indian concert music. Like Western jazz, Indian concert music is improvised. In some Indian music, one pitch, called a *drone*, is repeated in such a way that it is sounding continuously. This drone pitch provides a background for the creation and performance of rhythmic and melodic patterns. In *Madhu Kauns*, (mä′dōō käns), the pitch D-flat (the black key to the left of D on the keyboard) is repeated as the drone.

CD6:3

Listen for the D-flat drone in *Madhu Kauns*.

 Madhu Kauns

Play D-flat at the proper time on keyboard or bells as you listen again.

Rhythm patterns in Indian music usually are longer than those in Western music. Instead of two, three, or four beats to a group, Indian rhythm patterns can have ten, twelve, fourteen, or sixteen beats. These patterns are repeated and used as a basis for improvisation.

Perform the steady beat on percussion instruments with *Madhu Kauns*.
Next play the D-flat drone and the steady beat with the recording.

 CHALLENGE Try playing this rhythm pattern to *Madhu Kauns*.

Right hand
Left hand

213

MUSIC OF THE WORLD'S CULTURES

Focus: The Music of India

Objectives
To develop knowledge of repetition and tone color in Indian music
To introduce the sitar
To play music in an Indian style

Materials
Recordings: "Floe"
          Madhu Kauns
Bells or keyboard
Drumsticks, drums, or other unpitched percussion instruments

Vocabulary
Drone, sitar

1 SETTING THE STAGE
Review "Floe," page 127, and remind students that Philip Glass was influenced by the use of repetition in Indian classical music.

2 TEACHING THE LESSON
1. Introduce India and repetition as found in Indian music. Have the students:
• Discuss repetition in Indian music as presented in the text.
• Listen to *Madhu Kauns* and indicate the repeated pitch, D-flat, by raising their hands when they hear that pitch.
2. Perform the drone pitch and rhythm of Indian music. Have the students:
• Play D-flat on keyboard or bells with the recording.
• Discuss the information on rhythm patterns in Indian music.

- Perform the steady beat on percussion instruments with *Madhu Kauns*.
- Form two groups to practice and perform the steady beat and the D-flat drone pitch using appropriate instruments.
- Perform with the recording.
- Respond to the Challenge! by playing the rhythm pattern with the recording.

3. Introduce and listen to the sitar.
Have the students:
- Discuss the text and picture of the sitar.
- Listen to the sound of the sitar in *Madhu Kauns*.

Reinforcing the Lesson
Discuss traditional Indian music and its use of repetition.

3 | **APPRAISAL**

The students should be able to:
1. Distinguish repetition of rhythm and drone pitch in Indian music.
2. Identify and describe the sitar.
3. Perform rhythm and drone pitches to Indian music accurately.

CD6:3 **Tone Colors in the Music of India**

The melody of *Madhu Kauns* is performed on a *sitar* (si' tär). The sitar is a twenty-six-stringed instrument somewhat like a lute. The performer uses six of these strings to play a melody. The rest of the strings vibrate when the melody is played, resulting in a continuous layer of sound.

Top, girls from northern India. Above, Ravi Shankar (center), a world-famous sitar player. The other performers in his ensemble play the tambura (right), a stringed instrument that produces the drone pitches, and the tabla (left), drums.

- Listen again to *Madhu Kauns* and focus on the sound of the sitar.

 Madhu Kauns (excerpt)

The sitar melodies combine with the drone pitch and repeated rhythms played on hand drums to give Indian music its distinctive sound.

The traditional music of India is performed in concert settings. Members of an Indian audience are familiar with the repeated rhythms. As they listen they frequently move their hands silently in time to the rhythm. How is this different from the way an audience in the United States might respond? applause, shouts of "Bravo!" and so on

214

E X T E N S I O N

MORE MUSIC TEACHING IDEAS
Have the students:
1. Discuss the reaction of audiences in the United States to different types of musical events, such as orchestral concerts, music videos, school assemblies, and so on.
2. Identify the use of repetition in familiar music compositions.
3. Find compositions in Western music that use the sitar, for example, music of the Beatles from the mid-1960s.

CURRICULUM CONNECTION: SOCIAL STUDIES
India—a large country in southern Asia. It is the second largest country in the world in population. India has one of the great ancient civilizations, dating back to 2500 B.C. Its total present-day area is about 1,246,880 square miles, a little more than one-third the size of the forty-eight contiguous United States. Its capital city is New Delhi.

Xylophone ensembles are popular in many parts of Africa. These performers are members of the Senufo tribe from the Ivory Coast.

MUSIC OF MALI

In the African nation of Mali, *xylophone ensembles* frequently perform complex rhythmic and melodic patterns. Xylophones in an ensemble can vary. Sometimes other instruments perform with the xylophones, for example, guitar, metal clappers, drums, or voice.

Musicians in a xylophone ensemble perform rhythms in several different ways. They can repeat just one rhythm pattern or alternate between patterns. They can echo a pattern that another musician has just played or create new patterns.

Listen to *Kondawele*, a piece from Mali.

 Kondawele (excerpt)

You can use these rhythms to create a percussion ensemble in the style of those found in Mali.

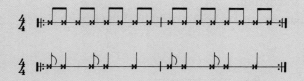

Perform both lines of rhythm. Use different melodic and percussion instruments for each line.

Notice how the sound of your ensemble changes when you use different instruments. Try other combinations of instruments.

215

EXTENSION

CURRICULUM CONNECTION: SOCIAL STUDIES

Mali—a large republic in western Africa. Half of Mali is covered by the Sahara desert. The rest of the country is rolling grassland. During the Middle Ages areas of present-day Mali formed part of three great black empires that controlled important African trade routes. In this period the city of Timbuktu flourished as a center of wealth and learning. In the late nineteenth century what is now Mali became a French colony known as French Sudan. When it gained complete independence in 1960, French Sudan changed its name to the Republic of Mali. Mali is about 478,000 square miles in area. Its capital city is Bamako.

MUSIC OF THE WORLD'S CULTURES

Focus: The Music of Mali

Objectives
To develop knowledge of instruments and tone colors in the music of Mali
To perform in a percussion ensemble similar to those found in Mali
To distinguish tone color changes in a percussion instrument ensemble

Materials
Recording: *Kondawele* (excerpt)
Orff instruments, bells, or other melodic percussion objects (pans, pan lids, metal objects, and so on)
Drumsticks, drums, or other rhythmic percussion objects

Vocabulary
Xylophone ensemble

1 SETTING THE STAGE
Introduce Mali, xylophone, and xylophone ensemble. Have the students discuss the text at the top of the page and the instruments in the picture. Then have them listen to *Kondawele*.

2 TEACHING THE LESSON
1. Play percussion instruments in an ensemble. Have the students:
• Identify melodic (pitched) and rhythmic (non-pitched) percussion instruments.
• Read the rhythmic notation for each line, saying the note values but not playing them.
• Practice the rhythm of each line on melodic, then rhythmic, percussion instruments.
• Form two groups with a combination of melodic and rhythmic percussion instruments to each line. Perform both lines at the same time.

2. Identify and discuss changing the ensemble sound. Have the students:
• Recognize and use words to describe the changes in sound when different combinations of instruments perform. (brighter, darker, light, heavy, and so on)

Reinforcing the Lesson
Summarize and discuss rhythmic and tonal characteristics of music from Mali.

3 APPRAISAL
The students should be able to:
1. Perform rhythm patterns characteristic of the music of Mali accurately in a percussion instrument ensemble.
2. Recognize tone color changes in performances of a percussion ensemble.

MUSIC OF THE WORLD'S CULTURES

Focus: Music of Gambia and Zimbabwe

Objectives

To experience instrumental and vocal tone colors of the music of Gambia and Zimbabwe

To listen to the kora and mbira

To perform a rhythmic accompaniment to Zimbabwean music

Materials

Recordings: *Kelefa ba*
          Cedo
          Chigamba

Bells or keyboard

Unpitched percussion instruments

Vocabulary

Kora, griot, mbira

1 SETTING THE STAGE

Tell the students they will be learning about two kinds of African music.

2 TEACHING THE LESSON

1. Examine the rhythmic complexity of *Kelefa ba*. Have the students:

• Discuss the text.

• Listen to *Kelefa ba* and recognize the changing rhythmic complexity as the number of parts is varied.

• Practice the three rhythm patterns.

• Form three groups and perform two of the patterns together, then all three.

• Perform *Kelefa ba,* paying attention to the rhythmic changes.

The Sounds of Gambia

Rhythmic variety is characteristic of traditional music from the African country of Gambia. *Kelefa ba* (ke-le′ fä bä) is an example of this style of music. Each of its rhythm parts is different from the others. When they are performed together, the result is a rhythmically complex and constantly changing musical sound.

• Listen to *Kelefa ba* to hear this rhythmic variety.

Kelefa ba

• Practice each of these rhythm patterns on unpitched percussion instruments.

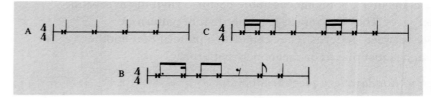

• Compare the rhythm patterns. Which has mostly short note values? Mostly long note values?

• Form three groups. Listen to the changing rhythmic sound as two groups perform two of the rhythm patterns at the same time. Have the third group add the third part.

• Perform the rhythm patterns with the recording of *Kelefa ba.* Listen for the changes in rhythm.

• Practice this melodic pattern on keyboard or bells. Play it with *Kelefa ba.*

• Form four groups to perform the three rhythm patterns and the melodic pattern with *Kelefa ba.*

216

Instrumental and Vocal Sounds of Gambia

Some Gambian music is performed by a solo voice and a stringed instrument called a *kora* (kô' rä). The kora, a kind of harp-lute, comes in several sizes with from five to twenty-one strings. A small metal disk with metal rings attached produces a rasping sound when the performer plucks or strums the strings.

Throughout West Africa, professional musicians are called *griots* (grē' ō). In Gambia, griots are very important, because one of their roles is to record the history of the Gambian people. They pass this history on through their music. In contrast, people of Western cultures write books to record their history. The griots compose songs to comment on historical events.

Listen to *Cedo* (kā' dō), a Gambian history, to hear the tone color of the kora.

🎵 *Cedo*

Koras are made in many sizes, from small (left) to large (below). *Cedo* is played on a large kora.

217

CD6:6

MUSIC OF THE WORLD'S CULTURES

2. Learn and perform an accompaniment to *Kelefa ba*. Have the students:
• Practice the melodic pattern on keyboard or bells.
• Form four groups, three to play the rhythm patterns and one to play the melodic pattern.
• Perform the rhythm patterns, then the melodic pattern, with the recording.
• Perform both with the recording.

3. Introduce and discuss the kora and griots. Have the students:
• Discuss the kora, and speculate on what it might sound like.
• Discuss griots and their role in Gambian society and relate this to folk songs that tell stories in the United States.
• Listen to and distinguish the buzzing sound of the kora in *Cedo*.

CURRICULUM CONNECTION: SOCIAL STUDIES

Gambia—a small country in western Africa that lies along the banks of the Gambia River, extending inland from the Atlantic Ocean for about two hundred miles. Once a British crown colony, Gambia gained its independence in 1965 and became a republic in 1970. Gambia is only about four thousand square miles in area, approximately twice the size of the state of Delaware. Its capital is Banjul.

MUSIC OF THE WORLD'S CULTURES

4. Listen to the use of the voice in Gambian music. Have the students:
• Listen and distinguish the qualities of the voice singing in *Cedo*.
• Summarize the sound qualities of the voice in the Gambian piece *Cedo*.
5. Introduce music of Zimbabwe and examine how the voice is used in *Chigamba*. Have the students:
• Discuss the material on Zimbabwe and the voice.
• Listen and distinguish the qualities of the voice singing in *Chigamba*.
• Summarize the sound qualities of the voice in the Zimbabwean piece *Chigamba*.
• Compare the pieces *Cedo* and *Chigamba* for similarities and differences.

A singer performs the melody in *Cedo*.

• Listen to *Cedo* again. Choose the words that best describe the quality of the voice: light or heavy, rough or smooth, strong or weak.

Cedo

In this Ivory Coast village, boys of the Yaou tribe listen as a storyteller recounts a tribal legend.

Instrumental and Vocal Sounds of Zimbabwe

Zimbabwe, also an African country, is about thirty-five hundred miles southwest of Gambia. In music from Gambia, stringed instruments are used, while in Zimbabwe, the *mbira* (m-bē´ rä), or thumb piano, is important.

The woman who sings the piece you are about to hear is named Stella Rambisai Chiweshe (stel´ lä räm-bē-sä´ ē chē´wä-shä). She is known as the "Queen of Mbira." Like *Cedo*, *Chigamba* (chē-gäm´ bä) has the feeling of improvisation, however, the tone colors of the instrumental accompaniments are very different.

• Listen to *Chigamba* and choose the words that best describe the quality of the voice: light or heavy, rough or smooth, strong or weak.

 Chigamba (excerpt)

218

The mbira is a melodic instrument. It has a wooden frame with metal tongs attached. The performer plays the mbira by pulling down or plucking each tong, causing it to vibrate. A dried gourd serves to amplify the sound, much like the body of a guitar. In other African cultures, the mbira is called the *sansa*, *likembe*, *budongo*, or *kalimba*.

In Zimbabwe, the mbira is used in many different musical ways. It can be used as a solo instrument to express personal feelings. Frequently it is used in religious settings. At other times it accompanies songs of love or politics.

Chigamba features the mbira and voice. Both perform variations of the same melody.

The mbira is found in many African cultures. Recently, it has become popular in Western musical styles.

Practice playing or singing this variation of the melody heard in *Chigamba*, then listen to the recording again and listen for it in its many forms.

Practice this rhythm accompaniment to *Chigamba*, then play it with the recording.

The mbira also has been used in American music. Both jazz and popular music groups have included its traditional sounds in a new context. With the MIDI, the sound of the mbira is readily available for use as a tone color in modern composition.

219

MUSIC OF THE WORLD'S CULTURES

6. Introduce the mbira and its use in Zimbabwean music. Have the students:
• Examine the picture and discuss the material on the role of the mbira in Zimbabwean music.
• Discuss using music for self-expression.
7. Listen to and perform music from Zimbabwe. Have the students:
• Learn and practice the melody heard in *Chigamba* on keyboard or bells.
• Identify the melody and its variations while listening to the recording of *Chigamba*.
• Practice the rhythmic accompaniment.
• Perform the rhythmic accompaniment to *Chigamba* while listening once more to the recording.
• Discuss the information on the use of the mbira in modern composition.

3 APPRAISAL

The students should be able to:
1. Identify and describe the sound qualities of the voice in songs from Gambia and Zimbabwe.
2. Identify and describe the kora and mbira, and to recognize their tone colors.
3. Perform a rhythmic accompaniment to Zimbabwean music accurately.

MORE MUSIC TEACHING IDEAS

Have the students:
1. Distinguish different uses of the voice in music performed in the United States.
2. Identify other cultures in which history is passed down through music.

CURRICULUM CONNECTION: SOCIAL STUDIES

Zimbabwe—an independent republic in southeast Africa. Zimbabwe's beautiful scenery includes the famous Victoria Falls on the Zambezi River along its northern border. From the 1890s until the 1960s Zimbabwe, then called Rhodesia, was under British Rule. In 1965 the Rhodesian government declared its independence from Great Britain, the first colony to do so since the American colonies declared their independence in 1776. The Rhodesian government underwent many changes over the next fifteen years. In 1980 Great Britain recognized the country's independence, and Rhodesia's name was officially changed to Zimbabwe.

MUSIC OF THE WORLD'S CULTURES

Focus: The Music of Turkey

Objectives
To develop knowledge of instruments and tone colors in Turkish music
To introduce the ney

Materials
Recording: *Taksim in Mode Segah*
Keyboard, recorder, or bells

Vocabulary
Ney, ornaments

1 SETTING THE STAGE

Listen to *Taksim in Mode Segah* to experience the scale and the sound of the ney.

2 TEACHING THE LESSON

1. Introduce Turkey and discuss the ney. Have the students:
• Examine and discuss the text and the picture of the ney.
• Discuss Turkey and the Middle East.
2. Introduce a scale from Turkey. Have the students:
• Play the scale shown on bells, keyboard, or recorder.
• Listen again to *Taksim in Mode Segah,* which is based on this scale.
• Recognize the sound of the ney.

THE MUSIC OF TURKEY

The *ney* (nā) is a flutelike wind instrument used in the music of Turkey and other countries of the Middle East. It is a hollow cane tube with six finger holes in front and one in back. Unlike the flute, which is held horizontally, the ney is held at an angle when it is played.

The classical music of Turkey is performed on the ney. In this music the performer frequently performs long solos. Sometimes a ney performance includes drums and stringed instruments. The ney is associated with a religious sect, and is played during certain religious services.

The ney is popular throughout the Middle East.

• Play this Turkish scale on keyboard, recorder, or bells. (B-sharp and C are the same key on a keyboard.)

• Listen to *Taksim* (täk′ sim), or improvisation, *in Mode Segah*. It is performed on the ney. This piece is based on the scale you just played, which is called mode *segah* (sā′ gä).

 Taksim in Mode Segah

220

E X T E N S I O N

The ney performer plays along melodic lines that are frequently improvised, or made up on the spot. Single tones of the scale are used as centers around which melodies are developed. In this example, each white note is the center of a melody, or tonal center.

Many times a performer uses *ornaments* with a melody. **Ornaments** are added notes that decorate a basic melody.

• Listen to *Taksim in Mode Segah* again. Try to hear each melodic line and its tonal center. Notice the ornaments the performer adds to the melody, and the long pauses.

Turkey has long been a meeting place between Europe and Asia. These ruins of a fortification are on the Mediterranean coast at Üçagiz near Kale.

221

3. Recognize the ney and its music. Have the students:
• Discuss music performed on the ney. Examine the notation and identify the center tones. (Center tones are those tones on which a performer bases a melodic improvisation. In this example center tones are shown as whole notes.)
• Discuss ornaments and their relationship to music. (An ornament is a form of decoration not basic to an object; in music, added notes ornament a melody or musical idea).
• Listen for ornaments in *Taksim in Mode Segah*. Emphasize the presence of center tones, long pauses, and ornaments in additional listenings.

Reinforcing the Lesson
Summarize the use of the ney in Turkish music.

3 **APPRAISAL**
The students should be able to:
1. Identify and describe the ney, a Turkish woodwind instrument.
2. Listen to and identify tone colors in Turkish music.

CURRICULUM CONNECTION: SOCIAL STUDIES

Turkey—located in both western Asia and southeastern Europe. European Turkey and Asian Turkey are separated by a strait called the Bosporus. Turkey is approximately three hundred thousand square miles in area, which is slightly larger than the state of Texas. Its capital city is Ankara.

MUSIC OF THE WORLD'S CULTURES

Focus: The Music of Japan

Objective
To develop knowledge of instruments and tone colors in Japanese music

Materials
Recording: *Sambaso*

Vocabulary
Nagauta, kabuki, o-tsuzumi, ko-tsuzumi, taiko, shamisen, bue

1 SETTING THE STAGE

Introduce Japan, the nagauta ensemble, and its instruments. Have the students discuss the text at the top of the page.

2 TEACHING THE LESSON

1. Introduce the percussion instruments of the nagauta ensemble. Have the students recognize the effect on pitch when the performer squeezes the laces on the ko-tsuzumi (pitch changes).
2. Introduce the sounds of a nagauta ensemble. Have the students:
• Discuss the shamisen and the bue.
• Listen to the recording of *Sambaso* with call numbers. Read the description by each number as it is called. Listen for percussion sounds in the music. Listen for the sounds of the shamisen and bue.

Reinforcing the Lesson

Compare the nagauta ensemble to the xylophone ensembles of Mali, page 215. Contrast the number and kinds of instruments and the circumstances in which each ensemble would perform.

CD6:9 THE MUSIC OF JAPAN

In Japan the *nagauta* (nä′ gä-ōō-tä) ensemble is used to accompany a popular form of operalike drama called *kabuki* (kä′ bōō-kē). The nagauta ensemble is similar to the xylophone ensemble of Mali in that it contains percussion instruments as well as pitched instruments. However, the nagauta ensemble performs only in very formal concert settings to accompany the kabuki plays.

The nagauta ensemble contains three different drums: the *o-tsuzumi* (ō′ tsōō-zōō-mē), the *ko-tsuzumi* (kō′ tsōō-zōō-mē), and the *taiko* (tī′ kō). The o-tsuzumi and ko-tsuzumi are doubleheaded laced drums. The player holds the drum on the shoulder and plays it with the other hand. The performer can make the pitch of the ko-tsuzumi high or lower by squeezing the laces while striking the head of the drum. The taiko also is double headed and laced, but is hung from a frame and played with sticks.
The nagauta ensemble also includes two pitched instruments. One is a stringed instrument, the *shamisen* (shä′ mē-sen), and the other, the *bue* (bōō′ ā), is a wind instrument.

Above, the nagauta To-On-Kai in performance. In the front row are one bue, three o-tsuzumi or ko-tsuzumi, and one taiko. The shamisen players in the upper row are awaiting their turn.

• Listen to *Sambaso* (säm′ bä-sō). Follow the description of the music.

 Sambaso

1. Ko-tsuzumi and taiko are heard; voice; drum calls; music becomes faster.
2. Vocal solo; drum calls are heard.
3. The bue is heard, along with the shamisen.
4. The shamisen presents an ascending pattern, then a melodic pattern.
5. Shamisen and bue continue melody; music gradually becomes faster.
6. Bue and drum calls are heard.

222

E X T E N S I O N

CURRICULUM CONNECTION: SOCIAL STUDIES

Japan—is an island country located off the northeast coast of Asia. Four large islands and thousands of smaller islands make up the country. The four main islands are Hokkaido, Honshu, Kyushu, and Shikoku. Japanese culture dates back many thousands of years. One of the great industrial nations of the world, Japan is approximately 141,000 square miles in area. Its capital is Tokyo.

MUSIC OF THE WORLD'S CULTURES

The students should be able to:
1. Identify the nagauta of Japan.
2. Identify and describe instruments in the nagauta ensemble.

Some scenes of Japan. Opposite page, umbrellas drying after painting at a factory. This page, top, a shamisen player. Above, Himeji Castle, near Osaka, the most famous medieval Japanese castle. Left, a festival scene at Sapporo, on Hokkaido island.

223

MUSIC OF THE WORLD'S CULTURES

Focus: The Music of Indonesia

Objectives
To develop knowledge of instruments and tone colors in Indonesian music
To introduce the gamelan
To play music in a gamelan style

Materials
Recording: Gênding KÊMBANG MARA
Unpitched percussion instruments
Orff instruments, bells, handbells, keyboard, or other pitched percussion objects

Vocabulary
Gamelan

1 SETTING THE STAGE

Discuss the text at the top of the page and the instruments in the photo.

2 TEACHING THE LESSON

1. Introduce Indonesia, gamelan, and gamelan ensemble. Have the students:
• Discuss the information on the gamelan.
2. Perform rhythms in gamelan style. Have the students:
• Discuss sharing rhythms. (Sharing is used here to specify notes on the same notation line which a performer omits. These notes are then performed, or shared, by another performer, either with the same or with a different tone color.)
• Read the rhythmic notation, saying the note values without clapping them.
• Clap the rhythm.
• Identify partners and decide which notes will be shared.

The Sound of the Gamelan

You heard a combination of Indonesian music and the music of the United States in *Kogoklaras* on page 211. This section concentrates on Indonesian sound alone.

The *gamelan* (gä' me-län) is the traditional instrumental ensemble of Indonesia. The ensemble consists of gongs and metallophones, rhythmic drums, flute, and stringed instruments. Some of the gongs play melodies, and others set the meter of the music.

A gamelan from Bali, Indonesia, with gongs, metallophones, and drums. The flute player is near the upper right-hand corner.

In Indonesia, the gamelan accompanies dance, drama, and puppet theatre. Although other types of musical ensembles are common in Indonesia, the gamelan is the most important. There are many different kinds of gamelans, and each kind uses a slightly different set of pitches. Some ensembles perform with five pitches and some use seven. Others use as few as four.

The sound of each instrument in the gamelan has a distinctive quality. As performers repeat rhythmic patterns, the sound joins with others to create layers of sound.

224

EXTENSION

CURRICULUM CONNECTION: SOCIAL STUDIES

Indonesia—a country of more than three thousand islands located in the southwestern Pacific Ocean. The main islands include Sumatra, Java, and Celebes. Indonesia is approximately 580,000 square miles in area, virtually the same size as Alaska. Its capital city is Jakarta.

Perform in Gamelan Style

One type of gamelan rhythm develops when the musicians read the same line of rhythm. Instead of performing all of the notes, however, they alternate with other ensemble members to share the notes of the rhythm pattern. The interlocking sounds of their instruments creates an interesting rhythmic and melodic quality.

- Clap this gamelan rhythm.

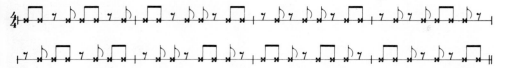

- Perform in gamelan style with a partner:

  1. Each of you should clap or pat every *other* note of the rhythm pattern. Listen closely to the change in the sound of the rhythm as you alternate.
  2. You and your partner should each choose an unpitched percussion instrument.
  3. Perform the rhythm pattern on percussion instruments. Alternate the notes.

  Melodic patterns on pitched instruments also are part of gamelan music. Some patterns are based on a four-pitch scale:

- Perform a two-pitch gamelan-style melodic pattern with a partner:

  1. Each of you should choose one pitch on a bell set, handbell set, xylophone, keyboard, or any pitched object.
  2. With your partner, decide which pitch will be played first.
  3. Perform the rhythm pattern at the top of the page. Alternate with your partner so that you each play every other note. Listen closely to the change in the sounds as you alternate the two pitches.

225

- Perform, listening closely to the change in sound from when one person clapped the entire rhythm.
- Share the rhythm on percussion instruments.

3. Introduce the four-note scale and perform melodic patterns in gamelan style. Have the students:
- Examine and discuss the four-note scale. (Emphasize the difference from our traditional twelve-pitch scale and the lack of half steps.)
- Identify a partner and share rhythms on pitched percussion instruments.
- Perform the rhythms, listening closely to the change in sound.

4. Create new gamelan-style sounds. Have the students:
- Choose pitched and unpitched instruments.
- Compose and perform additional rhythm patterns on these instruments.

Reinforcing the Lesson

Have the students:
1. Preview Gênding KÊMBANG MARA on page 226 to hear the layering of sounds in gamelan music.
2. Compare the use of different scales and instruments in the music of Indonesia and Turkey, pages 220–221.

3 APPRAISAL

The students should be able to:
1. Identify and describe the gamelan, an instrumental ensemble from Indonesia.
2. Perform accurately on percussion instruments in gamelan style.

MORE MUSIC TEACHING IDEAS

Have the students find examples of percussion and wind instruments from other countries.

MUSIC OF THE WORLD'S CULTURES

Focus: A Western Composer Uses Non-Western Ideas

Objectives
To introduce sources of musical ideas
To become familiar with the composer Claude Debussy and how he used ideas inspired by gamelan music
To perform a gamelan melody using stratification
To listen to melodic stratification in gamelan music
To listen to non-Western influences in Western music

Materials
Recordings: *Gênding KÊMBANG MARA*
             "Pagodes"
Bells or keyboard

Vocabulary
Stratification, impressionism

1 SETTING THE STAGE
Review the two-pitch pattern from the previous lesson.

2 TEACHING THE LESSON

1. Introduce borrowing musical ideas and melodic stratification. Have the students:
• Discuss borrowing musical ideas. (This practice is of long standing. Composers borrow not only from other sources but also from some of their own compositions. This practice was especially common prior to the mid-nineteenth century.)
• Discuss stratification.

BORROWING MUSICAL IDEAS

One composer who was deeply influenced by music of another culture was Claude Debussy (klôd də-byu-see). One of the aspects of Indonesian music that interested Debussy was the layering of sound. Stratification occurs when layers of melody or sound are heard.

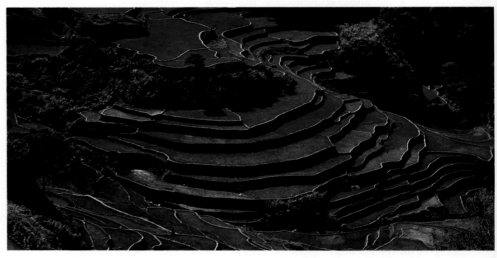

Stratification occurs not only in music but also in nature. These layered rice terraces are on Luzon, in the Philippines.

• Practice this melody on keyboard or bells.

• Form several groups and perform the melody in stratification. All start at the same time, but each group performs the melody at a different tempo and in different octaves. This creates different layers of sound.

The melody you just performed is similar to part of the melody found in *Gêndhing KÊMBANG MARA* (gen-ding´ kem-bang´ mä´ rä), gamelan music from the city of Solo on the island of Java, Indonesia.

• Listen to *Gêndhing KÊMBANG MARA*.

 Gêndhing KÊMBANG MARA (excerpt)

226

CLAUDE DEBUSSY

Claude Debussy (1862–1918) was one of the greatest French composers. Debussy was born in a suburb of Paris and was encouraged to play the piano at an early age. He entered the Paris Conservatory when he was eleven and studied there for eleven years. Debussy created a musical style known as *impressionism*. During his years in Paris he became acquainted with impressionist painters such as Claude Monet, whose works brought out the effects of light and color on nature. He created a style of music that used different harmonies and exotic rhythms to evoke delicate and mysterious moods.

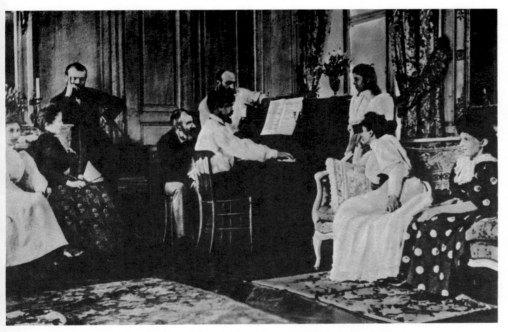

This photo shows the young Debussy playing the piano in a private home in Paris.

227

MUSIC OF THE WORLD'S CULTURES

2. Perform a melody in stratification. Have the students:
- Say the names of the notes without playing the notes.
- Practice the gamelan melody on bells or keyboard.
- Play the gamelan melody together at the same tempo.
- Form two groups with each group performing the melody in a different tempo. (Make the tempos as different as possible the first time they do this.)
- Form three or more groups and perform the melody (each group playing at a different tempo, and at different octaves).

3. Listen to *Gênding KÊMBANG MARA*. Have the students listen to *Gênding KÊMBANG MARA* and identify the melody that they have just performed.

4. Introduce Claude Debussy. Have the students discuss the text. (Emphasize Debussy's classical training at the Paris Conservatory, and his interest in music from another culture.)

5. Introduce "Pagodes." Have the students identify and discuss the gamelan characteristics Debussy used in "Pagodes."

6. Prepare the students for listening to "Pagodes" with call numbers. Have the students listen as you play each numbered

MUSIC OF THE WORLD'S CULTURES

melody below on the piano several times until the students can recognize the melodies when played at random.

Debussy's "Pagodes"

CD6:11 At the international Paris Exposition in 1889, Debussy had the opportunity to hear a gamelan ensemble from Java, one of the Indonesian islands. He was fascinated by the sounds of this exotic music. A different gamelan ensemble performed at the 1900 Paris Exposition. Again Debussy was intrigued by the music. The rhythms and melodies he heard challenged Debussy to include some of their characteristics in his own music.

Debussy wrote "Pagodes" (pä-gôd', "pagodas") in 1904, some years after he had heard the gamelan music that influenced this piano composition. Instead of imitating a gamelan ensemble, he included characteristics of gamelan music. He used scales that were not commonly found in Western music. He changed the rhythms of the melodies and added ornamental pitches to them. He also created layers of sound by having more than one melody sounding at the same time.

- Listen to "Pagodes" to hear how Debussy was influenced by gamelan music. Read the descriptions.

 "Pagodes," by Claude Debussy

A Section
1. Low gonglike pitches; melody 1; melody 1 with melody 2 below; altered melody 1 with melody 3 below; short melody 4
2. Altered melody 3, using high and low registers; altered melody 1; tempo slows down slightly

B Section
3. Melody 5; melody 1 reappears in part with melody 6 (very loud)
4. Melody 5 (lower); trills

A Section
   Low gonglike pitches; melody 1; melody 1 with melody 2 below; altered melody 1 with melody 3 below; short melody 4
5. Melody 3, using high and low registers; melody 6 (very loud)

Coda
   Melodies 1, 2, and 6, one after the other, with fast, high notes and low, soft gonglike pitches accompanying, to the end

228

EXTENSION

MORE MUSIC TEACHING IDEAS

Have the students:
1. Create melodies and perform them on bells or keyboard using stratification.
2. Find other examples of musical compositions that contain mixtures of different musical cultures.

Many peoples of the Far East have built pagodas. Left, below, and bottom, Borobudur Pagoda, on the island of Java, Indonesia

Left, Schwedagon Pagoda, in Rangoon, Burma

229

MUSIC OF THE WORLD'S CULTURES

7. Listen to the gamelan characteristics in "*Pagodes.*" Have the students listen to the recording of "*Pagodes*" with call numbers. Read each description as each number is called. Listen for melodic stratification and other characteristics of gamelan music.

Reinforcing the Lesson

Discuss the concept of borrowing non-Western musical ideas for use in Western music. (You may wish to mention other composers who incorporated nontraditional ideas into their music, such as Bartók, Schoenberg, Stravinsky, Varèse, and other composers active after World War I.)

3 APPRAISAL

The students should be able to:
1. Identify Claude Debussy and explain how he used gamelan techniques in his music.
2. Perform a gamelan melody accurately on bells or keyboard.
3. Recognize stratification in gamelan music and in music by Claude Debussy.
4. Define melodic stratification.

MUSIC OF THE WORLD'S CULTURES

LOOKING BACK

Objective
To review the skills and concepts taught in Music of the World's Cultures

Materials
Recording: Looking Back
Percussion instruments
Copying Master M-1 (optional)

TEACHING THE LESSON

1. Review the skills and concepts taught in Music of the World's Cultures. Have the students:
• Follow the recorded review with pages 230–231, perform the activities, and answer the questions.
• Review their answers.
(You may wish to use Copying Master M-1 at this time.)

LOOKING BACK

See how much you remember.

1. Perform these rhythms from Mali and Indonesia on a percussion instrument with the recording.

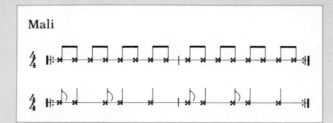

Mali

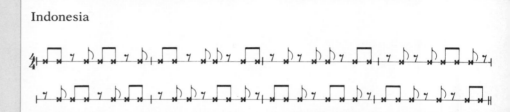

Indonesia

2. Pat the steady beat as you listen to *Madhu Kauns*.

230

3. Listen and identify the country of origin for each musical example.
   a. Japan or Turkey — Japan
   b. India or Mali — Mali
   c. Indonesia or Zimbabwe — Zimbabwe

4. Listen to this excerpt from *Kogoklaras* and identify the two cultures that contributed to this music. Indonesia and U.S.

5. Listen and identify the instruments you hear in these excerpts of music from three different cultures.
   a. xylophone ensemble or ney — xylophone ensemble
   b. kora or gamelan — gamelan
   c. nagauta ensemble or sitar — nagauta ensemble

6. Listen and decide which of these examples contain repetition. yes; no; no

7. Listen to a portion of *Sambaso* and identify the instrument families you hear. strings, woodwinds, percussion

8. Listen to a recording of a gamelan and describe the texture you hear. As performers repeat rhythmic patterns, the sound joins with others to create layers of sound.

9. Listen to a portion of *Cedo* and identify the tone colors in this musical example. Identify the country where you might find this musical style. vocal, kora; Gambia

MUSIC OF THE WORLD'S CULTURES

231

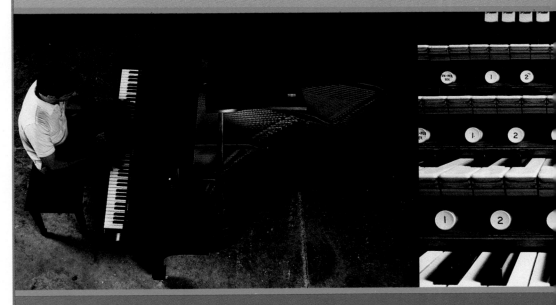

The piano was invented about 1720 and developed into the familiar instrument of today during the first half of the nineteenth century. The pipe organ had its roots in ancient Greece. The electronic organ was invented in the mid-1900s.

Keyboard instruments of today include pianos, organs, and synthesizers, which were developed during the 1960s. Today's synthesizers enable players to produce an almost unlimited variety

232

Detail from *Harpsichord*. Johann Christoph Weigel

of sounds, even the sounds of other instruments. Through rhythm units (drum machines), sequencers (recording devices), and a variety of tone colors, the synthesizer has become more complex.

Keyboard instruments are used by many popular music groups.

* Notice the many sizes and shapes of the keyboards shown here. The arrangement of black and white keys is always the same.

233

KEYBOARDS OF TODAY

Focus: Learning to Play Keyboard Instruments

Objective
To develop performance skills on the keyboard

Materials
Recordings: "Dream of Dreams"
"Harmonic Repetition Montage"
"Twelve-Bar Blues"

Vocabulary
Chord, twelve-bar blues

1 SETTING THE STAGE

Have the students:
* Discuss the information on the keyboard.
* Become familiar with the sizes and shapes of keyboards.

KEYBOARDS OF TODAY

2 TEACHING THE LESSON

1. Introduce learning to play keyboard instruments. Have the students:
• Listen to two selections to hear the sounds of different keyboard instruments.
• Discuss the information on keyboard basics.
• Locate each set of two black keys up and down the keyboard.
• Locate and identify the notes C, D, and E.
• Locate each set of three black keys up and down the keyboard.
• Locate and identify the notes F, G, A, and B.

CD6:28–29

• Listen to these two selections to hear the sounds of different keyboard instruments.

 "Dream of Dreams," by Joe Sample

 "Harmonic Repetition Montage"

The keyboard has sets of white and black keys. Center yourself in front of the keyboard and find each set of *two* black keys up and down the keyboard. C is always the white key to the left, D is the white key in the middle, and E is the white key to the right of the two black keys. Middle C is the C that is closest to the center of the keyboard.

Each set of *three* black keys is a reference point for finding F, G, A, and B. F is always the white key to the left, G and A are the white keys in the middle, and B is the white key to the right of the three black keys.

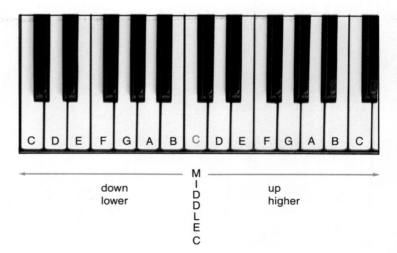

234

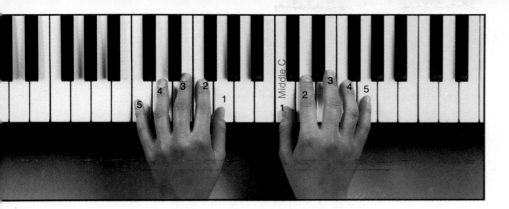

These hands show how the fingers are numbered for the keyboard.   CD6:30
Notice that both thumbs are numbered *1*.

You can learn to play chords on the keyboard. **A chord** consists of
three or more pitches played together. The twelve-bar blues is a
common chord progression, or pattern, used in popular music.

To start you can play one pitch at a time.

Find pitches C, F, and G on your
keyboard. Use the fingers of your
right hand as shown.

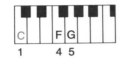
Right hand

Play the following pitches along with the recording of the
twelve-bar blues.

$\frac{4}{4}$ C C C C   C C C C   C C C C   C C C C

    F F F F   F F F F   C C C C   C C C C

    G G G G   F F F F   C C C C   C C C C

 "Twelve-Bar Blues," by Michael Treni

Play the same pitches again with the
twelve-bar blues, this time using the
fingers of your left hand as shown.

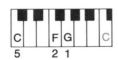
Left hand

235

**2. Introduce finger numbers for both
hands and the chord sequence for the
twelve-bar blues.** Have the students:
• Discuss the information on chords and
the twelve-bar blues.
• Identify the pitches C, F, and G.
• Read and play C, F, and G with the right
hand following the twelve-bar blues sequence. Use proper fingering and play each
pitch for four beats.
• Play the pattern twice with the recording.
(The recording has a four-measure introduction and a coda.)
• Read and play C, F, and G with the left
hand following the twelve-bar blues sequence. Use proper fingering and play each
pitch for four beats.
• Play with the recording.

3. Introduce the C, F, and G chords.
Have the students:
• Understand the meaning of a chord.
• Learn how the notes of a chord are arranged by skips.
• Learn to play the C, F, and G chords.

Learning to Play the C, F, and G Chords

You can play the C chord on the keyboard.
• Start with the left hand and play C with your fifth finger.
  Skip up one white key to the right and use your third finger. You should now be on E with your third finger.
  Skip up another key and use your thumb. You should now be on G with your thumb.
  Play all three notes at the same time.

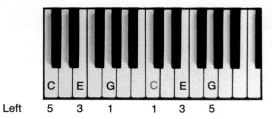

| Left | 5 | 3 | 1 | 1 | 3 | 5 | Right |

You have just learned to form and play the C chord.
• Now play the C chord with your right hand. Your thumb will be on C, your third finger will be on E, and your fifth finger will be on G.

You can play the F chord.
• Start with your left hand.
  Your fifth finger should be on F.
  Skip up one white key to the right. You should be on A with your third finger.
  Skip up another key and use your thumb. You should be on C with your thumb. Play all three notes together.
• Again, try the chord with your right hand, using your first, third, and fifth fingers.

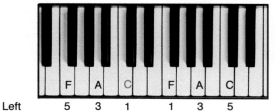

| Left | 5 | 3 | 1 | 1 | 3 | 5 | Right |

236

You can play the G chord.
Start with your left hand.
Your fifth finger should be on G.
Skip up one white key to the right. You should be on B with your third finger.
Skip up another key and use your thumb. You should be on D with your thumb. Play all three notes together.
Again, try the chord with your right hand, using your first, third, and fifth fingers, the same fingers you used for the C and F chords.

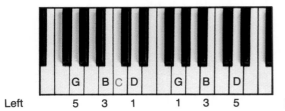

| Left | 5 | 3 | 1 | 1 | 3 | 5 | Right |

Now that you can play C, F, and G chords with either your left or right hand you can play the twelve-bar blues chord progression.

Many musicians play chords from chord charts. The following chord chart shows the 12 measures or bars of the twelve-bar blues. Three slashes after each chord's letter name indicate that the chord is to be played on every beat of each four-beat measure.

Twelve-Bar Blues

$\frac{4}{4}$ C/// C/// C/// C///
F/// F/// C/// C///
G/// F/// C/// C///

Play along with the recording of the twelve-bar blues.

 CHALLENGE Play the twelve-bar blues with both hands.

• Discuss the information on chord charts.
• Practice playing the C, F, and G chords following the twelve-bar blues sequence. Play on every beat of the measure using either the left or right hand.
• Play the pattern twice with the recording. (The recording has a four-measure introduction and a coda.)

Reinforcing the Lesson

Respond to the Challenge! by playing the twelve-bar blues with both hands.

3 APPRAISAL

The student should be able to:
1. Identify sets of two and three black keys on the keyboard.
2. Identify the pitches C, D, E, F, G, A, and B on the keyboard.
3. Read and perform the C, F, and G chords using the twelve-bar blues sequence.

237

KEYBOARDS OF TODAY

Focus: Reading Steps and Skips

Objective
To learn to read and play steps and skips on the keyboard

Vocabulary
Staff, stepwise, skipwise

1 **SETTING THE STAGE**

Review the information on skips, page 236.

2 **TEACHING THE LESSON**

Introduce reading steps and skips at the keyboard. Have the students:
• Discuss the information on reading music at the keyboard.
• Discuss the information on reading steps.
• Read and perform the exercises as indicated.

The pitches on the keyboard are notated on the **staff** as shown in the following diagram. Pitches can be notated either on lines or in spaces.

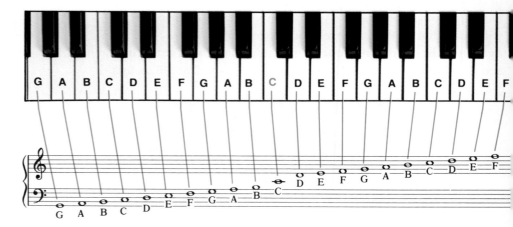

Pitches in the treble clef usually are played with the right hand. Pitches in the bass clef usually are played with the left hand.

Reading Steps

When a melody moves *up or down* on the keyboard from one white key to the next without skipping any notes in between, it is said to move **stepwise**. The steps from one key to the next are notated on the staff as either *line to space* or *space to line*.

• Place the third finger of your left hand on G in the bass clef. Play A, the next note to the right (up), with your second finger. You have moved up a step. Play B, the next note to the right (up), with your thumb. You have moved another step.

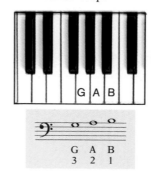

238

Read and play these patterns of steps in the bass clef. Say the names of the notes before you play them and again as you play them. Notice the upward and downward motion of each melody.

F	E	D	E	F	F	G	A	G	F	F	G	A	G	F	E	F
1	2	3	2	1	3	2	1	2	3	3	2	1	2	3	4	3

Place the thumb (finger 1) of your right hand on G in the treble clef. Play A, the next note to the right (up), with your second finger. You have moved up a step. Play B, the next note to the right (up), with your third finger. You have moved up another step.

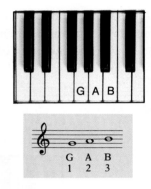

Read and play these patterns of steps in the treble clef. Say the names of the notes before you play them and again as you play them. Notice the upward and downward motion of each melody.

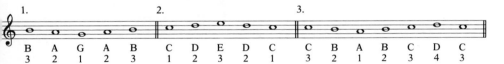

B	A	G	A	B	C	D	E	D	C	C	B	A	B	C	D	C
3	2	1	2	3	1	2	3	2	1	3	2	1	2	3	4	3

239

• Read and play the patterns of steps in the bass clef.
• Read and play the patterns of steps in the treble clef.
• Describe the direction of the step, for example, step up, step down.

KEYBOARDS OF TODAY

- Discuss the information on reading skips.
- Learn to play a broken C chord in the bass clef as indicated.
- Learn to play a broken F chord in the bass clef (using the chart on page 238 if necessary).
- Read and play the practice patterns in the bass clef.
- Learn to play a broken F chord in the treble clef as indicated.
- Learn to play broken C and G chords in the treble clef (using the chart on page 238 if necessary).
- Read and play the practice patterns in the treble clef.
- Learn to play broken C, F, and G chords in both clefs, then create and play practice patterns for each chord (using the chart on page 238 if necessary).
- Describe the direction of the skip, for example, skip up, skip down.

Reinforcing the Lesson

Have the students play C, E, and G together with the left hand to hear the C chord. Then have them play F, A, and C together with the right hand to hear the F chord.

3 APPRAISAL

The students should be able to read and perform melodies containing steps and skips in the bass and treble clefs.

Reading Skips

When a melody moves *up or down* from one note to the next and skips some notes, it is said to move **skipwise**. When you skip one key on the keyboard it is notated on the staff as either *line to line* or *space to space*.

- Play C with the fifth finger of your left hand. Skip a key up to the right and play E with finger 3. Skip another key up to the right and play G with finger 1.

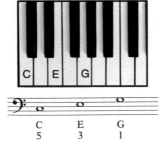

C	E	G
5	3	1

- Read and play these patterns of skips in the bass clef. Say the names of the notes before you play them and again as you play them. Notice the upward and downward motion of each melody.

1.
F	A	C	A	F
5	3	1	3	5

2.
F	D	B	D	F
1	3	5	3	1

- Play F with the first finger of your right hand. Skip a key up to the right and play A with finger 3. Skip another key up to the right and play C with finger 5.

F	A	C
1	3	5

- Read and play these patterns of skips in the treble clef. Say the names of the notes before you play them and again as you play them. Notice the upward and downward motion of each melody.

1.
G	B	D	B	D	B	G
1	3	5	3	5	3	1

2.
G	E	C	E	C	E	G
5	3	1	3	1	3	5

240

THE TWELVE-BAR BLUES

	1	2	3	4 beats
whole note	𝅝			
whole rest	𝄻			
half notes	𝅗𝅥		𝅗𝅥	
half rests	𝄼		𝄼	
quarter notes	𝅘𝅥	𝅘𝅥	𝅘𝅥	𝅘𝅥
quarter rests	𝄽	𝄽	𝄽	𝄽

This chart shows the relationships between notes and rests, or silences, of different durations.

CD6:30

- Read and play this blues progression. Practice each part separately before playing them together.
- Perform this progression with the twelve-bar blues.

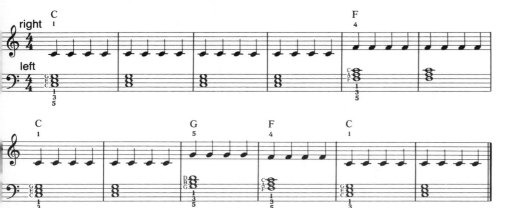

- Play these right hand melodies with the chord sequence. Pattern 1 contains steps. Patterns 2 and 3 contain skips.
- Choose pattern 1, 2, or 3. Play it with the twelve-bar blues. Be sure to play each chord enough times to fit the twelve-bar blues progression.

KEYBOARDS OF TODAY

Focus: Reading Music at the Keyboard

Objective
To read and play a blues progression on the keyboard

Materials
Recording: "Twelve-Bar Blues"

1 SETTING THE STAGE
Review the twelve-bar blues sequence in both the right and left hands.

2 TEACHING THE LESSON
Perform the twelve-bar blues. Have the students:
- Practice and then perform the twelve-bar blues sequence with the recording.
- Vary the right hand melody by reading and playing melodic patterns 1–3. (Inform the students that the starting note of each right hand melodic pattern is the root of the chord below.)

KEYBOARDS OF TODAY

- Practice and then perform the twelve-bar blues sequence with the recording.
- Vary the left hand by reading and playing melodic patterns 1–3. (Inform the students that the starting note of each left hand melodic pattern is the root of the chord above. Remind the students to play the melodic patterns the correct number of times to fit the sequence of the progression.)

Reinforcing the Lesson

Have the students create their own improvisation by combining alternate right and left hand patterns while performing the twelve-bar blues. (Encourage the students to refer to the patterns on these pages.)

3 APPRAISAL

The students should be able to read and perform melodies containing steps and skips in the bass and treble clefs using a twelve-bar blues sequence.

You can read and play this blues progression. Note that the chords are in the treble clef, and the melodic patterns are in the bass clef.

- Practice each part separately. Play the chords with your right hand. Play the melody with your left hand. Then play both parts together.
- Perform with the twelve-bar blues.

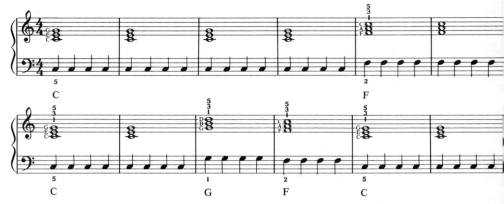

- Play these left hand melodies with the chord sequence. Pattern 1 measures contain steps and skips. Pattern 2 measures contain steps. Pattern 3 measures contain skips. Notice that when the chord changes to F or G, the beginning note of the left hand melodic pattern changes to F or G.
- Choose pattern 1, 2, or 3. Play it with the twelve-bar blues. Be sure to play each chord enough times to fit the twelve-bar blues progression.

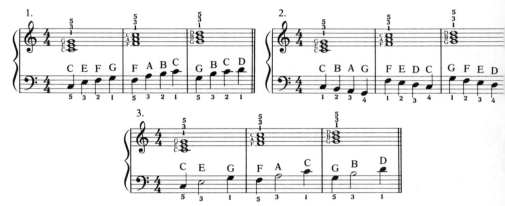

 Create your own melodies by combining right and left hand patterns to play with the twelve-bar blues.

TRIADS

The chords you have been playing are based on skips. The three notes are called a **triad**. The bottom note of the chord or triad is called the **root**, the middle note is called the **third**, and the top note is called the **fifth**.

CD6:30

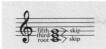

Each measure of melodic pattern 1 below begins on the root, each measure of pattern 2 begins on the third, and each measure of pattern 3 begins on the fifth of each chord.

Two eighth notes (♪♪) have the same duration as one quarter note (♩).

- Find the starting pitch of each melodic pattern before you play each chord change.

- Play the twelve-bar blues with each pattern.

KEYBOARDS OF TODAY

Focus: Reading Triads

Objective
To read and play triads on the keyboard

Materials
Recording: "Twelve-Bar Blues"

Vocabulary
Triad, root, third, fifth

1 SETTING THE STAGE
Review the definition of chords, page 235.

2 TEACHING THE LESSON
Introduce the triad. Have the students:
- Discuss the information on the construction of a triad.
- Practice finding the starting pitch and finger number of melodic patterns 1–3. (Inform the students that pattern 1 begins on the root, pattern 2 begins on the third, and pattern 3 begins on the fifth.)
- Read and perform melodic patterns 1–3.

Reinforcing the Lesson
Have the students play the twelve-bar blues sequence with melodic patterns 1–3. (Remind the students to play the melodic pattern the correct number of times to fit the sequence of the progression.)

3 APPRAISAL
The students should be able to define, read, and play triads at the keyboard.

KEYBOARDS OF TODAY

Focus: Reading Seventh Chords

Objective
To read and play seventh chords on the keyboard

Materials
Recording: "Twelve-Bar Blues"

Vocabulary
Seventh, flat

1 SETTING THE STAGE
Review the definition of chords, page 235, and tell the students that a chord can consist of more than three pitches.

2 TEACHING THE LESSON
Introduce the seventh chord. Have the students:
• Discuss the information on the construction of seventh chords.
• Examine this version of the twelve-bar blues and identify which measures contain a seventh chord. (measures 4 and 9)
• Practice the chords in the left hand and observe the fingering indicated.
• Examine right hand melodic patterns 1–3.
• Practice finding the starting pitch and finger number of each melodic pattern. (Inform the students that pattern 1 begins on the root, pattern 2 begins on the third, and pattern 3 begins on the fifth.)
• Practice each melodic pattern.

Reinforcing the Lesson
Have the students play the twelve-bar blues sequence with melodic patterns 1–3. (Remind the students to play the melodic pattern the correct number of times to fit the sequence of the progression.)

3 APPRAISAL
The students should be able to:
1. Define the seventh chord.
2. Read and perform chords and melodies that contain the seventh degree of the scale.

SEVENTH CHORDS

The triads you have been playing contain three pitches. When a chord contains four pitches, the fourth pitch is usually one skip above the fifth. It is the seventh scale tone above the root, called the **seventh**.

• Look at this version of the twelve-bar blues and identify which measures contain chords with four pitches or seventh chords.
• Play the left hand part shown.
Bb (B-**flat**) is the black key to the *left* of B.

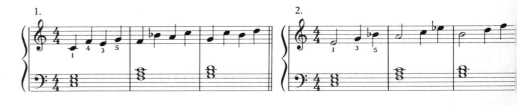

Melodic pattern 1 begins on the root, pattern 2 begins on the third, and pattern 3 begins on the the fifth of each chord. Eb (E-flat) is the black key to the left of E.

• Name the starting pitch of each melodic pattern. Refer to the chart on page 241 if necessary.
• Play each pattern with the twelve-bar blues.

244

"Several Shades of Blue"

The keyboard selection "Several Shades of Blue" uses the twelve-bar blues progression and several of the melodic patterns you have learned.

• Follow the suggestions in Part I through Part IV to prepare to play "Several Shades of Blue."

Part I: Play the individual notes in each measure all at the same time to form the chord.

Part II: Practice playing fingers 1, 2, and 5 in the right hand on all notes of the chord (Example 1). Later add finger 3 to form a four-note chord (Example 2).

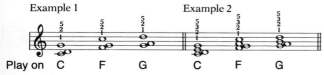

Part III: Practice moving the left hand from the root to the fifth.

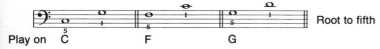

Part IV: Practice with descending quarter notes (Example 1) and then add the root in the right hand (Example 2).

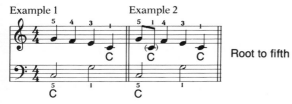

The mark ⎯⎯⎯ stands for **crescendo** (kre-shen' dō), meaning to play gradually louder. The mark ⎯⎯⎯ stands for **decrescendo** (dā' kre-shen-dō), meaning to play gradually softer. The term **simile** (sim' i-lē) means you should continue to follow the marks for crescendo or decrescendo.

245

KEYBOARDS OF TODAY

Focus: Reading Music at the Keyboard

Objective
To read and perform a song based on the twelve-bar blues sequence

Materials
Recording: "Several Shades of Blue"
Guitar, bass, or bells (or synthesizer)
Classroom percussion instruments

Vocabulary
Crescendo, decrescendo, simile

1 SETTING THE STAGE
Review the twelve-bar blues sequence, page 235.

2 TEACHING THE LESSON
Introduce "Several Shades of Blue."
Have the students:
• Observe the suggestions in Part I through Part IV before reading and performing "Several Shades of Blue."
• Discuss the information on the dynamics used while performing the piece.

KEYBOARDS OF TODAY

- Listen to the recording of "Several Shades of Blue."
- Read and perform "Several Shades of Blue."

Several Shades of Blue

L.H

246

- With a group, perform "Several Shades of Blue" by:
  1. playing the root of each chord on guitar, bass, or bells (or synthesizer)
  2. improvising a percussion accompaniment on classroom instruments
  3. playing along with the rhythm section of your keyboard

If you are using a synthesizer with a sequencer, record the root of each chord on your sequencer and replay in repeat mode. Change the keyboard voice on your synthesizer and play along with the sequencer.

247

Reinforcing the Lesson
Have the students form a group and perform "Several Shades of Blue" using the suggestions.

3 APPRAISAL
The students should be able to read and perform "Several Shades of Blue" based on the twelve-bar blues sequence.

KEYBOARDS OF TODAY

Focus: A New Chord Pattern

Objective
To read and perform chords and melodies on the keyboard

Materials
Recording: "New Chord Pattern"

Vocabulary
Tie, sharp

1 SETTING THE STAGE
Review the C, F, and G chords.

2 TEACHING THE LESSON

Introduce the new chord pattern.
Have the students:
• Listen to the recording of the pattern.
• Identify the new chords in this progression.
• Practice the chord changes.
• Perform the chords with the recording.
• Practice finding the starting pitch of melodic patterns 1–3.
• Discuss the information on the tie and the sharp.

Reinforcing the Lesson
Have the students read and perform melodic patterns 1–3 with chords.

3 APPRAISAL
The students should be able to read and perform the new chord progression accurately.

A NEW CHORD PATTERN

CD6:32 There are some new chords in this progression. They are shown in both the treble and the bass clef.

• Practice these chords.

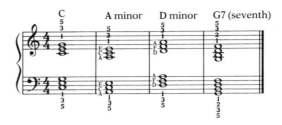

• Find and name the starting pitch of each melodic pattern below before you play it. C, E, G

In pattern 2, two notes of the same pitch are connected by a curved line called a **tie**. Hold that pitch for the *combined* value of the two notes. In pattern 3, F♯ (**F-sharp**), D♯ (**D-sharp**), and G♯ (**G-sharp**) are the black keys to the *right* of F, D, and G, respectively.

• Play this chord progression with each melodic pattern.

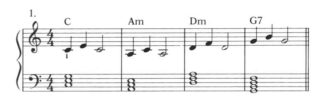

Start on the highest pitch of the chord

248

RESHAPING CHORDS

CD6:33

The pitches of a chord can be rearranged to make changes between chords smoother. This is called **revoicing**. It makes transitions from chord to chord sound smoother. It is important to remember that the names of chords do not change when they are revoiced.

- Practice this revoiced chord progression with the left hand.

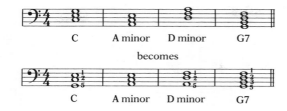

becomes

- Create your own melodic pattern in the right hand to play with the left hand chords. Use melodic patterns you have already learned.

- Practice this revoiced chord progression with the right hand.

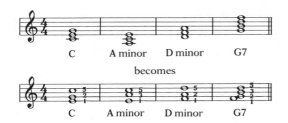

becomes

- Create your own melodic pattern in the left hand to play with the right hand chords. Use melodic patterns you have already learned.

'Blue Heart"

'Blue Heart" contains parts of the chord progressions you have learned, along with several of the melodic patterns you have learned. The **fermata** (𝄐) in the last measure tells you to hold those notes slightly longer than usual.

Practice patterns 1 and 2 before you perform "Blue Heart."

Pattern 1.   Pattern 2.

249

CD6

KEYBOARDS OF TODAY

Focus: Reshaping Chords

Objective
To read and perform chords and melodies on the keyboard

Materials
Recording: ''Blue Heart''
Guitar, bass, or bells (or synthesizer)
Classroom percussion instruments

Vocabulary
Revoicing, fermata

1 SETTING THE STAGE
Review the C, D minor, F, and G chords.

2 TEACHING THE LESSON

1. Introduce reshaping chords. Have the students:
- Discuss the information on reshaping chords.
- Practice the revoiced chord progression with the left hand.
- Create their own melodic patterns for the right hand to go with the chord progression.
- Practice the revoiced chord progression with the right hand.
- Create their own melodic patterns for the left hand to go with the chord progression.

2. Introduce "Blue Heart." Have the students:
- Practice patterns 1 and 2 in preparation for reading and performing "Blue Heart."

EXTENSION

MORE MUSIC TEACHING IDEAS
Revoice the chords in the twelve-bar blues sequence.

KEYBOARDS OF TODAY

- Listen to the recording of "Blue Heart."
- Read and perform "Blue Heart."

Reinforcing the Lesson

Have the students form their own groups and perform "Blue Heart" as indicated.

3 APPRAISAL

The students should be able to:

1. Perform a revoiced chord progression with the right and left hands.
2. Read and perform "Blue Heart" accurately.

Blue Heart

- With a group, perform "Blue Heart" by:
    1. playing the root of each chord on guitar, bass, or bells (or synthesizer)
    2. improvising a percussion accompaniment on classroom instruments
    3. playing along with the rhythm section of your keyboard

If you are using a synthesizer with a sequencer, record the root of each chord on your sequencer and replay in repeat mode. Change the keyboard voice on your synthesizer and play along with the sequencer.

250

ANOTHER FAMILIAR CHORD PROGRESSION

This chord progression uses chords from the twelve-bar blues. It is frequently found in popular music.

- Practice the chord changes before you play this progression.

- Practice the left hand melodic patterns below. Find the starting pitch of each measure before you play it. All patterns: Measure 1, C; Measure 2, F; Measure 3, G

Fine (End)

Da Capo al Fine
(Go back to the beginning and play to Fine)

The **natural** sign (♮) cancels a previous sharp or flat in the same measure.

 CHALLENGE Reverse the parts so that the right hand plays the melodic patterns while the left hand plays the chords.

251

CD6:34

KEYBOARDS OF TODAY

Focus: A Familiar Chord Progression

Objective
To read and play new chords and melodies on the keyboard

Materials
Recording: "Another Familiar Chord Progression"

Vocabulary
Natural

1 SETTING THE STAGE
Review the C, D minor, F, and G chords.

2 TEACHING THE LESSON

1. Introduce the new chord progression. Have the students:
- Listen to the recording.
- Identify the chords in this progression.
- Practice the chord changes.
- Practice the right hand chords and then add the root in the left hand.
- Perform the chord progression with the recording.
- Practice the left hand part in melodic patterns 1–3.
- Play the right hand chords with each left hand part.
- Perform melodic patterns 1–3 with the recording.
- Respond to the Challenge! by reversing the right hand and left hand parts.

Reinforcing the Lesson
Have the students improvise their own melodies to this chord progression.

3 APPRAISAL
The students should be able to read and perform a familiar chord progression accurately.

KEYBOARDS OF TODAY

Focus: Performing an Accompaniment

Objective
To read and perform a keyboard accompaniment to a song

Materials
Recording: "Mama Don't 'Low"
Guitar, bass, or bells (or synthesizer)
Classroom percussion instruments

1 SETTING THE STAGE
Review the G and C chords.

2 TEACHING THE LESSON
Introduce "Mama Don't 'Low." Have the students:
• Sing the song.
• Play the second measure of pattern 2 and identify it as the new chord D major.
• Practice the patterns in preparation for playing the accompaniment.
• Observe correct fingerings.

"Mama Don't 'Low"

You can play the American folk song "Mama Don't 'Low" as a solo or with other keyboard instruments or guitars.

• Sing the song first to become familiar with it.

Mama Don't 'Low

The keyboard accompaniment to "Mama Don't 'Low" is based on chords G major and C major, which you have learned, and new chord D major.

• Practice these patterns before you perform "Mama Don't 'Low."

252

Notice that the music has a new meter signature: $\frac{2}{4}$. In $\frac{2}{4}$ meter, the the quarter note has the steady beat, with two beats in each measure.

Pat the steady beat and clap the eighth notes to prepare for playing "Mama Don't 'Low."

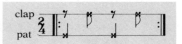

Keyboard Accompaniment to "Mama Don't 'Low"

You can also play this accompaniment with the version for guitar on page 263.

With a group, perform "Mama Don't 'Low" by:
1. playing the root of each chord on guitar, bass, or bells (or synthesizer)
2. improvising a percussion accompaniment on classroom instruments
3. playing along with the rhythm section of your keyboard

If you are using a synthesizer with a sequencer, record the root of each chord on your sequencer and replay in repeat mode. Change the keyboard voice on your synthesizer and play along with the sequencer.

KEYBOARDS OF TODAY

- Discuss the information on $\frac{2}{4}$ meter.
- Practice the rhythm pattern, using body percussion.
- Sing the song as they perform on the keyboard.
- Form two groups. Have one group perform the accompaniment on the keyboard while the other group performs on guitar (see pages 262–263).

Reinforcing the Lesson

Have the students form their own groups and perform "Mama Don't 'Low" as indicated.

3 APPRAISAL

The students should be able to accurately perform a keyboard accompaniment to a song.

CD6:36

PLAYING THE GUITAR

- Listen to these compositions for guitar. How do they sound alike? How do they sound different?

Concerto in D Major for Guitar and Orchestra, Third Movement, by Antonio Vivaldi

254

PLAYING THE GUITAR

Objectives
To identify the parts of the guitar and electric bass
To read and play simple accompaniments on guitar and/or electric bass

Materials
Recordings: Concerto in D Major for Guitar and Orchestra, Third Movement
"Hickory Hollow"
"Drunken Sailor"

Guitars
Electric basses and amplifiers (optional)
Keyboard

Vocabulary
Fret, strum, open string, tablature, chord diagram

1 SETTING THE STAGE

Introduce the guitar. Have the students:
• Discuss the photographs.
• Identify and discuss the types of instruments represented in the pictures.
• Listen to and compare the two recordings.

in the Temple, Vittore Carpaccio, ACCADEMIA, Venice

"Hickory Hollow," performed by Banks and Shane

255

THE ARTIST

Vittore Carpaccio (vē-to're kär-pä' chō) (ca.1455-ca.1526)—was an Italian painter. His work reflects the style of Venetian painting in his time, which emphasized the colors and textures of rich cloth, marble, and other materials. He painted many scenes of Venice as settings for religious figures.

EXTRA HELP

If your class is unable to complete Lesson 1 in one session, you may wish to teach pages 254–257 as one lesson, pages 258–260 as two lessons, and page 261 as a fourth lesson.

PLAYING THE GUITAR

2 TEACHING THE LESSON

1. Introduce or review the parts of the guitar and electric bass. Have the students:

• Discuss the information given.

• Identify and compare the parts of the guitar and electric bass.

In this section you will learn to play strum patterns, chords, and bass parts on the guitar. The four lowest strings of the six-stringed guitar can be tuned to the same pitches as the four strings of the electric bass. You can play bass parts on either instrument.

tuning machines

frets

nut

neck

fingerboard

strings

tuning machines

sound hole

nut

body

neck

bridge

frets

body

fingerboard

bridge

pickup

controls

256

TUNING YOUR GUITAR

he tuning most often used for guitar and bass is pictured here as
relates to the keyboard. The four strings of the electric bass are
uned to the same pitches (one octave below) as the four lowest
trings on a six-stringed guitar.

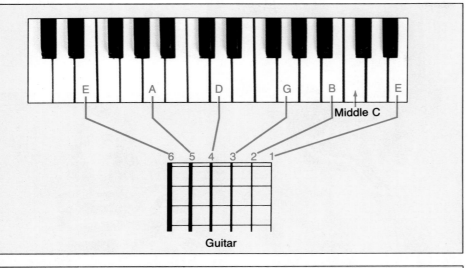

Guitar

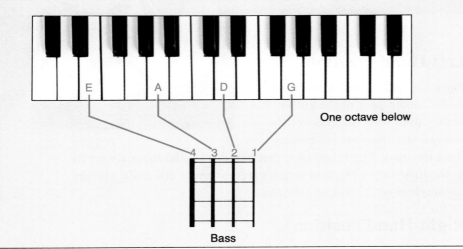

Bass

ou can use two alternate tunings for some of the songs in this
ection. You will find these tunings, as well as chord frames for the
ongs, on pages 276–277.

257

**2. Introduce or review tuning the
guitar and electric bass.** Have the students:
• Discuss the tuning diagrams and identify
the strings on the guitar and electric bass.
• Compare the string arrangements of the
guitar and electric bass.
• Tune their instruments as they are able.

PLAYING THE GUITAR

3. Introduce or review holding and playing the guitar and electric bass. Have the students:

• Discuss the photos of proper playing positions.

• Discuss the left-hand position and the order of left-hand fingering.

• Identify the meaning of *fret*.

• Discuss the right-hand position. (Some students may prefer to use a pick when playing the electric bass.)

• Identify the symbol for down strum and practice the down strum on the guitar.

• Identify the symbol for up strum and practice the up strum on the guitar.

Left-Hand Position

Place the pad of your left thumb in the center back of the guitar neck. Curve your fingers over the strings, keeping your palm away from the neck. The fingers are numbered from the index finger (1) to the little finger (4). Your fingers **fret**, or press down, the strings for single notes or to form chords.

Right-Hand Position

Curve the fingers and **strum**, or brush down across the strings with your fingernails. A down strum is indicated by this sign ⊓ .

Brush up across the strings with your thumbnail for an up strum (∨).

258

Strum Patterns for Guitar

Practice these rhythm patterns on **open** (unfretted) strings, or with any chords you already know. Play the downward (⊓) and upward (∨) strums where indicated.

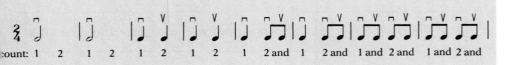

READING A BASS PART IN TABLATURE

Bass parts for either the six-stringed guitar or the electric bass can be written in *tablature*. **Tablature** is a picture of the guitar strings divided into measures of music.

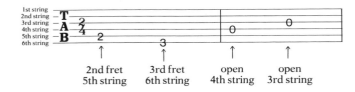

259

• Perform the rhythm patterns at the top of the page, using the down and up strums.
4. Introduce reading a bass part in tablature. Have the students:
• Discuss the information on tablature.

PLAYING THE GUITAR

- Discuss and compare the note durations and tablature symbols.
- Practice the short tablature sample at the bottom of the page.

The six lines represent the six strings of the guitar. The numbers on the line indicate the frets. An *O* indicates an open, or unfretted, string. In some tablature the rhythms are shown above the fret numbers. Here the rhythm is

More commonly, tablature symbols are used. They are shown with their equivalents in staff notation. The fret number is written inside the note head. The fret number replaces the note head for dotted quarter notes, quarter notes and eighth notes. The rests are the same as in staff notation.

NAMES	STAFF NOTATION	TABLATURE SYMBOLS
whole note	o	2 (just the number)
dotted half notes	𝅝. 𝄼·	②. ②·
half notes	𝅗𝅥 𝄼	② ②
dotted quarter notes	𝅘𝅥. 𝄽·	2. 2·
quarter notes	𝅘𝅥 𝄽	2 2
eighth notes	𝅘𝅥𝅮 𝄾	2 2
eighth notes	𝅘𝅥𝅮𝅘𝅥𝅮 𝄾𝄾	2 2 2 2

This is how the symbols look in tablature.

Unless otherwise indicated, the left hand fingering is the same number as the fret.

260

PLAYING CHORDS

A chord diagram or frame shows where to place your left fingers on the fingerboard to fret, or form, a chord. The number in the circle indicates which finger to use. The circle shows you where your finger belongs. An *X* means that a string is not played.

CD6:38

- Practice the E minor and D major chords and the accompaniment patterns for "Drunken Sailor." Then play them with the song.

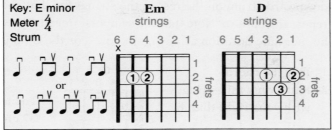

Drunken Sailor

Traditional

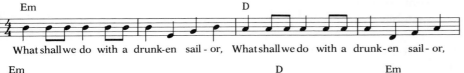

Em
What shall we do with a drunk-en sail - or, What shall we do with a drunk-en sail - or,

Em   D   Em
What shall we do with a drunk - en sail - or, Ear - lye in the morn - ing?

     Refrain   Way, hey, and up she rises, (*3 times*)
                      Earlye in the morning.
      2. Throw him in the longboat till he's sober, (*3 times*)
          Earlye in the morning.
      3. Pull out the plug and wet him all over, (*3 times*)
          Earlye in the morning.

ADD A BASS PART

You can play a bass part for this song on the four lowest strings of a six-stringed guitar or on the electric bass. The top line shows the part in staff notation.

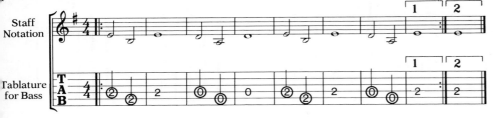

Staff Notation

Tablature for Bass

261

PLAYING THE GUITAR

5. Introduce or review playing chords and strum patterns on the guitar. Have the students:
- Discuss the information on playing chords and fret positions.
- Examine the diagrams for the E minor and D major chords and practice playing them on the guitar.
- Practice the chords with the strums indicated.

6. Introduce "Drunken Sailor." Have the students:
- Sing "Drunken Sailor."
- Sing the song again, playing the proper chord on the downbeat of each measure.
- Play "Drunken Sailor" with the two-chord accompaniment.

7. Introduce the bass accompaniment for "Drunken Sailor." Have the students:
- Examine the tablature for the bass accompaniment.
- Practice playing the bass part.

Reinforcing the Lesson
Have the students form two groups and perform both accompaniments with "Drunken Sailor."

3 APPRAISAL
The students should be able to:
1. Identify the different parts of the guitar and electric bass.
2. Read and play simple two-chord and bass accompaniments to "Drunken Sailor."

MORE MUSIC TEACHING IDEAS
You may wish to use the D minor tuning on page 277 for this song.

EXTRA HELP
If some students are unable to play the strum patterns for this song or any other song in this section, have them strum down on the proper chord on the downbeat of each measure.

PLAYING THE GUITAR

Focus: Alternating Bass Patterns

Objective
To read and play simple alternating bass patterns on the guitar

Materials
Recording: "Mama Don't 'Low"
Guitars
Electric basses and amplifiers (optional)
Keyboard

Vocabulary
Bass pattern

1 SETTING THE STAGE
Review fret positions, playing chords, and the down strum.

2 TEACHING THE LESSON

1. Introduce playing alternating bass patterns. Have the students:
• Identify the bass (lowest) notes in familiar chords, such as E minor and D major. (Note that the bass note will not always be the root.)
• Discuss the alternating bass patterns and examine the diagrams of the G, G7, D7, and C chords.
• Fret each chord and identify the bass note in each.
• Practice each chord, using alternating bass, in $\frac{2}{4}$ meter. Then practice changing from one chord to the next: G to G7, G7 to C, C to G, G to D7, and D7 to G.

BASS PATTERNS

Bass patterns involve playing the lowest notes of a chord separately from the other notes. In "Mama Don't 'Low," the chords are G major, G7, D7, and C major.

To play a bass pattern, first fret the chord. Then pluck *only* the single bass note shown in the tablature. Follow that with a downward strum on the rest of the strings for that chord. Then repeat the pattern. Note that the symbol ♪ means the strum should be the same duration as an eighth note. For the G major chord:

1. Fret the chord
2. Pluck *only* this string with your right thumb

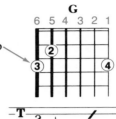

The left hand fingering for G and G7 chords is *not* the same as the fret number. The left hand fingering is shown in parentheses above the tablature.

3. Strum down on the remaining strings

Note that the G7 chord has the same bass note as the G major chord.

• Fret the D7 chord, pluck the fourth string bass note, and strum all the strings *except* the sixth string.

• Fret the C major chord, pluck the fifth string bass note, and strum all the strings except the sixth.

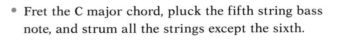

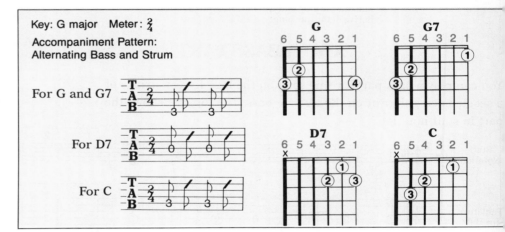

EXTENSION

Mama Don't 'Low

Key: G major   Starting Pitch: G   Scale Tones: *so, la, ti, do re ma mi so*

American folk song (arr. P.W.)

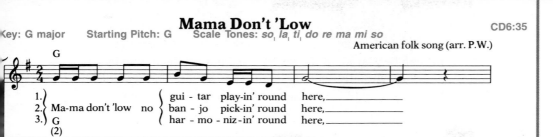

1.)
2.) Ma-ma don't 'low no
3.)
(2)

{ gui - tar play-in' round here,_____
{ ban - jo pick-in' round here,_____
{ har - mo - niz-in' round here,_____

Ma-ma don't 'low   no
(2)

{ gui - tar play-in' round here,_____
{ ban - jo pick-in' round here,_____
{ har - mo - niz - in' round here,_____

I   don't care what   Ma-ma don't 'low, Gon-na
(2)   (2)

{ play my gui - tar   an - y - how,
{ pick my ban - jo   an - y - how,
{ har - mo-nize songs   an - y - how,

Ma-ma don't 'low   no
(2)

{ gui - tar play-in' round here._____
{ ban - jo pick-in' round here._____
{ har - mo - niz - in' round here._____

263

PLAYING THE GUITAR

2. Play the alternating bass pattern.
Have the students:
• Sing the song, playing the proper chord on the downbeat of each measure.
• Sing the song again, playing the alternating bass accompaniment.
• Form two groups. Group I strums the chords on the beat while Group II plays the alternating bass pattern.

Reinforcing the Lesson

Have the students form three groups to play the chords, the alternating bass pattern, and the keyboard accompaniment on page 253.

3 APPRAISAL

The students should be able to read and play a simple alternating bass pattern as an accompaniment to "Mama Don't 'Low."

MORE MUSIC TEACHING IDEAS

Some students may want to improvise a bass part to "Mama Don't 'Low" on guitar or electric bass.

PLAYING THE GUITAR

Focus: Bass Runs

Objective
To read and play simple bass runs on the guitar

Materials
Recordings: ''Mama Don't 'Low''
''The Wabash Cannonball''
Guitars
Electric basses and amplifiers (optional)

Vocabulary
Bass run

1 SETTING THE STAGE

Review alternating bass by forming two groups, with one group strumming on the beat while the other plays the alternating bass and strum pattern to ''Mama Don't 'Low.'' Then switch parts if students are able.

2 TEACHING THE LESSON

1. Introduce the bass run. Have the students:
• Review the G, C, and D7 chords.
• Define and discuss a bass run and examine the bass runs shown.
• Practice playing these bass runs.

BASS RUNS

A **run** is a stepwise pattern of notes that connects two chords in a song. Runs can be played on the six-stringed guitar. Each note in a run is played individually, usually in an even rhythm. The symbol $\int$ means the strum should be the same duration as a quarter note.

To play Bass Run 1:
1. Fret and play the bass note and the chord in the previous measure.
2. With your right thumb, pluck the single notes shown in the tablature. Change the left hand fingers as necessary.
3. Fret and play the next bass note and chord.

Play Bass Run 2 in the same way:

• Practice these runs until they sound smooth, then play them where they are indicated in "The Wabash Cannonball."

Notice that in this song, the bass notes for each chord alternate.

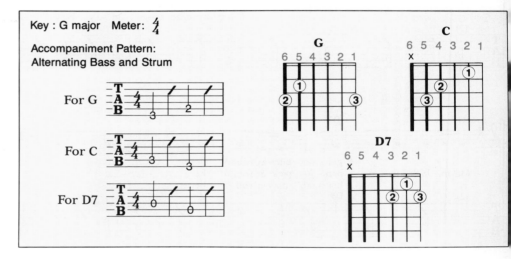

264

E X T E N S I O N

MORE MUSIC TEACHING IDEAS
You may wish to use the D major tuning on page 276 for this song. (Note that the bass runs cannot be played in this tuning.)

Key: G major   Starting Pitch: D   Scale Tones: *fa, so, la, ti, do re mi so*

The Wabash Cannonball

CD6:39

Traditional

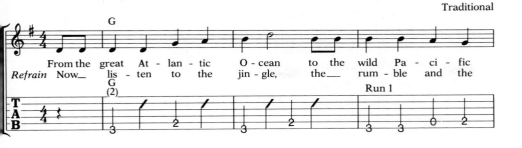

From the great At-lan-tic O-cean to the wild Pa-ci-fic
Refrain Now__ lis-ten to the jin-gle, the__ rum-ble and the

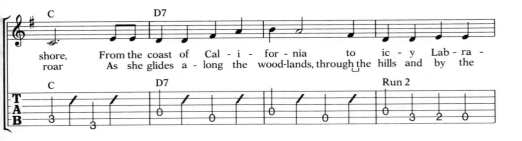

shore, From the coast of Cal-i-for-nia to ic-y Lab-ra-
roar As she glides a-long the wood-lands, through the hills and by the

-dor. She's long and tall and hand-some, she's known to one and
shore. Hear the might-y rush of en-gine, hear the lone-some ho-boes

all, that heav'n-ly com-bin-a-tion, the Wa-bash Can-non-ball.
call As they trav-el a-cross the coun-try on the Wa-bash Can-non-ball.

265

PLAYING THE GUITAR

2. Introduce "The Wabash Cannonball." Have the students:
• Sing "The Wabash Cannonball."
• Practice the G, C, and D7 chords with the song. Play the proper chord on the downbeat of each measure.
• Sing the song, playing the bass runs as they are able.
• Form two groups. Group I practices strumming the chords on the beat while Group II practices the bass runs.

Reinforcing the Lesson

Have the students perform "The Wabash Cannonball," combining the strummed accompaniment with the bass runs.

3 APPRAISAL

The students should be able to read and play simple bass run patterns as an accompaniment to "The Wabash Cannonball."

MORE MUSIC TEACHING IDEAS

Some students may want to improvise a bass part to "The Wabash Cannonball" on guitar or electric bass.

PLAYING THE GUITAR

Focus: The Slide

Objective
To read and play a simple slide on the guitar or electric bass

Materials
Recording: "The Golden Vanity"
"Follow the Drinkin' Gourd"
(performance mix)
Guitars
Electric basses and amplifiers (optional)

Vocabulary
Slide

1 SETTING THE STAGE

Review the E minor, C, D, and G chords, with students taking turns playing alternating bass and bass run patterns with these chords.

2 TEACHING THE LESSON

1. Introduce the slide. Have the students:
• Define a slide and discuss the three steps for playing one.
• Examine the tablature, on this page and in the song, that indicates a slide.
• Practice playing this slide on the guitar or electric bass. Observe that in this song it is used four times.
2. Introduce the B minor and A chords and strum patterns. Have the students:
• Examine the diagram and identify the bass note in the B minor and A chords.
• Practice the B minor and A chords.
• Practice playing all the chords with the strum patterns shown.

A slide is a kind of slur in which you fret two different pitches but pluck the string only once. The bass part in this song has a slide, ②-③ s, on the fifth and sixth strings. To play a slide:

1. Fret the string on the initial fret number indicated.
2. Pluck that string with your right thumb.
3. *At the same time*, slide the left hand finger up or down to the next fret number indicated. You will hear the pitch move up or down, too.

For example, to play ②-③ s, start on the second fret and slide to the third fret.

In this bass part for "The Golden Vanity," some of the left hand fingerings are *not* the same as the fret numbers. The left hand fingerings are shown in parentheses above the tablature when they are different.

This song has a meter of $\frac{4}{4}$. The song contains two new chords: A major and B minor.

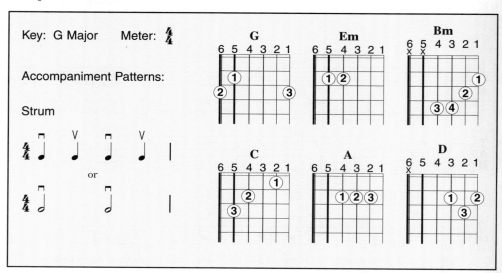

• Play "The Golden Vanity" with the bass part. Then play it again with the chord accompaniment.

266

The Golden Vanity

English Folk Song

1. There once was a ship, and a stur-dy craft was she; She
2. One day on the ship of the Gold-en Van-i-ty The

went by the name of the Gold-en Van-i-ty. And ne'er a fin-er ves-sel did
captain raised his spy-glass to see what he could see. And lo——— and be-hold, he did

sail up-on the sea. Oh, she sailed up-on the Low Lands
spy the en-e-my As they sailed up-on the Low Lands

Low. She sailed up-on the Low Lands Low.
Low. As they sailed up-on the Low Lands Low.

You will find the rest of the verses to this song on page 132.

267

PLAYING THE GUITAR

3. Review "The Golden Vanity." Have the students:
- Sing the song.
- Sing the song again, playing the proper chords on the guitar.
- Form two groups. Group I practices strumming the chords on the beat while Group II practices the bass accompaniment to the song, paying close attention to the bass slide.

Reinforcing the Lesson

Have both groups perform "The Golden Vanity." Then switch parts if the students are able.

3 APPRAISAL

The students should be able to read and play simple slides in the bass part of the accompaniment to "The Golden Vanity."

PLAYING THE GUITAR

Focus: Playing the Blues

Objective
To read and play a simple blues shuffle pattern on the guitar

Materials
Recording: "Worried Man Blues"
Guitars
Electric basses and amplifiers (optional)

Vocabulary
Blues shuffle

1 SETTING THE STAGE
Review the C, D, and G chords, with the students taking turns playing alternating bass and bass run patterns.

2 TEACHING THE LESSON

1. Introduce the blues. Have the students:
• Discuss the information on playing the blues. (You may wish to review the information on pages 104–105, and page 105 of the Teacher's Edition.)
• Examine the blues rhythm pattern.
• Practice playing the blues rhythm on the G, C, and D chords.

2. Introduce playing the blues shuffle. Have the students:
• Discuss the information on playing the blues shuffle.
• Examine the diagrams for root chords and chords with the added sixth.
• Practice playing the G and G6 chords, the C and C6 chords, and the D and D6 chords, using the blues rhythm pattern.

CD6   One basic rhythm pattern for the blues is

• Play it with a relaxed swing of long and short sounds.

• Practice this rhythm with the G, C, and D chords.
  You can play an accompaniment to "Worried Man Blues" using the rhythm pattern shown above.

The Blues Shuffle

The **blues shuffle** pattern combines the rhythm you have learned with two alternating chords, a root chord, and the same chord with an added tone, called the sixth.

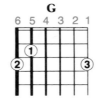

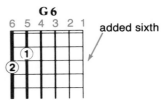

Play the root chord (G, C, or D) on the first and third beats of the measure. Play the sixth chord (G6, C6, or D6) on the second and fourth beats of the measure. You need to move only one finger back and forth to make the change from one chord to the other.

• Play the blues shuffle with these chords from "Worried Man Blues."

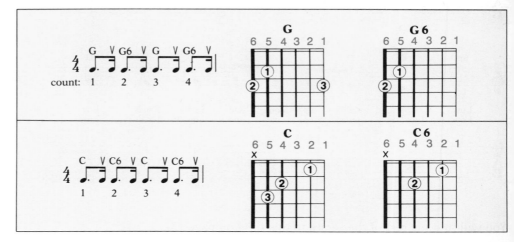

268

EXTENSION

MORE MUSIC TEACHING IDEAS
You may wish to use the D major tuning on page 276 for this song.

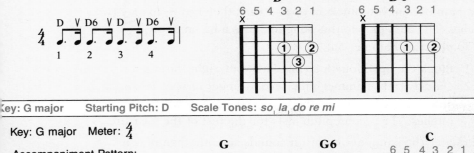

Key: G major   Starting Pitch: D   Scale Tones: *so, la, do re mi*

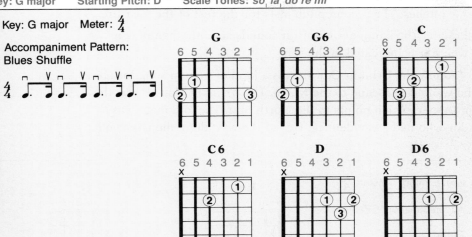

Key: G major   Meter: 4/4

Accompaniment Pattern:
Blues Shuffle

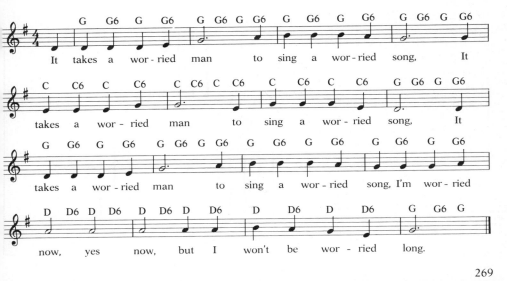

Worried Man Blues

Traditional

It takes a wor-ried man to sing a wor-ried song, It

takes a wor-ried man to sing a wor-ried song, It

takes a wor-ried man to sing a wor-ried song, I'm wor-ried

now, yes now, but I won't be wor-ried long.

269

PLAYING THE GUITAR

3. Introduce "Worried Man Blues."
Have the students:
• Sing "Worried Man Blues."
• Practice the blues shuffle as they sing the song again.
• Perform "Worried Man Blues" with the guitar accompaniment.

Reinforcing the Lesson
Some students may want to compose their own blues songs to perform with the blues shuffle, or use it as an accompaniment to blues songs they already know.

3 APPRAISAL
The students should be able to read and play simple blues shuffle patterns on the guitar as an accompaniment to "Worried Man Blues."

MORE MUSIC TEACHING IDEAS
Some students may wish to improvise bass patterns to "Worried Man Blues" by playing only the lowest note of each chord on the guitar or electric bass.

PLAYING THE GUITAR

Focus: The Hammer On

Objective
To read and play a hammer-on

Materials
Recording: "Follow the Drinkin' Gourd"
Guitars
Electric basses and amplifiers (optional)

Vocabulary
Hammer-on

1 SETTING THE STAGE

Review the E minor, B minor, G, D, and A chords. Practice the up and down strums with these chords.

2 TEACHING THE LESSON

Introduce the hammer-on. Have the students:
• Discuss the information on the hammer-on.
• Examine the tablature for the hammer-on on this page and in the bass accompaniment to the song.
• Practice the hammer-on on the guitar or electric bass, following the steps outlined. Continue until it sounds smooth.

THE HAMMER-ON

In a **hammer-on**, you pluck an open string, then fret it, to play two pitches. The bass part to this song includes a hammer-on.
To play this hammer-on:

1. Pluck the open fourth string with your right thumb.
2. *Quickly* fret ("hammer") the second finger of your left hand onto the second fret of the fourth string. You will hear two pitches. The second pitch lasts for the rest of the measure.

• Practice the hammer-on until it sounds smooth, then play it where it is indicated in the song.

"Follow the Drinkin' Gourd" was a kind of map in song for slaves who wanted to escape to the North. The "Drinkin' Gourd" was the Big Dipper, which points to the North Star. The "old man" was a sailor who had a wooden leg. He led the way along the riverbank.

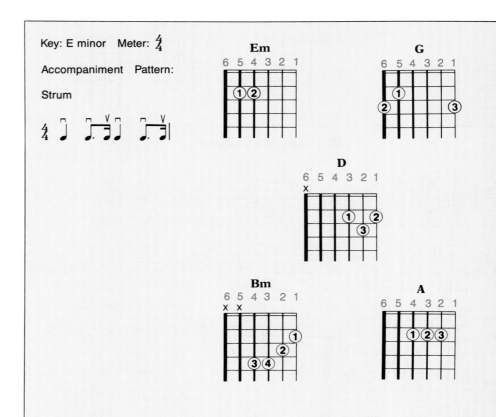

Follow the Drinkin' Gourd

Traditional

Verse 1. When the sun comes back and the first quail calls,_____
2. Now the riv-er bank-'ll make__ a might-y good road;____ The
3. Now the riv - er ends__ be - tween two hills;_____

Fol - low____ the Drink-in' Gourd.__Then the Old Man is a-wait-in' for to
dead trees____ will show you the way. And the left__ foot,_ peg - foot,_
Fol - low____ the Drink-in' Gourd._ And__ there's an-oth-er riv - er on the

car - ry you to free-dom, Fol - low the Drink - in' Gourd.
trav - el - in'____ on, ____ Fol - low the Drink - in' Gourd.
oth - er____ side, ____ Fol - low the Drink - in' Gourd.

Refrain Fol - low_____ the Drink - in' Gourd,_ Fol - low_____ the

Drink - in' Gourd,_ For the Old Man is a - wait - in' for to

car - ry you to free - dom, Fol - low the Drink - in' Gourd.

271

PLAYING THE GUITAR

3. Introduce "Follow the Drinkin' Gourd." Have the students:
• Sing the song, strumming the proper chord on the downbeat of each measure.
• Listen to or sing the song, strumming on the guitar as they are able.
• Form two groups. One group plays the chords in the strum pattern while the other plays the bass accompaniment, paying close attention to the hammer-ons.

Reinforcing the Lesson

Combine the groups and perform the song. Then switch parts if the students are able.

3 APPRAISAL

The students should be able to read and play the hammer-on as they accompany "Follow the Drinkin' Gourd."

PLAYING THE GUITAR

Focus: Interpreting the Mood of a Song

Objective
To play a guitar accompaniment in a manner that reflects the mood of a song

Materials
Recording: "The Ghost Ship"
Guitars
Electric basses and amplifiers (optional)

1 SETTING THE STAGE

Review the E minor, A, C, D, and G chords, with students practicing the down and up strums on each chord. Practice playing the bass notes of the chords on the guitar or electric bass.

2 TEACHING THE LESSON

1. Introduce the B7 chord. Have the students:
• Examine the diagram for this chord.
• Practice playing the chord, using the down and up strums.

2. Introduce the strum patterns for "The Ghost Ship." Have the students:
• Examine the strum patterns.
• Practice the strum patterns, first with the chords they know, then with the B7 chord.

3. Introduce "The Ghost Ship." Have the students:
• Listen to "The Ghost Ship," paying close attention to the mood of the song.
• Discuss the mood of the song (spooky, scary) and the kind of accompaniment that would be most appropriate.
• Sing "The Ghost Ship," using their voices to create an appropriate mood.
• Sing the song again, strumming the proper chord on the downbeat of each measure of verse 1, the refrain, and verse 2.

Key: E minor   Starting Pitch: B   Scale Tones: *mi, so, la, ti, do re mi*

SETTING THE MOOD OF A SONG

CD7:1 Try to catch the mood of "The Ghost Ship" as you play the guitar part or the bass part. This song has one new chord: B7.

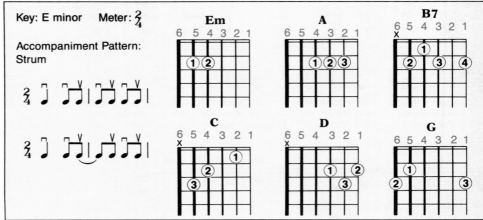

The Ghost Ship

Words and music by
Don Besig and Nancy Price

Verse Em ... A ... Em
1. Now lis-ten well as a tale I tell of a night I

B7 ... Em ... A
shook with fear._____ We were sail-ing west on the o-pen

C ... D ... Em ... G
sea, head-in' home from a long, long year._____ I was stand-ing

watch all a-lone that night when I heard a wail-ing cry._____ As I

strained to see what the sound could be, some-thing flashed and caught my eye._____

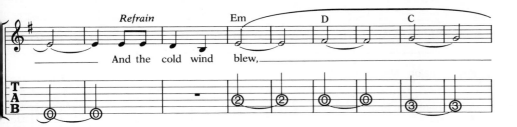

Refrain

And the cold wind blew,_____

and the cold wind blew._____

2. 'Twas then I spied off the starboard side a strange, mysterious sight.
   I froze with fear as it drifted near like a ghost in the dark of night.
   I could see a sail on a broken mast and deserted decks below.
   From all around came a mournful sound, but I saw not a living soul!

3. Well, I held fast to the forward mast as the ship moved slowly on.
   And I watched that way 'til the break of day, when I knew that it fin'lly
      had gone.
   Oh, they laughed and joked as I told my tale to the captain and the men.
   But the story's true, I can promise you, and it's sure to happen again.

273

PLAYING THE GUITAR

4. Prepare the accompaniment for "The Ghost Ship." Have the students:
• Practice the strum patterns and chord changes. Try to capture the mood of the song.
• Examine and practice the bass part to the song, interpreting the mood as best they can.
• Form two groups. One group plays the strum patterns while the other plays the bass part. Combine the two parts, using their ideas for interpreting the mood of the song.

Reinforcing the Lesson

Have the students perform "The Ghost Ship," combining the two guitar parts to create an appropriate mood for the song. Then switch parts if they are able, and try a different interpretation of the song. Compare the two versions.

3 APPRAISAL

The students should be able to play guitar and bass accompaniment in a style that accurately reflects the mood of "The Ghost Ship."

PLAYING THE GUITAR

Focus: Arpeggio

Objective
To read and play arpeggios on the guitar

Materials
Recording: "River"
Guitars
Electric basses and amplifiers (optional)

Vocabulary
Arpeggio

1 SETTING THE STAGE

Review the D, G, B minor, C, A, and E minor chords, with students practicing alternating bass and bass run patterns with these chords as they are able.

2 TEACHING THE LESSON

1. Introduce the arpeggio. Have the students:
• Discuss the information on the arpeggio and define it.
• Examine the tablature for the arpeggios.
• Practice the arpeggio pattern for each chord.
2. Review "River." Have the students:
• Sing the song. Compare the mood of this song with that of "The Ghost Ship" or another song in this section.
• Listen to the song or sing it again, playing the proper chord on the downbeat of each measure (and on the proper beat in measure 43).
• Sing the song again, playing the arpeggio accompaniment as they are able.
• Perform the song with the guitar accompaniment. Try to capture the mood of the song.

AN ARPEGGIO ACCOMPANIMENT

Key: D major   Starting Pitch: D   Scale Tones: *so, la, do re mi fa .*

An **arpeggio** is a chord whose notes are played one at a time, rather than all at once.

To play an arpeggio:

1. Fret the chord.
2. Pluck the strings indicated, one at a time and in rhythm, with your right hand fingers. Finger numbers for the right hand are shown in parentheses *below* the arpeggio. They are the same as for the left hand.

• Practice these arpeggios. Notice that the bass note changes from the fourth to the fifth to the sixth string. The upper strings remain the same for all the chords.

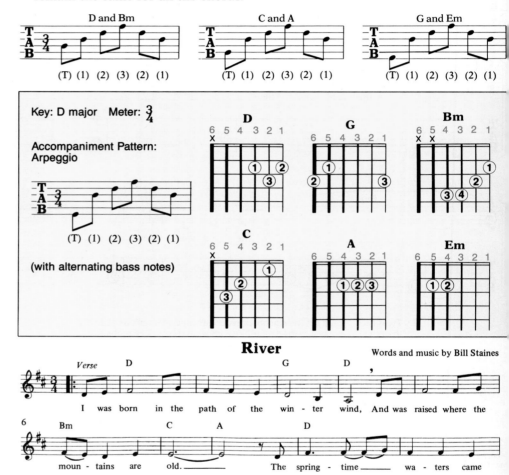

River

Words and music by Bill Staines

Verse
D   G   D

I was born in the path of the win-ter wind, And was raised where the

Bm   C   A   D

moun-tains are old.___ The spring-time___ wa-ters came

EXTENSION

MORE MUSIC TEACHING IDEAS

Some students may want to improvise a bass accompaniment for this song on the guitar or electric bass.

11 G   D   Bm   A   G   D

danc - ing down, I re - mem - ber the tales they told. _____ The

17 D   G   D

whis - tling _____ ways of my young - er days, Too quick - ly have

22 Bm   C   A   D

fad - ed on by. _____ But all of the mem - o - ries

27 G   D   Bm   A   G   D

lin - ger still, Like the light in a fad - ing sky. _____

33 *Refrain*   D   G   A   D

Riv - er, take me a - long, In your sun - shine

39 G   A   Em   A

sing me your song, Ev - er mov - ing and wind - ing and _____

44 D   Em   D   Em   D

free. You roll - ing old riv - er, You chang - ing old riv - er, Let's

49 Em   A   *1., 2.* D   **4**

you and me, riv - er, Run down to the sea. _____

3. D   *Coda* G   A   *ritard.*   D

sea. _____   Let's you and me, riv - er, Run down to the sea.

2. I've been to the city and back again;
   I've been touched by some things that I've learned,
   Met a lot of good people, and I've called them friends,
   Felt the change when the seasons turned.
   I've heard all the songs that the children sing
   And I've listened to love's melodies;
   I've felt my own music within me rise
   Like the wind in the autumn trees.

   Refrain

3. Someday when the flowers are blooming still,
   Someday when the grass is still green,
   My rolling waters will round the bend
   And flow into the open sea.
   So here's to the rainbow that's followed me here,
   And here's to the friends that I know,
   And here's to the song that's within me now;
   I will sing it where'er I go.

   Refrain

275

PLAYING THE GUITAR

Reinforcing the Lesson

Have the students form two groups. One group strums the chords on the beat while the other plays the arpeggio patterns. Perform "River," combining the two guitar parts to create an appropriate mood for the song.

3 **APPRAISAL**

The students should be able to read and play arpeggios on the guitar as an accompaniment to "River."

PLAYING THE GUITAR

Alternate Tunings

This section is provided for those teachers who may wish to teach D tuning. As the students tune their guitars to D major or D minor, point out that the fourth and fifth strings of the six-stringed guitar and the second and third strings of the electric bass do not have to be re-tuned.

When the students have re-tuned their guitars, have them examine the chord diagrams and practice playing these chords. Introduce the bar chord. When the students are familiar with the new chord fingerings, they can accompany "The Wabash Cannonball," "Worried Man Blues" (both in D major), "Drunken Sailor"(in D minor), and "Follow the Drinkin' Gourd" (in E minor).

ALTERNATE TUNING: D MAJOR

You can use this tuning to play "The Wabash Cannonball" and "Worried Man Blues."

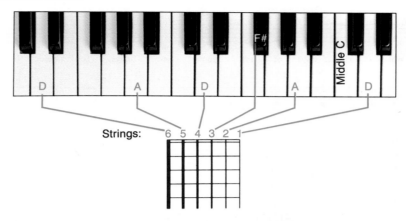

"The Wabash Cannonball"

To play the alternating bass and strum with your right hand, pluck the sixth string with your right thumb for all three chords, then strum the rest of the strings. Omit the bass runs in this tuning. G and C are bar chords. To fret a bar chord, press your index finger down firmly across *all* the strings on fret indicated.

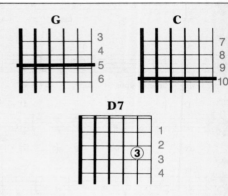

"Worried Man Blues"

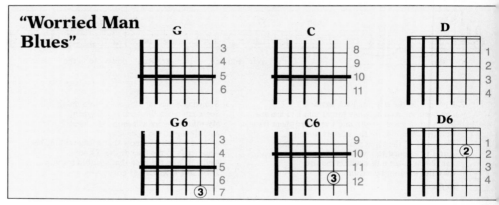

ALTERNATE TUNING: D MINOR

You can use this tuning to play "Drunken Sailor" and "Follow the Drinkin' Gourd."

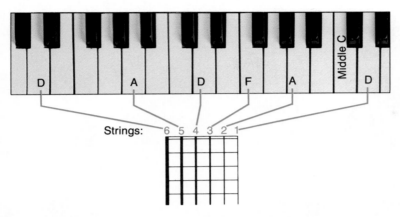

"Drunken Sailor"

E minor is a bar chord (as are A minor and G major below). To fret a bar chord, press your index finger down firmly across all the strings on the fret indicated.

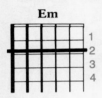

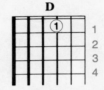

"Follow the Drinkin' Gourd"

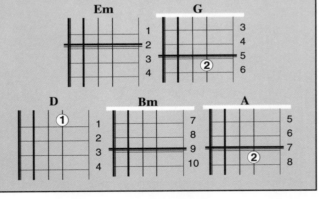

277

MUSIC IN YOUR LIFE

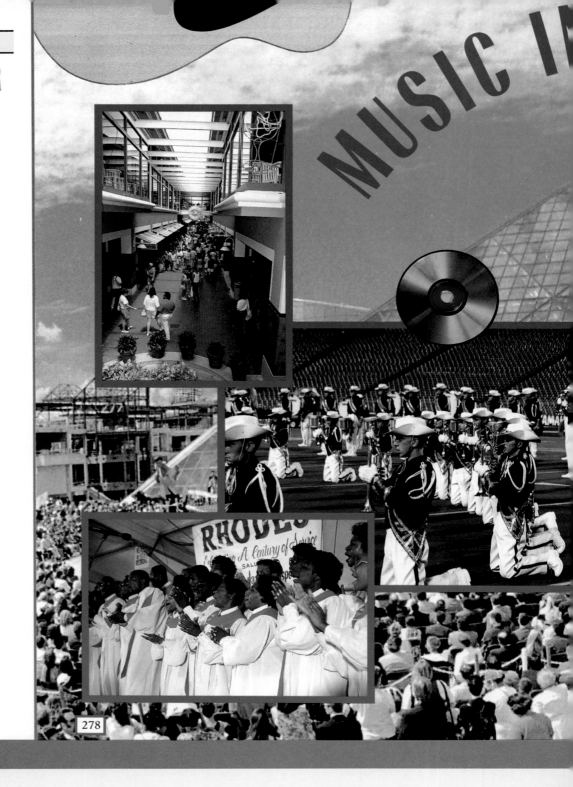

278

279

JOURNAL

The journal suggestions given throughout this unit will help the students extend their learning and apply it to their everyday lives. Journals might be used as part of the assessment.

Have the students keep a 24-hour log of any music they hear or participate in throughout the day. The log should be made into a chart with the following headings: time, source, type, and response (how they or other people responded to the music—tap their toe, ignore it, sing along, and so on). They should share their logs with the class as a volunteer makes a list on the board of the various types of music experienced.

MUSIC IN YOUR LIFE

Focus: Ways to Participate in Music

Objectives
To identify music in the environment
To identify decisions made to become active participants in music
To perform rhythmic accompaniments with different styles of music
To propose ways of participating actively in music in the future
To create a new rhythmic accompaniment
To explore the career of a vocalist
To discuss the future of music

Materials
Recordings: "Participation Music 1: 'When a Man Loves a Woman'"(Blue Devils Drum Corps)
"Participation Music 2: 'Climbing Up to Zion'"
"Participation Music 3: 'Head over Heels'"
"Participation Music 4: 'Cuequita de los Coyas'"
"Participation Music 5: Afro-Cuban Pop
"Participation Music 6: Mall Music"
"Get on Your Feet"

MUSIC IN YOUR LIFE

Identify ways that music is part of everyday life. Have the students:
• Discuss where they have heard music today. (class, cafeteria, home, on the way to school) Tell which sounds they *chose* to listen to and which were just parts of the environment.
• Categorize different music sources (television, radio, CD player, background music, supermarkets, shopping malls) as you list them on the board.
• Investigate the local concerts that are listed in the weekend newspaper.
• Discuss where they might hear music after school. (concert hall, car radio, theme park)
• Open to pages 278–279 and identify which musical situations they might actively participate in and which they would simply observe.

MUSIC IN YOUR LIFE

THE PARTICIPANTS

1. Identify decisions students might make to become active participants in music. Have the students:
• Discuss the questions at the top of page 280. Examine the differences between *hearing* music and *listening* to music. (Which involves a decision? Which requires their attention? Which is active?)
2. Perform rhythmic accompaniments to five different styles of music. Have the students:
• Learn to clap the rhythmic accompaniments on page 280. (There is no playalong for Participation Music 6, "Mall Music.")
• Perform the rhythmic accompaniments as they listen to "Participation Music." (See lengths of introductions and background information below.)
• Answer the follow-up question.
3. Propose ways to participate actively in music in the future. Have the students:
• Discuss how they currently participate in music. Discuss school options for participating in music. (singing in choir; playing an instrument in jazz, marching, or concert band; orchestras; taking part in musical plays, and so on)
• Discuss community options for participating in music. (singing in community or church choirs; playing an instrument in a summer band, drum corps, or garage band)
4. Create a new rhythmic accompaniment. Have the students:
• As a group, choose one of the "Participation Music" examples and listen to it again. (Allow as many additional listenings as are helpful throughout this exercise.)
• As individuals, improvise several different accompaniments while listening to the selection. Each accompaniment phrase should be four measures long.
• As individuals, choose one of their accompaniments and memorize it.
• Notate the improvised accompaniment with a single-line notation, using the examples on page 280 as models. Exchange scores with another class member to try with the recording.
• Perform the accompaniments for each other.
• Layer the new rhythmic parts, first two, then three, and so on. (One student may act as conductor, bringing in the parts phrase by phrase)
• Continue the rhythmic accompaniments after the recording has stopped to see what they sound like alone.
• Assess how well the accompaniments work together and whether they complement or detract from each other. Discuss the optimum number of parts for clarity and interest.

The Participants
CD7:2–7

How many times a day do you hear music? Think of each musical encounter listed below. Which ones offer an opportunity to participate by singing or by playing an instrument? By clapping or moving?

Your favorite group is performing at the mall.

You're waiting for a haircut. Background music is playing.

You stop to listen to the pep band practice for the big game.

You tune in to your favorite music television channel.

You get out your guitar and practice a few new chord changes.

You probably have many musical encounters every day. Some of them you will ignore. Some you will enjoy by listening. Others will invite further participation.

• Participate in active music-making by performing these rhythmic accompaniments.

 "Participation Music"

Participation Music

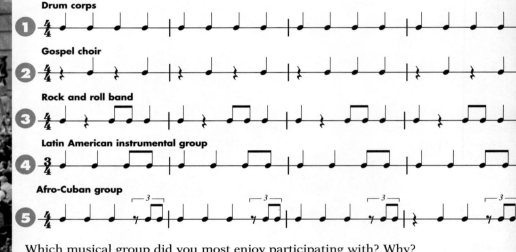

Which musical group did you most enjoy participating with? Why?

Create your own rhythmic accompaniment for one of the groups in "Participation Music." Perform your accompaniment with the group.

280

PARTICIPATION MUSIC

To facilitate performance of the playalongs, note the following:
1. Fade-in (no introduction)
2. Four-measure introduction
3. Fade-in (no introduction)
4. Four-measure introduction
5. Two-measure introduction
6. No playalong

BACKGROUND INFORMATION FOR "PARTICIPATION MUSIC"

Drum Corps: Every year thousands of youths ages 14–21 devote their summer to drum corps, an educational activity combining theater, musicianship, and competitive sport. A drum corps differs from a marching band in its instrumentation, with percussion and bugles only. Eight sizes of bugles are designed to project their sound forward. Drum corps began after World War I, when veterans formed corps to perform in parades to display the "Stars and Stripes." Modern corps perform a broad variety of music and dance, traveling throughout the country to participate in competitions. The *Blue Devils* featured here are seven-time winners of the World Championship. This performance was recorded at the 1992 World Championship.

People who love to participate in music often consider it as a possible career. Like any career in the arts, a career in music requires talent, hard work, persistence, and a great deal of training. A career as a musical performer is very demanding.

Gloria Estefan was the lead singer for Miami Sound Machine before launching her own career. She can project many moods to her audience—from energetic dance songs to slower, more serious selections. Her ability to do both reflects her versatility as a performer.

- **Play this rhythmic accompaniment part as you listen to Gloria Estefan sing "Get on Your Feet."**

"Get on Your Feet" Words by John De Faria, Music by John De Faria, Jorge Casas, and Clay Ostwald.

Introduction   *Verse 1: play 5 times.*
                   Verse 2: play 3 times.

Refrain 1: play 2 times.
Refrain 2: play 4 times. Last time improvise to end.   *Go back to verse 2.*

THINK IT THROUGH

Imagine what the career of a performer might be like in the future. What personal qualities and abilities will be needed? How might the training of a musician change over the next 50 years?

281

MUSIC IN YOUR LIFE

GLORIA ESTEFAN

1. Explore the career of a prominent vocalist. Have the students:
- Read the top of page 281.
- Discuss the hardships a performer might face. (lack of work, constant need to practice, long hours, and so on)
- Discuss the benefits a performer might enjoy. (fame, travel, rewarding work, and so on)

2. Perform a rhythmic accompaniment to a popular song. Have the students:
- Listen to "Get on Your Feet."
- Learn to clap the rhythmic accompaniment on page 281 and perform it as they listen to "Get on Your Feet."

3. Discuss the future of music. Have the students:
- Discuss the *Think It Through* questions. (What influence will the use of *technology* have on composing, performing, recording, distribution, and marketing?)

Andean Highlands Folk Music: "Cuequita de los Coyas," meaning "Dance of the Coyas," is a courtship dance. The instruments used in the recording are the bombo, a large double-headed drum; the charango, a small lute-like instrument; the guitarra, and the quena, a notched vertical flute which plays the melody in this recording.

Afro-Cuban Pop Have the students review triplets in preparation for "Afro-Cuban" playalong. They might try the exercise below.

JOURNAL

Have the students each choose and interview someone who sings in a choir, or plays in an orchestra, band, or any other musical organization. When they create the list of questions they will ask, they should be sure to avoid any that can be answered with a yes-or-no response. Students might ask why the person belongs to a musical organization, what they most enjoy about it, how much time they devote to music each week, how long they have belonged, and so on. They should then copy their interview questions and the responses into their journal.

MUSIC IN YOUR LIFE

Focus: Factors That Influence Our Musical Choices

Objectives

To summarize elements of the decision-making process when choosing music
To perform rhythmic accompaniments with five different styles of music
To become aware of advertising techniques
To create a commercial to sell a music product
To explore the career of record producer David Kahne

Materials

Recordings: "Musical Performances 1: 'Rocky Mountain'"
"Musical Performances 2: ACTE III: Symphony from *The Indian Queen*"
"Musical Performances 3: 'Rock and Roll Music'"
"Musical Performances 4: 'Light at the End of the Tunnel'"
"Musical Performances 5: 'Jazz in Five'"
"Commercial"
"Commercial Background Music 1: Rock Style"
"Commercial Background Music 2: Country Style"
"Commercial Background Music 3: Easy Listening Style"
Recorded Lesson: Interview with David Kahne

Vocabulary

Grammy®, record producer

Choosing Your Music

Because of the advances in recording and broadcasting technology, many more types of music are available today than ever before.

When you go to a record store, what types of music do you look for first? Which ones do you never look at? How important is each of the following in choosing music?

I heard this music on the radio.

A friend told me this music was good.

I want to learn to play this type of music.

I saw a video or TV show featuring this singer or group.

I saw a movie I like and want to get the soundtrack.

After thinking about these questions, take a class poll. Which is the strongest influence in your choice of music?

Look at these posters advertising musical events. Which performance would you like to attend? What factors influence your choice? Describe what you might hear and see at the performance you choose. Include in your description the type of music, number of performers, number of instruments and vocalists, and reaction of the audience. Will the music be loud or soft? Fast or slow? Dramatic or restful?

🎵 Musical Performances

- Listen to "Musical Performances Medley." Match each of the five short excerpts with one of the posters.

282

MORE MUSIC TEACHING IDEAS

1. Have the students review page 48 in preparation for $\frac{5}{4}$ meter found in example 5.
2. Have the students choose a selection from "Musical Performances," then perform the rhythmic accompaniment using feet instead of hands. Listen to the selection and improvise a second part with their hands while accurately sustaining the rhythmic ostinato in their feet.

Then have them choose one of their improvised accompaniments and memorize it. They can notate the improvised accompaniment with two single-line staves attached to make a single system. They should write the pattern from page 283 (the foot pattern) on the bottom and the improvised pattern (the hand pattern) on the top. Then they can perform the accompaniments for the class with the recording. Finally, they should layer the new rhythmic parts, first two, then three, and so on with the recording. Continue the rhythmic accompaniments after the recording has stopped to experience what they sound like without the music.

JAZZ FESTIVAL

August 13-15
Various locations throughout the city
Admission: free

*S*ymphony in the *P*ark

Once again the prize-winning Metropolitan Orchestra brings you a delightful evening of light classical favorites.

Every Friday in July
Webster Park Band Shell

Admission: free

An Evening of Broadway Highlights

The stars of Broadway bring you an evening of magical songs.

August 8
Fine Arts Center

Admission free

• Perform a rhythmic accompaniment with each of the excerpts.

Musical Performances

MUSIC IN YOUR LIFE

CHOOSING YOUR MUSIC

1. Explore elements that influence musical choices. Have the students:

• Read page 282. Discuss where they first heard or heard about some of their favorite songs. Discuss the suggestions on page 282.

• Discuss what influences them to want to obtain a recording (or to hear a performance live). Rank the strength of the influences listed on page 282, adding any of their own.

• Discuss factors that determine their choice of format when selecting a recording (CD versus cassette, for example) such as cost, time, convenience, sound quality, available equipment.

• Observe the concert posters. Discuss the questions on page 282. (Which posters catch their attention? Is it the design of the poster or the content? Which types of music are they already familiar with? Which are unfamiliar?) Justify their reasons.

2. Hear a variety of performance groups and perform rhythmic accompaniments. Have the students:

• Listen to the examples from "Musical Performances" and match them with the posters. Discuss preferences.

• Learn to clap the rhythmic accompaniments in the book and perform them as they listen to "Musical Performances."

• Answer the *Think It Through* questions and discuss the influence of familiarity on choices. (Many people tend to listen to musical styles they already are familiar with.)

T HINK IT THROUGH

Did you change your mind about which performance to attend after you heard the music? After participating as a performer? What is the biggest influence in your choice of music?

MUSICAL PERFORMANCES

To facilitate performance of the playalongs, note the following:

1. One-measure introduction
2. No introduction
3. No introduction
4. Fade-in (no introduction)
5. No introduction

JOURNAL

Have the students find a concert advertised in a local newspaper that they would *not* be tempted to attend. In their journal, have them compose a promotional article for the concert, including descriptions of the music and performers that might attract an audience to attend.

MUSIC IN YOUR LIFE

INFLUENCING CHOICES

Identify advertisement techniques.
Have the students:
• List concert tickets or music products they have purchased recently, or that they are interested in purchasing.
• Examine newspapers to find different methods of advertisement.
• Read page 284. Listen to the recording of a typical commercial and discuss the methods advertisers use to sell a product.

CREATE YOUR OWN COMMERCIAL

Create a commercial. Have the students:
• Form groups and choose a product to promote in a radio commercial.
• Plan strategies such as a special deal, or a limited-time offer. Be sure to mention such information as location or price.
• Write the commercial. Make a list of the various influencing techniques used.
• Listen to the three examples of commercial background music and choose one to use.
• Share the completed project with the class.
• Discuss the strategies each commercial used to influence a potential purchase. (Ask the writer or writers of the commercial to reveal the techniques used that the class was *not* able to recognize.)
• Discuss which commercial they thought was most convincing. Explain why they did or did not like what they heard. Explain whether or not they would buy the product.

Influencing Choices CD7:14–17

Commercials advertise a wide variety of products. Advertisers use commercials to persuade people to choose a particular product.

• Listen to this commercial. What is being advertised? What age group is being targeted? How is music used in the commercial?

 Commercial

Create Your Own Commercial

Design a commercial to sell a product. What will your product be? What age audience are you trying to reach? What strategies will you use to sell the product?

• Write a script for your commercial.

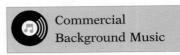 Commercial Background Music

• Listen to three types of music that might be used as background for an advertisement. Choose one to use in your commercial. Read your commercial with and without the background music. How did the music contribute to the commercial as a whole?

284

JOURNAL

Have the students create a diagram of the thought process used when deciding which music to listen to or purchase.

Celebrating Choices

Each year millions of people purchase recordings of their favorite music. Each time they do this, they cast a "vote" for their favorite recording. The music industry keeps track of the best-selling recordings and publishes a "Top 10 List" every week. The Grammy® awards, sponsored by the National Academy of Recording Arts and Sciences, are annual awards that recognize commercial success and other achievements in the recording industry.

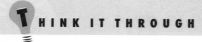

Meet David Kahne Record Producer

David Kahne is a Grammy®-award-winning record producer. David studied music and engineering in college and on the job. He has had a varied career as a keyboardist, composer, high school teacher, producer for a major record label, and as an independent producer. It is in this last role that he currently working with his own company in New York City.

A record producer directs the recording process. Acting as an artistic collaborator, a record producer uses the technology of the studio to create recordings that best show the artistic and entertainment qualities of the performer.

Mr. Kahne has worked with many performing artists including Tony Bennett, Shawn Colvin, Sugar Ray, and The Bangles. In 1995 Mr. Kahne won the Grammy® for "Album of the Year," with Tony Bennett's *MTV Unplugged*.

• Listen to David Kahne describe his career as a record producer.

THINK IT THROUGH

Create a "Top 10 List" of your favorite recordings. Arrange your list in order, starting with your favorite. Write a short statement describing why you chose a particular recording to be "Number 1."

MUSIC IN YOUR LIFE

MEET DAVID KAHNE

Investigate the musical career of a Grammy® award winner. Have the students:

• Read page 285.
• Make a list on the board of the personal qualities and abilities that would best suit a record producer.
• Listen to "Interview with David Kahne."
• Discuss the interview. (Describe what surprised them, what were the most interesting points, and whether this career sounds like it would be fun, difficult, stressful, or challenging.)
• Write a short response to the question on the bottom of page 285. Share responses with the rest of the class.

MUSIC IN YOUR LIFE

Focus: Enriching Your Entertainment

Objectives
To summarize the role music plays to enhance various forms of entertainment
To compare moods set by two pieces of music
To create a movie promotion using appropriate background music
To explore the career of film composer Alan Menken
To evaluate effectiveness of film music

Materials
Recordings: *Adagio for Strings*
"Spring" (First Movement), from *The Four Seasons*
Five Musical Moods 1 (Cheerful)
Five Musical Moods 2 (Slapstick)
Five Musical Moods 3 (Mysterious)
Five Musical Moods 4 (Melodramatic)
Five Musical Moods 5 (Epic)
Recorded Lesson: Interview with Alan Menken

Tape recorders

Vocabulary
Gleeful, mournful, adagio, detached, dynamics, texture

ENRICHING YOUR ENTERTAINMENT

1. Summarize the qualities music can bring to other forms of entertainment.
Have the students:
• Discuss their favorite entertainment, noting whether this entertainment *is* music or is *enhanced* by music.
• List some of the musical styles they have heard in these different kinds of entertainment—films may use classical, jazz, pop, or rock; sports events may have patriotic and pop.
• Read page 286 and describe how music enhances each form of entertainment shown. Discuss which kind of music might be appropriate for each of the examples. Choose answers from the list of adjectives found at the top of page 287, and add any others the students may suggest. (Possible answers: scary music to underscore the movie scene, and spirited music for a sporting event)
• Discuss whether these musical backgrounds would be interchangeable. Why or why not?

Enriching Your Entertainment

Music plays a role in many kinds of entertainment. Sometimes it is the featured entertainment. At other times it heightens the excitement or creates a mood. Imagine your favorite kind of entertainment. Is music a part of it?

• Look at these pictures. How is music used to enrich each event? List other kinds of entertainment that music enriches.

286

E X T E N S I O N

MORE MUSIC TEACHING IDEAS

1. Using MIDI equipment or acoustic instruments, students might create a music track as punctuation for a sports event, as background in a commercial of a type they specify, or to accompany a video they create.
2. Students can videotape some of their favorite television commercials and record excerpts from their favorite music. Then they can play the commercials with several different music backgrounds, choosing the music that provides the best match. Be sure they create criteria for evaluating the match of commercial music with the event that it is meant to accompany.
3. Have the students return to "Participation Music" on page 280 to describe the musical moods. Invite them to analyze musical characteristics that help to create the moods. (tone color, tempo, range, texture, expression, meter, tonality)

Music Enhances Mood

Music can be used to create or reinforce a mood. Here are two musical excerpts that might enhance the mood of a scene in a movie.

- Choose adjectives that describe the mood of each selection, for example: sad, mournful, lively, calm, happy, sorrowful, gleeful, spirited

CD7:19–20

 Adagio for Strings by Samuel Barber

 "Spring," from *The Four Seasons*, First Movement by Antonio Vivaldi

What musical characteristics contribute to the mood of each selection?

short sounds	**long sounds**
smooth sounds	detached sounds
slow tempo	fast tempo
loud dynamics	soft dynamics
thick texture	thin texture

- Choose one of the selections and imagine that it is background music for a movie. What kind of movie does the music suggest? Think of a theme for an imaginary film. Then give it a title. Read your title and description of the film as the music plays in the background.

287

MUSIC IN YOUR LIFE

2. Compare moods in two listening selections. Have the students:
- Read the text on page 287.
- Listen to *Adagio for Strings* by Samuel Barber and the first movement of "Spring" from *The Four Seasons* by Antonio Vivaldi.
- After hearing both selections, choose adjectives and musical characteristics from the lists on page 287 that best match each selection.
- Discuss whether either of these listenings would be appropriate for any of the pictured events. Explain why or why not.
- As individuals, choose to use either the Barber or the Vivaldi, and plan the film theme described in the last paragraph on page 287. Write a description of the film to read. Share their work with the class.
- After hearing all of the titles and descriptions, choose the five that seem to be the best match with the music. Justify their choices.

MUSIC IN YOUR LIFE

SELECTING FILM MUSIC

1. Investigate the process of adding music to film. Have the students:
• Read page 288. Listen to "Five Musical Moods" and describe the mood and musical characteristics of each section.

2. Create a movie promotion. Have the students:
• Read the directions given for the project on page 288.
• Working in groups of two or three, follow the directions for creating a movie promotion. (This project should be spread out over several class periods. Each group of students should have access to the musical selections they are using for frequent reference.)

Selecting Film Music

During a film, the music helps to set many different moods. The music may enhance the mood of the current scene. It may also set the mood for a scene to come. The film director and composer work together to ensure that the music sets the appropriate mood for each scene. Feature films are often preceded by a movie promotion. The five selections below can be used in a movie promotion.

• Listen to each selection. Describe the mood and musical characteristics of each.

 Five Musical Moods

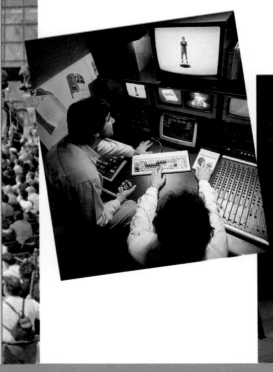

 Create

Follow these steps to create a movie promotion.

1. Think of an idea for a movie plot.

2. Think of two or more scenes, with different moods, that might be in this movie.

3. Write a few lines of dialogue for each of the scenes.

4. Decide on the mood of each scene. Select one of "Five Musical Moods" as background music for each scene.

5. Write a narration to introduce your movie promotion, connect the scenes and close it.

6. Revise the final promotion to be about 30 seconds long, including both narration and excerpts from the film music.

EXTENSION

Composing Film Music

Film music used to be recorded live. The conductor watched the film while conducting the orchestra. Today many film composers use computer programs that allow the composer to view the film as they compose. CD7:26–27

MEET

ALAN MENKEN

Theater and Film Composer

Alan Menken is known for his theater productions such as *Little Shop of Horrors* and Disney's animated movies. His first movie success was in 1989 with *The Little Mermaid*, on which he collaborated with lyricist Howard Ashman. A string of other successful Disney movies followed: *Aladdin, Beauty and the Beast,* and *Pocahontas.*

These animated films are done in the tradition of Broadway musicals. For this reason the music is a crucial element in bringing the story to life. For example "Under the Sea," a lively calypso number sung by musical crustaceans in *The Little Mermaid,* helps "animate" a scene in the film. Due to the tremendous success of Alan Menken's music, versions of his songs have been recorded by popular artists such as Vanessa Williams, Jon Secada and Celine Dion.

- Listen to Alan Menken as he describes the work of a film composer.

THINK IT THROUGH

The next time you go to the movies or watch a TV show, evaluate the background music. What worked well? What would you change? Why?

289

MUSIC IN YOUR LIFE

MEET ALAN MENKEN

Explore the work of a film composer. Have the students:
- Read page 289 and discuss their reactions to music of Alan Menken that they may have heard in the films mentioned.
- Discuss what they imagine the life of a composer is like.
- Make a list on the board of the personal qualities and abilities that would best suit a film composer.
- Make a list on the board of the kinds of equipment that might be necessary for a modern film composer.
- Listen to "Interview with Alan Menken."
- Check lists to see if their preconceptions were accurate.
- Discuss the interview. (Describe what surprised them, what were the most interesting points, and whether this career sounds like it would be fun, difficult, stressful, or challenging.)

ANALYZE BACKGROUND MUSIC

Evaluate the background music for a film or TV show. Have the students:
- Read the *Think It Through* questions.
- Articulate the qualities they would now look for.
- Carry out the assignment and share their ideas during the next class period.

JOURNAL

Have the students enter the results of the *Think It Through* in their journals. They should include the set of criteria that was used for their evaluation.

MUSIC IN YOUR LIFE

Focus: Music Through Technology

Objectives
To summarize the impact technology has made on composition
To categorize the processes of making a recording
To explore the career of a prominent vocalist/composer
To identify the elements of a MIDI system
To create a new composition that reflects the students' own sound environments

Materials
Recordings: Recorded Lesson: Interview with Peter Gabriel
"Don't Give Up"
"Snowy Twilight"
Tape recorders

Vocabulary
Composer, arranger, recording engineer, record producer, MIDI, controller, MIDI interface, sequencer program, tone generator, sound output device

MUSIC THROUGH TECHNOLOGY

1. Summarize the impact of technology on composition. Have the students:
• Read page 290 and answer the questions.
• Make a chart on the board of special sounds and effects that they have noticed in music, and list songs under each category that use each particular effect. (The students may remember which song was the first to use a particular effect.)
• Discuss any music-making technology they may use at home. Describe how they have used it. (What elements are of most use to them? Do they know enough about its use for serious composition? Do they have sequencers? sound banks? What are some of the sounds in their sound banks?)

DO IT YOURSELF:
Music Through Technology

CD7:28–29

Wherever music is heard today, technology was probably involved to create it, perform it, or record it. The influence of technology is especially strong in popular music.

• Think of your favorite popular recording. Describe some of the sounds and special effects in the recording. To what extent do you think technology played a part in creating these musical effects?

Creating Music Using Technology

Much as the word processor has helped writers to work, music technology has helped composers to work more quickly. Sequencers use digital language to allow any computer or electronic keyboard to act like a tape recorder. Unlike the tape recorder, however, a sequencer allows composers to hear and revise any part of the composition as soon as it is composed. Using sequencers, composers create, edit, store, and play back music digitally. Electronic sound banks are combined with sequencers. These sound banks give composers access to a wide variety of instrumental sounds.

Many electronic keyboards designed for home use have sequencers and sound banks built in. This new technology allows people to create their own music.

290

Peter Gabriel is a singer and a composer who has worked on a wide variety of projects that combine music from around the world. He established his own company to promote world music. The ability to combine musical ideas from distant parts of the world is made easier by today's rapidly advancing music technology.

• Listen as Peter Gabriel tells you about using technology to create his recordings. Which of these ideas can yo try by using technology in your classroom or home?

In "Don't Give Up" Peter Gabriel uses an innovative m of synthesized sounds, bass, and percussion to create a complex texture. Listen to h the instrumental and vocal tracks are layered to create rich blend of sounds.

 "Don't Give Up" (excerp by Peter Gabriel

EXTENSION

THE ARTIST

Peter Gabriel—was born in 1950 and rose to fame as the lead singer of Genesis, a group formed with friends at the Charterhouse School near London in 1966. While a member of the group, he was known for his theatrical style and eccentric costumes. In 1975 he left Genesis for a solo career which, since his 1980 album *Peter Gabriel*, has included much work with world music. The music on his albums has been influenced by diverse musicians from countries such as Egypt, India, Kenya, Russia, Senegal, and Turkey. Gabriel has also been able to bring the music of many previously unknown world music artists to the attention of the recording industry.

The chart below shows some of the key people involved in any recording. Which of these people use technology? Which career interests you most?

THE COMPOSER

writes the music. Using notation software, the composer can enter music directly into a computer and

THE ARRANGER

determines vocal combinations, the style of the accompaniment, and the instrumentation to help present the song to its best

THE PERFORMER

rehearses and records the arrangement, giving it his or her own artistic interpretation.

THE RECORDING ENGINEER

handles the technical aspects of a recording session: mike placement, sound levels, and effects such as reverb.

THE RECORD PRODUCER

directs the recording session by helping the musicians with creative decisions and by working with the engineer to get the desired sound.

291

MUSIC IN YOUR LIFE

2. Making a recording. Have the students:
• Read the text on page 291.
• Answer the questions at the top of the page after reading the flowchart.

MEET PETER GABRIEL

Explore the career of a prominent composer-vocalist. Have the students:
• Read the text in the box.
• Discuss how they imagine the life of a composer-vocalist might be different from that of a person who composes music for others to perform.
• Make a list on the board of the personal qualities and skills that would best suit a composer-vocalist.
• Listen to "Interview with Peter Gabriel."
• Discuss the interview. (What surprised them? What were the most interesting points? Does this career seem exciting, difficult, fun, stressful?)
• Read the final paragraph of the box in preparation for the musical listening.
• Listen to "Don't Give Up" by Peter Gabriel.
• Comment on the textures used, the meter, and the contrasting sections.
• Discuss the content of the song. (What is the meaning of the text? What role does the female voice play in the song? How does the music change to reflect different moods within the text?)

JOURNAL

Have the students choose five of their favorite recordings and discuss in their journal the musical choices that the artist made for each piece (texture, tone colors, rhythm, harmonies, special effects, melodic qualities, and so on). They should evaluate the quality of the composition as objectively as possible.

MUSIC IN YOUR LIFE

CREATE AND SHARE YOUR MUSIC

1. Learn about MIDI. Have the students:
• Read page 292.
• Identify the MIDI components visible in the photo using the vocabulary they have just learned. (*controller*—MIDI keyboard, *tone generator*—thin box to the right of monitor, and *sound output device*—speakers on either side of monitor)

2. Listen to a MIDI composition. Have the students:
• Listen to "Snowy Twilight."
• Discuss the various kinds of sounds and musical elements they hear.

Create and Share Your Music

MIDI (Musical Instrument Digital Interface) allows people to connect musical instruments to computers. Computers may be networked to allow users to share information. With MIDI, electronic instruments and computers may communicate digital-musical information. A typical MIDI system consists of five components:

1. a *controller* (a MIDI keyboard, guitar, saxophone, or other instrument)

2. a *MIDI interface* (a device that allows the controller to "talk" to the computer)

3. a *sequencer program* (software that enables a person to create, record, edit, and play back music)

4. a *tone generator* (a collection of different sounds)

5. a *sound output device* (speakers or headphones).

EXTENSION

MORE MUSIC TEACHING IDEAS

STUDENT EXHIBIT

Have students demonstrate their understanding of technology by planning, setting up, and supervising a hands-on music technology exhibit. This project could be presented in their classroom for an open house, parents evening, or similar event.

Have them follow these steps to set up the exhibit.
1. Make a list of the available technology equipment (MIDI, recording equipment, and so on). Decide which classroom percussion instruments or additional sources will be used to create sounds. Will pre-recorded sounds (CDs, radios, televisions, videos) be used?
2. Draw a map to show the location of all of the equipment in the exhibit, including recording equipment. Decide where they will place the microphones. Decide where they will place the accompaniment instruments. Decide whether the melodic sounds will be first or last to be created.
3. Write step-by-step instructions telling how to create and record music. Make the instructions clear for the entire process, and specific to each instrument and piece of equipment.
4. Test the instructions with the class by giving a mock presentation, making any revisions to the instructions or plan that seem necessary.
5. Give presentation at an appropriate occasion.

MIDI systems are used for all types of music making. "Snowy Twilight" was created using a MIDI setup like the one pictured. The 128 sounds available on General MIDI enabled the composer to combine electronic sounds with percussion instruments such as marimba and timpani. Notice the combinations of contrasting tone colors as you listen to "Snowy Twilight."

Create Your Own Music

In each period of history, music and other art forms express ideas and impressions that are important to people of that time. Imagine that you are the music representative on a time-capsule team. Your task is to create a short composition called "Sounds of My Time."

  CD7:30

1. Make a list of sounds that you will include. These could include excerpts from current music, environmental sounds, new music that you compose, or any other sounds.

2. Arrange your list of ideas in a pleasing order.

3. If original music is involved in your composition, plan and rehearse it.

4. Record the sounds and music that you want to use.

5. Revise your recording and share it with the class.

Share Your Music

Technology allows us to share music in ways we could not even imagine just a few years ago. Musicians can easily download and send music files via a computer on the Internet or World Wide Web.

THINK IT THROUGH

What ways can you share music in your community? Throughout the world? What ways do you think will be invented in the future?

MUSIC IN YOUR LIFE

CREATE YOUR OWN MUSIC

Plan and record music for a sound capsule. Have the students:
• Read and discuss page 293. Discuss what musical and environmental sounds are typical today. Identify kinds of music that their parents or grandparents would not have heard when they were growing up.
• Decide with the teacher whether to work individually or in groups. (Set guidelines for this project that are appropriate to the class. Standards should be set for the length, number of sound excerpts, and appropriate content.)
• Develop the project, using class time to plan the composition, and outside time to prepare and record it. (Encourage students to use as much original work as possible from both electronic and conventional sources.)
• Present the new composition to the class.
• Discuss the strong points of the composition. Discuss the purpose the composer had for including these particular musical excerpts and sounds in his or her composition.

SHARE YOUR MUSIC

Investigate the potential for creative exchange through technology. Have the students:
• Answer the *Think It Through* questions, basing their responses on technology they are familiar with, and technology that they can imagine for the future.
• Discuss how the Internet and the World Wide Web have changed the possibilities for sharing music. Contrast the advantages with the disadvantages of these possibilities for a composer living in this era.

BACKGROUND

"Snowy Twilight"—Musical compositions are generally more interesting when a composer takes into account the strengths and weaknesses of the musicians for whom the piece is written. When "Snowy Twilight" was composed and recorded, sounds and musical ideas were chosen that would sound best on the MIDI "orchestra." Some sounds, such as the timpani, were based on traditional instruments. Others, such as the dark bass line at the very beginning were created exclusively on electronic instruments. "Snowy Twilight" tells a musical story using a combination of traditional and modern tone colors.

MORE MUSIC TEACHING IDEAS

If you have Internet or World Wide Web access, ask your technology specialist for help finding information on music, music technology, music software and hardware, MIDI sequences, and sound files. Some schools have linked themselves together to collaboratively make music, exchange MIDI files, and share other music information. This access to other students' files will help the students share music worldwide with others their own age.

JOURNAL

As a final journal entry, have the students write an essay to examine their discoveries about the influence of technology and commercialism on music and on life in general, and on them in particular.

294

MUSIC LIBRARY

Focus: Experiencing the Singing Voice

Objectives
To use the singing voice to perform vocal music in unison and in parts
To evaluate vocal balance, vowel uniformity, and diction
To explore and describe music from different cultures

Materials
Recordings: "Harmony in C"
"Harmony in C"
(performance mix)
"Boat Song"
"Osebaba"
Recorded Lesson:
"Pronunciation: 'Osebaba'"
"Zol Zain Sholem"
Recorded Lesson:
"Pronunciation:
'Zol Zain Sholem'"
"Zol Zain Sholem"
(performance mix)

Vocabulary
Diction, balance, vowels, articulation

Music Library

295

MUSIC LIBRARY

TEACHING THE LESSON

1. Introduce "Harmony in C." Have the students:
• Examine and identify the musical notation in "Harmony in C." (Identify and define repeat sign, labels for Parts I, II, and III, *Last time to Coda* and *Coda*.)
• Listen to the song while following the score.
• Describe the order in which each vocal part is heard and combined with the others. (both Parts I and II alone; I and II combined; III alone; I, II, and III combined)

2. Teach "Harmony in C." Have the students:
• Follow the score as you model each of the vocal parts.
• Discuss appropriate singing posture (see below) and sing "Harmony in C."
• Establish singing posture and sing Parts I, II, and III with the recording. (Changing voices can perform Part I, Part II, measures 9 and 11, or Part III an octave lower.)
• Sing each part individually and in small groups with and without accompaniment. (Repeat and assist with vocal modeling as needed.)
• Divide into assigned groups and sing parts in various combinations. (Parts I and II, II and III, I and III)

3. Perform "Harmony in C." Have the students:
• Assigned to three groups, sing the song with accompaniment.
• Discuss the importance of balance in performing music.
• Sing "Harmony in C," listening for balance as individuals and small groups perform. (Discuss the results—Can all the parts be heard clearly ?)

Song Anthology

Each of us has a unique voice. Together our voices can produce rich harmony. The harmony in this song is created by singing three different melodies at the same time.

CD7:31, CD9:5

Key: C major   Range: C–C[I]   Piano Accompaniment on page PA 28

Harmony in C

Words and Music by M.J.

296

EXTENSION

POSTURE

Correct posture is the first step toward developing correct breathing for singing. Have students come forward in their chairs as though they are about to stand. They should sit tall with their shoulders relaxed and down. As soon as students know the correct posture, you can simply say "singing position" and they should automatically assume this position. If students are standing, ask them to stand firmly on both feet with feet slightly separated.

BREATHING

As soon as correct posture is established, work on proper breathing. Breathing deeply gives the energy necessary to support the singing tone. The following three exercises should make students aware of the meaning of diaphragmatic breathing.
1. Have the students place their hands on their abdomens and feel the impulse as they make the sound *ch ch ch*, like an old-fashioned locomotive. With their hands on their abdomens they can feel the intake and release of air.
2. Have them blow out old air, inhale new air to the count of 1–3, and exhale on a hiss to the count of 1–5. Repeat, exhaling to the count of 1–7. Extend the count each time to increase breath management.

3. Ask students to breathe in and then sing the alphabet up to the letter *k* on middle line B using a single breath. To further develop breath management, repeat, each time adding another letter of the alphabet. Remind students that breathing more deeply produces a fuller, more supported tone.

Create a routine for using dynamics and voice assignments in this folk song from Zaire.

CD7:32, CD9:6

Key: Mixolydian mode on G   Ranges I: G—B, II: B₁—D, III: D₁—G₁

Boat Song

Zairian Folk Song

THINK IT THROUGH: Evaluate the routine you created. Recommend ways to improve the routine to enhance the song.

297

PRONUNCIATION

Ai o le o le le le le
ī ō lā ō lā lā lā lā

MORE MUSIC TEACHING IDEAS

Have the students improvise and notate new percussion parts for the accompaniment. Discuss whether they seem to go well with the song or if they need to be changed to better fit the vocal parts.

4. Introduce "Boat Song." Have the students:
• Listen to the song three times, following a different vocal line each time.
• Speak the text of each vocal line in rhythm, then sing each line. (Sing an octave lower as needed. Remind students to keep their mouths open to sustain pure vowel sounds.)
• Discuss characteristics of the song. (major key, steady pulse, repeated rhythms)
5. Teach "Boat Song." Have the students:
• Sing each of the three vocal lines with the recording.
• Form three groups, each group singing a designated part alone without accompaniment. (Model as needed.)
• Sing designated Parts III and II combined with the accompaniment. (Observe progress and review parts as needed to promote success in combining parts.)
• Sing designated Parts III, II, and I with the accompaniment.
• Learn instrumental parts.
• Discuss and develop a routine for dynamics and assignment of parts. (Where might the voices become louder? Softer? Which voice group sounds best on Part I? II? III? Try different combinations.)
• Develop an introduction using the instrumental parts given with the song.
6. Perform "Boat Song." Ask for volunteers or select players for the instrumental parts. Have the students:
• Sing their designated parts with the instrumental accompaniment, as they follow conducting gestures and their previously agreed routine for dynamics.
• Listen to individuals or small groups perform. Discuss the dynamic changes and the assignment of parts. (Identify the sound changes as various voices are heard on different parts.)
• Discuss *Think It Through*.

ACCOMPANIMENTS

The piano accompaniments and recorded accompaniments help set the style of the songs.

Divided track recordings can be used to help teach parts. The vocal parts can be isolated by adjusting the balance between the left and right speakers. A group can sing with its own part to develop security, or that part can be turned down or off and the group can sing with the other part.

A performance mix can be used to develop independent singing and as an accompaniment for a performance.

Students may wish to create their own accompaniments on appropriate instruments.

MUSIC LIBRARY

7. Introduce "Osebaba." Have the students:
• Learn about the origin of the song.
• Listen to the song and discuss the style and text. (major key, repeated four-measure melodic/rhythmic pattern; six measures have a half note on pulses two and three)
• Identify songs they sing to celebrate joyous events. ("Happy Birthday," "The Star-Spangled Banner")

8. Teach "Osebaba." Have the students:
• Listen to "Pronunciation: 'Osebaba.'"
• Practice pronunciation as needed, then listen to and sing the entire song. (Emphasize singing on the vowels *oh, eh, ah, oo*.)
• Listen and follow the score as you or a student models the song or sections of the song using words.
• Sing "Osebaba" with the recording.
• Sing individually and in small groups. (Have the class evaluate the purity of the vowels. How close to the accompaniment model is the individual or group?)

9. Perform "Osebaba." Have the students:
• Sing the song with the accompaniment, following conducting gestures. (Emphasize eye contact, posture, and uniformity of vowels.)
• Listen for vowel uniformity as individuals or small groups perform. Discuss the performances.

10. Introduce "Zol Zain Sholem." Have the students:
• Learn about the origin of the song. (See *Background* below.)
• Listen to the song and discuss the style and text. (minor key, repeated melodic patterns, solo and group voices, repeated sections)
• Identify repeated melodic passages.
• Determine the form of the composition. (The ABA form is based on the melodic repetition: measures 1–5:A, 6–13:B, and 14–18:A.)

Ranges I: C–D¹, II: C–C, III: C₁–F, IV: C₁–C

EXTENSION

PRONUNCIATION

O-se, O-se- o, O-se- o, O-se- ba-ba
ō-shā, ō- shā-ō, ō-shā-ō, ō-shā-bä-bä

BACKGROUND

"Zol Zain Sholem" (Let There be Peace) is a traditional Yiddish folk song. The Yiddish language combines elements of Hebrew and German and has been spoken by Eastern European Jews for hundreds of years. "Zol Zain Sholem" is a joyous song of peace and jubilation. The call and response form and use of vocables (neutral syllables with no specific meaning) inspires audience participation.

PRONUNCIATION

Ya pa pa pa ya pa pa pa
yä pä pä pä yä pä pä pä

yam pam pam
yäm päm päm

Sho-lem, sholem
shō-lem, shō-lem

zol zain zol zain sho-lem
zōl zān zōl zān shō-lem

sho - lem, _____   sho - lem,   sho - lem,
free - dom, _____   free - dom,   free - dom,

sho - lem, _____   sho - lem,
free - dom, _____   free - dom,

sho - lem, _____   sho - lem,   sho - lem,
free - dom, _____   free - dom,   free - dom,

Refrain

zol zain zol zain   zol zain sho - lem.   Ya pa pa pa ya pa pa pa   yam pam pam
let us live in   free - dom. _____

zol zain zol zain   zol zain sho - lem.   Pa pa   pa pa   pam   pam
let us live in   free - dom. _____   Yam   pam pa pa pam pam

zol zain zol zain   zol zain sho - lem.   Yam   pam   pam pam
let us live in   free - dom. _____

1.   **2.**

ya pa pa pa ya pa pa pa   yam pam pam   yam pam pam.

1.   **2.**

pa pa   pa pa   pam   pam   pam pam.
yam   pam pa pa

1.   **2.**

yam   pam   pam   ya pa pa pa   yam pam pam.

💡 **THINK IT THROUGH:** Assess the diction and articulation in your performance. Propose ways to achieve greater clarity.

299

MORE MUSIC TEACHING IDEAS
FOLLOWING A CONDUCTOR

Remind students to watch the conductor for visual directions. Demonstrate the various conducting movements used and explain what they mean: meter patterns, dynamics, articulations, tempos, attacks, and cut-offs. Stress the importance of eye contact. Give students the opportunity to be conductors and refine their conducting techniques.

MUSIC LIBRARY

11. Teach "Zol Zain Sholem." Have the students:
• Listen to the song again, singing the melody of the A sections softly on the neutral syllable *loo*.
• Follow the score as you model measures 3 and 4, and 3 and 5 of the vocal parts. (Note how measures 4 and 5 differ slightly.) Have the students show the melodic direction with up and down hand movements. Sing each vocal passage after hearing the vocal model.
• Repeat listening and singing the melody of the A section on *loo*.
• Listen to "Pronunciation: 'Zol Zain Sholem.'"
• Practice pronunciation as needed for each section, then sing the melody of the A section with words.
• Follow the outlined procedure for the B section.
• Sing the entire song using words with the recording.

12. Teach the harmony parts of "Zol Zain Sholem." Have the students:
• Examine the score to find the unison and part-singing sections.
• Discuss singing in parts. (Part singing creates vocal harmony and musical interest.)
• Form four groups. (I—treble voices, II—treble voices, III—changing voices, and IV—baritone voices)
• Listen to the song and follow the appropriate part, singing softly on *loo*.
• Learn parts IV, III, and II separately for measures 14–18, and then measures 6–13 using words.
• Discuss the importance of diction in conveying the message of the text and the style of the composition. (Diction, through consonants, conveys meaning.)
• Identify words in the song whose pronunciation will require special attention to diction. (A sections: the explosive consonant *p* and pitched *m*; B sections: *sh, z d, t*)
• Listen for balance and diction as individuals and small groups perform; discuss the performances.

13. Perform "Zol Zain Sholem." Have the students:
• Sing the song in four parts with the accompaniment, following conducting gestures. (Focus on crisp diction.)
• Discuss performance in terms of clarity of diction. (Discuss ways of achieving greater clarity.)

APPRAISAL

The students should be able to:
1. Sing with increased confidence alone and in groups; sing in unison and in parts.
2. Demonstrate and evaluate balance, vowel uniformity, diction, and articulation.
3. Describe the musical characteristics of songs from the cultures studied.

Objectives
To identify and expand the vocal range
To explore technical aspects of vocal production
To perform vocal music in parts
To expand the expressive use of the voice

Materials
Recordings: "America, America"
"America, America" (performance mix)
"In the Mix"
"In the Mix" (performance mix)
"Freedom is a Constant Struggle"
"Freedom is a Constant Struggle" (performance mix)

Vocabulary
Phrase, vocal range

TEACHING THE LESSON

1. Introduce vocal exploration. Have the students:
• Read each statement on the page out loud. (While reading, use expressive qualities to emphasize the quality associated with each statement.)
• Discuss each statement in relation to the voice in general and the singing voice in particular.
• Listen and identify each vocal exercise after you have modeled the exercise on the neutral syllable *noo.*
• Sing each exercise using the words.
• Match the vocal exercise performed with a statement(s). (For example: *Breathing*: big sound, more breath; *Vowels*: emphasize clear voice; *Changing Voice*: lower.)
• Discuss *Think It Through.*

MORE TEACHING IDEAS

Sing each exercise in varied ways to explore different sensations in the singing experience. (Examples: try "Changing Voice" in different keys to identify changes in the voices, especially the boys; try "Breathing" at different tempos to experience different uses of the breath; have the class make up different words for "Diction," for example, *tumbleweed*, and *pots 'n' pans*. Explore new areas of articulation and diction. Connect "Stand Tall" and "Big Sound" with each of the exercises.)

Exploring Your Voice

Your voice is a complex musical instrument. Have you heard suggestions such as the following in your music class? What do you think is the purpose of each?

"Your pronunciation is great!"
"Stand tall."
"Try emphasizing the vowel more."
"Make a big sound here."
"Is your voice lower?"
"You have a very clear voice."
"Light on the top please."

Vocal Exercises

Explore your voice by practicing each of the following. After singing each exercise, choose the statement that best matches the exercise. Explain your choice.

Breathing

Sink - ing sun in ___ the sky, down ___ it comes, night ___ is nigh.

Diction

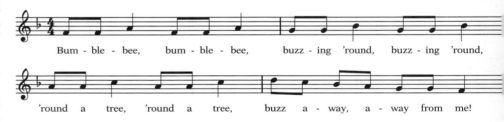

Bum - ble - bee, bum - ble - bee, buzz - ing 'round, buzz - ing 'round,

'round a tree, 'round a tree, buzz a - way, a - way from me!

300

Range

High — low, High — low, High — low, High — low, High — low, High — low.

Vowels

You, me, may I go? You, me, may I go? You, me, may I go?

Changing Voice

O ___ say, can you see, O ___ say, can you see,

As a singer, it's important to know your voice. As you grow older your voice will change. Continue to practice these and similar exercises as a way of monitoring and developing the most expressive instrument of all, your voice.

 THINK IT THROUGH: Create a plan to evaluate your progress over time.

MUSIC LIBRARY

MUSIC LIBRARY

2. Introduce "In the Mix" Have the students:

• Listen to the song and follow the score.

• Identify where unison and part singing are heard.

• Sing the melody with the accompaniment. (Focus on placing the tone, keeping an even quality of sound, and breathing properly to sustain the phrases. Changing voices may sing an octave lower.)

3. Practice placing the tone. Have the students:

• Discuss information on placing the tone. (Relate this to "In the Mix." Sing again as needed to demonstrate.)

• Listen, then sing as you model "I'm Shy" at varying pitch levels. (Help students sing with good breath control and focused vowels throughout their vocal ranges. They should place the tone either high or low in the voice and maintain a sustained vocal slide descending or ascending. Have the students sing in keys higher and lower as appropriate to include changing voices, and to expand all vocal ranges.)

• Sing individually and in small groups; focus on breathing and consistent tone throughout their ranges.

4. Introduce "America, America." Have the students:

• Listen and identify the phrases of "America, America." Learn the song by rote.

• Sing, listening to the change in tone quality between the lower and higher pitches of the melody. (You may wish to have half the class sing while the other half listens. Changing voices can sing the ostinato and alternate with other voices for variety.)

• Discuss how "Vocal Exercises" could be applied to this song.

PREPARING *to Sing "In the Mix"*

Some melodies move quickly between high and low pitches. To sing these melodies the singer must be able to place the tone comfortably from low to high pitches.

• Sing this pattern, moving higher and lower. The hum and vocal slide will help you place the tone over a wide vocal range.

Good vocal tone is produced when proper breathing and posture are combined with proper placement of the tone.

• Sing this short song while standing or sitting tall to help with your breathing. Stress the vowel sounds in each word to help develop your vocal tone.

America, America

Tradition

"In the Mix" contains melodies that cover a wide vocal range. Concentrate on placing your voice correctly to produce a good vocal tone while you sing.

302

In the Mix

Key: G major
Key: B♭ major
Key: E♭ major
Ranges I: A₁–C¹, II: G₁–E, III: F₁–C

CD7:38, CD9:9

"I Get Around," by Brian Wilson;
"Book of Love," Words and Music by Warren Davis,
George Malone, and Charles Patrick;
"Only You," Words and Music by Buck Ram and Ande Rand

Piano Accompaniment on page PA 34

"I Get Around" *(falsetto ad lib. throughout)*

Get a-round, round, round, I get a-round _ Get a-round, round, round,

I get a-round, _____ from _ town to town,

I get a-round. _ Get a-round, round, round, I get a-round, _

I'm a real cool head, _____

Get a-round, round, round, I get a-round, _ Get a-round, round, round,

Second time to ⊕

I'm mak-in' real good bread. _____ I'm get-tin'

Second time to ⊕

I get a-round, _ Get a-round, round, round, I get a-round.

bored driv-in' up and down the same old strip, I got-ta find a new place where the kids are _ hip.

My bud-dies and me are get-tin' real well known, Yeah, the

"Only You (And You Alone)" Words and Music by Buck Ram and Ande Rand
TRO-© Copyright 1955 (Renewed) Hollis Music, Inc., New York, NY. International Copyright
Secured. All Rights Reserved Including Public Performance For Profit. Used by Permission

303

• Emphasize breathing to sustain the tone through each phrase and then sing using the neutral syllables *tee* or *too*. Try to maintain the same vocal quality throughout the song. Sing with the words in higher and lower keys to experience differences in the use of breath and vowels.

• Sing as a two-, three-, or four-part round, following conducting gestures.

5. Teach "In the Mix." Have the students:

• Listen to the medley to identify the number of songs included. (three)

• Sing the unison melody sections. (Emphasize diction, vowels, phrasing, and tone placement throughout. The range should be appropriate for changing voices throughout most of this. Many students may know these songs and they may sing portions, especially the boys, in falsetto. Encourage all students to place the tone in the higher range whenever possible. Explore the lower and upper portions of the voice. Have students demonstrate this for the class.)

• Perform selected melodies individually and in small groups. Evaluate their performances.

• Discuss *Think It Through*.

MUSIC LIBRARY

THINK IT THROUGH: Evaluate the consistency of the tone quality in your vocal range. Recommend ways to improve the tone quality.

PREPARING *to Sing "Freedom Is a Constant Struggle"*

Vocal range describes the highest and lowest pitches a person can sing comfortably.

- Sing the opening passage of "Freedom is a Constant Struggle" in three different ranges. Listen to the quality of your voice in each range.

1.

2.

3.

THINK IT THROUGH: Which example contains the highest and lowest pitch you can sing comfortably? Which example is the most appropriate for your vocal range? Describe your vocal range. Compare your range to the range of others in your class.

305

6. Explore vocal range. Have the students:
- Discuss information on vocal range.
- Sing *Example 1* of "Freedom is a Constant Struggle." (Most voices should be singing comfortably here. Changing voices should sing at pitch.)
- Sing *Example 2*. (Identify those singing in the upper octave to determine highest pitch. Changing voices might sing an octave lower.)
- Sing *Example 3*. (Identify those who are singing in the lower octave to determine lowest pitch. Changing voices should be able to sing this at actual pitch.)
- Discuss the melody with the highest and lowest pitches and their own vocal ranges. Compare ranges with other class members. (Who has the widest range? Can sing the highest? The lowest?)

MUSIC LIBRARY

7. Teach "Freedom is a Constant Struggle." Have the students:

• Perform Warm-up 1 to develop skill in changing between bright and dark vowels.

• Locate the melody from *Example 1* in the score. (This appears two times—measures 1–4 and 7–10. Measures 4–7 have a variation.)

• Listen to the song and sing the melody they have learned.

• Divide into three parts and follow their parts in the score as they listen, then sing the song. (Descant: high trebles who sang *Example 3* comfortably; Melody: changing voices and low trebles; Baritone: boys who sang *Example 1* or *3* an octave lower.)

• Learn the baritone and the descant parts separately for each section. Sing these parts together slowly.

• Sing each part separately with the accompaniment, then combine parts.

• Perform "Freedom is a Constant Struggle" following conducting gestures, and emphasizing the placement of tone and vowels.

• Listen as the class or small groups perform. Discuss the performances.

APPRAISAL

The students should be able to:

1. Identify their vocal range from their highest to their lowest singing pitch.
2. Perform with attention to breathing, posture, vowels, diction, and balance.
3. Demonstrate increasing confidence in part singing.
4. Sing with increasing expressiveness.

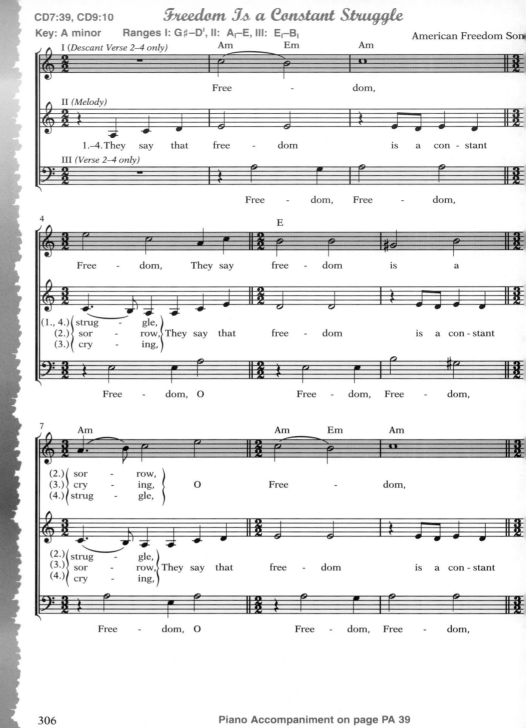

Freedom Is a Constant Struggle

Key: A minor   Ranges I: G♯–D', II: A₁–E, III: E₁–B₁

American Freedom Song

Piano Accompaniment on page PA 39

WARM-UP 1

Noo - ee - ah

Continue sequence to key of F.

Noo - ee - ah

Noo - ee - ah

307

MUSIC LIBRARY

Focus: Singing in Parts

Objectives
To develop and expand choral part-singing skills through performing rounds
To identify selected musical characteristics of two rounds

Materials
Recordings: "Big Ben"
"Big Ben" (performance mix)
"In Harmony"
"In Harmony" (performance mix)

TEACHING THE LESSON

1. Teach "Big Ben." Have the students:
• Speak the rhythm of the ⁶⁄₈ pattern.
• Clap the pattern as a two-, three-, and four-part round with and without speaking.
• Compare the rhythms of the preparation exercise with the rhythms of "Big Ben," and speak and perform the rhythm of "Big Ben" in two, three, and four parts.
• Listen to the song; sing the melody with and without accompaniment. (Boys with changing voices should sing measures 1–4 as written and measures 5–8 an octave lower. Baritone voices should sing parts as written.)
• Divide into parts and perform as a two-, three-, or four-part round.
• Perform in small groups. Discuss the blend and the balance between parts.
• Compare the scores of "In Harmony" and "Big Ben."
• Listen to "In Harmony" and sing the melody, repeat as necessary for confidence.
• Sing as a two-, three- and four-part round.
• Further compare the two rounds, relating the differences in mood to choral performance.

2. Perform "Big Ben" and "In Harmony." Have the students:
• Sing both rounds again focusing on the differences in mood.
• Discuss *Think It Through*.

APPRAISAL

The students should be able to:
1. Demonstrate confidence in singing parts in a two-, three-, and four-part round.
2. Describe selected musical characteristics of two rounds.

PREPARING *to Sing "Big Ben"*

In a round, one group of singers starts before the others. When all groups have entered the round, harmony is created. The round "Big Ben" has four parts, one for each group of singers.

• Speak this rhythm to feel the dance-like quality of the ⁶⁄₈ meter, then speak the round in four parts.

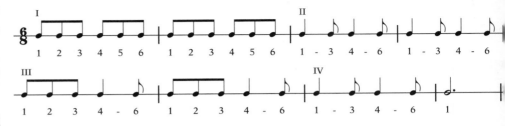

Key: C major   Range: E₁–C¹

Big Ben

Piano Accompaniment on page PA 44

Music by Louis Köhler
Words by MMH

I hear Big Ben from far a - way, I hear it chime, I hear it say, "E - lev - en o' - clock, Or sev - en o' - clock, I'll chime the time of day." _____

The round "In Harmony" also has four parts. Compare and contrast the styles of these two rounds. Describe the mood of each.

Key: G major   Range: D–C¹

In Harmony

Piano Accompaniment on page PA 45

Music by Thomas Tallis
Words by MMH

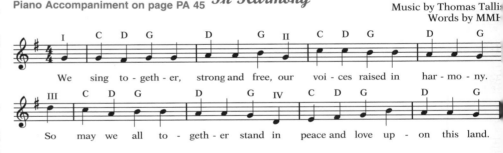

We sing to - geth - er, strong and free, our voi - ces raised in har - mo - ny.
So may we all to - geth - er stand in peace and love up - on this land.

THINK IT THROUGH: Assess how well your performance reflects the mood. Explain your point of view.

308

PREPARING *to Sing "Red Iron Ore"*

"Red Iron Ore" has various rhythm patterns in $\frac{6}{8}$ meter.

• Speak these rhythms from the melody.

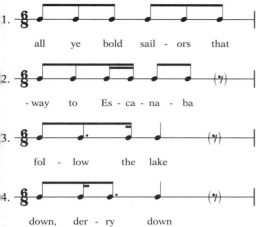

1. all ye bold sail - ors that

2. - way to Es - ca - na - ba

3. fol - low the lake

4. down, der - ry down

Most of the pitches in the melody of "Red Iron Ore" are in the range of a boy's changing voice, or **cambiata**.

• Sing this part of "Red Iron Ore" to help you focus your sound in the cambiata range.

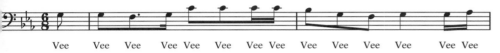

Vee Vee Vee Vee Vee Vee Vee Vee Vee Vee Vee Vee Vee Vee

The **refrain** section of "Red Iron Ore" is arranged for two vocal parts. One is for treble voices, and the other is for baritone. The cambiata voices can sing either part.

• Sing each part individually. Then sing both parts together.

Treble/Cambiata

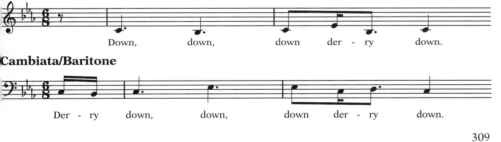

Down, down, down der - ry down.

Cambiata/Baritone

Der - ry down, down, down der - ry down.

MUSIC LIBRARY

Focus: The Male Voice: Cambiata and Baritone

Objectives
To reinforce confidence in singing
To expand skills in two-part singing
To further identify vocal ranges and classifications

Materials
Recordings: "Red Iron Ore"
"Red Iron Ore"
(performance mix)

Vocabulary
cambiata, refrain

TEACHING THE LESSON

1. Prepare to sing "Red Iron Ore." Have the students:

• Speak and perform rhythm patterns 1–4 from "Red Iron Ore" by clapping the eighth notes, snapping the sixteenth notes, and pat-sliding the dotted eighth notes and quarter notes.

• Form two groups and perform different combinations of the rhythms by speaking them at the same time. (Emphasize independence of parts and rhythmic accuracy.)

• Perform the patterns individually and in small groups (Perform each one separately and then in combination.)

• Locate patterns 1, 2, 3, and 4 in "Red Iron Ore."

2. Define cambiata. Have the students:

• Listen, follow the score as you model, then sing the melodic example on *vee*. (The neutral syllable *vee* promotes a bright sound as well as a focused tone.)

• Listen as only the boys sing the exercise in small groups. (Note for the students the change in sound quality and range of the unchanged treble and the baritone voices. Those boys who sing the example with a light, comfortable vocal quality and an evenness of sound have voices that may be changing.)

MUSIC LIBRARY

3. Introduce the refrain of "Red Iron Ore." Have the students:
• Listen, follow the score as you model, then sing each vocal line from the refrain.
• Divide into voice parts (treble, baritone, and cambiata) and visually identify which vocal line to sing. (Cambiatas may sing either part—if they sing with the baritones, they should sing an octave higher. Baritones sing the lower part.)
• In their appropriate parts, sing the refrain separately, and then combined.

4. Teach "Red Iron Ore." Have the students:
• Follow their parts in the score as they listen to the recording.
• Sing the first verse and refrain with the accompaniment. (The cambiatas should sing an octave higher as appropriate.)
• Sing solos on verses 1–6 with the accompaniment. (Have baritones, cambiatas, and treble voice boys sing solos to gain confidence.)
• Learn parts separately for measures 11–17. Look for repetition or similarity to parts previously learned. Sing parts combined.
• Perform with accompaniment. (Focus on maintaining good vocal balance between voice parts, and blend within each part.)
• Sing with and without accompaniment while following conducting gestures. (Emphasize eye contact with attention to attacks and releases.)

5. Perform "Red Iron Ore." Have the students:
• Perform in two parts with males only, then with mixed ensembles (with and without accompaniment.)
• Perform again with all students singing.
• Discuss the performances.
• Discuss *Think It Through*.

APPRAISAL

The students should be able to:
1. Demonstrate increased confidence in singing.
2. Sing in two parts with accuracy.
3. Demonstrate understanding of cambiata and baritone vocal ranges.

Key: C minor

Red Iron Ore   **Ranges I:** B♭₁–E♭, **II:** C₁₁–C

Piano Accompaniment on page PA 46

Boat Song from the Great Lakes Region
Arranged by M.

down der-ry down. Der-ry down, down, down der-ry down. Down,___ down,

down der-ry down. Down, down, down der-ry down. Der-ry down, down,

down der - ry down. Down,___ down, down der - ry down!

down der - ry down. Der-ry down, down, down der - ry down!

💡 **THINK IT THROUGH:** Evaluate the balance between the two parts in "Red Iron Ore." Suggest ways to attain better balance.

PREPARING *to Sing "Goin' Down to Cairo"*

The parts of "Goin' Down to Cairo" contain many repeated melody patterns. After practicing each pattern separately you'll be able to sing the entire composition more easily.

Sing these melodic patterns. Find them, and similar patterns, in "Goin' Down to Cairo."

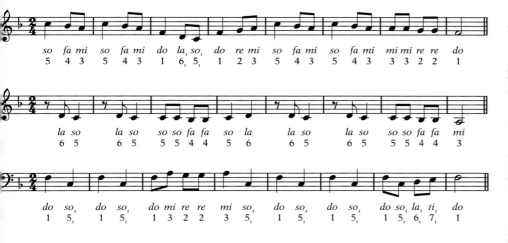

so fa mi so fa mi do la, so, do re mi so fa mi so fa mi mi mi re re do
5 4 3 5 4 3 1 6, 5, 1 2 3 5 4 3 5 4 3 3 3 2 2 1

la so   la so   so so fa fa so la   la so   la so   so so fa fa mi
6 5   6 5   5 5 4 4   5 6   6 5   6 5   5 5 4 4   3

do so, do so, do mi re re mi so, do so, do so, do so, la, ti, do
1 5,   1 5,   1 3 2 2   3 5,   1 5,   1 5,   1 5, 6, 7,   1

311

MUSIC LIBRARY

Focus: Singing in Three Parts

Objectives
To expand skills in singing in three parts
To reinforce melody reading

Materials
Recordings: "Goin' Down to Cairo"
"Goin' Down to Cairo" (performance mix)
Copying Master C1 (optional)

TEACHING THE LESSON

1. Prepare to sing "Goin' Down to Cairo." Have the students:
• Sing up and down the F-major scale to establish the key.
• Sing each of the three vocal examples with pitch syllables or numbers.
• Locate each part in "Goin' Down to Cairo."
• Learn and perform Warm-up 2.
• Focus on rhythmic and pitch precision while maintaining an even quality of sound.

WARM-UP 2

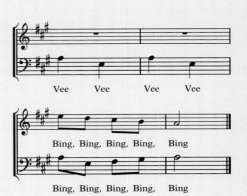

Vee   Vee   Vee   Vee

Vee   Vee   Vee   Vee
Continue sequence to the key of A.

Vee   Vee   Vee   Vee

Bing, Bing, Bing, Bing, Bing

Bing, Bing, Bing, Bing, Bing

Bing, Bing, Bing, Bing, Bing

Bing, Bing, Bing, Bing, Bing

Bing, Bing, Bing, Bing, Bing

Bing, Bing, Bing, Bing, Bing

MUSIC LIBRARY

2. Introduce "Goin' Down to Cairo."
Have the students:

• Form three groups and listen to the song, following their part in the score.

• Softly sing their part using a short neutral syllable *doo*. Focus on pitch and rhythmic accuracy.

• Learn Parts I, II, and III separately for the first section (measures 1–24). Use first the neutral syllable *doo*, and then the words.

• Combine two, and then three parts beginning with Parts II and III.

• Review and refine Parts I, II, and III separately for measures 25–32. Combine parts in varying combinations, with small groups, placing an emphasis on crisp diction and balance.

• Sing measures 1–32 in three parts with accompaniment.

Goin' Down to Cairo

Illinois Play–Party Song
Arranged by M.J.

- Learn Parts I, II, and III separately for measures 33–36.
4. Perform "Goin' Down to Cairo." Have the students:
- Sing all three parts with accompaniment. (Focus on crisp diction and maintaining good vocal balance between voice parts.)
- Follow conducting gestures and sing in three parts with and without accompaniment. (Emphasize eye contact and attention to attacks at the beginnings of phrases.)
- Identify the musical characteristics of "Goin' Down to Cairo."
- Listen as individuals and small ensembles perform. Discuss the performances and evaluate rhythmic precision.

APPRAISAL

The students should be able to:
1. Demonstrate expanded skills in singing in three parts.
2. Read and sing melodic patterns that move by steps and skips with more confidence.

MUSIC LIBRARY

Focus: Musical Style: Native American

Objectives
To experience a musical style of a Native American culture
To reinforce the reading and singing of repeated melodic patterns

Materials
Recordings: "Powama"
Recorded Lesson:
"Pronunciation: 'Powama'"

TEACHING THE LESSON

1. Introduce "Powama." Have the students:
• Read about the origin of the song. (See also *Background* below.)
• Listen to the song and discuss the style. (unison, repeated melodic and rhythm patterns, many of them syncopated)
• Identify repeated melodic patterns and repeated rhythmic patterns.
2. Teach "Powama." Have the students:
• Listen to the song again, singing the melody softly on the neutral syllable *too*. (Encourage students with changing voices to sing in their upper range throughout.)
• Listen and follow the score as you model short sections using the neutral syllable *too*. Locate each section being modeled. Sing it back and identity the measure or measures by number.
• Listen to "Pronunciation: 'Powama,'" and practice as needed, then sing the melody with the words.

APPRAISAL

The students should be able to:
1. Perform music of a Native American culture with attention to musical style.
2. Demonstrate improved skills in reading and in singing music containing repeated melodic and rhythmic patterns.

EXTENSION

BACKGROUND

"Powama" is a song of the Native American Cahuilla tribe of south-central California. "Powama" is of a genre of Cahuilla songs known as "Bird Songs." These songs relate to the origin of the world and life on earth and have accompanying dances. The text of Powama is translated to mean "these feathers move when you dance."

The Cahuilla (kä-wē´yə) tribe has lived in what is now south-central California for centuries. They still maintain many of their traditional ceremonies, songs, dances, and other forms of cultural expression. "Powama" comes from the body of Cahuilla songs known as "Bird Songs."

CD8:3–4

Powama

Key: Mixolydian mode on B♭   Range: B♭₁–B♭

Traditional Cahuilla Indian Song

y: B♭ major   Range: B♭₁–E♭¹   *The Seasons*

Music by William Byrd
Words by MMH

ano Accompaniment on page PA 53

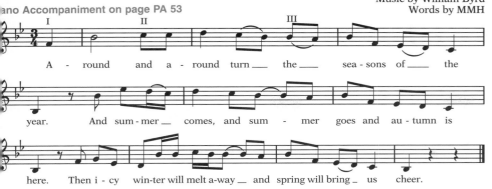

A - round   and   a - round   turn ___ the ___ sea-sons of ___ the

year.   And sum-mer ___ comes, and sum - mer goes and au-tumn is

here.   Then i - cy win-ter will melt a-way ___ and spring will bring ___ us   cheer.

THINK IT THROUGH: Experiment with varying tempos, dynamics, and word colors in "The Seasons." Choose an expressive combination for your performance. Justify your choices.

REPARING *to Sing "La Cigarra"*

'La Cigarra," is a favorite song in Mexico. The title refers to a cicada, n insect with a colorful song. This song has a characteristic $\frac{6}{8}(\frac{3}{4})$ Mexican beat. Practice these rhythms to help you feel the beat.

315

MUSIC LIBRARY

Focus: Musical Diversity: Mexican

Objectives
To explore expressive singing with a three-part round
To experience music of Mexico
To sing melodic patterns with changing meters and rhythms

Materials
Recordings: "The Seasons"
"The Seasons (performance mix)"
"La Cigarra"
Recorded Lesson: "Pronunciation: 'La Cigarra'"
"La Cigarra" (performance mix)
Copying Master C-2 (optional)

TEACHING THE LESSON

1. Teach "The Seasons." Have the students:
• Examine the score, describe and compare its phrases, then listen to the song. (Each of the three phrases ends in the same way.)
• Sing up and down the B-flat major scale to establish the key.
• Listen as you model measures 3, 6, and 9, then sing with emphasis on tone, phrasing, and musical style.
• Listen to the song and sing on measures 3, 6, and 9.
• Listen and sing the entire melody. (Repeat vocal modeling as needed.)
• Sing the song with accompaniment.
• Divide into three groups. Sing the song with accompaniment as a three-part round.
• Discuss *Think It Through*.
• Create a performance plan based on the decisions made in *Think It Through*, and perform "The Seasons" focusing on these qualities.
• Discuss and evaluate the performance.

BACKGROUND

Originally recorded in the 1940s, "La Cigarra" is among many favorite Mexican *huapangos*. It is a song of love, and of love of song. *Huapango* refers to traditional dance and music from the Huasteca region of northern Veracruz and its adjacent states in Mexico. It is commonly sung by two vocalists alternating verses, often in falsetto. Traditionally, the singers are accompanied by violin, five-string guitar (*jarana*), and an eight-string guitar (*huapanguera*). Its distinctive mixed-meter rhythm has been widely popularized.

MUSIC LIBRARY

2. Introduce "La Cigarra." Have the students:

• Practice the rhythms in the text.

• Listen to the song and discuss the style. (rhythmic, changing meter unison, long, sustained notes)

3. Teach the melody of "La Cigarra." Have the students:

• Listen to the song again, singing the melody softly on the neutral syllable *loo*. (Repeat as necessary.)

• Listen to "Pronunciation: 'La Cigarra.'" Practice Spanish pronunciation.

• Sing the melody using words. (Use teacher and student modeling to assist.)

• Sing with the recording.

• Listen for correct pronunciation and accurate rhythms as individuals or small groups sing.

4. Perform "La Cigarra." Have the students:

• Sing the song with accompaniment, following conducting gestures. (Emphasize pronunciation, breathing to sustain long phrases, and rhythmic accuracy.)

APPRAISAL

The students should be able to:

1. Perform a three-part round with confidence and attention to performing rhythmic patterns accurately.

2. Perform music of Mexico with attention to musical style.

3. Sing a song with changing meter and repeated rhythmic patterns.

La Cigarra (The Cicada)

Piano Accompaniment on page PA 54   Key: A minor/A major   Range: G_1–E^1 Words and Music by Ray Perez y Soto

1. Ya no me can-tes ci-ga-rra que a-ca-be tu son-so-ne-te que tu can-to a quien el al-ma co-mo un pu-ñal se me me-te sa-bien-do que cuan-do can---tas pre-go-nan-do vas tu muer-te.

2. Un pal-o-mi-to al vo-lar que lle-va-ba el pe-cho he-ri-do ya ca-si pa-ra llo-rar me di-jo muy a-fli-gi-do ya me can-so de bus-car---un a-mor cor-res-pon-di-do.

Ma-ri-ne-ro, ma-ri-ne-ro di-me si es ver-dad que sa-bes por-que dis-tin-guir no pue-do

Ba-jo la som-bra de un ar-bol y al com-pás de mi gui-ta-rra can-to a-leg-re es-te hua-pan-go

316

EXTENSION

PRONUNCIATION

"La Cigarra"
Verse 1
jyä nō mā kän' təs sē-gä'rrä kā ä-kä' bā tōo sōn sō nā' tā
kā tōo kän' tō ä kyen el äl' mä kō' mō ōon pōo-nyäl' sä mä mā' tä
sä-byen' dō kā kwän' dō kän' täs
prā-gō nän' dō bäs tōo mwer' tä
mä-rē-nā' rō dē' mä syes bər-däd' kä sä' vəs pōr-kä' dēs-tēn-gēr'
nō pwā' dō syen' el fōn' dō dä lōs mä räs äy ō' trō cō-lōr'
mäs nā' grō kãel cō lōr' dä mēs pä sä' rəs äy lä
Verse 2
ōon pä-lō-mē' tōal vō-lär' kä jyā bä väel pä chō-ä-rē' dō

jyä kä' sē pä' rä jyō-rär' mā dē' KHō mōoy äf-lē-KHē' dō
jyä mä kän' sō dä bōos-kär' ōon ä-mōr' cō-rrəs pōn-dē' dō
bä' KHō lä sōm' brä dä-ōon är' bōl yäl kōm-päs' dä mē gē-tä' rrä
kän' tō-ä-le'-grrä-es-tä hwä-pän' gō pōr-kä'
lä vē' dä sää-kä' bä ē kyä' rō
mō-rēr' kän-tän' dō kō' mō mwä' rä lä
sē gä' rrä ē mwä' rä
lä sē-gä' rrä

TRANSLATION

The Cicada

Don't sing to me anymore, cicada
Let your singsong end
For your song, here in the soul
Stabs me like a dagger
Knowing that when you sing
You are proclaiming that you are going to your death.

Sailor, sailor
Tell me if it is true that you know
Because I cannot distinguish
If in the depth of the seas
There is another color more black
Than the color of my sorrows.

317

A little dove upon flying
Bearing a wounded breast
Was about to cry
And told me very afflicted
I'm tired of searching for
A mutual love.

Under the shade of a tree
And to the beat of my guitar
I sing this huapango happily
And I want to die singing
Like the cicada dies.

MUSIC LIBRARY

Focus: Sight Reading

Objectives
To learn about careers in musical theater
To apply music-reading skills to a song
from a Broadway musical
To review syncopation

Materials
Recordings: "Milk and Honey"
              "Milk and Honey"
              (performance mix)

Vocabulary
Sight reading, syncopation

TEACHING THE LESSON

1. Introduce text on Broadway careers.
Have the students:
• Read and discuss the introductory information.
• Identify books or movies that might work as a musical and give reasons for their choices. (Discuss the different aspects of a musical: dancing, solo and group singing, costumes, and sets.)
2. Introduce "Milk and Honey." Have the students:
• Read and learn about the origin of the song.
• Follow the melody in the score as they listen to "Milk and Honey."
3. Introduce sight-reading exercises. Have the students:
• Establish a steady beat and then read and clap the rhythm from "Milk and Honey" on page 319 .
• Establish a steady beat and then read and perform the rhythm for each exercise by tapping the eighth notes in the palm of their hand, clapping quarter notes, and using a pat-slide movement for half notes and whole notes.

EXTENSION

MORE MUSIC TEACHING IDEAS

1. Challenge a group of students to develop a small-scale musical from one of their favorite stories as a long-term project. Listen to the interview with Alan Menken for ideas (page 289). They might also attend a local production of a musical or view a film version of a musical for ideas.
2. A backstage tour at a professional theater, including dressing rooms, pit, workshop, fly gallery, and lighting booth would add another dimension to this study of Broadway songs.

Choral Anthology

Careers on Broadway

People come from all over the world for the bright lights of Broadway in New York City. Broadway musicals have thrilled audiences for decades. Large-scale musicals involve many people with diverse careers, each bringing a variety of talents to the project.

Musicals start with story ideas. Often these ideas come from other plays or from books which are then adapted to create a musical. *Les Misérables* of Shöenberg and Boublil was based on the novel of the same name by Victor Hugo. Andrew Lloyd Webber's musical *Cats* was based on poems of Nobel Prize winner T. S. Elliot.

When the story ideas have been developed, the words for the songs are written by the lyricist and set to music by the composer. Once the words and the music are written, the **director** works with the **music director** and **choreographer** to bring the musical to life, combining many elements to create a balanced whole. The music director helps the **actors** learn their songs, and often conducts the **orchestra**. The choreographer creates the dance routines and teaches them to the actors and **dancers**.

Many people work on the look and sound of the production. The **set designer**, **lighting designer, sound technicians, costume designers, make-up artists** and **hair stylists** have the ideas that will help to transport the audience to a different time and place, and help the actor create a character that comes alive on stage. All work together to prepare for opening night. When it finally arrives, a hush falls in the theater, the lights are dimmed, and as the curtain rises, the audience is led on a journey of imagination and delight.

As you sing the following choral selections, think of a favorite book or movie that might work well as a musical. Decide how each of the songs could fit into your musical, and write new lyrics, adapting them to your story-line. Once you have the songs, create dance steps, costumes, and a set design. When you have rehearsed your musical, give a performance for your friends. Who knows? With time and effort, you might end up with a career under the bright lights of Broadway.

318

PREPARING *to Sing "Milk and Honey"*

The Broadway musical *Milk and Honey* depicts the strong spirit and determination of the people of Israel. This spirit can be heard in the song "Milk and Honey," which describes the plentiful land of Israel.

Practice Your Music Reading Skills—Sight-reading

• Sight-read this rhythm pattern.

The following patterns are similar to sections of the melody in "Milk and Honey."

• Clap, tap, and sing these patterns.

• Sing these patterns, then find them in "Milk and Honey."

A.

B.

C.

319

MUSIC LIBRARY

• Read and perform each rhythm pattern individually and in small groups.
• Sing up and down a C-major scale to establish the tonality. (Write the scale on the board.)
• Follow and sing melodic patterns you and student volunteers create by pointing to scale tones. (Include here isolated patterns from "Milk and Honey.")
• Read and sing each melodic line using pitch syllables and numbers. (You may wish to review pitch syllables and numbers. Focus on singing the syllables with pure vowels to help develop tone. Model as appropriate.)
• Find examples A, B, and C in "Milk and Honey" and perform each example once more.
4. Introduce Warm-Up 3. Have the students:
• Divide into assigned voice parts—Part I, trebles and boys with unchanged voices; Part II, lower trebles and boys with changing voices; Part III, changing voices and baritones.
• Sing Warm-Up 3 to assist in learning to perform "Milk and Honey." (Focus on developing an energetic quality of tone, quick vowel focus, and ensemble precision with the syncopated pattern.)
• Perform the song on different neutral syllables (*yoo, yee*), attempting to maintain the same qualities listed above.

WARM-UP 3

Yah Yah Yah Yah Yah

Continue sequence to key of F.

Yah Yah Yah Yah Yah

Yah Yah Yah Yah Yah

5. Teach "Milk and Honey." Have the students:

• Sing their parts softly while they listen to "Milk and Honey" and follow the score using the qualities practiced in Warm-Up 3 to improve their performance. (The goal at this point should be accurate reading of melodic and syncopated patterns. Repeat listening and singing on the neutral syllable *loo* as needed to develop confidence.)

• Learn Parts I, II, and III separately, emphasizing vowel accuracy.

• Combine Parts III and II, and then combine Parts III, II, and I.

• Review and refine Parts I, II, and III as needed.

• Sing again individually and with small groups.

6. Perform "Milk and Honey." Have the students:

• Sing the song with accompaniment.

• Discuss and evaluate the performance in terms of vowel focus and ensemble precision.

Key: C major

Piano Accompaniment on page PA 62

Milk and Honey
from *Milk and Honey*

CD8:8, CD9:17

Ranges I: A$_I$–E^I, II: A$_I$–B, III: C$_{II}$–D

Words and Music by Jerry Herman

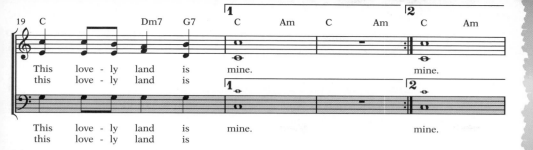

This love - ly land is mine. mine.
this love - ly land is mine. mine.
This love - ly land is mine. mine.
this love - ly land is

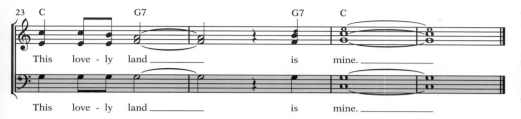

This love - ly land _____ is mine. _____
This love - ly land _____ is mine. _____

Music and Lyric by Jerry Herman
© 1961 (Renewed) JERRY HERMAN. All Rights Controlled by JERRYCO MUSIC CO.
Exclusive Agent: EDWIN H. MORRIS & COMPANY, A Division of MPL
Communications, Inc. All Rights Reserved.

 THINK IT THROUGH: Determine ways to highlight the syncopated rhythms best. Evaluate how effectively your performance conveyed the energy of the song.

Practice Your Music Reading Skills — Syncopation

"Milk and Honey" contains syncopated rhythm patterns. Syncopation emphasizes beats or parts of the beat that are not normally emphasized.

- Read these rhythm patterns to yourself. What words in "Milk and Honey" match these rhythm patterns?

- Clap each pattern as you say the words. Which part of the rhythm pattern contains syncopation? You can tell because it feels catchy and uneven.

- Practice these syncopated exercises. Tap a steady beat with your foot as you speak and clap the syncopation.

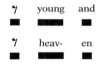

321

7. Practice syncopation. Have the students:
- Discuss *Think It Through*.
- Read each rhythm and identify the words from "Milk and Honey" that go with each rhythm. (Both occur several times.)
- Clap each pattern and speak the words to identify the syncopation.
- Practice syncopated patterns by tapping a steady beat as they speak and clap each example.
- Read and sing the score, focusing on accurate performance of the syncopation.
- Perform "Milk and Honey" with and without accompaniment.
- Evaluate each performance in terms of the rhythmic precision, energetic quality of tone, and quick vowel focus.

APPRAISAL

The students should be able to:
1. Identify careers in musical theater.
2. Demonstrate increased confidence maintaining their own voice part in three-part choral singing.
3. Accurately perform syncopated rhythm patterns.

MUSIC LIBRARY

Focus: Syncopation

Objectives
To read and perform syncopated rhythms in a Broadway song
To review the use of a tie in music

Materials
Recordings: "Together Wherever We Go"
"Together Wherever We Go"
(performance mix)

Vocabulary
Syncopation, tie

TEACHING THE LESSON

1. Introduce the preparation. Have the students:
• Read and learn about the origin of the song.
• Listen to the song and discuss the style, text, and use of syncopation.
• Establish a steady beat and then read and clap the two syncopated patterns on page 322. (Discuss why the tie is used here.)
• Sing a B♭-major scale to establish the tonality.
• Learn and sing the melodic excerpt from "Together Wherever We Go" by rote, noting the syncopation and melodic leaps.
• Discuss *Think It Through*.

2. Teach "Together Wherever We Go." Have the students:
• Sing the melody softly as they listen to the song again. (Encourage boys whose voices are changing to sing in their upper range throughout the composition.)
• Identify repeated rhythmic patterns. (Measures 1–6 are repeated in measures 9–14 and 33–38.)

PREPARING *to Sing "Together Wherever We Go"*

Ethel Merman's performance in *Gypsy* helped make her a Broadway legend. Jule Styne and Stephen Sondheim worked together to create the music and the lyrics for *Gypsy*. As with many musicals, there have been different versions on both the stage and in the movies. Many other great stars, such as Angela Lansbury, Natalie Wood, and Bette Midler have helped make *Gypsy* a well-loved classic. The song "Together Wherever We Go" expresses the friendship of the characters, who vow to stick together through "thick and thin."

Practice Your Music Reading Skills — Syncopation

• Clap this syncopated rhythm pattern.

• Clap this pattern. A tie between the two quarter notes makes this syncopated pattern more challenging.

In "Together Wherever We Go" this rhythm pattern is combined with a melodic pattern that contains many leaps.

• Sing this melody from "Together Wherever We Go" to experience the melodic leaps.

gon - na go through _ it to - geth - er.

 THINK IT THROUGH: Assess the accuracy of your performance of the rhythms and melodic leaps. Recommend ways to improve the precision.

322

Together Wherever We Go
from *Gypsy*

Words by Stephen Sondheim
Music by Jule Styne

Moderately

Wher - ev - er we go. ___ What - ev - er we do. ___ We're gon-na go through ___ it to -

geth - er. ___ We may not go far. ___ But sure as a star. ___ Wher -

ev - er we are, ___ it's to - geth - er ___ Wher - ev - er I go, ___ I know he goes. ___

___ Wher - ev - er I go, ___ I know she goes. ___ No fits, no fights, no

feuds and no e - gos. ___ A - mi-gos, ___ To - geth-er! Through

thick and through thin. ___ All out or all in. ___ And wheth-er it's win ___

___ place or show, ___ With you for me and me for you, We'll mud-dle through what-ev -

ad lib. ending

- er we do ___ To - geth - er, wher - ev - er we go! ___

323

MUSIC LIBRARY

• Follow the score as you model one or more measures from the song on a neutral syllable. (Have the students listen and identify which measures are being modeled, echo-sing the measure, and identify the measure by number.)
• Listen to the song again and learn the melody.
• Sing the song again, individually and in small groups.

3. Perform "Together Wherever We Go." Have the students:
• Sing the song with accompaniment. (Emphasize accurate performance of syncopation, crisp diction, and clear articulation.)
• Discuss and evaluate the performance.

APPRAISAL

The students should be able to:
1. Sing syncopated rhythms with increased confidence and accuracy.
2. Demonstrate an understanding of the use of a tie.

MUSIC LIBRARY

Focus: ⅜ Meter

Objectives
To read and sing a Broadway song that uses contrasting meters
To review identification of various meters, both aurally and in notation

Materials
Recordings: "Food, Glorious Food"
"Food, Glorious Food"
(performance mix)

TEACHING THE LESSON

1. Introduce "Food, Glorious Food."
Have the students:
• Read and learn about the origin of the song.
• Listen to the song and discuss the style, the text, and the use of different meters. (Students should note that in this recording, each soloist suggests his character's personality by using a unique singing style.)
• Establish a steady beat and then read and clap the rhythm pattern. Repeat at various tempos.
• Read and perform individually and in small groups, emphasizing accuracy of rhythm and maintaining a steady beat.
• Sing a C-major scale to establish the tonality.
• Sing the melody using pitch syllables and numbers.
• Sing individually and in small groups, (Emphasize accurate rhythm and pitch and maintaining a steady beat.)
• Discuss the accuracy of their performance.
• Discuss *Think It Through*.

PREPARING *to Sing "Food, Glorious Food"*

The musical *Oliver!* is based on Charles Dickens' novel *Oliver Twist*. Lionel Bart reworked this classic story about the orphan Oliver into a successful musical. It opened in London in 1960 and ran for 2,628 performances. This set a record for the longest running musical ever. In "Food, Glorious Food," Oliver Twist and his friends at the orphanage dream about how nice it would be to have delicious food, instead of their usual gruel. It is this strong craving for "glorious food" which sends Oliver on his wild journey where he encounters the evil Sikes, the mischievous Fagin, and the slow-witted Bumble.

Practice Your Music Reading Skills — ¾ meter

   Dotted half notes are often found in ¾ meter. A dot after a note means that one-half the value of the note is added to the original value. Since a half note equals two beats, a dotted half note equals three beats.

• Clap this ¾ rhythm pattern from "Food, Glorious Food."

• Sing this melody with the rhythms you just practiced.

There are three different meter signatures in "Food, Glorious Food." As you listen to the song, locate and identify the meter changes.

THINK IT THROUGH: In "Food, Glorious Food," the mood changes when the meter changes. Describe how the change of meter supports the new musical mood of each section.

324

Key: F major/C major   Range: C–E¹

CD8:10, CD9:19

Food, Glorious Food
from Oliver!

Piano Accompaniment on page PA 65

Words and Music by Lionel Bart

(solos and groups alternate)

Is it worth wait-ing for? If we live 'til eight-y - four, All we ev - er get is

gru - el! Ev - 'ry day we say a pray'r, will they change the bill of fare?

Still we get the same old gru - el! There's not a crust, not a crumb can we find, can we

beg, can we bor - row or cadge. But there's noth - ing to stop us from

rall.

get - ting a thrill when we all close our eyes and im - ag - ine;

mf

Food, glo - ri - ous food! ____ Hot sau - sage and mus - tard! ____

While we're in the mood, ____ cold jel - ly and cus - tard! ____

325

MUSIC LIBRARY

2. Teach "Food, Glorious Food." Have the students:
• Sing the melody softly while they listen to "Food, Glorious Food." (Encourage boys whose voices are changing to sing in their upper range throughout the composition.)
• Identify repeated patterns. (Measures 17–24 are repeated numerous times.)
• Contrast the rhythm of the first eight measures of the ¾ section with the first eight measures of the ¢ section.
• Follow the score as you model one or more measures on a neutral syllable, and echo-sing after each modeling. (As you sing, choose examples from each of the three meters. The students should listen closely for the meter and identify it after they sing.)
• Listen, learn, and sing the melody.
• Sing again with individuals taking turns singing solo.

3. Perform "Food, Glorious Food." Have the students:
• Create a performance plan for solo and group singing.
• Sing "Food, Glorious Food" with accompaniment. (Emphasize accurate performance of contrasting meters and of expressive singing.)
• Discuss and evaluate the performance in terms of accurate execution of meter changes and style.

APPRAISAL

The students should be able to:
1. Accurately sing a song that uses contrasting meters.
2. Identify meter changes by visual and aural cues.

reel - ing, _____ One mo - ment of know - ing that

full - up feel - ing! _____ Food, glo - ri - ous

food! _____ What would - n't we give for, _____

that ex - tra bit more, _____ That's all ___ that we live for, _____

Why should ___ we be fat - ed to do noth - ing but brood on

cresc.

food, mag - ic - al food, won - der-ful food, mar - vel-ous food, fab - u-lous

f

u-lous food, glo - ri-ous food, glo - ri - ous ___ food! _____

327

MUSIC LIBRARY

Focus: Patterns

Objectives
To recognize and perform melodic patterns
To reinforce understanding of good vocal ensemble

Materials
Recordings: "Freedom"
"Freedom" (performance mix)

Vocabulary
Patterns

TEACHING THE LESSON

1. Introduce "Freedom." Have the students:
• Read about the origin of the song.
• Listen to the song and discuss the musical style.
• Establish a steady beat and then read and clap rhythm patterns A and B from "Freedom."
• Read and perform each rhythm pattern individually and in small groups.
• Examine the musical score and locate each pattern. (A: measures 9–12; B: measures 13–16)
• Sing a G-major scale to establish the tonality.
• Learn and sing the melodic patterns A and B from "Freedom" on a neutral syllable. (Point out to the students that pattern A contains non-pitched notes that should be clapped.)
• Read and sing the patterns individually and in groups emphasizing accuracy of rhythm and pitch.
• Discuss *Think It Through*.

PREPARING *to Sing "Freedom"*

The musical *Shenandoah* tells the story of a household struggling with life during the American Civil War. In the song "Freedom," Gabriel, a youth who has recently been freed from slavery, sings about his new life. He says that freedom isn't a place to go, but a way of thinking about life.

Practice Your Music Reading Skills — Patterns

• Clap or tap the rhythms in these patterns from "Freedom." Then find these patterns in the song and sing them with the song text.

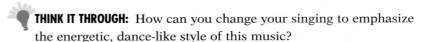

THINK IT THROUGH: How can you change your singing to emphasize the energetic, dance-like style of this music?

Freedom
from *Shenandoah*   Piano Accompaniment on page PA 72

Key: G major   Ranges I: B₁–G¹, II: D₁–D

Words by Peter Udell
Music by Gary Geld

Free-dom!

1. Free-dom ain't a state like Maine or Vir-gin-ia.
2. Free-dom ain't a boat that's leav-in' with-out ya,
3. Free-dom is a no-tion sweep-in' the na-tion,

Free-dom ain't a-cross a coun-ty line.   Free-dom is a flame that
Free-dom ain't a piece ya float to find.   Free-dom is the how ya
Free-dom is the right of all man-kind.   Free-dom is a bo-dy's

burns with-in ya.
think a-bout ya,   Free-dom is a state   of mind.   Free-dom,
'mag-i-na-tion.

free-dom.   Free-dom, free-dom.   Free-dom is a hope that

3rd time to Coda

burns with-in ya,   Free-dom is a state   of mind.

329

MUSIC LIBRARY

2. Teach "Freedom." Have the students:
• Divide into two groups. (Treble and unchanged voices should sing the upper line; changing voices and baritones should sing the lower line. Changing voices should sing an octave higher as needed.)
• Sing softly as they listen to the song again and follow their assigned voice part.
• Listen again while following the score and sing each part separately. (Focus on rhythmic and pitch accuracy.)
• Establish good singing posture and sing "Freedom" in two parts with accompaniment. (Repeat as needed to develop a sense of good choral ensemble.)
• Sing the song individually and in small groups.

3. Perform "Freedom." Have the students:
• Sing "Freedom" with accompaniment. (Emphasize good ensemble and clear articulation.)
• Discuss and evaluate their performance.

APPRAISAL

The students should be able to:
1. Identify melodic patterns in "Freedom."
2. Understand and apply the qualities of good ensemble to their singing.

330

PREPARING *to Sing "Lift Ev'ry Voice and Sing"*

James Weldon Johnson, a founder of the National Association for the Advancement of Colored People (NAACP), wrote these words in 1900 to commemorate the birthday of Abraham Lincoln. His brother J. Rosamond Johnson set the words to music. Many people refer to "Lift Ev'ry Voice and Sing" as the African American National Anthem.

Practice Your Music Reading Skills — $\frac{6}{8}$ meter

• Practice $\frac{6}{8}$ meter by clapping the following:

• "Lift Ev'ry Voice and Sing" has two different melodies. Sing both melodies and notice similarities and differences.

THINK IT THROUGH: What musical elements make these two melodies different?

MUSIC LIBRARY

Focus: $\frac{6}{8}$ **Meter**

Objectives
To read and sing an African American hymn in $\frac{6}{8}$ meter
To review the use of clear articulation for good diction

Materials
Recordings: "Lift Ev'ry Voice and Sing"
"Lift Ev'ry Voice and Sing"
(performance mix)

TEACHING THE LESSON

1. Introduce "Lift Ev'ry Voice and Sing." Have the students:
• Read about the origin of the song.
• Listen to the song and discuss the style and the text. (unison hymn style in three distinct sections)
• Establish a steady beat and then read and clap the two rhythmic examples.
• Establish a steady beat and then read and clap the rhythm of melodies A and B.
• Sing a G-major scale to establish the tonality.
• Establish a steady beat and then read and sing the two melodies from "Lift Ev'ry Voice and Sing" using pitch syllables and numbers.
• Read and sing melodies A and B individually and in small groups.
• Discuss and evaluate accuracy of rhythm and pitch in each performance. (Offer suggestions for improvement as needed.)

MUSIC LIBRARY

2. Teach "Lift Ev'ry Voice and Sing."
Have the students:
• Sing the melody softly while listening to the recording. (Encourage boys whose voices are changing to sing in their upper range as appropriate.)
• Follow the score as you model selected measures on neutral syllables. (Students should listen and echo-sing the example, and then identify the measures.
• Decide which consonants in this song will need extra attention.
• Follow the score and sing the song with accompaniment. (Repeat any difficult passages as needed, focusing on clear articulation and diction.)
• Sing individually and in small groups.
3. Perform "Lift E'vry Voice and Sing."
Have the students:
• Sing "Lift Ev'ry Voice and Sing." (Emphasize accurate rhythmic and melodic patterns and clear articulation.)
• Evaluate the performance in terms of articulation.

APPRAISAL

The students should be able to:
1. Show increased confidence when performing music in $\frac{6}{8}$ meter.
2. Show understanding and application of good articulation and diction when singing.

Lift Ev'ry Voice and Sing

Music by Rosamond Johnson
Words by James Weldon Johnson
Piano Accompaniment on page PA 7

Key: G major   Range: B♭–E♭

1. Lift ev'-ry voice and sing, till earth and heav-en ring,
2. Ston-y the road we trod, bit-ter the chas-t'ning rod

Ring with the har-mo-nies of lib-er-ty.
Felt in the days when hope un-born had died.

Let our re-joic-ing rise high as the list-'ning skies,
Yet with a stead-y beat have not our wea-ry feet

Let it re-sound loud as the roll-ing sea.
Come to the place for which our fa-thers sighed?

Sing a song full of the faith that the dark past has taught us;
We have come, o-ver a way that with tears has been wa-tered,

Sing a song full of the hope that the pres-ent has brought us;
We have come, tread-ing our path through the blood of the slaugh-tered;

Fac-ing the ris-ing sun of our new day be-gun,
Out from the gloom-y past, till now we stand at last

Let us march on till vic-to-ry is won.
Where the white gleam of our bright star is cast.

332

REPARING *to Sing "La Borinqueña"*

"La Borinqueña" achieves its unique rhythmic style by alternating two and three sounds to a beat.

Practice Your Music Reading Skills—Two and Three Sounds to a Beat

Tap your foot to create a steady quarter-note beat.

Tap the steady beat with your foot while you clap two sounds to a beat to perform a duple division of the beat.

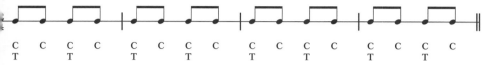

Snap your fingers, alternating hands, three times to a beat to perform a triple division of the beat.

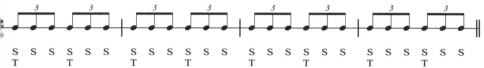

Perform this rhythm which contains both duple- and triple-beat divisions.

Create your own body percussion patterns that alternate between two and three sounds to a beat.

333

MUSIC LIBRARY

Focus: Duple- and Triple-Beat Divisions

Objectives
To read and perform duple- and triple-beat divisions in a song from Mexico
To create rhythm patterns using duple- and triple-beat divisions

Materials
Recordings: "La Borinqueña"
Recorded Lesson: "Pronunciation: 'La Borinqueña'"
"La Borinqueña" (performance mix)
Copying Master C-3 (optional)
Classroom percussion instruments (optional)

Vocabulary
duple, triple

TEACHING THE LESSON

1. Introduce "La Borinqueña." Have the students:
• Learn about the origin of the song.
• Softly sing "La Borinqueña" while they listen to the song and follow the score.
• Describe the style and the text. (Note the change from D major to D minor in measure 22.)

2. Introduce rhythmic exercises. Have the students:
• Establish a steady beat and then read and tap the example containing quarter notes.
• Establish a steady beat and then read and clap the second example (duple-beat division).
• Establish a steady beat and then read and snap the third example (triple-beat divisions, or triplets).
• Read and perform the example containing both duple-beat divisions and triplets. Continue to tap quarter notes, clap duple-beat divisions, and snap triplets.

MORE MUSIC TEACHING IDEAS

Try all of the exercises above with different sounds for the duple-beat divisions, the triplets, and the steady beat. Use wood blocks, claves, cymbals, or any other available rhythmic instruments. Emphasize the necessity of maintaining a steady beat at all times.

MUSIC LIBRARY

- Form small groups to create and perform four- or eight-measure patterns using duple-beat divisions, triplets, and combinations of both. (You may wish to have students notate these patterns.)
- Listen again to "La Borinqueña" as they read and clap the rhythm. (Repeat as needed, using various body percussion sounds to show duple-beat divisions and triplets.)

3. Teach "La Borinqueña." Have the students:
- Sing softly while listening to "La Borinqueña." (They can use the neutral syllable *loo* during the Spanish words and use the English words. Repeat passages that present a challenge.)
- Listen to "Pronunciation: 'La Borinqueña,'" and practice Spanish pronunciation as needed.
- Sing the melody using Spanish words while listening to the song. (Use teacher or student pronunciation modeling to assist.)
- Sing the song using words and accompaniment.
- Sing the song again individually and in small groups. (Emphasize clear articulation, and accurate duple-beat divisions and triplets.)

4. Perform "La Borinqueña." Have the students:
- Establish good singing posture and perform "La Borinqueña."
- Discuss and evaluate their performance in terms of rhythmic accuracy.

APPRAISAL

The students should be able to:
1. Identify and accurately perform duple- and triple- beat divisions.
2. Improvise a four- or eight-measure pattern using both duple- and triple- beat divisions.

La Borinqueña

Words by Manuel Fernandez Junc
Music by Felix Ast
English Words by MM

Key: D minor/D major   Range: C#–D¹

Piano Accompaniment on page PA

La tie-rra de Bor-in-quen don-de_he na-ci-do yo
Oh, land of Bor-in-quen, The___ land my child-hood knew.

Es un jar-dín flo-ri-do de má-gi-co pri-mor.
There in your fra-grant gar-dens, flo-wers of ev-'ry hue.

Un cie-lo siem-pre ní-ti-do le sir-ve de do-sel,
Heav-en-ly bree-zes blow-ing lul-la-bies soft and sweet.

Y dan a-rru-llo plà-ci-do Las o-las a sus pies.
Peace-ful and calm your sun-lit face, Waves at your grace-ful feet.

Cuan-do_a sus pla-yas lle-gó Co-lón, ex-cla-mó lle-no de_ad-mi-ra-
When to your bea-ches Co-lum-bus came, in ad-mir-a-tion he loud-ly

ción: ¡Oh! ¡Oh! ¡Oh! Es-ta_es la lin-da tie-rra, Que bus-co
cried: Oh! Oh! Oh! Now in this love-ly land my voy-age is

yo. Es Bor-in-quen la hi-ja, la hi-ja del mar y_el
done. Oh, Bor-in-quen, the daugh-ter, the daugh-ter of sea and

sol, del mar y el sol, del mar y el
sun, of sea and sun, of sea and

sol, del mar y el sol, del mar y el sol.
sun, of sea and sun, of sea and sun.

EXTENSION

PRONUNCIATION

la tē-ä' rrä dä bōr-ēn' ken dōn'dä nä-sē' do jyō

es ōōn här-dēn' flō-rē' dō dä mä' hē-kō prē-mōr'

ōōn sē-ä' lō sē em' prä nē' tē-dō lä sēr' vä dä dō-sel'

ē dän ä-rrōō' jyō plä' sē-dō läs ō' läs ä sōōs pē-äs'

kwän' dō-ä sōōs plä' jyäs jyä-gō' cō-lōn' ex-clä-mō' jyä' nō dä äd-mē-rä-sē-ōn'

ō ō ō äs' tä äs lä lēn' dä tē-ä' rrä kä bōōs' kō jyō

äs bōr-ēn-ken' lä ē' KHä lä ē' KHä del mär ē el sōl

REPARING *to Sing "A la Nanita Nana"*

Listen to "A la Nanita Nana" to find the musical characteristics that give it a dreamy, lullaby quality.

ractice Your Music Reading Skills—Singing in Minor

Sing this minor melody from Part I of the song.

la, la, ti, do re mi mi mi fa re mi mi mi fa re la mi
6, 6, 7, 1 2 3 3 3 4 2 3 3 3 4 2 6 3

Tap and sing these minor patterns from Parts II and III of the song.

la, la, ti, do re do do do re ti, do do do re re mi do
6, 6, 7, 1 2 1 1 1 2 7, 1 1 1 2 2 3 1

la, la, la, la, la, la, la, la, la, la, la, la, la, la, ti, do la,
6, 6, 6, 6, 6, 6, 6, 6, 6, 6, 6, 6, 6, 6, 7, 1 6,

Sing patterns I and III; I and II; II and III; and I, II, and III to experience two- and three-part singing in D minor.

ractice Your Music Reading Skills—Singing in Major

Sing this major melody from Part I of the song.

mi so do' ti la ti so la so fa mi fa so
3 5 1' 7 6 7 5 6 5 4 3 4 5

Tap and sing these major patterns from Parts II and III of the song.

mi so fa fa re mi fa mi
3 5 4 4 2 3 4 3

do mi re ti, do
1 3 2 7, 1

Sing patterns I and III; I and II; II and III; and I, II, and III to experience two- and three-part singing in D major.

335

MUSIC LIBRARY

Focus: Major and Minor

Objectives
To recognize the sounds of major and minor modes and sing their scales
To sing a three-part song from Cuba

Materials
Recordings: "A la Nanita Nana"
Recorded Lesson:
"Pronunciation:
'A la Nanita Nana'"
"A la Nanita Nana"
(performance mix)

Vocabulary
Major, minor

TEACHING THE LESSON

1. Introduce "A la Nanita Nana." Have the students:
• Listen to the song and follow the melody line. (Part I)
• Describe and discuss the style and the text. (legato, alternates between minor and major, lullaby)
• Learn about the origin of the song.
2. Introduce exercises in minor. Have the students:
• Listen (as you model) and then sing the D-minor scale below. (You may also wish to compare the D-minor and F-major scales.)
• Read and sing pattern I using pitch syllables, numbers, or the neutral syllable *loo*. (Repeat for patterns II and III.)
• Experience two- and three-part singing in minor by reading and singing different combinations of patterns I, II, and III.

D-minor scale

la, ti, do re mi fa so la ti do'

F-major scale

A la Nanita Nana

Key: D minor/D major; E minor/E major   Ranges I: D–E¹, II: D–C¹, III: A₁–C¹

Traditional Cuban Carol

Piano Accompaniment on page PA 82 Arranged by Michael Bra...

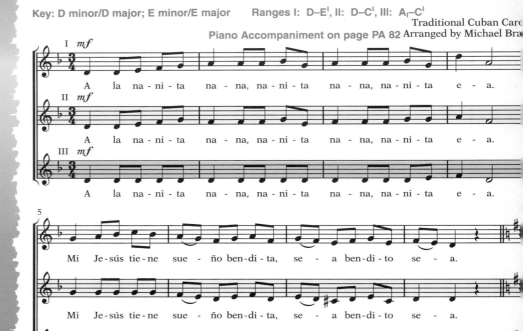

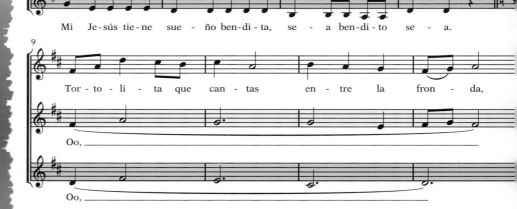

MUSIC LIBRARY

3. Introduce exercises in major. Have the students:
- Listen (as you model) and then sing the D-major scale below
- Compare the D-major scale with the D-minor scale.
- Read and sing pattern I using pitch syllables, numbers, or the neutral syllable *loo*. (Repeat for patterns II and III.)
- Experience two- and three-part singing in major by reading and singing the different possible combinations of patterns I, II, and III.

4. Introduce Warm-Up 4. Have the students:
- Learn and sing Warm-Up 4.
- Focus on maintaining an even quality of sound in moving between vowels and in using breath management to sustain a phrase.

5. Teach "A la Nanita Nana." (*Note: The remainder of this lesson is for trebles, altos and changing voices.*) Have the students:
- Divide into voice parts and listen to the song again, following their assigned voice parts.
- Sing up and down the D-minor scale to establish the key.
- Learn Parts I, II, and III separately for the first section (measures 1–8), emphasizing pitch and rhythmic accuracy. Use the neutral syllable *loo* to maintain stylistic accuracy. Combine two and then three parts beginning with Parts II and III.
- Listen to "Pronunciation: 'A la Nanita Nana'" for measures 1–8.
- Practice Spanish pronunciation as needed for this section, and then listen while singing Parts I, II, and III separately.
- Divide into voice parts, follow the score, and sing measures 1–8.
- Sing again individually and in small groups, emphasizing balance, pitch accuracy, and phrasing.

336

D-major Scale

do re mi fa so la ti do¹

WARM-UP 4

Mee Meh Mah Moh Moo

Continue sequence to key of G minor.

Mee Meh Mah Moh Moo

Mee Meh Mah Moh Moo

fuen- te- ci- lla que co- rres ru- mo- ro- sa.

Oo, _____

Oo, _____

p
Ca- lad que es-tá dor- mi- do el dul- ce in- fan- te.

p
Ca- lad que es-tá dor- mi- do Oo, _____

p
Ca- lad que es-tá dor- mi- do Oo, _____

Oo, _____ e - a.

A la na -ni -ta na - na, na -ni -ta e - a.

A la na -ni -ta na - na, na -ni -ta e - a.

337

MUSIC LIBRARY

• Repeat this teaching procedure as appropriate for the remaining sections (measures 9–24, 29–36, and 37–56).
6. **Perform "A La Nanita Nana."** Have the students:
• Perform the song with accompaniment.
• Discuss and evaluate the performance in terms of good balance and effective breath management.

APPRAISAL

The students should be able to:
1. Sing and classify scales as being major or minor.
2. Sing using a three-part vocal score.

PRONUNCIATION

ä lä nä-nē′ tä nä′ nä nä-nē′ tä ā′ ä
mē hä-sōōs′ tē-e-nä′ swä′ nyo ben-dē-tō sä′
ä ben dē′ tō sä′ ä
tōr-tō-lē′ tä kä cän′ täs en′ trä lä frōn′ dä
fwen′ tä sē′ jyä kä cō-rräs′ rroo-mō-rō′ sä
kä-jyäd kä es-tä′ dōr-mē′ dō el dōōl′ sä
en-fän′ tä
ō ā ä

MUSIC LIBRARY **337**

338

flow - ing, song - birds are sing - ing.

flow - ing, _____ song - birds sing - ing. _____

flow - ing, _____ song - birds sing - ing. _____

Rip-pling wa - ters and bird-song flow through my dream - ing.

Rip-pling wa - ters bird-song _____ through my dream - ing.

Rip-pling wa - ters bird-song _____ through my dream - ing.

mp
Hush now, be ver - y si - lent, he slum - bers so deep - ly.

mp
Hush now, be ver - y si - lent, he slum - bers so deep - ly.

mp
Hush, now, be ver - y si - lent, he slum - bers so deep - ly.

339

340

PREPARING to Sing "Take These Wings"

One of the characteristics of harmonious choral singing is **blend**. Notice the blending of voices as you listen to the recording of "Take These Wings."

- Listen to the choral blend as you sing the three-part section of "Take These Wings." What words can you use to describe the concept of choral blend?

Practice Your Music Reading — Choral Blend Skills

- Practice these patterns by singing them using pitch syllables or numbers. Then sing the following portion of "Take These Wings" on *loo*. Add each part one at a time, listening to the other parts as you sing.

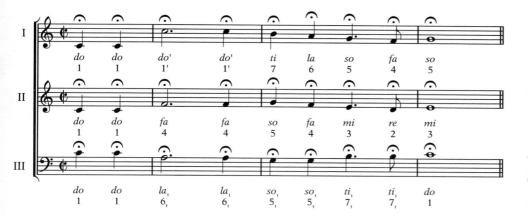

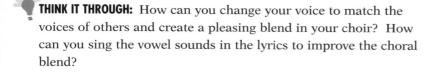

THINK IT THROUGH: How can you change your voice to match the voices of others and create a pleasing blend in your choir? How can you sing the vowel sounds in the lyrics to improve the choral blend?

MUSIC LIBRARY

Focus: Choral Blend

Objectives
To develop choral blend while singing a three-part song

Materials
Recordings: "Take These Wings"
"Take These Wings"
(performance mix)

Vocabulary
Blend

TEACHING THE LESSON

1. Introduce "Take These Wings." Have the students:

- Discuss choral blend.
- Listen to and then describe the refrain section. (legato, three-part harmony)
- Read and sing Part III from the excerpt on page 341 using pitch syllables and then numbers. (Remind the students to use good breath management to sustain a legato vocal line and pure vowels for good tone and vocal blend.)
- Read and sing Part II using pitch syllables and numbers.
- Divide into two sections and sing Parts III and II combined, emphasizing choral blend. (Have each half of the class sing both parts alternately so that the students experience singing all of the vocal lines, as well as the various combinations of parts. Use this teaching technique whenever appropriate.)
- Read and sing Part I using pitch syllables and numbers.
- Divide into three sections and sing Parts III, II and I together, emphasizing choral blend.

MUSIC LIBRARY

2. Introduce Warm-Up 5. Have the students:

• Perform Warm-Up 5 to practice choral blend and legato singing. (Guide students to strive for pure vowels throughout their vocal ranges.)

3. Teach "Take These Wings." Have the students:

• Sing Part III softly while they listen to the song and follow the score for measures 24–58. (Repeat this activity as needed to gain success in music reading and performance.)

• Divide into voice parts—Part I, both treble and unchanged voices; Part II, treble, unchanged, and changing voices; Part III, changing voices and baritones.

• Follow their assigned voice part in the score and sing measures 24–58 with accompaniment. (The focus throughout this lesson should be on choral blend and good balance among all voice parts.)

• Learn individual voice parts separately.

• Repeat procedure for measures 67–82.

• Read and sing measures 24–82 in three parts with accompaniment.

• Sing measures 9–24 in unison (all voice parts).

• Sing measures 9–24 in small ensembles, listening for and developing choral blend.

• Read and sing the Coda using pitch syllables or numbers. (Review pitch syllables and numbers from the opening of the lesson. Learn and practice individual voice parts as needed.)

CD8:17, CD9:24

Take These Wings

Key: C major   Ranges I: C–E^1, II: B$_1$–C^1, III: E$_1$–C

Words by Steve Kupferschmid
Music by Don Besig

Piano Accompaniment on page PA 89

342

WARM-UP 5

Mee-ay

Continue sequence to key of F.

Mee-ay

Mee - ay

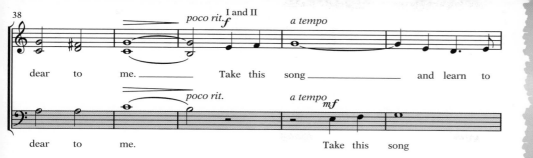

dear to me. _____ Take this song _____ and learn to

dear to me. Take this song

sing, _____ fill your voice with all the joys of spring; _____

and learn to sing, fill your voice with all the joys of spring; _____

Let it

___ Take this heart _____ and set it free _____

___ Take this heart _____ and set it free _____

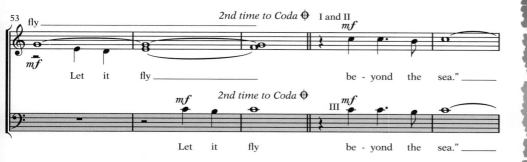

2nd time to Coda ⊕ I and II

fly _____ *mf*

mf
Let it fly _____ be - yond the sea." _____

mf *2nd time to Coda ⊕*
III *mf*
Let it fly be - yond the sea." _____

343

4. Perform "Take These Wings." Have the students:
• Sing the song with accompaniment. (Emphasize choral blend and maintaining an even quality of sound throughout each vocal range.)

APPRAISAL

The students should be able to:
Define and achieve improved choral blend in a three-part song.

PREPARING *to Sing "All the Good People"*

"All the Good People" has the quality of a folk song. This quality is due partly to the repeated patterns in the song, which help to make the song easy to sing and remember.

Practice Your Music Reading Skills — Rhythm Patterns

- Play these patterns from "All the Good People."

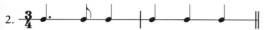

- Create new rhythm accompaniments by combining two or more of these patterns.

- Find all of these rhythm patterns in "All the Good People."

345

MUSIC LIBRARY

Focus: Rhythm Patterns

Objectives
To identify and perform rhythm patterns in music

Materials
Recordings: "All the Good People"
"All the Good People"
(performance mix)

TEACHING THE LESSON

1. Introduce rhythm pattern preparation. Have the students:
- Establish a steady beat and perform rhythm patterns 1–5. (They can snap the eighth notes, clap the quarter notes, and pat-slide both the dotted quarter notes and the half notes.)
- Listen while individuals read and perform selected patterns and identify the pattern being performed. (The performers should focus on accurate rhythm and keeping a steady beat.)
- Divide progressively into two, three, four, and five groups. (Each group establishes a steady beat and then reads and performs assigned patterns in different combinations. Then, each group should trade patterns so that all students experience performing each pattern.)
- Examine the score and identify measures containing these rhythm patterns.

MUSIC LIBRARY

2. Introduce "All the Good People."
Have the students:

• Follow the score and sing their assigned voice part with accompaniment.
• Learn individual voice parts separately. (Focus on rhythmic accuracy and score reading.)
• Read and sing the song with and without accompaniment in small groups.

3. Perform "All the Good People." Have the students:

• Sing the song with accompaniment.
• Listen as the entire class, sections, or small ensembles perform the song.
• Discuss and evaluate the performances in terms of rhythmic accuracy.
• Discuss *Think It Through.*

APPRAISAL

The students should be able to:
Recognize and accurately perform rhythm patterns in a composition.

Key: C major/F major
CD8:18, CD9:25   Piano Accompaniment on page PA 96

All the Good People   Ranges I: C–C¹, II: F₁–F, III: A₁₁–C

Words and Music by Ken Hicks

346

THINK IT THROUGH: How can you change your singing to emphasize the energetic style of this music? Suggest a place and time that might be appropriate to sing "All the Good People." Justify your answer.

347

MUSIC LIBRARY

Focus: Style

Objectives
To explore performance practice for a song in blues style

Materials
Recordings: "70 Times the Speed of Sound"
"70 Times the Speed of Sound" (performance mix)

TEACHING THE LESSON

1. Introduce "70 Times the Speed of Sound." Have the students:

• Review blues style on page 104.
• Divide into two voice parts—Part I, treble voices, including unchanged voices; Part II, baritones and changing voices.
• Softly sing "70 Times the Speed of Sound" while following their voice part in the score and listening to the song.
• Learn Parts I and II separately, emphasizing blues style.
• Sing the song with accompaniment while following the score.
• Sing again individually and in small groups.
• Review and refine Parts I and II as needed.

2. Perform "70 Times the Speed of Sound." Have the students:

• Sing the song with accompaniment. (Emphasize blues style and diction.)
• Sing the song silently and follow conducting gestures, breathing at phrase endings to indicate their attention.
• Follow conducting gestures and sing the song with accompaniment.

70 Times the Speed of Sound

Key: G major   Ranges I: D–D^I, II: G$_I$–F

Piano Accompaniment on page PA 105   Music and Lyrics by Linda Worsley

Bluesy, swinging sound

1. Ba - by said she loved me, ___ then she made me feel so bad.
2. Ba - by sent a let - ter, She mailed it from the moon.
3. I can see my ba - by, ___ see the one I love the best, ___

I made him ___ feel so bad. ___
I mailed it ___ from the moon. ___
I know that ___ he loves me best. ___

When she went and left me,
It said "I real - ly miss you,
see her go - ing o - ver in an

Right there on ___ the launch - ing pad.
I wish I ___ could see you soon!
I'm fly - in' o - ver ___ from east to west. ___

there on the launch - ing pad. ___
wish that I could see you soon! ___
or - bit from East to West. ___

My
And

at sev en ty times the speed of sound. ___
I'll go sev en ty times a round the sun. ___
at sev en ty times the speed of light. ___

Last time to Coda

ba - by left the ground ___ at sev-en-ty times the speed of sound.
But be - fore I'm done, ___ I'll go sev-en-ty times a round the sun.
then she's out of sight, ___ at sev-ent-y times the speed of light.

go on to **B** *Instrumental Interlude*

THINK IT THROUGH: Compare and contrast two performances of this song. First, sing the song with straight, even rhythms as notated, and short, staccato articulation. Then try singing the song in a freer, jazzier style. Which style suits this song best? Are there parts of the song that might sound better in one of these styles? Create a style performance plan. Evaluate the effectiveness of your performance.

349

MUSIC LIBRARY

- Explore performance styles as described in *Think It Through*.
- Perform once more in a swing style.
- Discuss and evaluate performance of this song in terms of style.

APPRAISAL

The students should be able to:
Describe and perform two-part music in a blues style.

MUSIC LIBRARY

Focus: Phrase Length

Objectives
To review and reinforce the concept of phrase length

To perform a three-part song focusing on choral blend, musical phrasing, and balance

Materials
Recordings: "Can You Hear the Music?"

"Can You Hear the Music?" (performance mix)

TEACHING THE LESSON

1. Introduce "Can You Hear the Music?" Have the students:

• Review the concept of phrase and phrase length. (pages 120–121)

• Discuss *Think It Through*.

• Sing up and down the D-minor and F-major scales to establish the keys used in this composition. (See page 335.)

• Divide into three sections—Part I, treble voices including unchanged voices; Part II, treble voices and some changing voices as appropriate; Part III, changing voices and baritones.

• Follow their assigned voice part and softly sing with accompaniment.

• Learn Parts I, II, and III separately for measures 3–18 emphasizing choral balance and blend.

• Repeat procedure for measures 19–44 and 45–62.

Can You Hear the Music?

Piano Accompaniment on page PA 100

Words and Music by Linda Worsley

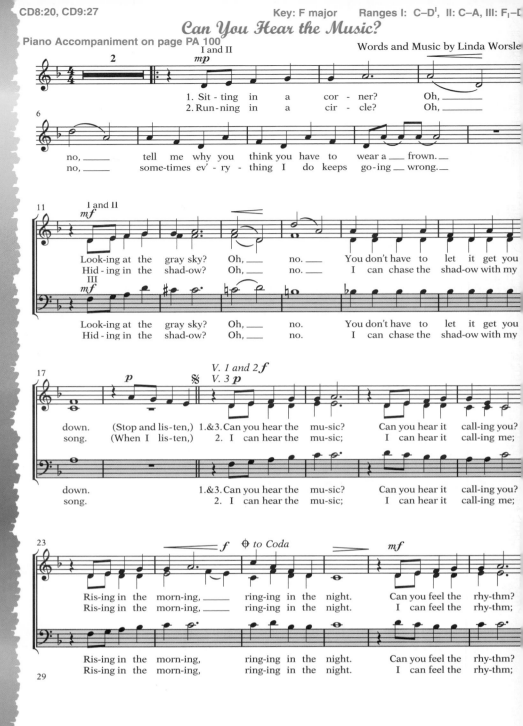

- Sing the entire song with and without accompaniment. (Emphasize the use of focused vowels.)
- Sing again individually and in small groups.
- Review and refine Parts I, II, and III as needed to enhance part singing and choral ensemble.

2. Perform "Can You Hear the Music?" Have the students:

- Sing silently and follow conducting gestures, breathing at phrase endings to indicate their attention.
- Sing the song with accompaniment. (Emphasize focused and sustained phrases, balance, and blend.)
- Discuss and evaluate the performance in terms of phrasing, balance, and blend.
- Discuss *Think It Through*.

APPRAISAL

The students should be able to:

1. Show understanding of and attention to phrase length.
2. Perform a three-part song with attention to choral blend, musical phrasing, and balance.

351

💡 **THINK IT THROUGH:** Are the questions in the text of this song ever answered? What performance techniques can you use to highlight the question and answer phrases in the text? Evaluate the effectiveness of your question and answer phrases.

352

REPARING ***to Sing "In Stiller Nacht"***

In Stiller Nacht" was composed by one of the most famous nusicians of the 19th century, Johannes Brahms. This piece is one of nany vocal works he composed in his native German language. The nusic is notated in $\frac{3}{2}$ meter. In $\frac{3}{2}$, the half note receives the steady eat.

ractice Your Music Reading Skills — $\frac{3}{2}$ meter

n $\frac{3}{2}$ meter:

the ♩ will sound for one-half of a beat

the 𝅗𝅥 will sound for one beat

the 𝅗𝅥. will sound for one and one-half beats

Sing this rhythm pattern on one pitch using the syllable *loo*. Try to feel three beats to a measure. Be sure your singing is *legato*, or sustained in quality.

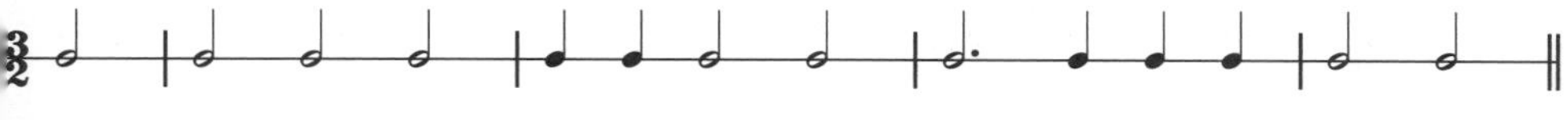

Sing this dotted rhythm found in the melody of "In Stiller Nacht." How can you emphasize or stress this new dotted rhythm?

ind this rhythm at the beginning of all three parts in the music.

Sing the third part in unison, stressing the dotted rhythm. Then divide into parts. Start with only Part III, then add Part II and finally Part I, maintaining the stress on this rhythm.

MUSIC LIBRARY

Focus: $\frac{3}{2}$ Meter

Objectives

To read and sing music in $\frac{3}{2}$ meter

To experience music of nineteenth-century Germany

To sing a three-part choral piece in a legato style

Materials

Recordings: "In Stiller Nacht"
Recorded Lesson: "Pronunciation: 'In Stiller Nacht'"
"In Stiller Nacht" (performance mix)

Vocabulary

Legato

TEACHING THE LESSON

1. Introduce the preparation. Have the students:

- Read and discuss the information on "In Stiller Nacht."
- Follow Part I and listen to "In Stiller Nacht."
- Establish a steady beat and starting pitch and then read and sing the first example on the neutral syllable *loo*. (Guide students to use breath management to sustain a legato vocal line and the pure vowel *oo* for good tone.)
- Repeat this procedure for the second example. (Shape the new rhythm with a crescendo on the dotted quarter note and a decrescendo on the eighth note. You may also wish to practice this rhythm in isolation.)
- Find the ♩. ♪ 𝅗𝅥 pattern in "In Stiller Nacht."

MUSIC LIBRARY

2. Introduce "In Stiller Nacht." Have the students:

• Softly sing Part III using the neutral syllable *loo* while following the score and listening to "In Stiller Nacht." (Repeat this activity as needed. Use modeling as appropriate to assist.)

3. Introduce Warm-Ups 6 and 7. Have the students:

• Focus on maintaining an even quality of sound from the higher to lower range when singing Warm-Up 6.

• Focus on maintaining an even quality of sound when changing vowel sounds in Warm-up 7.

4. Teach "In Stiller Nacht." Have the students:

• Listen to the song again, following the score, and apply the skills learned in Warm-Ups 6 and 7 as they sing Part III on the neutral syllable *loo*. (The emphasis should be on sustained, uniform sound. Repeat as needed.)

In Stiller Nacht

Key: E♭ major   Ranges I: C–F¹, II: C–A♭, III: G₁–E♭

Words and Music
Johannes Brahm
Arranged by David L. We

354

WARM-UP 6

Noo Noo Noo Noo Noo Nee Noo Nee Noo

Continue sequence to key of F.

NooNooNooNooNooNeeNooNeeNoo

Noo Noo Noo Noo   Noo Nee Noo Nee Noo

WARM-UP 7

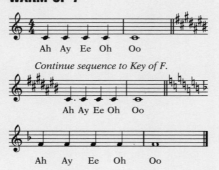

Ah Ay Ee Oh   Oo

Continue sequence to Key of F.

Ah Ay Ee Oh   Oo

Ah   Ay   Ee   Oh   Oo

PRONUNCIATION

in shtil' ler näKHt, tsōōr ar' shten väKHt
īn shtim be-goont' tsōō klä' gen
dār neKht' ge vind hät zēs ōōnt lint
tsōō mēr den kläng ge-trä' gen
fun hār' bem līt ōōnd trow' riKH-kīt
ist mēr däs härtz' tzer fläs' sen
dē ble' me-līn mit trä' nen rīn
häb iKH zē äl be-gos' sen

Blü - me - lein,   mit Trä - nen rein   hab ich sie all be - gos - sen.

Blü - me - lein,   mit Trä - nen rein   hab ich sie all be - gos - sen.

Blü - me - lein,   mit Trä - nen rein   hab ich sie all be - gos - sen.

THINK IT THROUGH: Choral composers often write melodies and rhythms in a way that places emphasis on certain words. Which words are stressed in this music? What do these words mean in English? What vocal skills can you use to emphasize these words?

• Divide into Parts I, II, and III. Learn Parts I and II separately, emphasizing pitch and rhythmic accuracy. (Use the neutral syllable *loo* to maintain stylistic accuracy. Combine two and then three parts beginning with Parts II and III.)
• Listen to "Pronunciation: 'In Stiller Nacht,'" and practice the German pronunciation.
• Listen to and sing each of the three voice parts using the German words.
• Follow the score while singing the song in German with accompaniment.
• Sing the song again individually and in small groups.
• Review and refine Parts I, II, and III, as needed. (Combine voice parts in different combinations, placing an emphasis on balance and phrasing.)
5. **Perform "In Stiller Nacht."** Have the students:
• Sing the song with accompaniment. (Emphasize breathing to sustain phrases, balance, and rhythmic accuracy.)
• Discuss and evaluate performance in terms of breath management and balance.
• Discuss *Think It Through*.

APPRAISAL

The students should be able to:
1. Perform basic rhythms in $\frac{3}{2}$.
2. Perform a three-part choral piece in German with attention to phrasing.
3. Recognize and perform in a legato choral style.

355

TRANSLATION—"In Stiller Nacht."

In still of night, before the first wake, a voice had begun to sound; a mighty wind had borne to me softly and sweetly the sound of the bell. My heart is flowing with bitter pain and sadness; I have drenched the little flowers with pure tears.

MUSIC LIBRARY

Focus: Imitation

Objectives
To experience imitation in music of the baroque period
To experiment with musical performance practices

Materials
Recordings: "Cum Sancto Spiritu"
Recorded Lesson:
"Pronunciation:
'Cum Sancto Spiritu'"
"Cum Sancto Spiritu"
(performance mix)

Vocabulary
Polyphony, fugue, imitation

TEACHING THE LESSON

1. Introduce the preparation. Have the students:
• Read and discuss the introductory information. (See also information below.)
•• Listen to the song and discuss the musical style.
• Identify and define imitation. (Imitation occurs when one voice repeats or slightly varies music that has been heard in another voice.)
• Sing up and down the D-minor scale to establish the tonality.
• Establish a steady beat and then read and sing Part I on page 356 using the neutral syllable *loo*. (You may wish to review time signature and note values with a half note pulse before beginning this exercise. Emphasize breath management to help sustain a legato vocal line and the use of a pure vowel *oo* to help develop tone.)
• Repeat for Parts II and III.
• Compare Parts I, II, and III. (Rhythm and words have similarities; starting pitches and intervals vary.)

PREPARING *to Sing "Cum Sancto Spiritu"*

The majority of early church music in Western civilization was composed and sung in Latin. "Cum Sancto Spiritu" composed by Antonio Lotti (1667-1740), comes from this tradition. Composers in Lotti's time often wrote using **polyphony** or independent melodic parts in the style of a round or canon. Popular forms of polyphonic music were the round and the **fugue**. "Cum Sancto Spiritu" is written in polyphonic style. Each part enters and imitates the previous part.

Practice Your Music Reading Skills — Imitation

• Sing Part I from "Cum Sancto Spiritu."

Cum   Sanc-to   Spi-ri-tu,   in   glo-ri-a   De-i   Pa-   tris

• Sing Part II, noting how it imitates Part I.

Cum   Sanc-to   Spi-ri-tu,   in   glo-ri-a   De-i   Pa-   tris

• Sing Part III, noting how it also imitates Part I.

Cum   Sanc-to   Spi-ri-tu,   in   glo-ri-a   De-i   Pa-   tris

• Find all three parts in "Cum Sancto Spiritu." Can you find other examples of imitation in "Cum Sancto Spiritu"?

THINK IT THROUGH: How can you use the expressive elements in music to highlight the independent polyphonic parts? Experiment by varying the tempos, dynamics, and word colors. Then create a plan that best highlights the important melodic lines in "Cum Sancto Spiritu." Justify your choices.

356

THE COMPOSER

Antonio Lotti (1667–1740)—was an Italian organist and composer. He was highly renowned for his work at the famous San Marco church of Venice, where he served in many capacities, including *maestro di capella* (head of music). His compositions included Masses, anthems, motets, and operas.

BACKGROUND

Polyphony—is a style of composition whose golden age spanned the 13th–16th centuries. Polyphony is achieved when there is a multi-voice texture featuring independent melodic lines. Counterpoint, fugue, and imitation are techniques that are frequently used. Some of the composers best known for this style are Palestrina, Morley, and Bach.

The Latin text of "Cum Sancto Spiritu" means "With the Holy Spirit, in the glory of God the Father." Most European choral music written prior to the nineteenth century was religious in nature. Many song texts were drawn from traditional prayers or from scripture.

Cum Sancto Spiritu

ano Accompaniment on page PA 118

Traditional Latin text
Music by Antonio Lotti

mf
Cum San - cto Spi - ri - tu, in glo - ri - a De - i

I
Pa - tris, De - i Pa -

II
mf
Cum San - cto Spi - ri - tu, in glo - ri - a

tris, De - i Pa - tris, in

De - i Pa - tris, De - i Pa -

III
mf
Cum Sanc - to Spi - ri - tu, in glo - ri - a De - i Pa -

f
glo - ri - a De - i Pa - tris. A -

f
tris, in glo - ri - a

f *mf*
tris, De - i Pa - tris. A -

Key: D minor   Ranges I: D–A , II: A₁–F, III: D₁–D

357

MUSIC LIBRARY

• Find Parts I, II, and III in "Cum Sancto Spiritu."
• Examine the score and find additional examples of imitation in the song. (Part I: measures 9–12, imitated in Part III in measures 20–22; Part I: measures 5–8, imitated in Part II: measures 23–26)

2. Introduce "Cum Sancto Spiritu." Have the students:
• Divide into appropriate voice parts. (This piece could be sung effectively by boys only—Unchanged, Part I; Changing/Cambiata, Part II; Baritones Part IV)
• Listen to the song, following the score, and sing their assigned voice part softly on the neutral syllable *loo*.

3. Introduce Warm-Up 8. Have the students:
• Sing Warm-Up 8 to assist in performing "Cum Sancto Spiritu." (Each time this is sung, focus on one of the following qualities: maintaining an even quality of sound and blend within each section and within the choir as a whole; maintaining vocal intensity; pitch and ensemble precision; vowel focus.)
• Perform Warm-Up 8 on different neutral syllables (*loo, lah*), while sustaining the same ensemble qualities.

4. Teach "Cum Sancto Spiritu." Have the students:
• Listen to the opening section again, following the score, and apply the techniques practiced in Warm-Up 8 as they sing (Part I: measures 1–21; Part II: measures 1–26; Part III: measures 1–22) softly on the neutral syllable *loo*.
• Listen to "Pronunciation: 'Cum Sancto Spiritu'" and practice the Latin pronunciation as needed.)
• Sing the opening section using words while listening. (Repeat as needed.)
• Follow the score and sing the opening section in Latin with and without accompaniment.

PRONUNCIATION

ko͞om sän' kto̅ spē' rē-to͞o
in glō' rē-ə dā' ē pä' trēs
ä-men'

WARM-UP 8

Vee Vee Vee Vee Vee _____

Vee Vee Vee Vee Vee Vee Vee Vee

Vee Vee Vee Vee Vee Vee Vee Vee

Vee Vee Vee Vee Vee

Vee _____

Vee _____

MUSIC LIBRARY

- Sing again individually and in small groups.
- Using the same procedure, learn measures 23–42.
- Combine two and then three parts, beginning with Parts III and II. (Review and refine each part as needed.)
- Sing the song again, individually and in small groups.

5. Introduce performance options for "Cum Sancto Spiritu." Have the students:
- Discuss *Think It Through*.
- Identify changes they could make in their performance to draw attention to important moments of the melodic lines. (dynamics)
- Experiment with each suggestion, and discuss each performance experiment. (They can evaluate the suggestions in terms of the success and appropriateness of the changes in highlighting each voice at its important moments.)
- Identify the most appropriate performance practices. (steady tempo, pure vowels, imitation brought out, vowels sustained, balance, and choral blend)

6. Perform "Cum Sancto Spiritu." Have the students:
- Sing the song with accompaniment, focusing on the previously identified performance practices.
- Sing the song unaccompanied.
- Discuss and evaluate each performance experience in terms of the desired performance characteristics.

APPRAISAL

The students should be able to:
1. Perform with attention to expressive characteristics of polyphonic musical style.
2. Propose, perform, evaluate, and re-apply expressive decisions.

358

The rhythm used in "I Hear America Singing" can be described as strong and syncopated. This helps to give the composition energy and vitality.

Practice Your Music Reading Skills — Syncopated Rhythm

- Perform this syncopated rhythm pattern from "I Hear America Singing" by clapping the eighth notes and patting the quarter-note durations.

- Clap and pat the syncopated rhythm in the bottom voice starting in measure 25, "Great camp meeting." Add the upper parts, one at a time. Find and practice other measures that contain syncopation.

💡 **THINK IT THROUGH:** Assess the accuracy of your rhythmic performance as a group. Recommend ways to improve the rhythmic precision.

Key: E♭ major   Ranges I: C–G♭¹, II: B♭₁–D♭¹, III: E♭₁–E♭, IV: B♭₁–D♭

I Hear America Singing

Piano Accompaniment on page PA 111

Words and Music by André J. Thomas
based on the Spiritual "Walk Together Children"

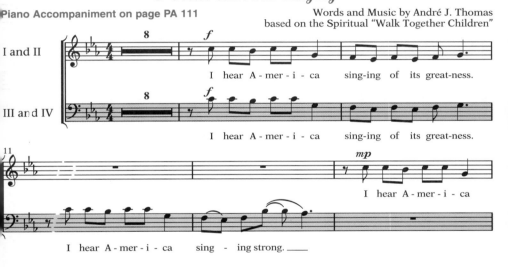

359

MUSIC LIBRARY

Focus: Syncopation

Objectives
To read and perform a song based on an African American Spiritual
To practice syncopated-rhythm skills

Materials
Recordings: "I Hear America Singing"
"I Hear America Singing" (performance mix)

Vocabulary
Syncopation, Spiritual

TEACHING THE LESSON

1. Introduce the syncopation exercises. Have the students:
- Listen to "I Hear America Singing" and discuss the style. (four-part, based on a Spiritual, syncopated)
- Divide into two groups, one clapping a steady beat while the other taps the rhythm notated on page 359. Exchange parts on each repetition.
- Divide into four voice parts—Parts I and II, both trebles and unchanged voices; Part III, changing voices; Part IV, baritones.
- Follow the score as you model the rhythmic pattern for Part IV in measures 25–36.
- Establish a steady beat and then read and perform the rhythmic pattern of Part IV for measures 25–36.
- Repeat this procedure for Parts III, II, and I, adding each newly learned part to those previously learned. (Modeling will be very important for learning each new part.)
- Establish a steady beat and then perform all parts together. (Begin with Part IV, adding Parts III, II, and I with each repeat.)

MUSIC LIBRARY

- Identify, read, and perform other examples of syncopation in the score. (measures 15, 53, 55, and 58–63.)

2. Teach "I Hear America Singing." Have the students:

- Listen to the song, following the score, and softly sing their assigned voice part
- Follow the score as you vocally model Part IV, measures 25–36.
- Echo-sing Part IV. (Emphasize accurate syncopated rhythms through crisp diction.)
- Learn and sing measures 25–36 of Part III.
- Sing Parts IV and III together with accompaniment. (Begin with Part IV singing alone, and then repeat, adding Part III. Have Part IV sung by students assigned to Parts IV and II; Part III by those assigned to Parts III and I.)
- Sing this combination of Parts IV and III as individuals and in small groups (unaccompanied and accompanied).
- Repeat this procedure for learning and adding Parts II and I.
- Follow the score and sing measures 25–36 in four parts with accompaniment.
- Sing the song again individually and in small groups. (Use both unaccompanied and accompanied singing.)

360

3. Teach measures 9–24 and 36–65. Have the students:
• Learn individual voice parts separately using the procedures outlined previously. (Work on each of the following as units: 9–16, 17–24, and 36–65.)
• Sing the entire song individually and in small groups, using both unaccompanied and accompanied singing.
4. Perform "I Hear America Singing." Have the students:
• Sing the song with accompaniment, following conducting gestures and emphasizing syncopation, crisp diction, balance, and blend.
• Discuss and evaluate their performance.

APPRAISAL

The students should be able to:
1. Perform a Spiritual with attention to musical style.
2. Read and perform syncopated rhythms.

PREPARING *to Sing "I've Got a Robe"* CD8:26, CD9:31

Gospel music had its beginnings in African American church services during the 1930s. Gospel singers ornament traditional spirituals such as "I've Got a Robe" with their own rhythmic and melodic improvisations.

• Clap these rhythms from the first part of "I've Got a Robe."

Key: B♭ major   Ranges I: B♭–F¹, II: F–C¹, III: B♭₁–A♭, IV: E♭₁–B♭₁

I've Got a Robe

Piano Accompaniment on page PA 122

Traditional Spiritual
Arranged by David Parker

1. I've got a robe, ___ you've got a robe, ___ all of God's chil-dren got a
2. I've got shoes, ___ you've got shoes, ___ all of God's chil-dren got

robe. ___ When I get to heav-en goin' to put on my robe, I'm goin' to
shoes. ___ When I get to heav-en goin' to put on my shoes, I'm goin' to

363

MUSIC LIBRARY

Focus: Gospel Style

Objectives
To sing a song in gospel style

Materials
Recordings: "I've Got a Robe"
"I've Got a Robe"
(performance mix)

Vocabulary
Gospel style

TEACHING THE LESSON

1. Introduce the rhythm exercise. Have the students:
• Listen to "I've Got a Robe," following the score, and note the layering technique used in measures 27–34.
• Discuss characteristics of the gospel style that they may already have experienced. (See also *Background* below.)
• Establish a steady beat, then read and clap the rhythm notated on page 363.
• Identify and perform other rhythms that need extra attention in the song.
2. Introduce "I've Got a Robe." Have the students:
• Divide into four voice parts—Parts I and II, both trebles and unchanged voices; Part III, boys with changing voices; Part IV, baritones.
• Sing measures 5–12 of Part IV while listening and following the score. (Emphasize accurate rhythmic and stylistic performance.)
• Perform Warm-Up 9 to develop additional vocal and stylistic qualities associated with performing "I've Got a Robe" in a gospel style. (Emphasize the open quality of sound associated with the vowel *ah.*)

WARM-UP 9

Fa Fa Fa Fa Fa

Fa Fa Fa Fa Fa

Continue sequence to key of E-flat.

Fa Fa Fa Fa Fa

Fa Fa Fa Fa Fa

BACKGROUND

Gospel music—is a highly emotional and improvisatory form of music which first developed during the Depression in black Baptist and Pentacostal churches. A typical instrumentation for a gospel band includes organ, percussion, bass, piano, and various solo instruments such as trumpet or saxophone. The gospel singing style is highly ornamented with improvised shouts, glissandos, improvised words, and falsetto obbligatos. The singing is very often accompanied by energetic movement, either spontaneous or choreographed. Many well-known Rhythm and Blues and Soul singers got their start as gospel singers, including Dinah Washington, Lou Rawls, LaVerne Baker, Sam Cooke, Wilson Pickett, and Aretha Franklin. Although highly popular as entertainment, gospel music is most frequently heard in the African American churches where it was born.

Presenting authentic materials to a student population of diverse ethnic and religious backgrounds can present special challenges. Before presenting such materials, you may wish to review with your students the cultural and historical context out of which the music arose. African American spirituals, for example, are an important part of our American heritage. They express universal feelings of the hope for a life of freedom, toleration, and well-being.

MUSIC LIBRARY

3. Teach measures 5–12 of "I've Got a Robe." Have the students:

• Listen again to measures 5–12 of Part IV, following the score, and sing them using both unaccompanied and accompanied.
• Listen and read measures 5–12 of Part III as those assigned to Parts I and III sing those measures. (Use teacher modeling as needed.)
• Establish a steady beat and then read and sing measures 5–12 of Parts IV and III together. (Have students assigned to Parts IV and II perform Part IV; students assigned to Parts III and I perform Part III. Sing unaccompanied and accompanied.)
• Continue by learning Parts II and I as outlined, combining each newly learned voice part with those previously learned.
• Sing measures 5–12 combining all parts. (Begin with Part IV alone, repeat adding Part III, repeat adding Part II, repeat adding Part I. Use unaccompanied and accompanied singing.)
• Sing the song again individually and in small groups. (Emphasize maintaining a steady beat, rhythmic and stylistic accuracy, and an open vocal quality.)

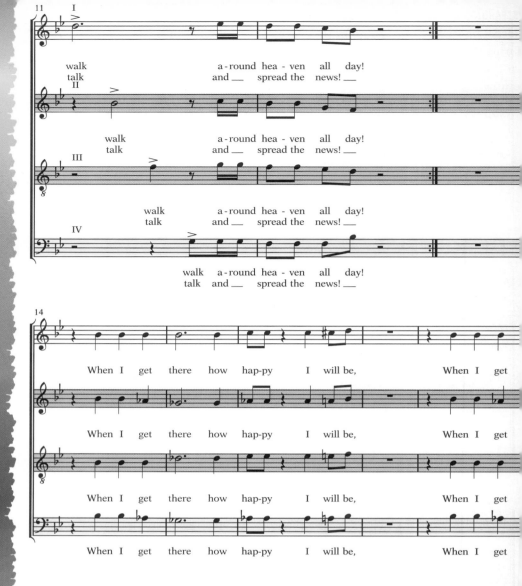

19

there my Sav-ior's face I'll see. Well!

there my Sav-ior's face I'll see. Well! Walk

there my Sav-ior's face I'll see. Well!

there my Sav-ior's face I'll see. Well!

Rest first time through
Sing second and third times through

23

Hea - ven! all day!

Solo, first time through (sing these four measures three times)

_ a-round hea-ven all day! Walk _ a-round hea-ven all day! Walk _

Rest first and second times through
Sing third time through

talk, and tell the sto - ry,

Rest three times through

25

Hea - ven! all day!

_ a-round hea-ven all day! Walk _ a-round hea-ven all day! Walk _

Talk, 'bout how I made it o - ver.

365

4. Teach measures 14–42. Have the students:

• Learn all voice parts separately, following the same procedure for measures 14–22, 23–34, and 35–42. (Measures 35–42 are the same as measures 14–22 and use a glissando at the end of the phrase. The recording together with teacher modeling will assist in learning this stylistic characteristic.)

• Establish singing posture and then listen to and sing the song.

• Sing again individually and in small groups. (Use unaccompanied and accompanied singing.)

• Follow the score and sing the song emphasizing strong rhythm and gospel-style characteristics.

5. Perform "I've Got a Robe." Have the students:

• Sing the song with accompaniment, following conducting gestures, focusing on strong rhythms and consonants, and performing with an open vocal quality.

• Discuss *Think It Through*.

• Perform the song again and evaluate the performance in terms of expressive elements.

APPRAISAL

The students should be able to:
Identify characteristics of, and perform music in a gospel style.

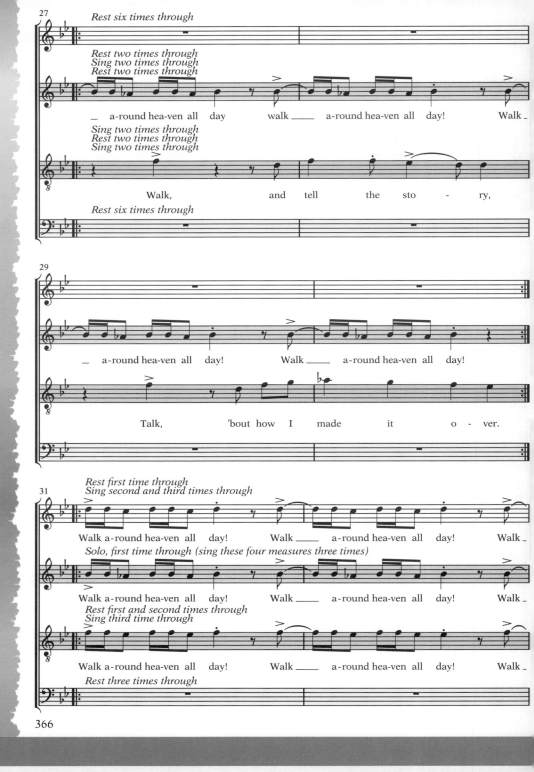

367

MUSIC LIBRARY

Focus: Rhythm Skills

Objectives
To experiment with musical performance practices while singing a traditional Chinese song of celebration

Materials
Recordings: "Drum Song"
    "Drum Song" (performance mix)

Vocabulary
Vocables

TEACHING THE LESSON

1. Introduce the preparation. Have the students:
• Listen to "Drum Song" while following the score.
• Read and discuss the introductory information.
• Establish a steady beat, then read and clap rhythmic example 1. (You may wish to review note values. Model as needed.)
• Establish a steady beat for rhythmic example 2 and then (a) read and clap, (b) read, clap and speak, and (c) read and speak.
• Find rhythmic examples 1 and 2 in "Drum Song." (example 1: measures 3–6, example 2: measures 7–8)
2. Introduce "Drum Song." Have the students:
• Divide into four voice parts—Parts I and II, both trebles and unchanged voices; Part III, changing voices; Part IV, baritones.
• Listen to the song, following the score, and sing assigned voice parts on the neutral syllable *doot*. (Focus on an accurate performance of the rhythmic patterns of examples 1 and 2.)

This traditional Chinese "Drum Song" is remembered by many as the triumphant song sung as soldiers marched home at the end of World War II. The vocables, or syllables, mimic the loud banging and clashing of the drums. These noises are associated with driving away evil and setting the stage for a joyful and triumphant celebration.

Practice Your Music Reading Skills — Rhythms

"Drum Song" has combinations of quarter-, eighth-, and sixteenth-note rhythms in both the melody and percussion parts.

• Clap the following rhythms in preparation for reading "Drum Song," then find them in the song.

1.

2.

We're　com - ing home　and we　all　are　full　of　joy

THINK IT THROUGH: What expressive musical elements can you use to engage your audience in your performance of "I've Got a Robe"? Create a chart of musical elements and create plans for adding expressive elements. Evaluate the success of each plan.

Key: F major　　　Ranges I: D–F^I, II: C–D^I, III: B♭$_I$–F, IV: C$_I$–D

Drum Song

Piano Accompaniment on page PA 129

Traditional Chinese
Translation by Lucy J. Ding and Julian Harvey
Arranged by Julian Harvey

With joy and a somewhat raucous tone

I and II

Rum　ta　da　rum　ta　rum　ta　rum,

III and IV

Small Cyms.

Hand Drum

368

Rum ta da rum ta rum ta rum, Rum ta da rum ta rum ta da rum ta

Rum ta da rum ta rum. We're com - ing home and we

all are full of joy. Let the drum sound, let the cym-bals ring.

369

3. Teach "Drum Song." Have the students:
• Follow the score as you vocally model measures 3–6 of Part IV on the neutral syllable *doot*.
• Echo-sing Part IV. (All sing, with an emphasis on accurate rhythms, crisp diction, and precision of ensemble.)
• Follow the score as you vocally model measures 3–6 of Part III on the neutral syllable *doot*.
• Echo-sing Part III (only those assigned to Parts I and III).
• Combine Parts IV and III with accompaniment. (Begin with Part IV singing alone; repeat adding Part III. Students assigned to Parts IV and II sing Part IV; those assigned to Parts III and I sing Part III.)
• Sing the combined Parts IV and III as individuals and in small groups, unaccompanied and accompanied.
• Continue by learning Parts II and I as previously outlined, combining each new voice part with those already learned.
• Combine singing all parts with accompaniment. (Begin with Part IV singing alone, then repeat, adding Part III, repeat adding Part II, repeat adding Part I.)
• Sing again individually and in small groups using unaccompanied and accompanied singing.
• Sing measures 3–6 using the vocables.
• Follow the score and sing measures 1–6 individually and in small groups, unaccompanied and accompanied
• Learn all voice parts separately following the previously outlined procedures for measures 7–14 and 19–25. (Emphasize rhythmic and pitch accuracy, and ensemble.)

MUSIC LIBRARY

4. Explore the vocables in "Drum Song." Have the students:

• Identify changes they could make in their vocal performance to imitate drum sounds. (Experiment with the use of more percussive, explosive, consonant sounds.)

• Experiment with each performance suggestion by using it as they sing measures 3–6. (Continue attention to pitch and rhythmic accuracy as well as maintaining choral ensemble at all times.)

• Discuss and evaluate each performance experiment in terms of how it could contribute to the desired musical style.

• Identify the most appropriate drum-like performance practices.

• Sing the song again individually and in small groups.

Men and wo-men, ev-ery-one you see, Young and old are hap-py as can be.

Man and wo-man, girl and boy, Now we sing our songs of joy, (shout) Heh!

370

Songs of __ joy and songs of __ tri - umph, songs of __ tri - umph songs of

joy!

5. Teach percussion parts for "Drum Song" (optional). Have the students:
• Establish a steady beat and then read and perform the hand drum part. Repeat for the small cymbal part. (Emphasize careful performance of dynamics and accents.)
• Divide into two sections, establish a steady beat and then perform each part separately; then combined.
• Explore different percussion performance options. (Use hand drums, claves, sticks, anvil or other available percussion.)
• Perform the percussion parts with accompaniment while listening to the song.
• Identify and decide which of the percussion choices seems the most appropriate for use with this Chinese folk song and why.
6. Perform "Drum Song." Have the students:
• Discuss *Think It Through*.
• Sing the song with accompaniment. (You may wish to include student percussion performers at this time.)

APPRAISAL

The students should be able to:
1. Perform a song from China with attention to musical style.
2. Perform identified changes involving expressive elements.

THINK IT THROUGH: Many of the words in the text of "Drum Song" imitate percussion sounds. What interesting vocal tone colors can you use to imitate the drum and cymbal sounds in the text? Plan a performance that uses both real and vocally imitated percussion sounds. Evaluate the effectiveness of your performance.

371

MUSIC LIBRARY

Focus: Rhythm Patterns

Objectives
To identify and sing polyphonic and homophonic music of the Renaissance
To sing a song in Latin and German

Materials
Recordings: "Psallite"
            Recorded Lesson:
            "Pronunciation: 'Psallite'"

Vocabulary
Polyphonic, homophonic

TEACHING THE LESSON

1. Introduce the preparation. Have the students:
• Read and discuss the introductory information. (Review polyphonic and homophonic textures from page 83.)
• Follow the score while listening to "Psallite."
• Examine the score for "Psallite" and identify polyphonic and homophonic passages. (polyphonic: measures 1–4, 16–20; homophonic: measures 6–8, 21–23)
• Establish a steady beat, then read and clap pattern 1. (You may wish to review time signatures before these exercises.)
• Perform patterns 2–4 using the tone colors suggested on page 372. (Use an explosive *sss* sound for pattern 4.)

PREPARING *to Sing "Psallite"*

"Psallite" expresses the joy that surrounds the Christmas season. Michael Praetorius was a composer and musician who lived during the late Renaissance. Like many composers of that era, he often alternated between polyphonic style with its independent melodic parts, and homophonic style with its chordal parts. Look for passages in "Psallite" that show both of these ways of writing.

Practice Your Music Reading Skills — Rhythm Patterns

Perform each:

• Clap this pattern.

• Tap this pattern.

• Snap this pattern.

• Say this pattern using an *sss* sound.

• Create your own musical composition by combining two or more of these patterns.

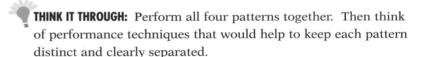 **THINK IT THROUGH:** Perform all four patterns together. Then think of performance techniques that would help to keep each pattern distinct and clearly separated.

372

BACKGROUND AND TRANSLATION

The text of "Psallite" is a combination of Latin and German. A paraphrase of the text follows.

Sing praises together to Christ, the son of God, the child Redeemer lying in a crib, a little child lying in a small crib. All the angels love this little child.

Christmas in Europe in the late 1500s– early 1600s was primarily a religious celebration. Choral works using texts such as "Psallite" reflected both the joy and the solemnity of the season. The use of both homophonic and polyphonic writing enabled composers to emphasize contrasting phrases of text with different textures of sound.

Psallite

Key: G major   Ranges I: D–D^I, II: B$_I$–A, III: G$_I$–D, IV: C$_I$–A$_I$

Words and Music by
Michael Praetorius

373

MUSIC LIBRARY

• Divide into groups of four to create, practice, and perform an original sixteen-measure sequence choosing from these patterns. (Any of the patterns may be used once or more.)

• Listen for and identify the sequence of patterns used. (For example, one group might choose the sequence of rhythm patterns 4, 3, 2 and 3.)

• Combine the sequences of two, three or more groups.

• Divide into four groups to read and perform patterns 1–4 simultaneously. (Repeat the exercise, trading parts so that all students experience each rhythm.)

2. Introduce "Psallite." Have the students:

• Clap rhythms of all parts in measures 1–4.

• Divide into four voice parts—Parts I and II, both trebles and unchanged voices; Part III, changing voices; Part IV, baritones.

• Listen while following the score, and sing their assigned voice part softly on the neutral syllable *doot*.

• Follow the score as you model Part IV, measures 1–9, on the neutral syllable *doot*.

• All echo-sing Part IV. (Emphasize crisp diction and precision of ensemble.)

• Repeat procedure as students assigned to Parts III and I learn Part III.

• Combine Parts IV and III with accompaniment. (Begin with Part IV singing alone. Repeat adding Part III. Students assigned to Parts IV and II sing Part IV; those assigned to Parts III and I sing Part III.)

• Learn Parts II and I, combining each newly-learned voice part with those previously learned.

PRONUNCIATION

säl' lē-tä ōō-nē ja' nē-tō
kris' tō dā' ē fē' lē-ō
rä-demp-tō' rē dō' mē-nō pōō-ä-rōō' lō
yä-chen' tē
in prä-sä' pē ō
īn klī n'es kin' də-līn
lēKht in dem krip'pe līn
äl' le lē' be an' ge līn dē' nen dem
kin' de līn
ōōnt sin'g gen im fīn

MUSIC LIBRARY

- Combine singing all parts with accompaniment. (Begin with Part IV singing alone, repeat adding Part III, repeat adding Part II, repeat adding Part I.)
- Sing again individually and in small groups, unaccompanied and accompanied.
- Listen to "Pronunciation: 'Psallite,'" and practice the Latin pronunciation as needed.
- Sing measures 1–9 using words.
- Follow the score and sing measures 1–9 with accompaniment.
- Sing Warm-Up 10 to help with diction and energetic singing for measures 1–9. (Emphasize breath and diction energy to create a light, crisp singing style for this section of "Psallite.")
- Sing again individually and in small groups, unaccompanied and accompanied.
- Repeat this procedure to learn measures 9–17 and 16–24.
- Sing the composition with and without accompaniment, emphasizing the difference between the polyphonic and homophonic sections.

3. Perform "Psallite." Have the students:
- Sing the song with accompaniment, following conducting gestures while focusing on appropriate performance practices. (crisp diction, polyphonic clarity of line, balance in homophonic sections, and clear, unified Latin and German diction)
- Discuss *Think It Through*.

APPRAISAL

The students should be able to:
1. Perform music of the Renaissance with attention to musical style.
2. Sing a song in Latin and German with accurate pronunciation.

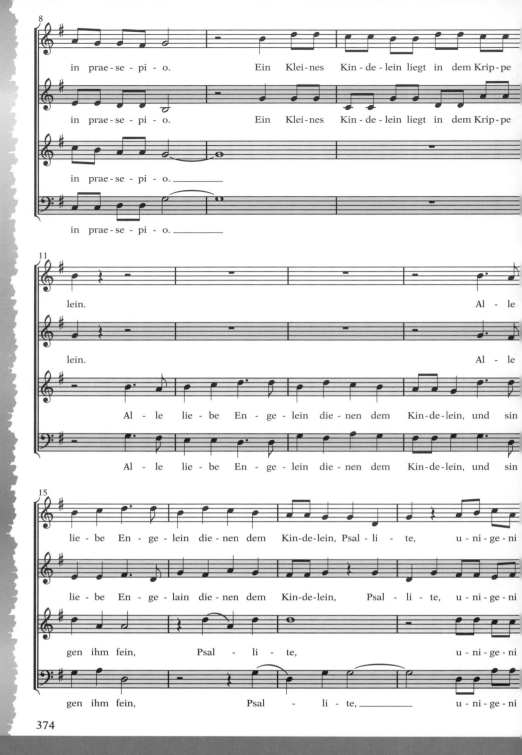

374

WARM-UP 10

Ss Ss Ss Ss Ss Ss Ss Ss

Tee kee Tee kee Tee kee Tee kee Teh

Ss Ss Ss Ss Ss Ss Ss Ss

Tee kee Tee kee Tee kee Tee kee Teh

Ss Ss Ss Ss Ss Ss Ss Ss

Continue sequence to key of D.

Tee kee Tee kee Tee kee Tee kee Teh

to, Chris-to De - i Fi - li - o. Psal - li - te, Re-demp-to-ri

to, Chris-to De - i Fi - li - o. Re-demp-to - ri

to. Chris-to De - i Fi - li - o, Re-demp-to - ri

to. Chris-to De - i Fi - li - o, Re-demp-to - ri

Do - mi - no pu - e - ru - lo ja - cen - ti in prae - se - pi - o.

Do - mi - no pu - e - ru - lo ja - cen - ti in prae - se - pi - o.

Do - mi - no pu - e - ru - lo ja - cen - ti in prae - se - pi - o.

Do - mi - no pu - e - ru - lo ja - cen - ti in prae - se - pi - o.

THINK IT THROUGH: Evaluate the clarity of each part. Try singing the imitative sections using a sustained bell-like vocal quality. Sing the fast-moving sections in a light and detached manner. How does this plan change the quality of the performance? Create a plan for your performance and decide the most appropriate techniques for this style of music.

375

TIMELINE

Michael Praetorius 1571–1621
Thomas Weelkes 1576–1623

1600

1620 Mayflower lands at Plymouth Rock
1643 Louis XIV becomes king of France at age 5

1666 Newton discovers Law of Gravity

Jean Baptiste Lully 1632–1687
Johann Pachelbel 1653–1706
Henry Purcell 1659–1695
Antonio Vivaldi 1678–1741
Johann Sebastian Bach 1685–1750
George Frederick Handel 1685–1759

1700

1707 United Kingdom of Great Britian formed

Franz Joseph Haydn 1732–1809
John Stafford Smith 1750–1836
Wolfgang Amadeus Mozart 1756–1791
Ludwig van Beethoven 1770–1827

1769 James Watt patents his steam engine
1775 American Revolution (ended 1783)
1776 American Declaration of Independence
1787 American Constitutional Convention
1788 John Fitch invents steamboat
1789 French Revolution; George Washington
     first president of United States
1791 Biil of Rights
1793 Eli Whitney invents the cotton gin

Franz Schubert 1797–1828

1800

1803 Louisiana Purchase
1804 Napoleon crowned emperor; Lewis and
     Clark expedition
1807 Robert Fulton builds first commercial
     steamboat; London streets lighted by gas

Fanny Mendelssohn Hensel 1805–1847

Felix Mendelssohn 1809–1847
Frédéric Chopin 1810–1849
Robert Schumann 1810–1856
Richard Wagner 1813–1883

1812 War of 1812
1815 Napoleon defeated in Battle of Waterloo
1819 First steamship crosses Atlantic

1825

1825 Opening of the Erie Canal
1825 First public railroad opened in England
1838 Daguerre takes first photographs

Johannes Brahms 1833–1897
Georges Bizet 1838–1875
Modest Mussorgsky 1839–1881
Peter Ilyich Tchaikovsky 1840–1893
Edvard Grieg 1843–1907
Nicolai Rimsky-Korsakov 1844–1908

1844 First telegraph message transmitted
1846 First use of ether as an anesthetic
1848 California Gold Rush; first Women's
     Rights Convention

1850

John Philip Sousa 1854–1932
Cécile Chaminade 1857–1944
Giacomo Puccini 1858–1924
Claude Debussy 1862–1918

1860 Lincoln elected president;
     Civil War (ended 1865)

377

TIME LINE

Scott Joplin 1868–1917
James Weldon Johnson 1871–1938
Ralph Vaughan Williams 1872–1958
W.C. (William Christopher) Handy 1873–1958
Arnold Schoenberg 1874–1951
Charles Ives 1874–1954
Robert Frost 1874–1963

Igor Stravinsky 1882–1971
Ferdinand ("Jelly Roll") Morton 1885–1941
Gertrude ("Ma") Rainey 1886–1939

Ernst Toch 1887–1964
T.S. (Thomas Stearns) Eliot 1888–1965
Sergei Prokofiev 1891–1953
Bessie Smith 1894–1937
William Grant Still 1895–1978
George Gershwin 1898–1937
Duke Ellington 1899–1974

Louis Armstrong 1900–1971
Harry Partch 1901–1974
Langston Hughes 1902–1967
Ogden Nash 1902–1971

Harold Arlen 1905–1986

Milt Hinton 1910–

John Cage 1912–1992
Morton Gould 1913–1996
Benjamin Britten 1913–1976
Lester Flatt 1914–1979
Milton Babbitt 1916–
Eve Merriam 1916–
Lou Harrison 1917–
Leonard Bernstein 1918–1990
Dave Brubeck 1920–
Katsutoshi Nagasawa 1923–
Earl Scruggs 1924–
Paul Desmond 1924–1977
Pierre Boulez 1925–

Burt Bacharach 1928–

Claude Bolling 1930–

1875

1900

1925

1863 Gettysburg Address; Emancipation Proclamation
1865 Abraham Lincoln assassinated
1869 First American transcontinental railroad opening of Suez Canal

1876 Alexander Graham Bell invents telephone
1877 Thomas Edison invents the phonograph
1879 Edison invents improved incandescent electric light bulb
1885 Louis Pasteur develops milk "pasteurization"
1886 Statue of Liberty unveiled in New York Harbor
1889 Completion of Eiffel Tower in France

1895 Wilhelm Roentgen discovers X-rays
1898 Spanish-American War

1901 Guglielmo Marconi transmits wireless telegraph signals across Atlantic
1902 Pierre and Marie Curie discover radium
1903 Wilbur and Orville Wright make first successful airplane flight
1904 First sound moving picture
1905 Albert Einstein offers Theory of Relativity
1906 San Francisco earthquake and fire
1908 Model T Ford produced
1909 Robert Peary and Matthew Henson reach North Pole
1910 Discovery of the South Pole; discovery of protons and electrons
1912 Titanic disaster

1914 Opening of the Panama Canal; World War I (ended 1918)

1917 Russian Revolution

1920 First commercial radio broadcast; suffrage (19th Amendment)

1927 Charles Lindbergh's flight across the Atlantic; first television transmission
1928 Sir Alexander Fleming discovers penicillin
1929 New York stock market crash; beginning of worldwide depression

378

Stephen Sondheim	1930–
Shel Silverstein	1932–
Isao Tomita	1932–
John Williams	1932–
Krzysztof Penderecki	1933–
Terry Riley	1935–
Philip Glass	1937–
Leo Brouwer	1939–
Trevor Nunn	1940–
Bob Dylan	1941–
David Fanshawe	1942–
George Harrison	1943–
Vangelis	1943–
James C. Pankow	1947–
Elton John	1947–
Andrew Lloyd Webber	1948–
Stephen Schwartz	1948–
Stevie Nicks	1948–
Billy Joel	1949–

1950

Peter Gabriel	1950–
Bernie Taupin	1950–
Dewey Bunnell	1952–
Bruce Hornsby	1954–
Gloria Estefan	1957–

1975

1932 Franklin D. Roosevelt elected president

1933 Nazi Revolution in Germany

1939 World War II (ended 1945)

1950 Korean War (ended 1953); Vietnam War (ended 1975)

1954 First polio vaccine developed by Jonas E. Salk

1957 Launching of Sputnik, first earth satellite

1961 First successful manned orbital space flight

1962 Cuban missile crisis

1963 President John F. Kennedy assassinated

1965 First "walk" outside spaceship by an astronaut

1968 Martin Luther King, Jr., and Robert F. Kennedy assassinated

1969 First men land on the moon

1971 Voting age lowered to 18 years

1976 U.S. celebrates its bicentennial on July 4; Viking I and II landers set down on Mars

1981 Sandra Day O'Connor becomes first woman appointed to the Supreme Court; first reusable spacecraft, space shuttle Columbia, travels into space and returns to earth

1983 Sally Ride becomes the first American woman to travel in space

1984 First mechanical heart implanted in a human

1985 Worldwide Live Aid concert to benefit famine victims in Ethiopia

1986 Statue of Liberty centennial celebration

1987 Voyager makes first nonstop flight around the world without refueling

1990 Germany reunited; dissolving of the Soviet Union; spacecraft Magellan maps Venus

379

TIME LINE

GLOSSARY

ABA form a three-part form in which there is repetition after contrast, **21**

absolute music makes no attempt to tell a story, describe an event, or paint a picture, **153**

accent (>) placement of emphasis or stress on certain beats, **3**

aria solo song from an opera or oratorio, **196**

arrange to re-set a composition for a different combination of musical resources, **206**

art song music written for solo voice and instrumental accompaniment, usually keyboard, **111**

atonal music characterized by the absence of a tonal center and equal emphasis on all twelve tones of the chromatic scale, **92**

ballad a song that tells a story, **130**

bar lines lines separating measures, **18**

baroque style the common musical characteristics reflected by the music composed between 1600 and 1750, **17**

bitonality harmony created by playing two different tonalities at the same time, **108**

blues a melancholy style of American music characterized by flatted notes and a syncopated, often slow jazz rhythm, **104**

cambiata the range of a boy's changing voice, **309**

calypso style of folk music from the Caribbean Islands, **10**

canon a form of music in which different vocal or instrumental parts take up the melody, successively creating harmony, **82**

380

chamber music compositions for small groups, **194**

chord three or more pitches sounding together, **4**

classical style the common musical characteristics reflected by the music composed between 1750 and 1830, **17**

coda concluding section, **20**

composer writes the music, **290**

compound meter meter whose beat is divided into threes and/or sixes, **61**

consonance the sounding of a combination of tones that produces little tension, **80**

controller element of the MIDI system on which the music is played, **290**

crescendo (————) getting louder, **13**

dancehall melodic form of rap music from the Caribbean Islands, **5**

decrescendo (————) getting softer, **13**

development the expanded treatment of a musical idea, **147**

dissonance the sounding of a combination of pitches that creates harmonic tension and sounds incomplete, **108**

dominant chord a chord built on the fifth tone of a scale, **11**

dotted quarter note (♩.) a symbol for a sound equal in length to three eighth notes; represents the basic beat in compound meter, **60**

dotted quarter rest (♩·) a symbol for an interval of silence lasting as long as a dotted quarter note, **60**

GLOSSARY AND INDEXES

GLOSSARY AND INDEXES

natural (♮) symbol indicating that a sharp or a flat should be canceled, **25**

neoclassical style of composition exhibiting the characteristics of classical piece, but composed after the close of that period, **149**

opera a drama with scenery and costumes in which all or most of the words are sung to the accompaniment of an orchestra, **196**

oratorio a dramatic musical composition usually set to a religious text and performed by solo voices, chorus, and orchestra, without action, special costumes, or scenery, **83**

ostinato repeated pattern, **54**

phrase a complete musical idea, **120**

piano (p) soft, **13**

pipe organ keyboard instrument whose sound is produced by wind moving through pipes, **172**

pizzicato music played by plucking the strings of a stringed instrument with the finger instead of bowing the strings, **106**

polyphonic music having two or more independent melodic parts sounding together, **83**

polyrhythm a combination of two or more different rhythm patterns played at the same time, **70**

prepared piano piano whose sound has been altered by placing items of wood, metal, rubber, between the strings of the piano, **175**

program music a composition whose title or accompanying remarks link it with a story, idea, or emotion, **50, 152**

quadruple meter beats that are grouped into sets of four, **40**

quarter note (♩ or ♩) a symbol for a sound in music that is one fourth as long as the sound of a whole note, **3**

382

quarter rest (𝄾) a symbol for an interval of silence lasting as long as a quarter note, **3**

record producer directs the process of making a recording, **290**

recording engineer handles the technical aspects of the recording session, **290**

reggae style of popular music from the Caribbean Islands, **5**

register the high to low range of a voice or instrument, **102**

Renaissance style the common musical characteristics reflected by the music composed between 1450 and 1600, **17**

repeat sign (𝄇) play or sing the pattern again, **3**

retrograde a backwards version of a melodic pattern, **88**

ritardando gradual slowing of the tempo, **20**

ritornello section of a baroque concerto played by all the players, **192**

rock and roll style of music combining the styles of many other forms including rhythm and blues, blues, rockabilly and others, **30**

romantic style the common musical characteristics reflected by the music composed between 1830 and 1900, **17**

root the lowest pitch of each chord, **11**

salsa style of Latin dance music characterized by exciting rhythms and tone colors, **70**

sequencer program software that enables one to create, record, edit, and play back music, **290**

serial music atonal music written using a technique based on the successive repetition of all twelve tones of the chromatic scale in a fixed order, **90, 238**

ska fast, lively style of music originating in Jamaica, **5**

skipwise melodic movement using skips between pitches, **240**

sonata allegro a musical form that uses the overall design of exposition, development, and recapitulation, **149**

sound output device speakers or headphones, **290**

staccato music that sounds crisp and detached, **141**

steady beat an unchanging beat or pulse, **3**

steel drums "homemade" percussion instruments found in the West Indies, **182**

stepwise melodic movement using only adjacent pitches, **238**

stratification layering of melody or sound, **226**

strophic form form in which the music is repeated with each new verse or stanza of text, **130**

style quality that is characteristic of a culture, individual, or historical period, **2**

subdominant chord chord based on the fourth tone of the scale, **104**

suite a musical composition consisting of a succession of short pieces, **24**

symphony long orchestral work organized into three to five movements, **149, 194**

syncopation off-beat rhythm pattern that has unexpected sounds and silences, **10**

synthesizer an instrument for producing electronic music that combines sound generators and modifiers in a single control system, **178**

tempo the speed of the beat, **8**

ternary form (ABA) a three-part form in which there is repetition after contrast, **21**

texture the character of the different layers of sound in music, **83**

Theremin first electronic musical instrument, invented by and named for Leon Theremin, **178**

tonality the relation of melodic and harmonic elements to a home tone, **80**

tone color the unique sound of each instrument or voice, **13**

tone generator collection of sounds to be accessed by the computer, **290**

tonic chord a chord built on the first tone or key tone of a scale, **11**

triple meter beats grouped into sets of three, **18**

twelve-bar blues chord pattern often used in blues music based on the I, IV, and V chords, **104**

twelve tone row a type of pitch organization made up of all of the tones of the chromatic scale that has no tonal center and in which all pitches are equal, see also **serial music**, **90**

twentieth-century style the common musical characteristics reflected by the music composed since 1900, **17**

whole note (o) a symbol that represents a sound that lasts for four quarter notes, **4**

383

CLASSIFIED INDEX

LISTENING SELECTIONS

385

ALPHABETICAL SONG INDEX

African American Music (See also Multicultural Music)

Bebey, Francis. *African Music: A People's Art.* Chicago: Chicago Review Press, 1975.

Edet, Edna S. *The Griot Sings: Songs from the Black World.* Collected and adapted. New York: Medgar Evers College Press, 1978.

Glass, Paul. *Songs and Stories of Afro-Americans.* New York: Grosset & Dunlap, 1971.

Johnson, James Weldon, and J.R. Johnson, eds. *The Books of American Negro Spirituals.* 2 vols. in 1. Jersey City, N.J.: Da Capo Press, 1977.

Jones, Bessie, and Bess L. Hawes. *Step It Down: Games, Plays, Songs, and Stories from the Afro-American Heritage.* Athens, Ga.: Univ. of Georgia Press, 1987.

Nketia, Joseph H. *The Music of Africa.* New York: W.W. Norton & Co., 1974.

Southern, Eileen. *The Music of Black Americans.* 2d ed. New York: W.W. Norton & Co., 1983.

Cooperative Learning

Gibbs, Jeanne. *Tribes: A Process for Social Development and Cooperative Learning.* Santa Rosa, Calif.: Center Source Publications, 1987.

Johnson, David W., Robert T. Johnson, and Edythe Johnson Holubec. *Circles of Learning: Cooperation in the Classroom.* Alexandria, Va.: Association for Supervision & Curriculum Development, 1984.

Slavin, Robert E. *Cooperative Learning: Student Teams.* 2d ed. Washington, D.C.: National Education Association, 1987.

Dalcroze (See also Movement)

Abramson, Robert M. *Rhythm Games.* New York: Music & Movement Press, 1973.

Aronoff, Frances W. *Move with the Music: Songs and Activities for Young Children, A Teacher-Parent Preparation Workbook Including Keyboard.* New York: Turning Wheel Press, 1982.

Bachmann, Marie-Laure. *Dalcroze Today: An Education Through and into Music.* Oxford: Clarenon Press, Oxford University Press, 1991.

Jaques-Dalcroze, Émile. *Rhythm, Music, and Education.* rev. ed. Translated by Harold F. Rubenstein. London: The Dalcroze Society, 1980.

Early Childhood Music

Andress, Barbara. *Music Experiences in Early Childhood.* New York: Holt, Rinehart & Winston, 1980.

Aronoff, Frances W. *Music and Young Children: Expanded Edition.* New York: Turning Wheel Press, 1979.

Bayless, Kathleen M., and Marjorie E. Ramsey. *Music: A Way of Life for the Young Child.* 3d ed. Columbus, Ohio: Merrill Publishing Co., 1987.

Birkenshaw, Lois. *Music for Fun, Music for Learning: For Regular and Special Classrooms.* 3d ed. Toronto: Holt, Rinehart & Winston of Canada, 1982.

McDonald, Dorothy C., and Gene M. Simons. *Musical Growth and Development: Birth Through Six.* New York: Schirmer Books, 1989.

Nye, Vernice T. *Music for Young Children.* 3d ed. Dubuque, Iowa: William C. Brown Publisher, 1983.

Kodály

Choksy, Lois. *The Kodály Context.* Englewood Cliffs, N.J.: Prentice-Hall, 1981.

——. *The Kodály Method: Comprehensive Music Education from Infant to Adult.* 2d ed. Englewood Cliffs, N.J.: Prentice-Hall, 1988.

Daniel, Katina S. *Kodály Approach, Method Book One.* 2d ed. Champaign, Ill.: Mark Foster Music Co., 1979.

——. *Kodály Approach, Method Book Two.* Champaign, Ill.: Mark Foster Music Co., 1986

——. *Kodály Approach, Method Book Three.* Champaign, Ill.: Mark Foster Music Co., 1987.

——. *Kodály Approach, Method Book Two—Song Collection.* Champaign, Ill.: Mark Foster Music Co., 1982.

Szonyi, Erzsébet. *Musical Reading and Writing.* Translated by Lili Halápy. Revised translation by Geoffrey Russell-Smith. 8 vols. London and New York: Boosey & Hawkes Music Publishers, 1973–1979.

Listening

Copland, Aaron. *What to Listen for in Music.* New York:

McGraw-Hill Book Co., 1988.

Hoffer, Charles R. *The Understanding of Music.* 5th ed. Belmont, Calif.: Wadsworth Publishing Co., 1985.

Miller, Samuel D. "Listening Maps for Musical Tours." *Music Educators Journal* 73 (October 1986): 28–31.

Movement (See also Dalcroze)

Boorman, Joyce L. *Creative Dance in the First Three Grades.* Toronto: Harcourt Brace Jovanovich, Canada, 1969.

——. *Creative Dance in Grades Four to Six.* Toronto: Harcourt Brace Jovanovich, Canada, 1971.

——. *Dance and Language Experiences with Children.* Toronto: Harcourt Brace Jovanovich, Canada, 1973.

Joyce, Mary. *First Steps in Teaching Creative Dance to Children.* 2d ed. Mountain View, Calif.: Mayfield Publishing Co., 1980.

Weikart, Phyllis. *Teaching Movement and Dance: Intermediate Folk Dance.* Ypsilanti, Mich.: High/Scope Press, 1984.

Multicultural Music (See also African American Music)

Anderson, William M. *Teaching Asian Musics in Elementary and Secondary Schools.* rev. ed. Danbury, Conn.: World Music Press, 1986.

Anderson, William M., and Patricia Shehan Campbell. *Multicultural Perspectives in Music Education.* Reston, Va.: Music Educators National Conference, 1989.

Fulton Fowke, Edith, and Richard Johnston. *Folk Songs of Canada.* Waterloo, Ontario, Canada: Waterloo Music Company, 1954.

George, Luvenia A. *Teaching the Music of Six Different Cultures.* rev. ed. Danbury, Conn.: World Music Press, 1988.

Heth, Charlotte, ed. *Native American Dance: Ceremonies and Social Traditions.* Washington, D.C.: National Museum of the American Indian, Smithsonian Institution with Starwood Publishing, Inc., 1992.

Horse Capture, George P. *Powwow.* Cody, Wyo.: Buffalo Bill Historical Center, 1989.

Rhodes, Robert. *Hopi Music and Dance.* Tsaile, Ariz.: Navajo Community College Press, 1977.

Speck, Frank G., Leonard Broom, and Will West Long. *Cherokee Dance and Drama.* Norman, Okla.: University of Oklahoma Press, 1983.

Titon, Jeff Todd, ed. *Worlds of Music: An Introduction to the Music of the World's Peoples.* 2nd ed. New York: Schirmer Books, 1992.

Orff

Frazee, Jane, and Kent Kreuter. *Discovering ORFF: A Curriculum for Music Teachers.* Valley Forge, Pa.: European American Music Distributors Corp., 1987.

Keetman, Gunild. *Elementaria, First Acquaintance with Orff-Schulwerk.* Valley Forge, Pa.: European American Music Distributors Corp., 1974.

Keller, Wilhelm. *Introduction to Music for Children.* Translated by Susan Kennedy. Valley Forge, Pa.: European American Music Distributors Corp., 1974.

Nash, Grace C., Geraldine W. Jones, Barbara A. Potter, and Patsy S. Smith. *Do It My Way: The Child's Way of Learning.* Sherman Oaks, Calif.: Alfred Publishing Co., 1977.

Orff, Carl, and Gunild Keetman. *Music for Children.* English version adapted from Orff-Schulwerk by Margaret Murray. 5 vols. London: Schott & Co., 1958–1966.

——. *Music for Children.* Canadian (North American) version adapted from Orff-Schulwerk by Doreen Hall and Arnold Walter. 5 vols. London: Schott & Co., 1956.

Regner, Hermann, ed. *Music for Children.* Vol. 2, *Orff-Schulwerk.* Valley Forge, Pa.: European American Music Distributors Corp., 1977.

Shamrock, Mary. "Orff Schulwerk: An Integrated Foundation." *Music Educators Journal* 72 (February 1986): 51–55.

Recorder

King, Carol. *Recorder Roots* (Books I–II). Memphis, Tenn.: Memphis Musicraft Publications, 1978 and 1984.

Signing

Gadling, Donna C., Pastor Daniel H. Pokorny, and Dr. Lottie L. Riekehof. *Lift Up Your Hands: Inspirational and Patriotic Songs in the Language of Signs.* Washington, D.C.: National Grange, 1975.

Kannapell, Barbara M., and Lillian B. Hamilton. *Songs in*

Signed English. Washington, D.C.: Gallaudet College Press, 1973.

Riekehof, Lottie L. *The Joy of Signing.* 2d ed. Springfield, Mo.: Gospel Publishing House, 1987.

Sternberg, Martin. *American Sign Language.* New York: Harper & Row Publishers, 1987.

Weaks, Donna Gadling. *Lift Up Your Hands.* Vol. 2, *Favorite Songs with Sign Language Interpretation.* Washington, D.C.: National Grange, 1980.

Special Learners

Atterbury, Betty W. *Mainstreaming Exceptional Learners in Music.* Englewood Cliffs, N.J.: Prentice-Hall, 1990.

Cassidy, J.W., and W.L. Sims. "What's In a Name?" *General Music Today* 3 (3–1990). 23–24, 32.

Darrow, Alice-Ann. "Music for the Deaf." *Music Educators Journal* 71 (February 1985): 33–35.

Graham, Richard M., and Alice S. Beer. *Teaching Music to the Exceptional Child: A Handbook for Mainstreaming.* Englewood Cliffs, N.J.: Prentice-Hall, 1980.

Hughes, J.E. "Sing everyone." *General Music Today,* 4 (2–1991), 8–9.

Jellison, J.A. "A Content Analysis of Music Research with Handicapped Children and Youth (1975–1986): Applications in Special Education." In C.K. Furman (ed.), *Effectiveness of Music Therapy Procedures: Documentation in Research and Clinical Practice* (pp. 223–279). Washington, D.C.: National Association for Music Therapy, 1988.

——. "Functional Value as Criterion for Selection and Prioritization of Nonmusic and Music Educational Objectives in Music Therapy." *Music Therapy Perspectives,* 1 (2–1983), 17–22.

——, B.H. Brooks, and A.M. Huck. Structure Small Groups and Music Reinforcement to Facilitate Positive Interactions and Acceptance of Severely Handicapped Students in Regular Music Classrooms." *Journal of Research in Music Education* 39 (1984), 322–333.

——. "Talking About Music: Interviews with Disabled and Nondisabled Children." *Journal of Research in Music Education,* 39 (1991), 322–333.

——. "Writing and Talking About Children with Disabilities. *General Music Today* 4 (1–1990), 25–26.

Lam, Rita C., and Cecilia Wang. "Integrating Blind and Sighted Through Music." *Music Educators Journal* 68 (April 1982): 44-45.

Pennington, H.D. "Acceptance and Expectations of Disabled Students in Music Classes" *General Music Today* 5 (1–1991), 31.

Technology

JVC Video Anthology of World Music and Dance. Victor Company of Japan and Smithsonian/Folkways Recordings, 1991. Distributed by New England Networks, 61 Prospect Street, Montpelier, Vt. 05602

MetroGnomes' Music (MS-DOS, 640K, CGA, or better display, 3.5" or 5.25" drive, hard drive and sound card recommended). Fremont, Calif.: The Learning Co.

Note Play (MS-DOS/Windows, MIDI keyboard optional). Available through Educational Resource, Elgin, Ill.

Piano Works (MS-DOS, 640K, CGA, or better display, 3.5" or 5.25" floppy drive and hard drive, MIDI interface and keyboard). Bellevue, Wash.: Temporal Acuity Products.

Soloist (MS-DOS, 286K, Sound Blaster sound card, microphone). Ibis Software, available through Educational Resource, Elgin, Ill.

Vocal Development/Choral Music

Bartle, Jean Ashworth. *Lifeline for Children's Choir Directors.* Toronto: Gordon V. Thompson Music, 1988.

Cooksey, John M. *Working with the Adolescent Voice.* St. Louis: Concordia Publishing House, 1992.

Heffernan, Charles W. *Choral Music: Technique and Artistry.* Englewood Cliffs, N.J.: Prentice-Hall, 1982.

May, William V., and Craig Tolin. *Pronunciation Guide for Choral Literature.* Reston, Va.: Music Educators National Conference, 1987.

Rao, Doreen. *Choral Music Experience Education Through Artistry.* Vol. 1, *Artistry in Music Education;* Vol. 2, *The Artist in Every Child;* Vol. 5, *The Young Singing Voice.* New York: Boosey & Hawkes, 1987.

Swears, Linda. *Teaching the Elementary School Chorus.* Englewood Cliffs, N.J.: Prentice-Hall, 1984.

ACKNOWLEDGMENTS

Grateful acknowledgment is given to the following authors, composers, and publishers. Every effort has been made to trace the ownership of all copyrighted material and to secure the necessary permissions to reprint these selections. In the case of some selections for which acknowledgment is not given, extensive research has failed to locate the copyright holders.

Arc Music Corp. for *Book of Love*. © 1957 (Renewed) Arc Music & Windswept Pacific. All Rights Reserved. Used by Permission.

Boosey & Hawkes, Inc. for *Birth of Kijé and Wedding of Kijé* from LIEUTENANT KIJÉ SUITE by Sergei Prokofieff. © Copyright 1936 by Edition A. Gutheil; Copyright Renewed. Copyright and Renewal assigned to Boosey & Hawkes, Inc. Reprinted by Permission.

Bug Music for *River* by Bill Staines. © 1978 MINERAL RIVER MUSIC (BMI)/Administered by BUG. All Rights Reserved. Used by Permission.

Dunvagen Music Publishing Inc. for *Floe* from GLASSWORKS by Philip Glass. Copyright © 1982 Dunvagen Music Publishing, Inc. Reprinted by permission. All rights reserved.

Folk-Legacy Records for *All the Good People*. © 1987 KEN HICKS, FOLK LEGACY RECORDS, INC. Sharon, CT 06069.

Hal Leonard for *La Borinqueña*. Music by Felix Astol. Lyrics by Manuel Fernandez Juncos. Copyright © 1957 by Edward B. Marks Music Company. Copyright Renewed. International Copyright Secured. All Rights Reserved. Used by Permission. For *(Life Is a) Celebration*. Words and Music by Rick Springfield. Copyright © 1976 Songs of Polygram International, Inc., 40 West Music Corp., Children of Charles Music and 212 Music. International Copyright Secured. All Rights Reserved. For *Milk and Honey*. Music and lyric by Jerry Herman. © 1961 (Renewed) JERRY HERMAN. All Rights Controlled by JERRYCO MUSIC CO. Exclusive Agent: EDWIN H. MORRIS & COMPANY, A Division of MPL Communications, Inc. All Rights Reserved. For *Only You (And You Alone)*. Words and Music by Buck Ram and Ande Rand. TRO– © Copyright 1955 (Renewed) Hollis Music, Inc., New York, NY. International Copyright Secured. All Rights Reserved Including Public Performance For Profit. Used by Permission (Canadian rights only). For *Our World*. Words by Jane Foster Knox. Music by Lana Walter. Copyright © 1985 by Jenson Publications. International Copyright Secured. All Rights Reserved. For *Run Joe*. Words and music by Dr. Walt Merrick, Joe Willoughby, and Louis Jordan. Copyright © 1947 (Renewed) CHERIO CORP. International Copyright Secured. All Rights Reserved. For *Together Wherever We Go*. Words by Stephen Sondheim. Music by Jule Styne. Copyright © 1959 by Norbeth Productions, Inc. and Stephen Sondheim. Copyright Renewed. All Rights Administered by Chappell & Co. International Copyright Secured. All Rights Reserved.

HarperCollins Publishers for *Backward Bill* from A LIGHT IN THE ATTIC by SHEL SILVERSTEIN. COPYRIGHT © 1981 BY EVIL EYE MUSIC, INC. SELECTION REPRINTED BY PERMISSION OF HarperCollins Publishers.

Julian Harvey for *Drum Song* from FOUR CHINESE FOLK SONGS. © 1994 by Julian Harvey and Lucy J. Ding.

Hollis Music, Inc. for *Consider Yourself* and *Food, Glorious Food* from the Columbia Pictures–Romulus Film OLIVER! Words and music by Lionel Bart. © Copyright 1960 (Renewed) Lakeview Music Co., Ltd., London, England. TRO–Hollis Music, Inc., New York, controls all publication rights for the U.S.A. and Canada. Used by Permission. For *Only You (And You Alone)*. Words and music by Buck Ram and Ande Rand. TRO–© Copyright 1955 (Renewed) Hollis Music, Inc., New York, NY. International Copyright Secured. All Rights Reserved Including Public Performance For Profit. Used by Permission.

Henry Holt and Co., Inc. for *Bravado* from THE POETRY OF ROBERT FROST edited by Edward Connery Lathem. Copyright 1947 © 1969 by Henry Holt and Co., Inc. Copyright © 1975 by Lesley Frost Ballantine. Reprinted by permission of Henry Holt and Co., Inc.

Hinshaw Music for *A la nanita nana*. Copyright © 1995 by Hinshaw Music, Inc. Used by Permission.

Irving Music Inc. for *I Get Around* © 1964, Renewed 1992 Irving Music Inc. (BMI) All Rights Reserved. International Copyright Secured. Used by Permission.

Julie Music Corporation for *Mi Caballo Blanco*. Words and music by Francisco Flores. Copyright © 1971 Julie Music Corporation (BMI) Administered by Next Decade Entertainment, Inc. All Rights Reserved. Used by Permission.

The Lorenz Corporation for *I Hear America Singing* by André Thomas. Copyright 1993 Heritage Music Press, a division of Lorenz Corporation, All rights reserved. Reproduced by Permit #327661.

Music Sales Corporation for *The Ghost Ship* from REFLECTIONS OF A LAD AT SEA by Don Besig and Nancy Price. Copyright © 1982 by Shawnee Press, Inc. (ASCAP). International Copyright Secured. All Rights Reserved. Reprinted by Permission. For *Take These Wings*. Music by Don Besig. Lyrics by Steve Kupferschmid. Copyright © 1984 by Shawnee Press, Inc. (ASCAP) International Copyright Secured. All Rights Reserved. Reprinted by Permission. For *Tonight* from WEST SIDE STORY by Leonard Bernstein. Lyrics by Stephen Sondheim. Copyright © 1956, 1957 (Renewed) by Leonard Bernstein and Stephen Sondheim. Jalni Publications, Inc., U.S. & Canadian Publisher. G. Schirmer, Inc. worldwide print rights and Publishers for the rest of the World. International Copyright Secured. All Rights Reserved. For *Un bel di vedremo* from MADAMA BUTTERFLY by Giacomo Puccini. English version by John Gutman. Copyright © 1964 (Renewed) by G. Schirmer, Inc. (ASCAP). International Copyright Secured. All Rights Reserved. Reprinted by Permission.

David Parker for *I've Got a Robe*. Musical arrangement by David Lee Parker.

Random House for *April Rain Song* and *Dreams* from THE DREAM KEEPER AND OTHER POEMS by Langston Hughes. Copyright 1932 by Alfred A. Knopf, Inc. and renewed 1960 by Langston Hughes. Reprinted by permission of the publisher.

Marian Reiner for *Rainbow Writing* by Eve Merriam. Copyright © 1976 by Eve Merriam. Reprinted by permission of Marian Reiner.

Silver Burdett Ginn for *The Golden Vanity*. Arrangement by George Douglass. © 1974 by GENERAL LEARNING CORPORATION, an imprint of Silver Burdett, Simon Schuster Elementary. Used with permission.

Jerry Silverman for *Freedom Is a Constant Struggle*. Arranged by Jerry Silverman.

Somerset Press for *In Stiller Nacht*. Arrangement © 1985 by Somerset Press (A Division of Hope Publishing Company), Carol Stream, IL 60188. All rights reserved. Used by permission.

Songs of Freedom Publishing (ASCAP) for *Climbing Up to Zion*. Words and Music by Wintley Phipps.

Sundance Music for *Can You Hear the Music?* by Linda Worsley. Copyright Sundance Music. For *70 Times the Speed of Sound* by Linda Worsley. Copyright Sundance Music.

J. Weston Walch for *Eraser Piano Tee*s from ZOUNDS by Dorothy Gail Elliott. Copyright © 1994 J. Weston Walch, Publisher. Used by permission.

David Ward-Steinman and Susan Lucas Ward-Steinman for *The Web*. Copyright 1976 by D. Ward Steinman.

Warner Bros. Publications for *Believe* by Elton John and Bernie Taupin. © 1995 Williams A. Bong Ltd. (PRS) & Hanis (ASCAP). All Rights administered by WB Music Corp. (ASCAP). All Rights Reserved. Used by Permission. For *Cum Sancto Spiritu* edited arrangement by Patrick M. Liebergen. © 1991 Studio 224. All Rights Reserved. Used by Permission. For *La Cigarra* by Ray Perez y Soto. © 1958 Promotora Hispana Americana de Musica S.A. © Renewed/controlled by Peer international Corp. (BMI). All Rights Reserved. Used by Permission. For *Love Song*. Music and lyrics by Stephen Schwartz. © 1972 Stephen Schwartz. All Rights administered by Jobete Music Co. Inc. & EMI Mills Music, Inc. All Rights Reserved. Used by Permission. For *That's What Friends Are For* by Burt Bacharach and Carole Bayer Sager. © 1985 WB Music Corp. (ASCAP), New Hidden Valley Music (ASCAP), Carole Bayer Sager Music (BMI). All Rights jointly administered by WB Music Corp. (ASCAP) & Warner-Tamerlane Publishing Corp. (BMI). All Rights Reserved. Used by Permission. WARNER BROS. PUBLICATIONS U.S. INC., Miami, FL 33014.

World Music Press for *Zol Zain Sholem*. © 1994 World Music Press, P.O. Box 2565 Danbury, CT 06813.

SPECIAL CONTRIBUTORS

Consultant Writers

Dr. Betty Atterbury
Mainstreaming
Gorham, Maine

Alex Campbell
Choral Music
Lakewood, Colorado

Mary Frances Early
African American Music
Atlanta, Georgia

Dr. JaFran Jones
Ethnomusicology
Toledo, Ohio

Consultants and Contributing Writers

Dr. Clifford Alper
Towson, Maryland

Dr. James Anthony
Towson, Maryland

Teri Burdette
Rockville, Maryland

Glenn Cashman
Baltimore, Maryland

Gregory Clouspy
Reisterstown, Maryland

Marilyn Copland Davidson
Bergenfield, New Jersey

Ruth Landis Drucker
Baltimore, Maryland

Dr. Robert A. Duke
Austin, Texas

Nancy E. Ferguson
Tucson, Arizona

Donna Brink Fox
Rochester, New York

Larry Harms
Los Angeles, California

Bernard Hynson, Jr.
Baltimore, Maryland

Dr. Judith A. Jellison
Austin, Texas

Tom Kosmala
Pittsburgh, Pennsylvania

Gilbert Meerdter
New Windsor, Maryland

Carl J. Nygard, Jr.
Fleetwood, Pennsylania

Belle Ortiz
San Antonio, Texas

Jane Pippart-Brown
Lancaster, Pennsylvania

Edwin J. Schupman, Jr.,
of ORBIS Associates
Spokane, Washington

Dr. Susan Snyder
Norwalk, Connecticut

Cynthia Stephens
Ellicott City, Maryland

Mollie G. Tower
Austin, Texas

José A. Villarrubia
Towson, Maryland

Michael Yockel
Miami, Florida

TEACHER'S NOTES

TEACHER'S NOTES

TEACHER'S NOTES